YALE HISTORICAL PUBLICATIONS

LEWIS PERRY CURTIS, EDITOR

HISTORY OF ART

V

PUBLISHED UNDER THE DIRECTION OF
THE DEPARTMENT OF HISTORY FOR
THE DEPARTMENT OF THE HISTORY OF ART
IN THE GRADUATE SCHOOL
FROM THE INCOME OF
THE FREDERICK JOHN KINGSBURY MEMORIAL FUND
AND
THE HISTORY OF ART PUBLICATION FUND

AIDED BY A GRANT FROM
THE AMERICAN COUNCIL OF LEARNED SOCIETIES

Tepeaca, S. Francisco, view of nave

MEXICAN ARCHITECTURE OF THE SIXTEENTH CENTURY

BY

GEORGE KUBLER

I

GREENWOOD PRESS, PUBLISHERS
WESTPORT, CONNECTICUT

The Library of Congress has catalogued this publication as follows:

Library of Congress Cataloging in Publication Data

Kubler, George, 1912-
Mexican architecture of the sixteenth century.

Original ed. issued as no. 5 of History of art. Yale historical publications.
Bibliography: p.
Includes bibliographical references.
1. Architecture--Mexico. 2. Architecture, Colonial --Mexico. I. Title. II. Series: Yale historical publications. History of art, 5.
NA753.K8 1972 720'.972 70-171517
ISBN 0-8371-6256-4

Originally published in 1948
by Yale University Press, New Haven

Reprinted with the permission
of George Kubler

Reprinted from an original copy in the collections
of the University of Illinois Library

First Greenwood Reprinting 1972

Library of Congress Catalogue Card Number 70-171517

ISBN 0-8371-6256-4 Set
ISBN 0-8371-6257-2 Vol. 1

Printed in the United States of America

TO MANUEL TOUSSAINT

AND MY MEXICAN FRIENDS

PREFACE

THE architecture of a colonial people is usually studied only in terms of final causes. If the colony becomes a great nation, with a style of life and art peculiar to itself, then the humble colonial beginnings will attract students, as in the case of Italo-Byzantine painting, or of Roman architecture in the Rhineland. In Mexico the architecture of the sixteenth century needs no justification from final causes, compelling as these may be. The accomplished mastery of European building crafts, manifested by native builders as early as 1560, and the originality of many Mexican forms of structure and ornament at this early period, are striking enough for detailed study without reference to later events in national history.

This work is not the first of its kind. It stands upon the broad platforms built first by Manuel Toussaint, and later by Robert Ricard. The major difference from these predecessors appears in the effort to relate demography, urbanism, and institutional history to an analysis of the monuments. The study of the monuments, in turn, differs from other treatments in the search for exact chronology, and in the effort to generalize upon the cultural significance of such chronological sequences. Thus the first four chapters deal with social processes, human equipment, and the collective forms of architectural effort; the last four treat more closely of the individual monuments, whether civil or religious.

The geographical scope is not identical with that of modern republican Mexico. The states of the peninsula of Yucatan (Campeche, Yucatan, and Quintana Roo), and the southernmost states of continental Mexico (Chiapas and Tabasco) are scarcely discussed. Little attention has been paid to the northern states (Lower California, Sonora, Chihuahua, Tamaulipas, Nuevo Leon, etc.) or to the extreme western provinces of Mexico. The reason for these omissions is that Yucatan and southernmost Mexico pertain more directly to another colonial tradition in Latin America, namely that of the Captaincy-General of Guatemala, or of Central America in general. The tropical or Cordilleran environment, the presence of Maya-speaking peoples, and many specific traits of architectural style would make it difficult to treat the colonial architecture of Central America in a volume dedicated principally to the building history of the sixteenth century in highland Mexico. The reader will also note that the geographical scope does not fully coincide with the territorial definition of colonial New Spain itself. We do not deal with northern Mexico or with the provinces of the southwestern United States, for the good reason that the traces of sixteenth-century building are either negligible or non-existent. In short, the geographical definition for these studies is based upon the diffusion of monumental building in New Spain during the sixteenth century. That area is roughly defined by a great triangle drawn from Nombre de Dios in the northwest, to Tampico in the northeast, and Tehuantepec to the south. The historical center lies in the Valley of Mexico, and with distance from the Capital, the number and size of sixteenth-century buildings diminish.

The field work in 1941 was aided by a grant from the American Council of Learned Societies. My wife and I visited as many monuments as possible, working particularly in the States of Mexico, Puebla, and Morelos, and in Michoacan, Hidalgo, and Oaxaca. We maintained residence in the Capital, returning to it for short periods of archive and library study between motor trips. In each settlement, we tried to gain some idea of sixteenth-century size, then to seek out the individual buildings. Photographs, measurements, and sketch plans were taken on the spot, usually in the course of a single day's visit. Our efforts to locate older archives in the churches were rarely rewarded, and then only with baptismal books or late inventories. Needing more detailed understanding of certain questions we spent two weeks at the Franciscan church in Tepeaca, preparing measured drawings with plane table and alidade sight. Similar drawings of parts of the Dominican establishment of Cuilapan were also made, in less detail. In the Appendix, the monuments visited and studied by the author are indicated by an asterisk before the place name.

The writing during 1943–44 was done with the help of a John Simon Guggenheim Memorial Foundation Fellowship. The continued support of the officers of Yale University has been invaluable. Many kinds of aid were given in Mexico City by the staffs of the Dirección de Monumentos Coloniales, the Museo Nacional, the Departamento de Bienes Nacionales, and the Instituto de Investigaciones Estéticas. My friends Wendell C. Bennett, Lewis P. Curtis, John McAndrew, and Elizabeth Wilder made many suggestions for the improvement of the work. Mr. McAndrew and Miss Wilder gave me much help during a short field trip in 1945. Charles Gibson II donated his time and energy to the field work, to proofreading, and to the index.

For permission to include certain paragraphs in Chapters I, II, and III, I am indebted to the *Hispanic American Historical Review*, the *Art Bulletin*, and the *Journal of the Warburg and Courtauld Institutes*. Mrs. Alice K. Bennett, Mrs. Elizabeth Shaffer Carnell, and Miss Jeannette Fellheimer helped with innumerable details of editing. For other assistance I am indebted to Miss Jayne Kuchar, Noel Dant, Charles Stousland, and Terry Keenan.

Yale University,
New Haven, Connecticut,
September 30, 1947.

G. K.

CONTENTS

VOLUME I

VOLUME II

ILLUSTRATIONS

Italicized numbers refer to text figures; other numbers to plates.

VOLUME I

VOLUME II

The following maps will be found at the end of Volume I:

ABBREVIATIONS

AC	Mexico (City) Cabildo, *Actas de cabildo de la ciudad de México*
CDHM	J. García Icazbalceta, ed., *Colección de documentos para la historia de México*
CDIHE	*Colección de documentos inéditos para la historia de España*
CDIAI	*Colección de documentos inéditos de Indias del archivo de Indias*
CDIU	*Colección de documentos inéditos relativos al descubrimiento, conquista y organización de las antiguas posesiones españolas de ultramar.* Segunda serie
NCDHM	J. García Icazbalceta, ed., *Nueva colección de documentos para la historia de México*
PNE	F. del Paso y Troncoso, ed., *Papeles de Nueva España . . .* Segunda serie. *Geografía y estadística*
Publ. AGN	*Publicaciones del archivo general de la nación*

MEXICAN ARCHITECTURE OF THE SIXTEENTH CENTURY

INTRODUCTION: THE MENDICANT FRIARS

The Indians haue the friers in great reuerence: the occasion is, that by them and by their meanes they are free and out of bondage; which was so ordeined by Charles the emperor: which is the occasion that now there is not so much gold and siluer comming into Europe as there was while the Indians were slaues.

HENRY HAWKS, 1572.[1]

ONE generation after the Conquest of Mexico, by 1550, a great colonial state stood upon the ruins of Indian civilization. The rapid creation of this ordered polity was beset by factional disputes, contradictory methods, and the familiar struggle for power.

The civilian colonists tended to form a hereditary class of great wealth and privilege. The Crown government thwarted such feudatory tendencies by expropriation and the centralization of power in the viceregal government. The status of the populous and civilized Indian peoples of Mexico became a central issue. The civilian colonists wished to control Indian labor: the Crown sought to establish the freedom of the Indian's person and the integrity of his communal lands. In the struggle the Indian's spokesmen and defenders were for a time the Mendicant friars of the Franciscan, Dominican, and Augustinian Orders. Opposed to the Mendicants stood the secular priests of the episcopal hierarchy, whose sacramental functions had been usurped by the friars in Indian communities throughout the land. Henry Hawks, quoted above, states the conflict clearly: the Crown and the friars were allied against civilian interests in the defense of Indian welfare, and at the expense of Crown revenues. But Hawks fails to mention the fourth party to the conflict: the secular clergy whose rise to Crown favor in the second half of the sixteenth century coincided with the collapse and disintegration of Mendicant enterprise.

At no time were Europeans more than a tiny minority. In 1570, the white population of New Spain numbered about seven thousand adult male colonists, interspersed among a known Indian population of some three and a half million souls.[2] Among

1. R. Hakluyt, *Hakluyt's Collection of the Early Voyages, Travels, and Discoveries of the English Nation. A New Ed.* (London, 1809–12), III, 553.

2. These and other figures are taken from the account by López de Velasco (*Geografía y descripción universal de las Indias* [Madrid, 1894], J. Zaragoza, ed.), whose totals contain copyists' or other errors. Wherever alternate estimates were given by López de Velasco, we have taken the larger. The term "colonist" or "white" here signifies "householder" to correspond with López de Velasco's "vecino," and it does not include women or children, although it does include single men and religious.

the religious, over eight hundred belonged to the three Mendicant Orders in 1559, and the secular clergy numbered about five hundred.[3] The civilian settlers (*encomenderos*) enjoying labor grants (see p. 85) were seven hundred in 1572.[4] The remaining five thousand whites may be distributed among civil servants, artisans, miners, farmers, and merchants. The miners lived mainly in the archbishopric of Mexico, in Oaxaca, and in New Galicia, but in 1570, their number did not exceed seventeen hundred. Farmers of European extraction were most abundant in the fertile valleys of the bishopric of Puebla, where twenty-four hundred had settled, about Atlixco, Otumba, Tepeaca, and Tecamachalco. Mexico City sustained a European population numbering about seventeen hundred in 1570, of whom most were civil servants, merchants, and artisans. There remain, in all territories, twelve hundred white colonists, mostly servants, some merchants, and a few craftsmen.

The Mendicant Orders, Franciscan, Dominican, and Augustinian, planned the towns, built the churches, governed the communities, and educated the Indians. Organized during the religious revival of the late Middle Ages, the institutes of the Mendicant friars all specified the practice of poverty and a return to the life of Christ and the Apostles. Their great differences from the monastic orders of an earlier Christianity appeared in preaching activity among urban populations, and in renunciation both of monastic retreat and of the wealth of the secular clergy. In Mexico their missionary foundations and educational establishments were the centers of the emergent patterns of colonial culture.

Although the friars were assisted by Crown grants, and by the encomenderos, who were ordered after 1536 to support the religious foundations within their jurisdictions,[5] the true source of Mendicant power lay, of course, not in its financial backing, but in the autocratic privileges accorded under *patronato real* of the Church in America. By this institution (1508) the Papacy conceded radical privileges to the Spanish Crown, including the collection of tithes and the fundamental right of presenting or nominating the candidates for all benefices in the American colony. The Crown, at the insistence of Cortés, elected the Mendicants to fulfill the mission. By special dis-

3. In 1575, the archdiocese of Mexico supported 158 clerics (M. Cuevas, *Historia de la iglesia en México* [El Paso, 1928], II, 136; Tlaxcala contained 103 parishes; Oaxaca, 37; Michoacan; 94; New Galicia, 90. The figures for New Galicia were compiled in 1584. See *ibid.*, pp. 151–152. We shall assume one cleric for each parish, which is perhaps too generous an estimate.

4. The encomendero is the trustee for a number of Indians whose labor is assigned to him under fiduciary commission. Encomienda designates the commission: the term repartimiento describes the assignable labor of Indians. C. Pérez Bustamante, *Los Orígenes del gobierno virreinal en las Indias Españolas, Don Antonio de Mendoza, primer virrey de la Nueva España (1535–50)* (Santiago [de Compostela] 1928) (Anales de la universidad de Santiago, III), p. 88 ff.; L. B. Simpson, *The Encomienda in New Spain* (Berkeley, 1929) (University of California Publications in History, XIX), p. 92, n. 18.

5. G. de Mendieta, *Historia eclesiástica indiana* (Mexico, 1870), pp. 482–483; M. Cuevas, comp., *Documentos inéditos del siglo XVI para la historia de México* (Mexico, 1914), p. 277.

pensation, members of the regular clergy were permitted to be ordained as parish priests. Thus the Crown confirmed the Mendicants in the exercise of total authority.[6]

Patronato real led to certain abuses.[7] Grave consequences resulted from the crippling of episcopal authority; the Church tended to become the instrument of the royal rather than the pontifical will; the litigiousness of the clergy was encouraged; the financial structure of the Church in America was held in tutelage, and the long periods *sede vacante* in the bishoprics provoked many disorders. But the power of the missionaries in their jurisdictions was unlimited save by the human weakness of the missionary himself. Labor could be impressed without pay. Recalcitrants were whipped or imprisoned. As early as 1533, the municipal council of the City of Mexico complained to the King that Franciscans had arrogated civil authority, interfering with justice and holding prisoners on their own initiative. At Ocuituco before 1541, conditions were so bad that the Augustinians were replaced by a curate.[8]

In short, the authority of the Mendicants was practically absolute, and, equally important, it was buttressed by spiritual imperatives of an apostolic intensity. Civilian immigrants were incapacitated for the labors of a sound colonization by the administrative frustration of their absolute, Roman sense of private property. The weakening of this drive to action did not affect the regular clergy. On the contrary, the Mendicant vows of renunciation, the Christian doctrine of a compassionate deity, and the institutional authority of the sacraments were for a time masterfully supported by the Crown. The agrarian collectivism of the native peoples of America was ideal material within which to realize the Christian community. In the effort the missionary drew closer to the Indians than to his fellow-Europeans, against whom he held the Indians in protective custody until the time of their spiritual and temporal maturity should have arrived. The moral aims of all three Orders were identical; differences manifested themselves in the ways and means of their work.

The Mendicant evangelization of Mexico began in earnest with the arrival of twelve Franciscans in 1524. The Dominicans followed in 1526, and the Augustinians in 1533. As a whole, the pattern of Mendicant activity was defined and established

6. See J. Lloyd Mecham, "The Church in Colonial Spanish America," *Colonial Hispanic America* (Washington, 1936), pp. 200–239, A. C. Wilgus, ed. (Studies in Hispanic American Affairs, IV). The texts of the bulls of concession are available in the Spanish translation by Solórzano, in *Don fray Juan de Çumárraga . . . documentos inéditos* (Mexico, 1941), pp. 95–106. A. M. Carreño, ed. See also L. B. Simpson, *Many Mexicos* (New York, 1941), p. 70.

7. Cuevas, *Historia de la iglesia en México*, II, 58–59.

8. Genaro García, "El Clero de México durante la dominación española," *Documentos inéditos ó muy raros para la historia de México* (Mexico, 1907), XV, 139–140; F. del Paso y Troncoso, comp. *Epistolario de Nueva España, 1505–1818* (Mexico, 1939–42) (Bibliotéca histórica mexicana de obras inéditas, segunda ser., I–XVI), III, 85; also IV, 168 ff.; Cuevas, *op. cit.*, I, 360–361.

by the Franciscans. The Apostolic Twelve (Figs. 1, 237), under the leadership of Martín de Valencia (Fig. 3), rapidly penetrated among the great centers of Indian settlement. The first Bishop of Mexico, fray Juan de Zumárraga (Fig. 2), was a Franciscan. The Franciscan missionaries early established the widest and closest network of foundations, covering the vast triangle of Mexico from Durango to Tampico and Tehuantepec (Map 6). It is therefore to the Franciscans that we must look for some definition of the spiritual drives animating Mendicant activity.

Singularly little has been written about the European antecedents of the Apostolic Twelve. Writers upon the subject have always assumed that the men were simple Franciscans, and that their motives were identical with those of other Franciscans elsewhere in the world. The failure to examine the European preparation of the men under Martín de Valencia, and of fray Juan de Zumárraga in particular, has prevented students from perceiving the reformist and Humanist training of this extraordinary troop of Mendicant radicals.[9]

These men were exalted by a spiritual unrest closely akin to that of the Northern Reformation in Europe. Their story may be said to reach its European climax with the reformatory action of Cardinal Ximénez de Cisneros before 1510. Confessor to Queen Isabella after 1492, Franciscan Provincial in Castile, Archbishop of Toledo, Primate of Spain, Inquisitor General after 1507, twice regent, founder of the University of Alcala, and instigator of the Polyglot Bible, Cisneros was one of the pre-Reformation protagonists of the Humanist *Philosophia Christi* in Europe.[10] As Bataillon has pointed out, Cisneros sought to achieve the purification of the clergy by strengthening the preaching mission and austerity of the Mendicant Orders. How this latter was achieved, we shall see in a moment. Among the Franciscans, he favored the Observance against the lax Conventual branch of the Order. Similar internal movements of reform appeared *ca.* 1500 among Dominicans, Benedictines, and Jeronymites. Hence an enormous increase in reformed Mendicant population occurred in Cisneros' lifetime, an increase that Bataillon has related to the formation of a spiritual militia in the New World. To Cisneros' action, Bataillon also attributes the emergence of a spiritual elite of evangelical tendency, that would sympathize with Erasmus, and come under suspicion of Lutheranism later in the century. Bataillon says this *avant garde* of Catholicism in Spain has profound affinities with the Protestant Reformation. In particular, the reform movement among the Franciscan Observants was the central

9. Thus Simpson, *Many Mexicos*, p. 69, could write that the Franciscans "had few preconceived notions of their mission, and no blueprints . . . practical men . . . of . . . comfortable humanity."

10. See M. Bataillon, *Erasme et l'Espagne; Recherches sur l'histoire spirituelle du XVIe siècle* (Paris, 1937), chap. i. Bataillon notes (p. 5 n.) that the study of the Mendicant reform movement cannot yet be undertaken. Monastic archives are not accessible to scholarship—neither are the documents confiscated by the secularizations of the nineteenth century, and deposited in the Archivo Histórico Nacional in Madrid, as property of the Ministry of Finance.

1. Huejotzingo, mural in the convento, showing the Apostolic Twelve

2. Archbishop fray Juan de Zumárraga

3. Fray Martín de Valencia, mural portrait in the cloister at Tlalmanalco

DE OPTI
MO REIP. STATV, DEQVE
noua insula Vtopia, libellus ue-
re aureus, nec minus salutaris
quàm festiuus, clarissimi disertissimiq; uiri THOMAE MORI in
clytæ ciuitatis Londinensis ciuis
& Vicecomitis.

EPIGRAMMATA clarissimi
disertissimiq; uiri THOMAE
MORI, pleraq; è Græcis uersa.

EPIGRAMMATA. Des. ERA-
SMI Roterodami.

Apud inclytam Basileam.

Es del obpo de Mexico frai Joã Zumarraga.

4. Titlepage of Zumárraga's copy of the Frobenius edition of More and Erasmus

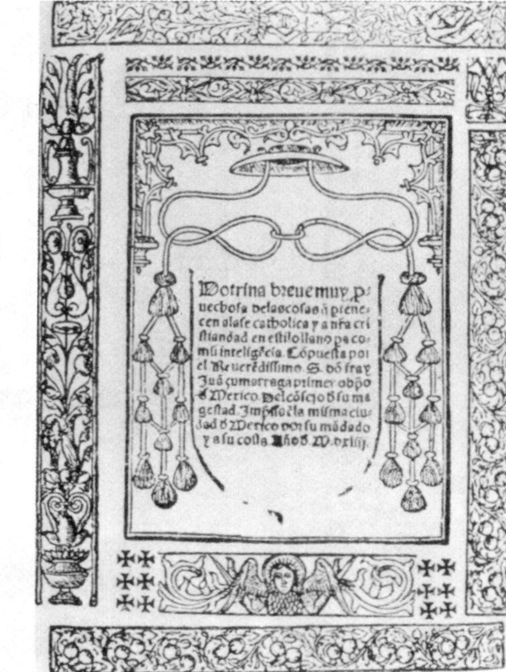
Dotrina breue muy p-
uechosa delas cosas q pertene-
cen ala fe catholica y a nra cri
stiandad en estilo llano pa co-
mũ inteligẽcia. Cõpuesta poi
el Reuerẽdissimo S. dõ fray
Juã çumarraga primer obpo
d Mexico. del cõsejo d su ma
gestad. Impssa ẽla misma ciudad d Mexico por su mãdado
y a su costa. Año d M.d.xliiij.

5. Titlepage of Zumárraga's *Doctrina breve* of 1544

6. Bishop Vasco de Quiroga

phenomenon, in a widespread cult of austerity to which Cardinal Cisneros gave administrative and political form.

The origins of the rift between Conventuals and Observants show in events of the lifetime of St. Francis. Such factions were the Italian Cesarenes after 1289, and many other Observant movements reaffirming the original Franciscan renunciation of property. After the mid-fourteenth century, such tendencies of Observant reform were powerfully impelled by the epidemics and secular disorders of the age. Separate branches increased greatly throughout Europe, such as the Coletani in Cologne and Saxony; the Clarenes in Umbria and Ancona; the Amadeists in Rome; the Neutri, the Caperolani, the Celestines, Martinianists, Narbonenses, Gentiles, etc.[11] In 1506, Julius II ordered these many minor reforms to ally themselves either with the Conventual or the Observant branch of the Order, and to discontinue their separate existences.

In Spain, the history of the Regular Observance is most complicated, especially in its late fifteenth-century stages. Originating as a separate movement, the Spanish return to the strict rule of St. Francis was nominally complete by 1517, when no Conventual house was left in Spain. The special group from which Mexico later drew her friars, was founded in 1487 by fray Juan de la Puebla, and came to be known as the Minorites of the Blessed John of Puebla.

Known in secular life as the Count of Belalcazar, John of Puebla (born 1453) became a Jeronymite in 1476, but gained Sixtus IV's permission to change to the Italian Observance in 1480, when he was received at Subiaco near Assisi. Returning to Spain in 1487 with three Italian friars, to assume his nephew's guardianship, he organized a new reform, the Custodia de los Angeles, with the permission of the General Chapter of the Observance, held in Touraine in 1489. Two houses were founded, one near Hornachuelos in the Sierra Morena of Andalusia, called S. Maria de los Angeles, in 1490, and the other in 1493 at Belalcazar, where the Blessed John died in 1495. Among the purposes of the reform the friars acted to ameliorate the condition of the sparsely settled mountain dwellers of Andalusia, whose religious education had long been neglected for want of priests. In addition, the rule by which the custody was governed prescribed extreme poverty and spiritual retreat. Each week, four friars were selected to go into four separate hermitages, for one week each. At the entrance to the refectory, these friars kissed the feet of all the other friars in the establishment. In retreat, silence was observed, and the friars ate nothing cooked or alive, abstaining even from milk products, disciplining themselves thrice daily, and relieved only from the general obligation to manual labor. The Custodia ultimately included fourteen foundations, when it was incorporated as the Provincia de los Angeles in 1518.[12]

11. See H. Holzapfel, *Handbuch der Geschichte des Franziskanerordens* (Freiburg i/B, 1909), pp. 136 f. M. J. Heimbucher, *Die Orden und Kongregationen der Katholischen Kirche* (3d ed. Paderborn, 1933–34), I, 717–719.

12. P. Hélyot, *Histoire des ordres monastiques,*

After the Blessed John's death his disciple Juan de Guadalupe (born 1450), wishing to extend the reform to the province of Granada, introduced an even severer rule. Hence, although John of Puebla is often taken as the spiritual father of the Discalced or Barefoot movement in the Observance, many incline to credit Juan de Guadalupe with the definitive formulation of this way of life. In creating the *Observantia strictissima,* Guadalupe introduced the pointed cape, short mantle, patched robe, and barefoot practice that were later to be taken over by the Discalced and Capuchin friars. The members of his reform assumed the name of Minorites of the Holy Gospel. In 1496, they secured release from Observant jurisdiction, and proceeded, first to convert the Moslems of Granada, and then to found hermitages at Oropesa and Plasencia. Later foundations were made, after 1500, near Trujillo and in Portugal. Guadalupe and his followers made a practice of preaching an austere and simple Christianity to the spiritually neglected peasants and townsfolk of the western provinces. In such endeavors, the friars prepared unconsciously for the great evangelical mission that was to become theirs in 1523.[13]

Meanwhile the Observants took alarm at the scores of recruits flocking to Juan de Guadalupe. In 1502, after several earlier efforts, they secured a brief from Alexander VI, revoking Guadalupe's privileges as accorded by the same pope in 1496. The reforming friars then were expelled from their Castilian houses, and took refuge in Portugal.[14] Guadalupe died in 1506, but his followers succeeded in securing papal permission to found new establishments. Returning to Castile, they found their houses in Trujillo (N. S. de la Luz) and Salvaleon (Montesion) ruined, and met further persecution from the Observants, because of an earlier allegiance given to the Conventual branch of the Order, precisely in order to escape Observant jurisdiction. Julius II finally accorded them provincial status in 1508, with two *Custodias,* the Piedad in Portugal, and the Santo Evangelio in Castile. The two custodies then met pressure by the Chapter General of the Franciscans to join either the Conventuals or the Regular Observance. For strategic reasons, the Portuguese custody became Observant, and the Castilian custody continued its alliance with the Conventuals. In 1517, upon the initiative of Leo X, all the reforming branches once again considered the choice of aligning either with the Observants or the Conventuals. Provincial status was given both custodies, in Portugal and Castile, and both threw in their lot with the Observ-

religieux et militaires, et des congregations seculières (Paris, 1714–19), VII, 117–120; M. Angel, "La vie franciscaine en Espagne entre les deux couronnements de Charles-Quint ou le premier commissaire general des provinces franciscaines des Indes occidentales," *Revista de archivos, bibliotecas y museos,* XXVI (1912), 180; J. Torrubia, ed., *Chrónica seraphica* (Madrid, 1725–56), IX, 261–278.

13. Holzapfel, *op. cit.,* pp. 141, 323; *Chrónica seraphica,* IX, 282–283, 288.

14. T. Motolinia, "Historia de los indios de la Nueva España," *CDHM,* I (1858), 152–153, L. García Pimentel, ed. (*Documentos históricos de Méjico,* I).

ance. The Castilian group became the Province of S. Gabriel, and the Portuguese became the Province of Piedad. At about the same time, the followers of John of Puebla formed another province, under the advocacy of N. S. de los Angeles.[15]

Hence the remarkably severe reform inaugurated by John of Puebla ultimately found expression in three separate provinces, of which none really wished to be identified with either the Conventuals or the Observants, but only to maintain the integrity of its preaching mission and austerity of retreat, independently of all institutional interference.

With one or another of these *Observantias strictissimas,* all members of the Apostolic Twelve and many friars of the other early missions show intimate connection. They participated in the desperate struggle for autonomy and jurisdictional independence, and they spent their lives as friars within the reform, before their departure to America. Significantly enough, they adopted the name of the Castilian custody, the Santo Evangelio, when naming their Mexican territory, in honor of the custody that had been absorbed by the Regular Observants as the Province of S. Gabriel in 1517.[16] It is again to be stressed that the reformed groups in Spain and Portugal worked among neglected rural and village folk, and that the friars' privileges expressly conceded their status as *predicadores apostólicos,* in order that, in the words of the bull issued by Alexander VI in 1496, they might "throughout the world among the faithful and the infidel, preach the word of God and the Holy Gospel."[17] In such terms was it possible for the reforming Franciscans to prepare for their American mission, by defining a labor of evangelization in Europe itself, that none of their Franciscan colleagues would undertake. The rule established by Juan de Guadalupe is by far the more important, in that he originally worked in the newly-conquered province of Granada, among the Moslem farmers and townspeople who had no other religious attentions. Here, then, is the specific preparation for the American work, among a non-European people in Spain itself, in the territory designated as the Custodia del Santo Evangelio.[18]

The Apostolic mission of the Twelve was very clearly present to the authorities

15. Hélyot, *op. cit.,* VII, 120–129; *Chrónica seraphica,* IX, 278–386.

16. A. de Vetancurt, *Chrónica* (Mexico, 1697), *Teatro,* Pt. IV, pp. 2–3, "resuscitando este Soberano titulo que tuvo la provincia de S. Gabriel." See L. Wadding, *Annales Minorum seu trium ordinum a. s. Francisco institutorum* (3d ed. Quaracchi, Italy, 1931–33), XVI, 182 ff. (1523). The naming of Puebla in 1531 may honor the founder of the Spanish province, the Blessed John of Puebla (suggested by J. McAndrew).

17. Text of bull in *Chrónica seraphica,* IX, 291–293.

18. *Ibid.,* IX, 294–295. Their activity among the Moslems of Granada, however, was shortlived, because of opposition from fray Hernando de Talavera, 1st Archbishop of Granada. Andrés de Cordova, who went to Mexico in 1524, accompanied Guadalupe to Granada (*ibid.,* p. 303). Using the biographies of the early bishops in America, R. Ricard, "Granada y America," *Sociedad mexicana de geografía y estadística, Primer centenario . . . 1833–1923* (Mexico, 1933), I, 245–247, has made the same point. In this he follows P. Leturia in *Razón y Fe* (Madrid, 1927).

and to the friars themselves. Their number explicitly appears in 1523, at the time of their appointment, as twelve, "quoniam hic fuit numerus discipulorum Christi."[19] The plan probably comes from the General of the Order, Francisco de Quiñones, who later became the Cardinal de Santa Cruz. Quiñones himself wished to go to the Indies, and in effect, received the permission of Leo X on April 25, 1521. Later, in 1526, he wished to take charge of the entire missionary enterprise in America, in the spirit of the primitive Apostolic Church. The plan remained the constant obsession of his later career.[20] But Quiñones was an anti-Erasmian in his dealings with Charles V and the Papacy, even if he advanced the Cisnerian pre-Reformation by his belief that Christianity might revive through the strict Franciscan Observance.[21]

In any event, it was Quiñones, who, when attending the chapter meeting of Province of S. Gabriel at Belvis in 1523, ordered Martín de Valencia to take his following and go forth upon the Mexican mission. Fray Martín was the first provincial elected in S. Gabriel, taking office in 1518, and insisting upon an extreme severity of discipline in the houses of the Province.[22] In 1523, the Province had but one hundred seventy-five friars in eleven *conventos,* from which fray Martín drew his Apostolic band.[23] Without exception, every one of the twelve had taken refuge in the reform group from the lax and secular life of conventual establishments elsewhere; indeed one of them, Alonso Suárez, quite like Martín de Valencia, once entertained the thought of becoming a Carthusian in the quest for a greater severity of rule.[24] Both Martín de Valencia and Andrés de Cordova, furthermore, were disciples of Juan de Guadalupe.[25] It was a tightly knit, radical little band of men who had worked together for many years as apostolic preachers and in the intention of effecting great conversions.[26] By 1543, the fame of their work was proclaimed by Alonso de Isla in the following words,

I do believe that it stands with them as it did in the primitive church, as we read in the Acts of the Apostles [2, 44] where it is said, "And all that believed were together; and had all things common." It does not seem to be otherwise in these [countries] converted and taught by the twelve apostolic friars.[27]

19. Wadding, *op. cit.*, par. 163, p. 188. On the legal aspects of the Mexican conversion, see S. A. Zavala, *Las Instituciones jurídicas en la conquista de América* (Madrid, 1935) (Junta para ampliación de estudios e investigaciones científicas. Centro de estudios históricos. Sección hispano-americano, I).

20. Angel, "La Vie franciscaine en Espagne entre les deux couronnements de Charles-Quint," *Revista de archivos, bibliotecas y museos,* XXVI (1912), 167, 178–179, 188–189, 192–183. Clement VII described him in 1526 as "ymitando en ello a los santos apostoles de dios la evangelica virtud."

21. Bataillon, *op. cit.*, pp. 354, 399; Angel, *op. cit.*, XXVI, 171.

22. See Motolinia, *op. cit.*, pp. 154–155, and the biography by Martín's close friend, Francisco Jiménez, published by A. Lopez, "Vida de fray Martín de Valencia, escrita por su compañero Fr. Francisco Jiménez," *Archivo ibero-americano,* XIII (1926), 48–83.

23. Angel, *Revista de archivos, bibliotecas y museos,* XXVIII (1913), 185–186.

24. F. Serrate de San Nicolás, *Compendio histórico de los santos* (Seville, 1729), p. 135. López, *Archivo ibero-americano,* XIII (1926), 54.

25. Serrate, *op. cit.*, pp. 116, 143.

26. See Motolinia, *op. cit.*, p. 151, on Martín's vision of his future mission in Mexico, vouchsafed him before 1500.

27. Alonso de Isla, *Thesoro de virtudes* (Medina del Campo, 1543), cited from Angel, *Revista de archivos,*

Thus the grand program of Cardinal Cisneros came to realization, beyond even his intentions, carried by the obscure friars from western Spain. But in 1524, the Franciscan missionaries were not, to our knowledge, in contact with the political and religious thought of North European Humanism. If the Apostolic Twelve represented Cisnerian Spain, a later group of missionaries under Juan de Zumárraga represented Erasmian thought in Mexico.

In 1527, the year of Zumárraga's nomination by Charles V as first Bishop of Mexico, the court of Spain carried on an extraordinary discussion of the work and philosophy of Erasmus. The powerful Chancellor, Gattinara, not only read Erasmus, but was aided in Latin correspondence by Alonso de Valdes, the great admirer of Erasmus.[28] Erasmus' name was again much discussed, when the monastic orders undertook to demonstrate errors in Erasmus' writings; in March, 1527, their presentation before the Grand Inquisitor oddly took the form of strong praise. Not only was the Emperor favorably disposed towards Erasmus, but the Archbishop of Toledo and the Grand Inquisitor followed the paths of admiration laid out by Cardinal Cisneros. The Conference of Valladolid, held in June and July, brought Erasmus' writings under close scrutiny by large numbers of his supporters and enemies in Spain. As Bataillon has shown in great detail, these events precipitated the "Erasmian invasion" of Spain after 1527. For our purposes, it is important that the Emperor spent Holy Week in the monastery at Abrojo, near Valladolid.[29] This monastery, in the strict Observant province of Concepción,[30] had Zumárraga as its guardian at that moment, following his term of office as Provincial (1520–26).[31] The Emperor's attention was first drawn to Zumárraga by his charity and austerity, and Zumárraga accepted an Inquisitorial commission to punish the sorcerers of Biscaya, whose language and customs he knew well as a native of Durango. His nomination to the see of Mexico came at the end of 1527.[32] It is this friar who has been listed with the Grand Inquisitor Manrique, Archbishop Fonseca, Bishop Cabrero, Archbishop Merino, and Alonso

bibliotecas y museos, XXVI, 171: "Cierto a mi se me figura que sera entre ellos lo que era en la primitiva yglesia. Segun se lee en las Actas de los apostoles, donde dize. Que eran todos de un coraçon e de vna anima: e que todas las cosas eran a ellos en comun [Acts 2, 44]. No creo que sera menos en estos convertidos y enseñados por aquellos doze varones apostolicos." Alonso de Isla made these remarks upon publishing Martín de Valencia's letter to the Chapter of Toulouse (1532). In 1528, at least six more missionaries were recruited in the Provincia de S. Gabriel. See Serrate, *op. cit.,* pp. 144–149.

28. Bataillon, *op. cit.,* pp. 246–247. In this connection, Bataillon speaks of a "moment aigu de l'érasmisme espagnol. Il y a quelques années pendant lesquelles l'érasmisme, pour l'élite intellectuelle de la cour, est une atmosphère idéologique permettant de concilier le zèle antiromain avec la volonté d'orthodoxie et la ferveur évangélique," p. 249.

29. M. Foronda y Aguilera, *Estancias y viajes del emperador Carlos V* (Madrid, 1914), p. 289. April 18–23.

30. In 1528, the province was staffed by 1100 friars in thirty-four conventos. Angel, *Revista de archivos, bibliotecas y museos,* XXVIII (1913), 185–186. It was constituted in 1518 from territory previously held by the Province of Santiago (Holzapfel, *op. cit.,* p. 390).

31. Angel, *Revista de archivos, bibliotecas y museos,* XXIX (1913), 205.

32. J. García Icazbalceta, *Don fray Juan de Zumárraga, primer obispo y arzobispo de México* (Mexico, 1881). Andrés de Olmos accompanied him on the witch hunt.

Ruiz de Virues, as among the outstanding Erasmian prelates of Spain in the reign of Charles V.[33] As Zumárraga was born *ca.* 1461, it is likely that he became aware of the thought of Erasmus long before his episcopal nomination. Unfortunately, his early biography is unknown, but several events in his Mexican career indicate an audacious and radical policy of action, founded upon the *Philosophia Christi* promulgated by Erasmus and diffused throughout the literate world of Spain by 1525.

The main documents of Zumárraga's contact with Spanish Erasmianism are the doctrinal books printed in Mexico under his direction, and a copy of More's *Utopia* and Erasmus' *Epigrammata* in his possession (Fig. 4).[34] The Mexican imprints have been the subject of exhaustive study by Marcel Bataillon,[35] both the *Doctrina breve* of 1544 (Fig. 5) and the *Doctrina cristiana,* of 1545 and 1546.[36] The *Doctrina breve* purported to instruct the priests of the Mexican diocese. From Erasmus' *Enchiridion* Zumárraga adapted the chapters upon the remedies against vices; and the *Paraclesis* yielded the conclusion. In compiling the little work, Zumárraga availed himself of the modified translation by Alonso Fernández de Madrid (Arcediano del Alcor). In general, Zumárraga departed from Erasmus in insisting upon the gentility of the Platonic, Stoic, and Pythagorean philosophers. He changed Erasmus' *Filosofía cristiana* to "doctrina cristiana," and deleted the name of Erasmus, but confirmed the denunciation of scholasticism. Zumárraga also approved Erasmus' advocacy of the unlimited diffusion of Scripture, as in the *Paraclesis,* and kept the doctrine of interior Christianity intact. On the whole, the Pauline formulas of Charity appear as in the *Enchiridion.* The unfavorable remarks about Mendicants were, of course, suppressed.

The *Doctrina cristiana,* on the other hand, was prepared as a catechism for Indian use. It rests upon the *Suma de doctrina christiana* by Dr. Constantino Ponce de la Fuente, confessor to Charles V, and head of the so-called "Lutheran" movement in Seville. This little summary of essential Christianity, conceived in the spirit of Erasmus, insists upon the primacy of faith over works. It had a wide distribution in Spain, appearing in at least five editions between 1543 and 1551. When Zumárraga author-

33. Bataillon, *op. cit.,* p. 580.

34. The earliest modern reference to Zumárraga's "heterodoxy," in 1887, is reported by J. García Icazbalceta, in "Códice franciscano," *NCDHM,* II (1889), 295–303. Icazbalceta came to the correct conclusion that at the time Zumárraga was active, the "heterodoxy" of his position had not yet been clearly defined in European Catholicism. The University of Texas owns the copy of the *Epigrammata* (Basel, Frobenius, 1518); the book has been described by S. A. Zavala, *Ideario de Vasco de Quiroga* (Mexico, 1941), pp. 51–54.

35. Erasmus, *El Enquiridion . . . y La Paráclesis . . .,* ed. D. Alonso (Traducciones españoles del siglo XVI) (Madrid, 1932) (*Revista de filología española,* Anejo XVI), Appendix III. Also M. Bataillon, "Erasme au Mexique," Société historique algérienne, Algiers. *Deuxième congrès national des sciences historiques, 1930* (Algiers, 1932), pp. 31–34. Bataillon here gives parallel passages from Erasmus and Zumárraga, and suggests that Zumárraga knew the *Diálogo de doctrina cristiana* by Juan Valdés.

36. For exact descriptions, see García Icazbalceta, *Bibliografía mexicana del siglo XVI* (Mexico, 1886), pp. 6, 10; as well as his *Don fray Juan de Zumárraga.*

ized its printing in Mexico, it was enriched by a conclusion drawn again from the *Paraclesis.*

Zumárraga's own copy of Erasmus' *Epigrammata* is the Froben edition of 1518, which contains More's *Utopia.* In the two sections of the English humanist's book, two contrasting worlds intersect: the world of Henry VIII with its gross inequalities and the depredations of court and clergy; and the ideal world of humanism. A Lucianic irony enhances the contrast—England and Utopia mirror one another in reversed and opposite images; England's misery and the serenity of Utopia in More's intention, represent actual and possible worlds, perhaps in the relation of nightmare—from which the sleeper will awake—to reality.

For the Mexican humanists, such complexities in the English political situation were irrelevant. They attended only to the possible and ideal world of Utopia. The marginal notations to the *Utopia* are nearly all in the same rapid hand, and bear an unmistakable resemblance to Zumárraga's known holographs.[37] Zumárraga's notations show him especially sensitive to More's remarks upon the foolish estimation of gold, upon crafts and hospitals, social organization, and religious exercises. They are the notes of a straightforward, simple man of action, revealing a decidedly naive curiosity about the natural and historical identification of Utopia, as on p. 63, where he glosses More's navigational distances. Zumárraga failed to comment upon More's esthetics, or his speculations on health and the pleasures of the mind. Significantly, there is no comment upon the passages treating of war and religious tolerance, but much upon the industry of Utopians (one marginal note reads "none is idle"), the manner of dying, the laws, the forms of religious community, the size of the *familia* ("30 families eat together"), the status of priests, and the form of towns, where Zumárraga has underlined the passages describing Utopian architecture with heavy, rapid, agitated strokes.

We are still ignorant of the main details of Zumárraga's spiritual biography. Was he an "erasmianizing" prelate before leaving Spain in 1528, or did he come under Erasmus' influence after beginning his American mission? Were fray Andrés de Olmos, the linguist, and fray Juan de Alameda, the builder, chosen to accompany him in 1527, from among a circle of humanist friars in the Provincia de la Concepción?[38] How long before 1540 did Zumárraga's intention to mediate the *Philosophia Christi* to Indians take shape in his mind? The answers to these and many other questions lie in the conventual archives of Spain.

37. See Carreño, ed., *Don fray Juan de Çumarraga,* n.p., "poder otorgado al chantre Cristobal de Pedraza, 1536." Zavala, *Ideario,* p. 53, was unable to identify them with the hand of Quiroga, and admitted the possibility that they were written by Zumárraga.

38. Cf. Mendieta, *Historia eclesiástica indiana,* pp. 644, 654.

One incident in Franciscan recruitment for the Mexican mission deserves mention. In 1532, at the General Chapter of the Regular Observance held in Toulouse, letters from Martín de Valencia and Juan de Zumárraga arrived, asking for missionaries to work in the Indies. The Latin letters at once appeared in French and German, the latter in several editions, and thus circulated widely throughout Europe.[39] The date and place of promulgation are significant. In the 1530's Toulouse was among the foremost university cities of the world, especially in jurisprudence; extravagantly pious, with a pan-European population.[40] It was also the scene of great religious unrest. Between 1528 and 1532, evangelical ideas had spread among the university students, and scriptural studies were secretly conducted in the Augustinian monastery. An inquisitorial trial brought the discovery of a religious movement throughout southwestern France. Its leader, Jean de Cahors, was burned alive in 1532, and decrees of arrest were issued against some forty students, friars, and professors of law.[41] The moment coincides with the most active recruitment of friars by the Franciscan mission in Mexico, and it suggests that an investigation of the European antecedents of the many dozens of Franciscans arriving in Mexico after 1532 would throw much light upon the religious motivation of the Mexican mission.[42]

Similar uncertainties surround the biography of the first Bishop of Michoacan, Vasco de Quiroga (Fig. 6), Zumárraga's friend, and the disciple of Thomas More. About Quiroga we know nothing between 1492 and 1530, and yet, as Zavala has shown, he was one of the most effective agents of humanist Christianity in Mexico.[43] In 1531, the Audiencia commissioned him to establish a center for the Indians just released from monastic schools. The object was to provide a place of passage between the atmosphere of the schools and the still pagan environment of the Indians' families.[44] The settlement, called Santa Fe (Fig. 99), was later duplicated upon the north shore of Lake Patzcuaro. The special interest of these communities is that they are the earliest manifestations now known in Mexico, of Humanist and Erasmian ideas of social reform, for Zumárraga's catechisms did not appear until the mid-1540's. Quiroga

39. H. Harrisse, *Biblioteca americana vetustissima* (New York, 1866), pp. 244, 168, 177, 186, Add. 98.

40. H. Tollin, "Toulouser Studentenleben im Anfange des 16. Jahrhunderts," *Historisches Taschenbuch*, XLIV (1874), 77–98.

41. V.–L. Bourrilly and N. Weiss, "Jean du Bellay," *Société de l'histoire du protestantisme français, Bulletin*, LIII (1904), 102–103.

42. See A. Génin, *Les Français au Mexique du XVIe siècle à nos jours* (Paris, 1933), pp. 55–97, and this volume, pp. 96–97, for names of French friars in Mexico.

43. S. A. Zavala, *La "Utopia" de Tomás Moro en la Nueva España, y otros estudios* (Mexico, 1937) (Biblioteca historica mexicana de obras inéditas, IV); *idem, Ideario de Vasco de Quiroga*. J. Fernández and E. O'Gorman, *Santo Tomás Moro y "La Utopia de Tomas Moro en la Nueva España"* (Mexico, 1937). R. Aguayo Spencer, ed., *Don Vasco de Quiroga, Documentos* (Mexico, 1939). J. Xirau, "Humanismo español," *Cuadernos americanos*, I (1942), 147, supposes the men were all acquainted in Spain, Zumárraga, Las Casas, and Quiroga, Vives, and others. No proof is offered.

44. H. Ternaux-Compans, *Voyages, relations et mémoires originaux pour servir à l'histoire de la découverte de l'Amérique* (Paris, 1837–41), sér. II, Vol. V, 166.

stated explicitly in later life that he had patterned his towns upon More's *Utopia* (Fig. 4), of which a copy was in the possession of his friend, Zumárraga. The municipal ordinances composed by Quiroga before 1565 also reveal the closest affinities with the social thought of Thomas More.[45] An interesting estimate of the character of Quiroga comes from the pen of his colleague, the Oidor Salmerón, who wrote in 1531, that Quiroga was "virtuous and most solicitous for the welfare of the Indians; but timid and scrupulous, therefore more apt to carry out orders than to give them."[46] It is the familiar judgment made at all times of idealists by their busy colleagues. But the unsolved question immediately arises, whether Quiroga was acting upon his own initiative, or "carrying out orders" of the Audiencia when he founded the Utopian Santa Fe.

Thus the two Franciscans, Martín de Valencia and Juan de Zumárraga, and the humanist lawyer, Vasco de Quiroga, carried to New Spain the idealist social and religious theory of their day. The part played by the Augustinians and the Dominicans is less well known. That the Cisnerian reform, if not the *Philosophia Christi,* extended to the other Mendicant Orders in Spain, has been suggested, but not demonstrated in detail.[47] Among the Dominicans, an Observant movement took form at the close of the fifteenth century, in the foundation of new houses at Granada, Avila, and Valladolid. The head of the first Dominican mission to Mexico in 1526, Domingo de Betanzos (Fig. 359), was an austere exponent of monastic reform. Born *ca.* 1480, he resolved, when still a student of law at Salamanca, to become a hermit. After examining the conditions at the monastery of Montserrat, he rejected the thought of becoming a Benedictine and continued to Rome. Upon an island near Naples, he withdrew in eremitic retreat for five years. Returning to Spain, he took the Dominican habit in 1510, and applied for passage to Hispaniola in 1515,[48] where he is reported to have influenced Bartolomé de las Casas to enter the Order. In Mexico, Betanzos' policy was to introduce the strictest possible observance. He wished to establish twelve great conventos, each with thirty resident friars, who should go forth in pairs to administer the district. Although he never fully realized his desire, Betanzos, as much as Martín de Valencia, may be regarded as an instrument of the Cisnerian reform.[49]

The internal history of the Spanish Augustinians at this period still remains

45. *Colección de documentos inéditos de Indias del archivo de Indias* (Madrid, 1864–84), X, 493, 511. See our Chapter II, pp. 223–224. Later reference in the text to this work will be made as *CDIAI*. See also R. P. Adams, "Designs by More and Erasmus for a New Social Order," *Studies in Philology,* XLII (1945), 131–145.

46. Ternaux-Compans, *Voyages,* sér. II, Vol. V, 195.

47. Bataillon, *Erasme et l'Espagne,* pp. 5, 7.

48. A. M. Carreño, *Fray Domingo de Betanzos* (Mexico, 1924), pp. 21–31.

49. Another Dominican was the first bishop of Tlaxcala; fray Julian Garcés had taught in Paris and was so accomplished a Latinist that the great grammarian, Antonio de Lebrija, said he must study further to equal Garcés, at least according to P. de la P. C. Beaumont, *Crónica de Michoacán* (Mexico, 1932) (*Publ. AGN,* XXVII–XIX).

obscure. A reformed or Observant branch of the Order was introduced into Spain in 1430 by Juan de Alarcón. By 1505, its houses were so numerous that a division into four provinces was necessary—New Castile, Old Castile, Leon, and Andalusia. The strict Observance of the Discalced or Recollect Augustinians did not come to Spain until 1588.[50] For our purposes, the most striking figure in the Augustinian mission of Mexico was fray Alonso de la Vera Cruz. Educated at Alcala, in the University founded by Cardinal Cisneros, and under Francisco de Vitoria at Salamanca, he was invited in 1535 by the head of the Mexican mission to accompany him to America, as a secular priest who would instruct the friars in arts and theology. Taking the Augustinian vows in Mexico in 1537, fray Alonso first worked among the Tarascans at Tiripitio. In 1542 Bishop Quiroga put him in charge of the diocese during Quiroga's contemplated absence in Spain. After a life of productive scholarship and vigorous missionary activity, fray Alonso was sent to Spain in 1562, and gained the favor of Philip II. Before returning to Mexico he became *Visitador y Reformador de los conventos del Reino de Toledo*. Escobar adds the interesting comment that this office was given him in order that he might introduce into Europe the stricter Augustinian Observance of America.[51] That this Mexican Observance was not out of touch with Erasmian circles in Spain is revealed by the attitude of Alonso de la Vera Cruz, upon hearing of the arrest of fray Luis de León by the Inquisition. The Augustinian mystic, as Bataillon has shown, became the proponent of a veiled Erasmian illuminism, and fray Alonso, when he learned the distressing news of fray Luis' arrest, spoke out before the assembled University in Mexico, saying that the Inquisition might burn him if they burned fray Luis, for he agreed with the manner of the propositions for which the poet had been arrested.[52]

With respect to the other Mendicants in Mexico, moreover, the Augustinians displayed a radical humanism, insisting more upon the high moral capacity of the Indians than did their Franciscan and Dominican colleagues, and admitting the Indians to Communion and Extreme Unction,[53] sacraments which the Franciscans sometimes refused the Indians. The late-coming Augustinians carried a Christian humanism that in certain respects reached far deeper than that of their Mendicant

50. See P. Hélyot, *Dictionnaire des ordres religieux* (Paris, 1847–59), I, cols. 301–332. J. Bricout, *Dictionnaire pratique des connaissances religieuses* (Paris, 1925–28), I, cols. 534–535. Heimbucher, *op. cit.*, I, 543–545.

51. M. de Escobar, *Americana thebaida* (2d ed. Mexico, 1924), p. 337. For the life of fray Alonso, see García Icazbalceta, *Bibliografía mexicana*, pp. 77 ff. Fray Alonso returned to Mexico in 1573 and died in 1584.

52. J. de Grijalva, *Crónica de la orden de N. P. S. Augustín en las provincias de la Nueva España, en quatro edades desde el año de 1533 hasta el de 1592* (2d ed. Mexico, 1924–30), p. 327. Cf. Bataillon, *Érasme et l'Espagne*, pp. 803–811. The *Nombres de Cristo*, which Bataillon analyzes, was begun at the time of fray Luis' imprisonment. See A. F. G. Bell, *Luis de Leon (a Study of the Spanish Renaissance)* (Oxford, 1925), pp. 143, 146. The charges against fray Luis were that he had translated the *Song of Songs* (giving literal interpretation), and had belittled the authority of the Vulgate.

53. R. Ricard, *La "Conquête spirituelle" du Mexique* (Paris, 1933), p. 132.

colleagues, in assuming the spiritual readiness of the Indians, and shortening their tutelage.

Hence it is fairly easy, in the light of the recent investigations by Bataillon and Zavala, to demonstrate that the intellectual leaders of the Mexican colonization were governed by the most novel religious and social ideas of their day in Spain, and that they formed a spiritual *avant garde* for the late Renaissance in America.

Much less edifying is the history of the friars' political behavior in their complex struggle for colonial power—a struggle in which the friars' enemies were the encomenderos and the parish priests or secular clergy.

The class of encomenderos consisted principally of armed citizens whose subsistence was derived from the usufruct of Indian labor, rather than from the exercise of productive trades. Among the exhaustive autobiographical notices compiled between 1546 and 1550,[54] the most common qualification is that the subject possesses no trade or other means of support, but bears arms, maintains horses, and stands at the disposition of the Crown for military service. The encomenderos preferred to live in the cities, many congregating in the capital, rather than near Indian towns or among their Indians. A few more lived in the provincial towns founded by and for the whites. Puebla, Valladolid, Guadalajara, Zacatula, Colima, Veracruz, Villa Alta de San Ildefonso, La Purificación, Compostela, Panuco, Santiago de los Valles, and a few mining settlements are examples. Compared with the large Indian towns, these were mostly villages of impermanent construction.

The centripetal tendency of the white colonists was most pronounced among the craftsmen; they were European bourgeois, of whom few resided before 1550 outside the capital. Mexico City had the only concentration of currency; it was the only large urban white settlement: in other places the demand for manufactured products was long satisfied by Indian labor or by imports.

It is axiomatic, in pre-industrial societies, that a polity dominated by the military caste discounts the ethical value of manual labor. Such was surely the case in sixteenth-century Mexico. But the social behavior of the entire civilian population of the colony was further conditioned by the erratic policy of the Crown with regard to private property. Until late in the century, no European enjoying the use of Indian labor was certain that his control over that labor would be made permanent. As early as 1530, the Crown undertook to restrict, curtail, and ultimately absorb outstanding encomiendas. Secret instructions to the Second Audiencia[55] could not be realized, because en-

54. F. A. de Icaza, *Conquistadores y pobladores de Nueva España; diccionario autobiográfico* (Madrid, 1923). Artisans composed about one per cent of this class before 1550.

55. See Simpson, *Encomienda,* for a historical treatment of the events to the end of the reign of Viceroy Mendoza. S. A. Zavala, *La Encomienda indiana* (Madrid, 1935) (Junta para ampliación de

comienda was a uniquely efficient instrument of colonization. No adequate substitute had yet been devised. The enforcement of the reform laws of 1542,[56] which were animated by an impractical and lofty humanitarianism, would have caused all private grants vacated through decease or maladministration to revert to the Crown. These *Nuevas leyes* met with such violent disapproval that the pertinent clauses were revoked in 1546. Later on, an effort to suspend the inheritance of encomienda after the third generation led to renewed disturbances. Thus the driving power of the colonists was checked and retarded; the processes of economic stabilization were frustrated, and the ethical values of the *Conquista* survived beyond their prime. In the encomenderos' view, the incipient absolutism of the Crown threatened the survival of the colony.

By the seventeenth century, however, the gradual process of Crown absorption advanced considerably.[57] The encomienda gave way to *corregimiento,* or Crown property, administered by Crown officials.[58] With corregimiento, the Crown acquired control of large labor reserves for the mines and other enterprises. The inception of a feudal order based upon encomienda was arrested. Thus the effort of the Crown to reduce private demands upon Indian labor has a double aspect. On the one side, in the representations made by Bishop Las Casas, the anti-encomienda legislation of 1542 had a humanitarian and idealist countenance; but on the other, and in terms of long-range colonial policy, the gradual incorporation of outstanding encomiendas enhanced the power of the Crown, and put the major resource of the colony, i.e., Indian labor, largely at the disposal of the State. In the process, the civilian colonists who once held encomiendas, became government officials or constables. It cannot be overemphasized that the institution of encomienda was the most powerful single instrument of the Spaniards in the colonization of the Indians, a fact known to the Second Audiencia in Mexico, to Fuenleal, to Mendoza, and to the agent, Tello de Sandoval, who was sent to Mexico with the New Laws in 1544; in short, to every realistic administrator engaged in colonial government. Thus the anti-feudatory legislation promoted at Court by the humanitarian faction met opposition in the colony until the mid-century from the administrators entrusted with its execution. These administrators realized that without encomienda, there would be no colonization. The truth was that when an Indian community, or a group of communities fell within an encomienda grant, the Indians' control of their land was gravely endangered. If the

estudios e investigaciones científicas. Centro de estudios históricos. Sección hispano-americana, II), treats the juridical problems of the same period, as well as the later history of the institution. The two books are complementary.

56. Pérez Bustamante, . . . *Don Antonio de Mendoza,* chap. viii; Simpson, *op. cit.;* Zavala, *op. cit.*

57. *Ibid.*, pp. 312–314. In 1546, 537 encomiendas were in private hands; by 1572, their number had dropped to 351 in the same area (New Spain excluding Yucatan and Tabasco); and in 1602, only 140 encomiendas survived.

58. Simpson, *Encomienda,* p. 113; G. Kubler, "The Quechua in the Colonial World," *Handbook of South American Indians,* J. H. Steward, ed. Vol. II, *The Andean Civilizations* (Washington, 1946), pp. 331–410 (Smithsonian Institution. U. S. Bureau of American Ethnology. Bulletin 143).

community could not meet its tribute obligations, or if its headmen could be bribed, the community lands might without restraint be offered for sale.[59] The widespread institution of encomienda therefore signified the progressive dissolution, or the enforced dispersal of Indian land rights. Encomienda may rightly be compared to the *latifundismo* of the nineteenth century: any incorporation of Indian lands by a private colonist signifies some progress in the dissolution of an economically free Indian society. The Crown, for humanitarian and economic reasons, wished to arrest this progress. Colonial officials, clergy, and colonists more or less agreed to hasten dissolution through perpetuating the institution of encomienda.[60]

But among the Mendicant Orders, at least, unanimous agreement and a consistent plan of action developed slowly. In the Dominican Order, for instance, Las Casas was the main propagandist for the New Laws, but his colleague and mentor, Domingo de Betanzos, bitterly opposed expropriation of the encomenderos as early as 1531.[61] Ultimately, at the time of the propagation of the New Laws in 1544, Betanzos' views were adopted by the three Orders acting in unison. But it is important to remark that the Franciscans in particular came only gradually to this pro-encomendero view. In 1531, when the Second Audiencia first attempted to follow the secret instructions to incorporate outstanding encomiendas, they reported to the King that the irate encomenderos believed the bishop and friars to be responsible for the ordinances.[62] Another indication of early Franciscan opposition to the institution of encomienda appears in the case of land at Huejotzingo. Just before 1535, fray Antonio de Ciudadrodrigo approved a distribution of idle community lands among the leadmen of the settlement. Viceroy Mendoza was asked, shortly after his arrival, to approve the deed. This he was glad to do in his desire to aid the Indians. But on second thought, and in 1550, he judged the action most prejudicial to the "república" and advised his successor to beware of repeating his mistake.[63] The implication is that any such vacant, idle, or unclaimed lands should be converted to European use, either by sale or appointment, rather than returned to Indian communities. Hence the Viceroy condemned a Mendicant effort to reënforce the economic basis of Indian society.

59. See V. de Puga, ed., *Provisiones, cédulas, instrucciones de Su Majestad, ordenanças de difuntos y audiencia para la buena expedición de los negocios y administración de justicia y governación de esta Nueva España, y para el buen tratamiento y conservación de los Indias dende el año de 1525 hasta este presente de 63* (2d ed. Mexico, 1878–79), I, 367–368.

60. In 1550, Viceroy Mendoza wrote that the only revenue from the colony was produced by the Spaniards, in mines, silk-growing, and cattle-raising. Indian enterprise produced little or nothing. His implication is that European enterprise is to be favored at the expense of Indian labor. Mexico (Viceroyalty), *Instrucciones que los vireyes de Nueva España dejaron á sus sucesores* (Mexico, 1873) (Biblioteca histórica de la Iberia, XIII–XIV), I, 29.

61. His opinion is printed in *CDHM*, II, 190–197. Zavala, *op. cit.*, p. 65, has interpreted this letter as a plea for the constitution of a medieval body politic in New Spain. Actually, it corroborates only the opinion of Viceroy Mendoza that royal income is best to be increased by European private enterprise.

62. Ternaux-Compans, *Voyages*, Sér. II, Vol. V, 132. Cf. Simpson, *Encomienda*, pp. 121, 132.

63. *Instrucciones que los vireyes*, I, 27.

At the time of the first effort to cancel encomienda between 1530 and 1535, many Mendicants supported the Crown in its anti-feudatory campaign. By 1544 their views had changed to an outright advocacy of perpetual encomienda status for Indian peoples.[64] The Franciscans reported to the King that in their opinion, the Spaniards would lose, and the Indians suffer from the creation of corregimientos. The Dominicans submitted a similar opinion, in which they argued that royal income depended upon the number of wealthy, taxable colonists, and that the creation of corregidores would lead to a shrinking of the European colony and the growth of military government. At once after promulgation of these laws, the three Orders sent a mission to Europe to appeal directly to the Emperor.[65]

The conditions for this change in the attitude of the Mendicants are difficult to establish. L. B. Simpson wrote that the Church "accepted the encomienda, because it continued the familiar feudal organization, and because the notion of the spiritual wardship of backward peoples is not incompatible with Christianity."[66] But we have just seen that the churchmen of the period, secular and regular, came from liberal and humanist circles in European Catholicism. The date of the Mendicant defense of encomienda, furthermore, coincides closely with the printed Erasmian manuals of Christianity published by fray Juan de Zumárraga.[67] The sudden Mendicant defense of the new feudatories is inconsistent with their earlier intention to create the Christian Utopia among the Indians of New Spain.

Article XXXI of the New Laws[68] decreed the Crown incorporation of encomiendas awarded to all prelates, monasteries, and houses of religion. It is difficult to relate this legislation to Mendicant behavior. The examples of encomienda owned by the Orders were very rare before 1550, as when the tribute of Texcoco accrued to the Augustinians for three years after 1541, or when, *ca.* 1535–36, Ocuituco was given to the Augustinians, and later, after 1536, to Zumárraga.[69] These cases are exceptional, and do not alone account for the Mendicants' emphatic support of perpetual encomienda in 1544. The friars drew their strength from other sources than encomienda, from patronato real, and from the original bulls of 1521, conceding them the rights of priests, as well as from their unparalleled moral authority among the Indians.

In 1544 the friars were beginning to strike an understanding with the encomenderos, in contrast to the open enmity between the two groups in the early 1530's. Thus Juan de Alvarado at Tiripitio provided the materials for the convento in 1537, after having requested the Viceroy to permit the Augustinians to establish upon

64. *CDIAI,* VII, 528 (Franciscans); 532–542 (Dominicans).

65. Zavala, *Encomienda indiana,* p. 102, and Escobar, *Americana thebáida,* p. 193.

66. Simpson, *Encomienda,* p. 189; cf. Zavala, *op. cit.,* pp. 67, 105.

67. Note, however, that Zumárraga urged perpetual encomienda in 1529. Simpson, *op. cit.,* pp. 104, 240. No later opinion from him is recorded.

68. Text in *CDHM,* II, 213, following edition of Valladolid, 1603; faulty version in *CDIAI,* XVI, 376 f.

69. See Chapter IV, p. 137.

his grant.[70] In 1540, again, Cristóbal de Oñate asked the Augustinians to establish at Tacambaro.[71] The Franciscans in Jalisco were likewise allied with an encomendero, Hernando Ruiz de la Peña, in the construction of a simple establishment at Autlan in 1545–46.[72] On the other hand, the Dominicans, desiring in 1541 to build at Yanhuitlan, were at first frustrated by Francisco de la Casas, but later on, they took much help from his son Gonzalo.[73] In general, the Augustinians seem to have benefited most from such alliances with the great encomenderos: at Atotonilco el Grande in 1564, Pedro de Paz endowed the Augustinian establishment with an annual income of four thousand pesos.[74] It is likely that the Mendicants were discovering the advantages of a working alliance with civilian colonists. These advantages were not material alone, but political and strategic. The friars were seeking to allay civilian opposition to their program, an opposition that had found vituperative expression since the beginning of their work, especially in the abusive letters of Gerónimo López, who, writing to the King, condemned the friars and the work of higher education then proceeding under Mendicant direction.[75]

The friars' anxiety arose not only from civilian attacks:—the main threat to their exceptional powers and privileges was to come from the episcopacy, to whom the friars' status as priests outside the hierarchy was an irritation and an affront.

The role of the secular clergy during the first half of the century was an unimportant one. Until 1555 or thereabouts, secular curates were few in number. They were variously described as being wicked, stupid, inconstant, and ignorant. Their low quality has been attributed to a variety of causes, among them, the decadence of the Peninsular clergy, the inconsistent and badly enforced emigration policy of the Crown, and the absence of seminaries in New Spain.[76] After 1550, a double process may be observed: on the one hand, the sacerdotal and territorial privileges of the Mendicants came under increasing criticism and restriction; and on the other, the numbers, training, and powers of the secular clergy augmented steadily at Mendicant

70. Escobar, *Americana thebaida,* pp. 80, 74–76; 144: D. Basalenque, *Historia de la provincia de San Nicolas de Tolentino de Michoacan, del orden de N. P. S. Augustín* (Mexico, 1673), p. 4a.

71. *Ibid.,* p. 17b.

72. E. Mendoza, *Fragmentos de la crónica de la provincia de franciscanos Santiago de Xalisco* (Mexico, 1871), pp. 66–67; N. A. de Ornelas Mendoza y Valdivia, *Crónica de la provincia de Santiago de Xalisco* (Guadalajara, 1941), p. 27.

73. F. de Burgoa, *Geográfica descripción* (Mexico, 1934) (*Publ. AGN,* XXV, XXVI), I, 292; W. Jiménez Moreno and S. Mateos Higuera, ed., *Códice de Yanhuitlán* (Mexico, 1940), p. vii.

74. *Sociedad mexicana de geografía y estadística, Boletín,* época 5, IX (1919), 467.

75. *CDHM,* II, 148. Teaching Indians to read and write he regarded as "muy dañoso como el diablo . . ." Other letters by López may be found in *Epistolario, passim.*

76. See Cuevas, *Historia de la iglesia en México,* II, 133–138, citing Viceroy Mendoza, the Bishop of Tlaxcala, and Bishop fray Diego de Landa. A useful list of curates *ca.* 1570 is found in (A. de Montúfar, *abp. of Mexico) Descripción del arzobispado de Mexico hecha en 1570 y otros documentos* (Mexico, 1897). L. García Pimentel, ed.

expense.[77] The secular-regular conflict first broke out over the issue of episcopal tithes: the bishops were unable to collect them, and blamed the dominion of the friars over their Indian charges.[78] Other complaints concerned the sacramental privileges arrogated by the friars. In 1557, the Crown sought to restrict Mendicant activity by a decree subjecting the foundation of new establishments to the approval of the bishop concerned. The bishops then attempted (1557) to place secular clerics in Mendicant jurisdictions, whereupon the Crown sought to restrain the bishops.[79] Conversely, Mendicant encroachment upon populations already assigned to the clerics was forbidden by the Crown in 1559. The Viceroy soon complained to Philip that the schism developing between the two parties was a matter of serious concern.

The 1560's mark the new strength of the secular clergy:—many new priests immigrated, and the creole priests now had the advantages of the foundation of the University, the discipline of the Holy Office, and the legislation of the church councils in Mexico.[80]

In 1574, a royal cedula, pursuant to the resolutions of the Council of Trent, subjected the Mendicants to viceregal and diocesan control, as to nominations, numbers and movements. Finally a decree of 1583 ordered outright preferential treatment of the secular clergy in Mexico.[81] Thus were the Mendicants gradually shorn of their privileges. By the end of the century, they faced the choice of retiring to their remaining conventual retreats, or of going forth to new conversions at the periphery of the colonial world. The secular clergy now numbered about five hundred. Many administered parishes taken over from the Mendicants.

During the course of these events, if we may judge from an *información secreta* taken in 1569,[82] the Mendicants lost the support of the encomenderos. Of nine important civilians queried upon the question, only one defended the friars' privileges, and even he urged that the question of tithes be settled in favor of the episcopacy. All other informants agreed that more clerics, of higher cultivation than those then available, were the main need of the colony, rather than more friars.

Within the Orders, these troubles took piteous expression. In 1562, Mendieta complained of chaos in the affairs of his province, observing that chapter-meetings

77. The course of events has been admirably charted by Ricard, *La "Conquête spirituelle" du Mexique*, pp. 286–310. Cf. Cuevas, *Historia de la iglesia en México*, II, 153 ff.

78. See the letters of Archbishop Montúfar to the King, e.g., *Epistolario*, VII, 311, to the King in 1554; *ibid.*, VIII, 72, Montúfar to the Consejo de Indias, pp. 72 ff., 1556.

79. Grijalva, *Crónica de la orden de N. P. S. Augustín*, pp. 287–288; Puga, *Cedulario*, II, 288, 291–292.

80. Contrast Mendieta (*Historia eclesiástica indiana*, p. 546), whose estimate pertains to a new administrative division of benefices. See also "Cartas de religiosos de Nueva España," *NCDHM*, I, 59, 63–65. Also Vetancurt, *Chrónica*, *Teatro*, Pt. IV, p. 29.

81. Cuevas, *op. cit.*, II, 172–193; *Documentos* (1914), pp. 245, 304. On the decree of 1583 see Grijalva, *op. cit.*, pp. 544 ff.

82. F. del Paso y Troncoso, comp., "Papeles de Nueva España," MS, Vol. III, in the Library of the Museo Nacional de Arqueología, Mexico City.

were filled with the resignations of the guardians of conventos. Everywhere, friars were demanding to return to Spain; none was learning languages; and the primitive apostolic fervor had died.[83] Fray Miguel Navarro, in 1568, likewise noted the decadence of his Order, assigning its causes to the death of many old workers, and to the unfair treatment by the bishops and Audiencia, and noting that the process had been going on for about ten years.[84]

The same process of incorporation that struck the institution of encomienda, overtook the friars. Whether encomenderos or friars, their drives to action were frustrated by the incipient centralization of authority in the Crown. Hence the "golden age" of the colonization of Mexico, as Ricard has called it, came to an end with the abrogation of the Mendicants' power.[85] Their privileges were under sustained attack as early as 1555; by 1565, they foresaw the decay of their work. The melancholy dispersal of Mendicant energies left a void. For eleven generations no equivalent agency emerged to resume the humanization of Indian society. Only in the twentieth century was the work of rural education and welfare begun again, by a government whose unacknowledged archetype is the Mendicant organization of the sixteenth century.

The voluminous record of the disputes and controversies among the various factions contains singularly little mention of the most tangible achievement of the men of the sixteenth century. This achievement was the building of new towns, with all the specialized structures that were part of the Renaissance concept of urban life. To discover the chief conditions of this extraordinary campaign of architectural activity will be the immediate concern of Chapter I.

83. "Cartas de religiosos de Nueva España," *NCDHM,* I, 3–4. Mendieta to Comisario general, from Toluca, 1562. ". . . el fervor y ejercicio en la obra de la salvacion de las animas ya parece del todo que ha cesado: ya murió el primitivo espiritu."

84. *Ibid.,* p. 59.

85. Ricard, *op. cit.,* p. ix. Ricard assumes 1572, the date at which the Jesuits became effective in Mexico, as the critical point in the process.

I

DEMOGRAPHIC PROBLEMS

El único punto en que se han (*sc.* las crueldades) disminuido es Méjico: allí hay justicia, y las inhumanidades públicas no son toleradas: las exacciones de tributos son inmensas é insoportables, pero los homicidios no son tan frecuentes.

B. de las Casas, *Colección de las obras* (Paris, 1822), I, 198.

THE eye of the traveller needs but little practice to distinguish the buildings of the sixteenth century from those of all other periods in Mexico. The forms are but generically Spanish; they are specifically Mexican in the simplicity of their masses and profiles, in the sober allocation of profusely ornamental panels. It quickly becomes apparent that these great churches and conventual establishments are out of all proportion to the communities now sustaining them. Usually in a square somewhat removed from the center of activities in the town or village, they stand aloof, immense, and as if forgotten by the townspeople. At Tepeaca the cult images and the altars have been removed from the great Franciscan establishment (*Frontispiece*). The church doors are open only at rare intervals, when a few women and children come to worship. In southern Mexico, the gigantic, incomplete church at Cuilapan (Fig. 216) seems to lack a town altogether. At Acolman, where the paved road to the pyramids of Teotihuacan branches from the International Highway, few signs may be seen of the community that once sustained the sumptuous Augustinian establishment (Fig. 159). And yet, since these churches were the work of the Mendicant Orders, whose mission impelled them towards the great urban centers, it must be supposed that the edifices themselves are the physical remnants proving the existence of once-great and crowded towns. The tides of population surely rose high at these points: today the churches remain as the chief landmarks of an older beach-level.

It is a situation that is faced by every student of older cultures. Wherever beauty and form were created in the past, there throve dense populations whose only record is often a monumental surplus, an excess of usable artifacts. To provide a quantitative statement of the relationships between ancient population and its material culture is usually impossible. In Mexico an abundance of information justifies the attempt.

A fact sometimes overlooked by the students of Spain's colonial empire is that the colonists secured remarkably detailed and accurate population counts. Administrative policy was often governed by knowledge gained from these census reports, and in the case of architectural activity, it can be shown that the closest correlation exists between the magnitude of the building enterprise in a given community and the size of the population locally available to carry out the project. It is of course impossible to assert that these correlations were the fruit of a systematic plan of colonization, elaborated by central authorities and rationally executed according to forethought and regulation.[1] On the contrary, adaptations of the architectural program to the conditions of local population were attained intuitively by individual planners who, in each instance, had to face the prospect of failure, should the design be too ambitious for the resources of the community. Each of the great colonizing agencies, furthermore, faced a different population problem. These agencies were the Mendicant Orders. Franciscans, Augustinians, and Dominicans each developed a highly characteristic and individual method of utilizing the available population densities.

These ordinal peculiarities are most easily displayed in tabular form. Table *A* shows that the kind of religious architecture built by the Mendicants is related to the size of the community where the building was done. These relationships are indicated by cross-reference. The character of the establishment (indicated as I, II, or III) and the size of the community (indicated as *A, B, C,* or *D*) are classed. To emphasize the differences in the behavior of the various Mendicant Orders, the towns and establish-

TABLE A

MONUMENTS OF THE FIRST CLASS: the largest churches, with vaults or richly decorated wooden ceilings; elaborate conventual layouts in two stories with one or two courts and vaulted walks; rich and abundant ornament

FRANCISCAN		
Cholula (A)	12,000 tributaries	(1569)*
Cuernavaca (A)	8,000	(1569)*
Huejotzingo (A)	8,000	(1569)*
Tepeaca (A)	6,000	(1569)*
Texcoco (A)	6–7,000	(1569)*
Tlaxcala (A)	14,666	(1574)†
Tula (A)	8,000	(1569)*
Xochimilco (A)	5,000	(1569)*

1. According to Rodrigo Gil de Hontañon, the Spanish architect of the sixteenth century, the size of the church was calculated with respect to available population ("Algunos avisados modernos suelen mirar la gente que hay en el tal pueblo"). When the growth of the settlement had been forecast in the coming century, a computation of the area of the church was made in terms of the estimated number of burials that would be needed. See Simón García, "Compendio de arquitectura," *Arte en España,* VII (1868), chap. ii, 126.

AUGUSTINIAN		
Acolman (B)	2,560	(1570–72)‡
Actopan (A)	7,190	(1570–72)‡
Atotonilco el Grande (B)	4,200	(1571)§
Ixmiquilpan (B)	2,546	(1571)§
Metztitlan (A)	7,251	(1597)‖
Yecapixtla (C)	1,283	(1597)‖
Yuriria (D)	900	(1580)¶
DOMINICAN		
Coixtlahuaca (B)	2,600	(1570–72)‡
Cuilapan (B)	3,001	(1597)‖
Tlaxiaco (B)	3,575	(1574)†
Yanhuitlan (A)	6,184	(1570–72)‡

MONUMENTS OF THE SECOND CLASS: medium-size, well built churches of permanent construction; two-storied conventual buildings with or without vaulting; may include large establishments of which construction extended over several generations

FRANCISCAN		
Acatzingo (B)	4,000 tributaries	(1569)*
Atlihuetzia (B)	2,468	(1574)†
Atlixco (C)	1,071	(1574)†
Calpan (B)	3,000	(1569)*
Calpulalpan (B)	2,290	(1571)‖
Chalco Atenco (D)	550	(1574)†
Cuautinchan (B)	2,500	(1569)*
Huaquechula (B)	3,000	(1569)*
Jilotepec (A)	7,000	(1574)†
Otumba (A)	5,400	(1569)*
Patzcuaro (B)	4,000	(1574)†
Quecholac (B)	4,000	(1569)*
Tecali (A)	6,000	(1569)*
Tecamachalco (A)	5,000	(1569)*
Tepeapulco (A)	6,400	(1574)†
Tepeji del Rio (B)	3,500	(1569)*
Tepeyango (B)	2,060	(1574)†
Tlalmanalco (B)	4,000	(1574)†
Tlaquiltenango (B)	4,500	(1569)*
Tochimilco (B)	3,000	(1569)*
Totimehuacan (D)	1,000	(1569)*
Zacatlan (B)	3,000	(1569)*

Zempoala (B)	3,000	(1569)*
Zinacántepec (B)	3,000	(1569)*
AUGUSTINIAN		
Atlatlauca (D)	651 tributaries	(1571)§
Cuitzeo (D)	780	(1597)‖
Epazoyucan (C)	1,350	(1570–72)‡
Huejutla (B)	2,300	(1574)†
Malinalco (D)	1,000	(1570–72)‡
Molango (B)	2,600	(1553)‖
Tiripitio (C)	1,200	(1574)†
Tlayacapan (C)	1,500	(1574)†
Totolapan (B)	3,000	(1574)†
Tutotepec (B)	4,000	(1570–72)‡
DOMINICAN		
Amecameca (C)	1,500	(1574)†
Etla (C)	1,138	(1597)‖
Oaxtepec (A)	9,000	(1574)†
Teposcolula (B)	4,000	(1570–72)‡
Tepoztlan (B)	2,600	(1574)†
Yautepec (B)	4,500	(1574)†

MONUMENTS OF THE THIRD CLASS: small edifices of permanent construction but casual form; full conventual program incompletely realized, or provisional church; limited ornamental program

FRANCISCAN		
Acambaro (C)	2,800 tributaries	(1570)‡
Erongaricuaro (D)	512	(1546–47)**
Etzatlan (C)	1,000	(1569)*
Huichapan (A)	7,000	(1569)*
Milpa Alta (C)	2,800	(1574)†
Tehuacan (C)	2,730	(1574)†
Tlahuelilpa (D)	380	(1569)*
Tlajomulco (C)	1,400	(1574)†
Tulancingo (A)	5,500	(1574)†
Uruapan (C)	1,700	(1570)*
Zacapu (C)	1,000	(1570)*
AUGUSTINIAN		
Acatlan (D)	211	(1546–67)**
Chiautla (C)	2,016	(1574)†
Chilapa (C)	1,250	(1569)*

Chucandiro (D)	400	(1570–72)‡
Huango (D)	111	(1597)‖
Jantetelco (D)	295	(1597)‖
Jonacatepec (D)	505	(1597)‖
Mixquiahuala (D)	800	(1570–72)‡
Ocuituco (C)	1,600	(1574)†
Singuilucan (D)	757	(1570–72)‡
Tezontepec (D)	807	(1570–72)‡
Ucareo (D)	400	(1546–47)**
Zacualpan Amilpas (C)	1,700	(1571)‖
DOMINICAN		
Chimalhuacan Chalco (C)	1,000	(1570–72)‡
Coyoacan (B)	3,334	(1597)‖
Tacubaya (D)	640	(1597)‖
Tlahuac (D)	912	(1597)‖

* "Códice franciscano," *NCDHM*, II.
† López de Velasco, *Geografía.*
‡ García Pimentel, ed., *Relación . . . Tlaxcala, Michoacán, Oaxaca.*
§ *PNE*, III.
‖ *Epistolario*, VIII (1553), XIII (1597), XVI (1571).
¶ Paso y Troncoso, comp., "Papeles de Nueva España," MS, VIII.
** *PNE*, I.

ments have been grouped by ordinal filiation. Within the listings of Franciscan towns and establishments, moreover, subdivisions by province appear, to show the differences between the mother-province (Santo Evangelio), and the more sparsely populated western provinces, in Michoacan and New Galicia.

In order to maintain all these comparisons, a point in time was chosen which yielded the most abundant and reliable population figures for the various communities. This point theoretically lies in the years between 1569 and 1574, at a moment when the great campaigns of building activity had begun to subside, and when the general population of the colony was relatively stable. It was of course necessary occasionally to utilize figures from periods both before and after this half-decade, and it was also necessary, in the absence of all figures, to omit mention of several communities in which important building enterprises were undertaken. The European towns, moreover, such as Mexico, Puebla, Morelia, Guadalajara, or Oaxaca, are not relevant in this immediate context of Indian population. Hence, of 273 foundations by the Mendicants (Franciscans, 138; Augustinians, 85; Dominicans, 50), about twenty may be disregarded as serving Europeans. Of the remainder, serviceable figures are available for slightly more than half, or 128 Indian communities. These are the principal towns, and we lack figures mainly for the small Indian towns and for villages.

Table *A* therefore represents about two-thirds or more of the Indian population under Mendicant control, and may serve as a reliable indicator of generalized events.

The first observation concerns the Franciscan domination of virtually all the great centers of Indian population. The towns that numbered over five thousand families were not very numerous, and of twenty-two such towns, the Franciscans occupied nineteen. This fact is to be explained largely by Franciscan priority in the conversion of Mexico. Theirs was the Order favored by the Crown, and theirs was the first choice among evangelical fields.

The Franciscans never pretended to establish their major foundations in lesser population centers. On the contrary, they often erected rather modest edifices in some of the greatest towns, as in Otumba (Fig. 365) or Tulancingo. This practice contrasts with the Augustinian habit of initiating pretentious construction in towns of medium size. The most striking case is at Yuriria (Figs. *118*, 453) where a gigantic church and convento arose among Indians whose numbers never exceeded fourteen hundred families during the period of missionary activity. The Dominicans likewise imposed ambitious building programs upon small settlements, as at Oaxtepec (Fig. 163), where the sumptuous church buildings served a population numbering 367 families in the latter part of the century. In the western provinces, furthermore, the Franciscans sacrificed all pretensions to important building activity. The Franciscan foundations in Michoacan do not bear comparison with the lesser churches in the metropolitan province, and even farther west, in New Galicia, provisional churches of adobe and wood were the rule, with rare exceptions, as among relatively large towns such as Poncitlan or Tlajomulco.

Hence the Franciscans treated the size and ostentation of their buildings as the direct function of locally available populations. In the most densely settled areas, an intricate monastic plan, with a vaulted church or a classicizing basilica, was normal. The scale of such buildings depended not only upon the size of the settlement, but upon its distance from the capital. Thus small settlements near the capital might display more elaborate buildings than settlements of the same size at great distance from the center. The reason for this is that the three factors, population density, technological level, and distance from the capital are intimately related. The thinly peopled areas of Mexico lacked the advanced pre-Conquest building techniques. Conversely, the thickly settled areas of high technological attainments contained few peoples who did not participate in a generally high level of material culture. The exceptions to this last proposition are marginal: in southern Mexico the Chinantec might be named, or in Tlaxcala the Otomies, but their habitats were topographically remote and sparsely settled, with the result that such peoples maintained few contacts among their highly civilized neighbors in the rich valleys. The Franciscans respected these limitations among their charges. Where large towns were infrequent, as in Michoacan, the builders insisted upon a simple conventual plan, and on trabeated rather than the expensive vaulted construction. If local tradition and the labor supply permitted, masonry walls were built. In the most remote, least civilized, and most sparsely populated districts, such as Jalisco, where settlements of five hundred families were exceptionally large, adobe walls and provisional roofing were the standard.

The notable exceptions to our rule occur in the urban settlements designed for European use, as Puebla or Morelia, where the labor of construction was paid for and subsidized from Crown funds. An eccentrically large settlement in a thinly peopled area (Poncitlan), or an unusually small one in a densely settled region (Chalco Atenco) may contain religious edifices conforming to the pattern of their whole area rather than to the size of the settlement *per se*. In short, the areal or regional population is the critical factor, rather than purely local density, for the obvious reasons of competitive ostentation, easily available neighboring labor supplies, and the general level of technological training in the area.

Worth noting in addition is the wide range of peoples with whom the Franciscans worked, in contrast to their Augustinian and Dominican rivals, who came later, and worked with fewer missionaries. The Franciscans labored not only among the highly civilized and densely settled central southern Indians, but also among the sparser Tarascans, and among many rude tribes of the western and northern frontiers.

Turning to the Augustinians, we see immediately that the scale of their establishment does not bear the close relation to size of settlement that characterized Franciscan activity. Three of their greatest foundations were built in medium settlements, containing less than five thousand families, and two were imposed upon small towns with less than two thousand families. In their defense it may be said that the Augustinians sought to relieve the burden, and to shorten the building period, by importing metropolitan labor, as at Tiripitio, and by sending local labor to the capital for advanced training. In this sense, their great building enterprises served to raise the technological level, especially in Michoacan.

The Augustinians were more often blamed for ambitious building than the other Mendicants; Table *A* gives weight to these charges. On the other hand, certain peculiarities of their style, such as their failure ever to have built a completely rib-vaulted church, and their excessively long building campaigns, as in Michoacan, where construction continued long into the seventeenth century, now become understandable. The deficiencies of their supply of building labor are at fault. In short, the Augustinians not only lacked access to the best supplies of labor; they never commanded the manpower accessible to the Franciscans. It is all the more remarkable, therefore, that at the Chichimec border, such small populations were induced to build the vast establishments at Cuitzeo or Yuriria. As we shall see later on, certain military considerations favored the Augustinian frontier mission.

The Dominican achievement of such imposing edifices as those at Yanhuitlan, Coixtlahuaca, Cuilapan, Teposcolula, and Tlaxiaco may be related to their undisputed control of the highly civilized Mixtec tribespeople. Large settlements, artisans long familiar with stoneworking, and competent European directors after 1550, lent to Dominican work in southern Mexico a distinction that it never attained elsewhere in New Spain. The exception is the edifice at Oaxtepec (Fig. 207), a completely rib-vaulted church built under influence from nearby Franciscan centers. Like Tepoztlan, Oaxtepec was situated in the great marquesate awarded to Cortés, and the friars benefited from the peculiar conditions prevailing in the administration of that estate. Dominican building is all the more remarkable for the fact that its chief monuments arose after the great epidemic crises which depleted the population of New Spain.

The achievement of the three Mendicant Orders with respect to the populations they commanded may now be examined. The Franciscans, who disposed of the largest urban agglomerations and the greatest territory, exacted less from the Indians than did the other friars. The humanistic direction of their enterprise in Mexico may be largely responsible (see pp. 9–15). The Franciscans labored more than their rivals to record native culture, and to conserve the indigenous populations. In relative terms, the Franciscans may be said to have under-exploited their charges, while the Augustinians over-exploited them. Still, the Augustinians were prepared to admit the Indians to a status far more autonomous within Christianity than the Franciscans, and we must acknowledge remarkable feats of moral persuasion in the Augustinian architectural achievement. The Dominicans, finally, demanded more than the Franciscans, but less than their Augustinian colleagues. Yanhuitlan (Fig. 171), for instance, is more elaborate than Tula (Fig. *240*) or Tepeaca (Fig. 162), but less so than Yuriria or Actopan (Fig. 166). These particular edifices may be regarded as the showpieces of their respective Orders. The relative populations laboring upon their construction are an index to the ambition as well as to the evangelical tyranny of the various friars.

The foregoing pages incur the danger of suggesting that the population patterns of New Spain were stable, ready-made entities among which the missionaries had only to discover the relative magnitudes. Nothing could be farther from the truth. The missionaries brought innumerable settlements into being; other agglomerations vanished at the approach of the friars, and throughout the colony, an appalling mortality among the Indians marked the first century of Spanish colonization. The sources are unanimous about the fact.[2] Even the hyperbolic statements of interested parties could only suggest a reality that defied any exhaustive statistical approach. Measurement and tabulation were incapable of keeping pace with the successive population disasters that struck New Spain, New Galicia, and the other territories of what is today the republic of Mexico. The diction of the historians of the time is replete with allusions to calamity; Motolinia, for instance, enlarged upon the ten various "plagues" that had beset the affairs of the colony, Mendieta dedicated an entire chapter to the problem of depopulation, and Domingo de Betanzos, the eminent Dominican missionary, prophesied the total extinction of the Indian race if the disasters were to continue without abatement.

On the other hand, during these troubled years of the sixteenth century, a great colonial state was brought into being, with its administrative and spiritual center in Mexico. The foundation of hundreds of new urban settlements took place. A stable and highly productive colonial economy was established. Many specialized institutions came into being, and the tangible economic returns from the colony soared to a peak at the end of the century.[3] In other words, more and more of the equipment of civilization was being produced among a race that simultaneously underwent a diminution of numbers rarely equalled in the history of mankind. It is an anomalous situation. If Mexico were as thinly peopled at the time of the Conquest as recent studies would indicate,[4] how may the fact of severe losses of population be made to agree with the accompanying phenomenon of a vigorous colonial culture?

2. Jerónimo López wrote Prince Philip on September 10, 1545, to the effect that 400,000 Indians had been stricken by epidemic disease in seven months within ten leagues of Mexico City alone. F. del Paso y Troncoso, comp., *Epistolario de Nueva España 1505–1818* (Mexico, 1939–42) (Biblioteca histórica mexicana de obras inéditas, segunda serie, I–XVI), IV, 232. See also T. Motolinia, *Memoriales de fray Toribio de Motolinia* (Mexico, 1903), pp. 17–28, L. García Pimentel, ed. (Documentos históricos de Méjico, I); Mendieta, *Historia eclesiástica indiana*, pp. 513–519; A. Dávila Padilla, *Historia de la fundación y discurso de la provincia de Santiago de México* (2d ed. Brussels, 1625), p. 100. A somewhat fuller account of the sources and figures used in this section will be found in G. Kubler, "Population Movements in Mexico, 1520–1600," *Hispanic American Historical Review*, XXII (1942), 606–643.

3. Simpson, *Encomienda; idem*, "Studies in the Administration of the Indians in New Spain," *Ibero-americana*, VII (1934); XIII (1938). R. D. Hussey, "Colonial Economic Life," *Colonial Hispanic America* (Washington, 1936), pp. 308–309. A. C. Wilgus, ed. (Studies in Hispanic American Affairs, IV). The net proceeds from Spanish exploitation of the New World reached 7,000,000 pesos annually between 1590 and 1600, and fell back to 1,000,000 pesos by 1651.

4. A. L. Kroeber, *Cultural and Natural Areas of Native North America* (Berkeley, 1939), pp. 150–151 (University of California Publications in American Archaeology and Ethnology, XXXVIII). The cultivable land of Mexico was capable of yielding maize and beans for the support of 10,000,000 persons, a figure which Kroeber wishes to reduce by four-fifths for antiquity. Contrast Paul Rivet, in A. Meillet and M. Cohen, *Les Langues du monde* (Paris, 1924), pp. 599–602 (Collection linguistique . . . Société de linguistique de Paris, XVI), who gives Mexico 4,500,000 inhabitants in 1492. See also H. J. Spinden, "The Population of Ancient America," *Smithsonian Institution, Annual Report*, 1929, pp. 451–471; K. Sapper, "Die Zahl und Volksdichte der indianischen Bevoelkerung in Amerika vor der Conquista und in der Gegenwart," *International Congress of Americanists, Proceedings*, XXI (1924), 95–104. Dino Camavitto, *La Decadenza delle popolazioni messicane al tempo della conquista* (*Pubblicazioni del comitato italiano per lo studio dei problemi della popolazione*, ser. 1, Vol. IV), Rome, 1935, is based upon a wide range of sources, but adds little that is new to the method or the findings. M.

The analysis of the sources can best be approached through an examination of the peculiar difficulties involved in taking the census among these scattered peoples. It is necessary to understand, for instance, how fluid and unstable the tribal population was. The new economic pressures of various kinds often forced previously sedentary peoples into a state of nomadism. To escape the burdens of taxation, the inhabitants of an entire town would flee to the mountains. Such behavior was severely punished, but even then, the law allowed Indians who had recently changed residence for legitimate reasons, to enjoy one year of exemption from tribute.[5] In addition, the creation of a mercantile economy greatly enlarged the number of migrant Indians, who travelled constantly from one occupation to the next, seeking work in the mines, or on cattle farms, or again as carriers and harvesters.[6] Beyond these factors of dispersal, it should not be overlooked that the fundamental agricultural technology of the time hindered the farmers from living in urban groups;[7] rather was it necessary for the farming population to live in the fields. Even today, the visitor to Mexico may witness this agrarian dispersal, as in the mountains of the eastern Sierra Madre, where the population of the settlements is far exceeded by that of families living the year around upon inaccessible mountainside fields, and coming into the towns only upon ceremonial occasions. Everywhere, furthermore, Indian property consisted of such casual elements that abrupt changes of residence were constantly in progress.[8]

Hence no census pretending to accuracy could be made until after the resolution of the many problems of property ownership and jurisdiction that remained unsettled until nearly the middle of the century. It was above all necessary that a Spanish population be thoroughly settled among the Indians in every region. No real census could be taken until the missionaries, the secular clergy, the civil administration, and the encomenderos had established the boundaries of their jurisdictions and made

Mendizabal, "La Demografía mexicana, época colonial, 1519–99," *Boletín de la sociedad mexicana de geografía y estadística,* XLVIII, 1939, 301–341, estimates 9,170,400 people in Mexico in 1519, by extrapolation from López de Velasco's figures of *ca.* 1570.

5. *CDIAI,* XIV (1870), 330–331. *PNE,* V (1905), 220.

6. A. de la Mota y Escobar, *Descripción geográfica de los reinos de Nueva Galicia, Nueva Vizcáya y Nuevo León* (2d ed. Mexico, 1940), pp. 34–35.

7. *PNE,* V, 100; *Epistolario,* II, 181.

8. ". . . no se puede averiguar ni saber los pueblos, casas ni número de los naturales que hay por ser muchos y vivir apartados y en una casa hay ocho y diez y más, y porque se encubren y porque hacen y deshacen sus casas con poco trabajo y viven en lugares y partes tan apartados y escondidos que no se saben ni alcanzan." Report of the Audiencia, July 5, 1532, *Epistolario,* II, 181.

These obstacles to an accurate taking of the census have not yet been removed in many outlying parts of the Republic. Hans Gadow described essentially similar conditions in 1904: ". . . the numbers of the less civilized natives especially are mere guess work, let alone those of the still really wild tribes. The Prefect sends in the return for his district, himself relying upon the returns of the municipal presidents, who certainly do not overestimate their people, many of whom live in lonely hamlets, scattered among the mountain fastnesses. The census of the towns is just as difficult. The Indians shrewdly suspect that a census may be connected with increased taxation, with military service, vaccination, and similar blessings of civilization, and those who feel that they are 'wanted' think that this is a dodge for catching them. Consequently, there is an exodus, and they vanish. Those authorities who know the prevailing conditions, consider the population of brown natives to be several millions larger than the official returns." H. F. Gadow, *Through Southern Mexico* (London, 1908), pp. 259–261.

the acquaintance of the peoples living in those territories. It is unlikely that any reliable census figures earlier than 1545 will ever be found, for a contemporary writer says that within twenty leagues of the capital, Indians lived in such confusion and ignorance about their status in the colony that they held their encomendero as a kind of sovereign. Large numbers of Indians were still unaware of the Conquest; they had never been visited by Spaniards, and their ignorance of Christianity was complete. In this text, reference was not to the distant, unconverted provinces, but to districts within a few days' journey from Mexico City.[9]

It would be futile to attempt to prove that the population lists were accurate, exhaustive, or unbiased. At all times, the efforts of the viceregal administration to secure accurate information regarding population were frustrated in various ways, as by the state of economic nomadism described above, the agrarian dispersal of large parts of the population, by inadequate census methods, and by fraudulent reports whether from Europeans or Indians. Still, the figures gathered under these conditions are far from completely useless for our purpose. Surprising agreement is sometimes manifest in reports written by different authorities at the same time.[10] Among reports compiled at different times by the same interests, the degree of biased distortion may be taken as constant. That is, those lists prepared under the influence of the encomenderos will always show inflation, but the degree of inflation may be assumed to be uniform, so that it does not disguise the real, underlying rate of change in the population. For if the bias of an interested party does not materially alter during a number of years, then it makes little difference what his total figures may be, since we are primarily interested in the rate of change. It seems safe to calibrate the available sources as follows. If a churchman estimates the size of his flock, the highest available figure will be closer to reality than the lowest, since the clergy was usually pro-Indian, striving constantly to moderate the burden of tribute. When an encomendero, however, volunteers information regarding the number of Indians in his service, the lowest figure is most acceptable.

It happens to be true that the clergy submitted relatively few reports regarding population. Civilian authorities prepared many more in connection with the prolonged controversy over tenure of the *encomiendas*. We are, therefore, almost entirely dependent upon encomienda lists, and in effect, the conclusions of this study rest upon

9. *Epistolario*, IV, 210–213. Tello de Sandoval to Philip II, September 9, 1545. Jacques Soustelle reports upon the survival of these conditions in many parts of modern Mexico. Soustelle, *Mexique, terre indienne* (Paris, 1936).

10. Among twenty-five towns listed in the Archbishopric of Mexico by López de Velasco, *Geografía*, pp. 194–206, and B. de Ledesma, "Descripción del arzobispado de México," *PNE*, III (1905), the totals differ by less than ten per cent. This is of special interest since López de Velasco's report, though sketchy, covers all America, and Ledesma's, which includes but a few settlements in the northern parts of the Archbishopric, is admirable for the exhaustive classificatory treatment of population.

such sources. Their chief defect, and it is a defect they share with other classes of statistical material from the period, is that they tell nothing of abandoned settlements,[11] or of urban regroupings, where the remains of a dozen settlements were gathered into one. Nor do the encomienda lists reveal the magnitude of the flow of scattered, non-urban peoples into cities at certain periods,[12] and vice versa; they yield an unequivocal index only to the size of certain conveniently documented encomiendas at given times. It is as if the population movements of England in the sixteenth century were to be estimated from the number of tenant farmers upon selected manors at different times during the century.

The accompanying table shows the populations of 156 settlements as of the years 1546–47, 1569–71, and 1595–97 (Table *B*). These particular settlements were selected for tabulation simply because they are the ones which figure in all of the available encomienda lists. Occasionally the figures stand only for an encomendero's share in the population of a town. His share, however, remained constant, even in the estate transmitted to his heirs, so that the part may be taken to remain constantly proportional to the whole.

TABLE B

SELECTED ENCOMIENDA POPULATIONS

ARCHBISHOPRIC OF MEXICO

	1546–47	1569–71	1595–97
Tepetitlan	352	766	324
Taxcaltitlan	824	1,509	1,429
Ocuila	823	850	298
Guachinango	1,143	3,700*	2,242
Michimaloya	1,390	1,547	249
Quamuchtitlan	2,247	1,600†	862
Tlapanaloya	118	150	273
Tenanpulco	160	150	73
Coatepec	260	500	167
Tlahuelilpa	271	433	241
Aculma	1,617	2,560	1,221
Zacualpa }	180		108
Guazulco }	223		203
Tlacotepeque }	190		107
Temoaque }	700	1,630	428
Tlamaco	400	793	182
Zinacantepeque	815	1,500	1,191
Zacualpa }	1,000		319
Tenancingo }	786	2,150	307
Malinalco	950	1,000	1,217
Xiquipilco	2,800	3,500	1,290
Mizquiaguala	114	400	438
Tocaliyuca	503	527	198
Acamistlahuaca	245		272
Teçontepeque	80	300	195
Atotonilco de Pedraza	820	1,550	343
Atotonilco	1,415		1,596
Acatlan	211		288
Quaquezaloya	155	5,200	203
Tepexi	2,000	3,980	748
Nestalpa	200	410	125
Chila	331	350†	289
Metztitlan	6,308	6,980‡	7,251
Tlachinolticpac	1,033	4,500‡	3,191
Huepustla	1,927	3,070	789
Tequisquiaque	1,090	1,650	856

11. E.g., Xahualtepec, near Acapulco, completely wiped out *ca.* 1574 by smallpox. *PNE*, VI (1905), 156.

12. Certain settlements grew steadily throughout the century, regardless of the effects of disease. Such was Zimapan, a mining town, in the Archbishopric of Mexico. *PNE*, VI, 3.

Axacuba	2,985	4,365	747
Apazco	532	1,155	331
Tezcatepeque			
Tuzantlalpa	2,313	3,071	286
Chilguautla	961	1,200	346
Tlalchichilpa	905	1,555	958
Pachuca	432	710	142
Tepechpa	965	927‡	480
Tianguiztengo	543	600	527
Micaoztoc	28	30	20
Cacahuatepeque	116	600	64
Chilapa	1,130	4,009†	2,794
Ayutla	120		373
Suchitonaca	100		90
Tututepeque	107	400	140
Tistla	158	394†	1,120
Çipaçucalco	93	200	230
	45,169	72,471	38,161

BISHOPRIC OF OAXACA

	1546–47	1569–71	1595–97
Ocotlan	1,556	2,020*	806
Tamazulapa	800	1,672	1,036
Totolapa	272	550	202
Chicomesuchil	682	550	239
Etlatongo	104		60
Guautla			233
Zensontepeque	21		267
Tamazola	302	727	51
Coyotepeque	707	500	175
Mitlantongo	355	300*	175
Ocelotepeque	393	1,200*	1,364
Apuala			223
Coatlavista			143
Jocoticpac	709	1,526	115
Tlacochahuaya	855	600*	372
Yztlan	420	400*	149
Miaguatlan	913	1,400*	914
Coatlan	4,600	2,000	1,012
Otlatitlan	82	500	168
Xicaltepeque	43	50	6
Tlaxiaco	5,870	3,575*	1,678
Chicahuastla	671	450*	331
Nopala	695		629
Tututepeque	900	3,463	2,386
Yanguitlan	3,052	6,184	3,354
Achiutla	402	1,000*	585
Tiltepeque	72	240	
Atoyaquillo	30	200	131
Tlapanala	106	250	139
Tehuilotepeque	125	150	95
La Chichina	148	50	78
Ayacastla	125	140*	100
Xareta	60	100	45
Tequepanza-cualco	59	50*	34
Totolinga	105	60*	73
Nespa	80	125	31
Ometepeque	340	800*	774
Amusgos	240	300	307
	25,894	31,132	18,480

MICHOACAN

	1546–47	1569–71	1595–97
Uruapan	473	1,700	1,129
Tzirosto	1,064	2,500	1,570
Huango			111
Purandiro	283	845	393
Taximaroa	530	3,000*	1,527
Acambaro	508	2,800	1,557
La Guacana	45	500	122
Tacambaro	325	800*	351
Indaparapeo	96	370	186
Turicato	131	425	371
Zacapu	316	1,000	263
Periban	291	1,400	880
	4,062	15,340	8,460

BISHOPRIC OF TLAXCALA

	1546–47	1569–71	1595–97
Quechola	4,392	3,360*	1,255
Tecamachalco	13,982	8,700	5,108
Tututepeque	2,535	4,000	2,167
Achachalintla	696	1,500	925
Çuatinchan	3,120	2,568	1,459
Xuxupango	534	700*	100
Piasla	108	355	295
Çapotitlan	1,346	2,000*	1,353
Acolzingo	204	300†	100
Teupantlan	470	524	545
Totomehuacan	835	1,000	516
Chiapulco	228	200	348
Çacatlan	2,081§	3,150	348
Tepexuxuma	685	800	465
Huaquechula	1,646	3,665*	1,895
	32,862	32,822	16,879

PROVINCE OF PANUCO

	1546–47	1569–71	1595–97
Tantala } Tampaca }	290	450	287
Moyutla }	54		
Oceloama }	181	100	104
Tamalol }	150		
Cuacaxo }	107	120	162
Tanta	32	30	50
Calpan	40	40‡	19
Tamazunchale (Cervantes)	102	200‡	510
Tançetuco	91	50	25
Guautla	169	100	233
Coatzalingo	1,531	800	444
Tancaxen	50	35	32
	2,807	1,925	1,866

Tenamaztlan, Tecolutla, Ayutitlan, Ayutla, Istlahuaca, Atengo }	724	930	532
Chipiltitlan	102	50	23
Comala	117	150	137
Popoyutla	27	20	15
Xicotlan	150	50	35
Axixic, Atoyaque, Zacualco‖, Cocula‖, Sayula‖, Chapala‖, Tepeque, Teoquititlan, Techalutla, Xocotepeque }	3,773	3,167	3,497
	5,275	4,605	4,378

PROVINCE OF COLIMA

	1546–47	1569–71	1595–97
Alcoçani	78	108	72
Tlacoloastla	73	30	50
Apatlan	231	100	17

ZACATULA AND MAR DEL SUR

Zacaltepeque	550	923	366
Huiztlan	87	60	45
	637	983	411
Grand Total	116,706	159,278	88,635

* Figures from López de Velasco, *Geografía y descripción universal de las Indias* (Madrid, 1894).

† *Papeles de Nueva España* (Madrid, 1905), Vol. V.

‡ *Papeles de Nueva España* (Madrid, 1905), Vol. III (Bartolomé de Ledesma).

§ In 1555, from *Epistolario*, VIII, 4.

‖ Settlements located in New Galicia, but belonging to the encomienda of Alonso Dávalos. The province of Colima actually belonged to the bishopric of Michoacan, but it has been listed separately here, in order to present peripheral conditions. The encomiendas of the bishopric of New Galicia are fully listed only in the *Suma* of 1546–47.

N.B. Spellings of place-names are given as in the *Suma de visitas*. Brackets signify towns belonging to one encomendero.

From the information presented in Table *B*, a graph was drawn (Fig. 7), to clarify the changes in population density. As graphs go, it is an odd composition, based partly upon figures, partly upon historical surmise. Only three of its points are fixed by statistical evidence of any degree of accuracy and completeness. All other positions rely upon non-statistical estimates, contemporary assertions, and general sixteenth- and seventeenth-century impressions. The three known points are plotted upon the strength of the encomienda populations as of 1546–47, 1569–71, and 1595–97. The sharp drop in population as of 1545 was plotted by virtue of a number of authoritative sources, all agreeing that the mortalities suffered in the plague of 1545 were less than one-half as numerous as those of the plague of 1576.[13] Of course, the actual population loss of 1576 is not directly given by our figures, but is projected backward in time from the conditions prevailing in 1595–97. Between 1546 and 1575, an extraordinary rise in population occurred. This, to be sure, is the movement to be noted only in certain encomienda towns, but there is no compelling reason, within present knowledge, for not assuming that the ratios involved are typical and proportionally accurate with regard to total population.[14] Furthermore, the trajectory between 1546 and 1575, although lacking in detailed incidents supported by further documentation, represents the most secure portion of the graph. Remarkable, moreover, is the long period, between 1546 and 1563, in which no epidemics are recorded. This must be regarded as an important cause for the striking recovery made by nearly all the populations of Mexico prior to 1570.[15] Concerning the movement between 1577 and 1595, no such rise can be

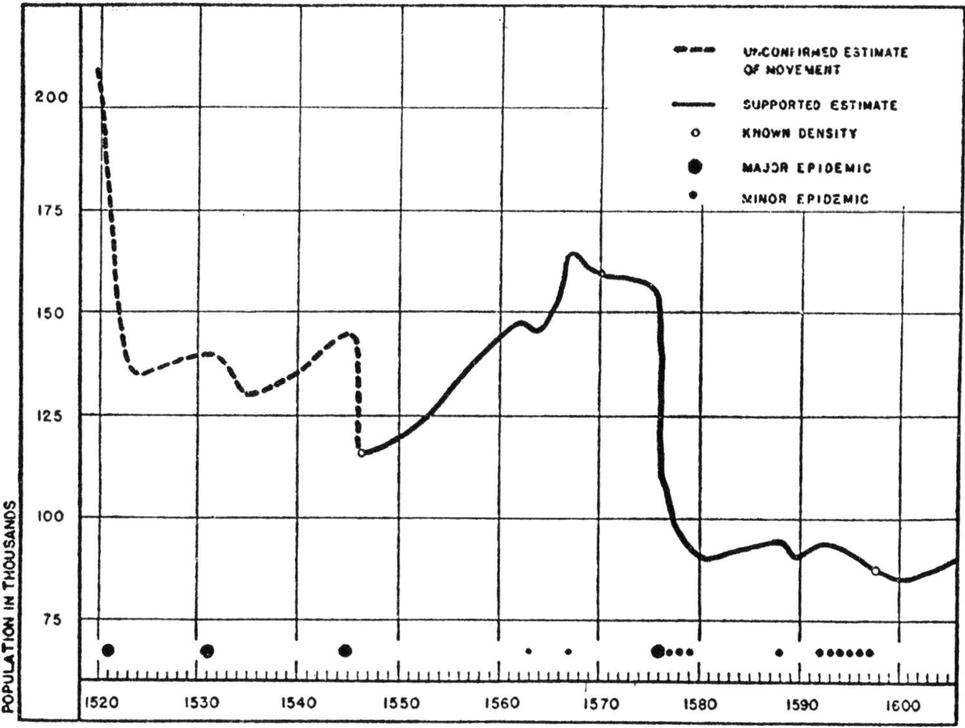

7. Population changes in Mexico, 1520–1600

13. See pp. 42–43.

14. Compare, for instance, the totals suggested by López de Velasco, *Geografía,* against those of 1597. López de Velasco counted 711,000 tributaries in the bishoprics of Mexico, Tlaxcala, Oaxaca, Michoacan and New Galicia, while in 1597, according to *Epistolario,* XIII, 17, the total number of tributaries belonging to the Crown, the Marquesate, and the private encomiendas barely touched 500,000 in the same areas.

15. See pp. 39–41.

documented. Our interpretation of the period 1575–95, then, is supported only by the many historical indications of minor but persistent epidemics of limited range but considerable intensity.

At the left-hand extreme of the curve, the section representing population at the time of the Conquest was determined by a series of inferences from extremely vague data. This section of the graph, to 1546, has therefore less validity than other sections, and contains a possible error of unknown magnitude, since we are deprived even of contemporary guesses as to the size of population losses at that time.[16] Thus the most reliable positions along the curve are the points corresponding to the well-documented years in Table *B*. The next most credible indications are those of the plague years, plotted along the horizontal axis. All the rest is conjecture, more or less supported by historical information of non-statistical character.

In the next step all conjecture, beyond the initial assumption that the encomienda figures are reliable indicators of population movement, was dispensed with. Only the ratios contained among the totals of the three "known" points (1546–47, 1569–71, 1595–97) are shown, plotted from a common index in 1546–47, and resolved into separate curves according to the sub-totals for the various geographical or administra-

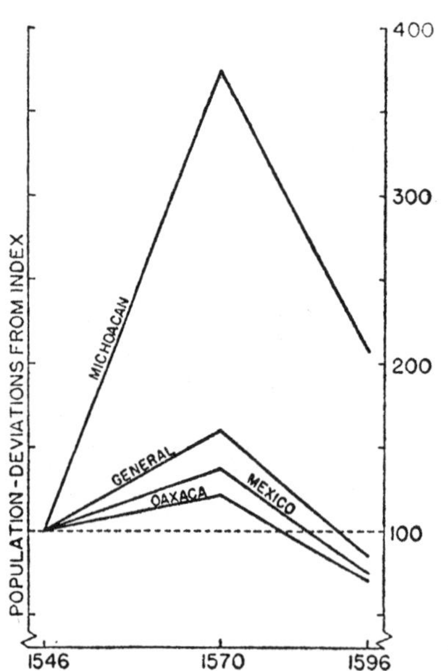

8. Population changes in the bishoprics of Mexico, Michoacan, and Oaxaca, 1546–96

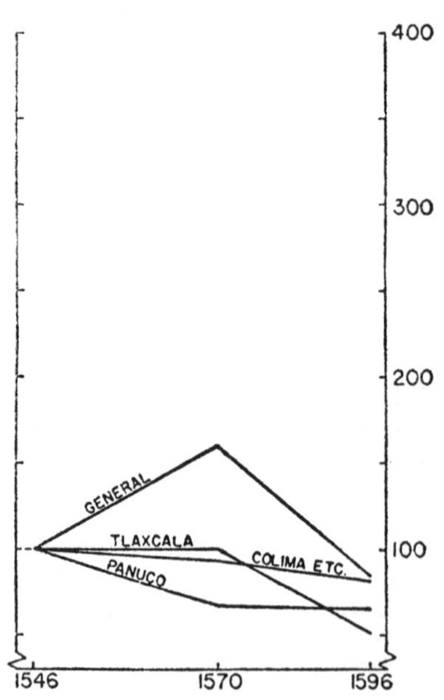

9. Changes in bishopric of Tlaxcala and provinces of Panuco, Colima, etc., 1546–96

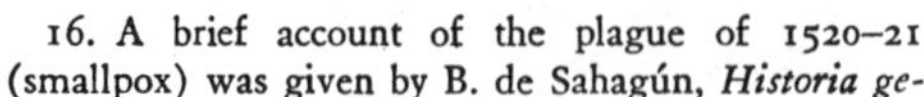

16. A brief account of the plague of 1520–21 (smallpox) was given by B. de Sahagún, *Historia general de las cosas de Nueva España* (Mexico, 1938), IV, 191–193.

tive areas (Figs. *8, 9*). It will be proper to analyze these separate curves with reference to other information regarding the areas in question.

In the bishoprics of Michoacan, Mexico, and Oaxaca (Fig. *8*), population rose steeply after 1546, and dropped abruptly sometime following 1570. These dioceses were the largest single administrative areas within the viceroyalty of New Spain. The remarkable fact in all three areas is the recovery effected between 1546 and 1570. The opposite holds true in Panuco, Colima, the province of Mar del Sur, and the bishopric of Tlaxcala (Fig. *9*), where the population either remained stable during the period in question, as in the bishopric of Tlaxcala, or else dropped suddenly. The phenomenon of recovery is most apparent in the curve for Michoacan (Fig. *8*), where the density of urban population was more than tripled by 1570.

The fact may be explained by any combination of the following causes. In the first place, the bishopric possessed extensive frontiers upon untouched, if thinly populated country (Fig. *10*). That is, following a depletion by disease, the colonists, notably the missionaries, could readily replenish their settlements by drawing upon these peripheral reserves of population. The process is well documented in the activity of fray Juan Bautista de Moya.[17] In the second place, if the colonial regime really enabled the Indians to produce more abundantly with the new technology introduced by the European settlers, then Michoacan, a rich country, would have been made to support a far larger population than in pre-Conquest antiquity. It is striking, even today in Michoacan, to observe how thinly populated its fertile landscapes are, in contrast to the swarming populations of much poorer areas of the republic of Mexico.[18] Now among the Tarasca and Matlatzinca peoples of Michoacan,[19] the level of material culture that had been attained in antiquity was far lower than that of the high civilizations of the central southern plateaus, in the Valley of Mexico, and in the country about Puebla and Cholula. In other words, the technological expansion of the colonial regime was slight with regard to the Aztec peoples of central southern Mexico, but it was greater with regard to the tribes of western Mexico. That differential may be of some importance to the question at hand.

In the third place, Michoacan was the theater of the extraordinary social experiments of Vasco de Quiroga.[20] The communities he founded, and the many others he

17. Escobar, *Americana thebaida*, p. 128. After 1552, the Augustinian friar, Juan Bautista de Moya ". . . fundó las doctrinas de Nucupétaro, Turicato, Cutzio, Sirándaro, Guacana y Purungueo, adonde edificó iglesias y conventos, y bajando hasta Acapulco, fundó a Coaguayutla, Petatlán y Tecpan, hasta . . . la Guacana, y allí cerca fundó a Urecho y a Santa Clara y Ario, y en Sinagua hasta hoy perseveran las pequeñas celdas que labró." Full biographical details of the life of this remarkable missionary appear in the same work, p. 447.

18. See S. W. Cushing, "The Distribution of Population in Mexico," *Geographical Review*, XI (1921), 227–242.

19. L. Mendieta y Núñez, ed., *Los Tarascos* (Mexico, 1940). J. García Payón, *La Zona arqueológica de Tecaxic-Calixtlahuaca y los matlatzincas*, Pt. I (Mexico, 1936).

20. See Introduction, p. 13, n. 45.

influenced,[21] were primarily dedicated to Christian perfection, and served as efficient organizations for the propagation of the faith among unsettled groups of new converts. All property was held communally, and the Indians were relieved from personal service and tribute. The exercise of crafts and agriculture provided subsistence, while leisure was employed in doctrinal exercises and the care of the sick. The experiment of Bishop Quiroga was so successful that the Mendicant Orders in western Mexico adopted the form of these communities, and as late as the eighteenth century, the community meetings, the landholding system, and other characteristic arrangements survived intact in many areas.[22] Thus the work of Quiroga cannot be overlooked in relation to the extraordinary increase of urban population reflected in our figures. It created a stable mode for Indian life unparalleled elsewhere in the colonial world.[23]

The striking movement observed in Michoacan relates, then, to open frontiers,

10. The bishoprics of Mexico, *ca.* 1580

21. D. Basalenque, *Historia de la provincia de San Nicolas de Tolentino de Michoacán, del orden de N.P.S. Augustín* (Mexico, 1673), p. 102a. At Patzcuaro, Quiroga "Hizo . . . un Hospital de santa Martha, dedicado à la Concepcion de N. Señora, de donde tuvieron principio todos los Hospitales de esta Provincia . . . de modo, que vezinos, y forasteros todos hallā alli remedio."

22. Zavala, *La "Utopia" de Tomás Moro en la Nueva España,* p. 15.

23. The special distinction of the "Hospitals" of Michoacan would appear to be their relative freedom from onerous supervision. Other "Utopian" efforts, such as that of the Jesuits in Paraguay (1610–1767), were achieved only by keeping the Indians in a prolonged state of tutelage.

general underpopulation at all times, and a systematic program of social improvement unprecedented elsewhere in Mexico. Conditions were perhaps roughly analogous in the bishopric of Oaxaca. An intense urban program, directed by the Dominican missionaries,[24] was maintained by replenishing the depleted populations from an extensive back country, southward to the Pacific, and eastward to the Isthmus of Tehuantepec. As regards the archbishopric of Mexico, an important factor in the population rise between 1546 and 1570 would have been the metropolitan character of the Valley of Mexico. Whether forced or voluntary, the migration of Indians to the capital would at all times have been greater than to any provincial center.[25] It is also true that the archbishopric of Mexico, like Michoacan and Oaxaca, possessed extensive frontiers upon virgin country (Fig. *10*) with unconverted populations. But the limited recovery can perhaps be assigned to a more rapid spread of epidemic disease among these urban populations.[26]

It will be seen that the phenomenon of recovery was missing for the bishopric of Tlaxcala and for certain peripheral provinces, such as Colima, Mar del Sur (Zacatula) and Panuco (Fig. *9*). The diocese of Tlaxcala did not have a great back-country from which nomadic or semi-nomadic reserves could be recruited (Fig. *10*). The map reveals how the bishopric was wedged, without indefinite territories, between two other great dioceses barring it from expansion into any *terra incognita.* Another factor is the dense concentration in the area; it is the most thickly populated region of Mexico, and in its great towns, such as Cholula, Tepeaca, Tecamachalco, and dozens of others, epidemic disease took a steady, unremitting toll.[27] Although the area surely benefited from certain factors of increase, these impeding conditions were such that its population remained static.

The peripheral districts ordinarily should be included in the figures for the great bishoprics, but I have listed them separately here because the movements revealed are so widely divergent from those indicated for the larger areas (Table *B*). It was really only in these border-lands that population declined steadily without redress. Elsewhere, the decline was corrected by moments of remarkable recovery; at the fron-

24. See Dávila Padilla, *Historia . . . Santiago de México,* pp. 64–65.

25. F. Cervantes de Salazar, *México en 1554* (Mexico, 1875), p. 141. J. García Icazbalceta, ed.

26. In speaking of missionary activity during the period 1590–1620 in the area from the Sinaloa River north to the Yaqui country, Carl Sauer notes that "European epidemics probably preceded the white man into this area, but their seriousness was certainly much aggravated by the mission system. Prior to the missions these natives (except so far as they had been reduced in encomiendas) lived in scattered rancherías." Thus urbanization exposed the Indians to infections gathered in gregarious living, and the daily assemblies for church-building, instruction and ritual dissolved the "protective isolation of aboriginal living." C. O. Sauer, "Aboriginal Population of Northwestern Mexico," *Iberoamericana,* X (1935), 12.

27. See A. Chimalpahin Quauhtlehuanitzin, *Annales de Domingo Francisco de San Anton Muñon Chimalpahin Quauhtlehuanitzin, sixième et septième relations (1285–1612)* (Paris, 1889). R. Siméon, tr. (Bibliothèque linguistique américaine, XII); and A. Peñafiel, ed., "Anales de Tecamachalco," *Colección de documentos para la historia mexicana,* V (México, 1903).

tiers of the colony, however, it is not unlikely that the various general causes for decline operated with unchecked vigor.

In general, only in Michoacan did the population show a net increase from 1546 to 1595 (Fig. *8*); elsewhere its net diminution was considerable and uniform (Fig. 9). If the figures upon which these curves are based bear any valid relation to reality, the graph here is the most remarkable confirmation of the effectiveness of the social program instituted by Bishop Quiroga.

In order to present the statistical material, such as it is, some casual references were made to the causes of population loss. Widespread and repeated epidemics were of course the major cause of elimination and the most obvious one. Pestilence was almost constant during the sixteenth century. To be sure, there were spells when the colony was free from plague, but the longest of these recesses lasted only seventeen years, between 1546 and 1563. The normal interval between general attacks was ten years or less, and the records suggest frequent localized epidemics[28] of which little account will be taken here, since no measure for the mortality incurred during such incidents can be deduced.

Although no detailed impressions survive as to the extent of the epidemic of 1520–21, fairly consistent estimates of the relative intensity of the pestilences of 1545 and 1576 are available. Torquemada, Escobar, Dávila Padilla and Clavigero all indicated that the mortality in 1576 was about two-and-one-half times as great as that in 1545.[29] Their estimates are confirmed by an important contemporary account, the *Anales de Tecamachalco,*[30] a year book which records the various epidemics at the time of their occurrence. According to this source, the deaths by disease at Tecama-

28. Viceroy Luis Velasco II wrote to Philip II on Nov. 6, 1591, as follows: "En algunas partes hay siempre enfermedad entre los indios, como ahora sucede en la Mixteca y algunos pueblos de la comarca de la Ciudad de los Angeles." Cuevas, *Documentos inéditos,* p. 434. Indications of pre-Conquest epidemics are not uncommon. See *PNE,* IV (1905), 236, for Guatulco, and *PNE,* VI (1905), 220, for Teotihuacan.

Hans Gadow travelled through an area stricken by smallpox in 1906, and his description of the effects is worth quotation. The region is southern Oaxaca. ". . . in nearly all the villages and hamlets along the track there raged smallpox of the virulent black and confluent kind. It is no exaggeration to say that people were dying on the roadside. The huts in this somewhat poor district were loosely, and often carelessly, constructed reed shanties. Outside some of these, in the little courtlike enclosures, we saw lying on the ground both men and women, some in the shade, others left in the glaring sun, in the last stage of the disease, with their relations squatting round them in dumb despair. This had been going on for several weeks; naturally some had recovered—at least, many of those that we met were in the peeling stage—but many huts were deserted, the reed-curtains used as doors being left open and aslant. The entire population of one village was said to have been exterminated, with the exception of a little girl who was found there, and who, when rescued, was quite prostrate by starvation. Yet there had been no stampede, the people stoically waiting for what was going to happen; in some villages they had had a few sporadic cases, and after the victims of these had died, the remainder were left in peace." Gadow, *Through Southern Mexico,* p. 224.

29. J. de Torquemada, *Primera* [*segunda, tercera*] *parte de los veinte i un libros rituales i monarchia indiana* (Madrid, 1723), I, 643. Escobar, *Americana thebaida,* p. 3. Dávila Padilla, *Historia . . . Santiago de México,* pp. 516–518. F. S. Clavigero, *Storia antica del Messico* (Cesena, 1780–81), IV, 282. Clavigero may have had access to the mortality lists kept in each settlement by order of Viceroy Enríquez. Dávila Padilla, *op. cit.,* pp. 100, 516–518.

30. See n. 27

chalco in 1545 numbered forty daily, striking chiefly among the children, whereas in 1576, the plague struck all ages, carrying away at least one hundred persons daily during the crisis. In fact, a rather full account of the plague of 1576 can be written.[31] It broke out in August, rapidly attained a climax in September, and did not spend its force until the end of 1577. The disaster was general throughout New Spain and New Galicia, from northwestern Mexico to Yucatan. The symptoms of infection were stomach pains, violent coughing, and high fever; death came after six or seven days. All ages and classes of Indians were affected, although the Spaniards seemed immune. Famine, as always, accompanied the infection, and deaths were so numerous that the corpses were buried in trenches. Relief work was organized by the friars and by civilians, with support from the viceregal government. Hostile Indians sought to turn the crisis to their advantage, with attempts to infect the Europeans by throwing corpses into the water supply, or by kneading infected blood into the bread.

The nearly constant presence of disease naturally perturbed the white colonists, although epidemic was no novelty for Europeans of the sixteenth century. It was rather more the normal condition of civilized society. Troels-Lund estimates that the nations of the time were more steadily and disastrously swept by epidemic diseases than at any other time in modern history.[32] Typhus, pox, the sweating disease (1529), bubonic plague (1552–64), and influenza (1580–82) were not the occasional ailments of vulnerable individuals; they were the diseases of the whole European community. A nation, such as Spain or England, suddenly fell ill, agonized, and recovered, but meanwhile the disease had swept communities bare, sometimes taking the children, sometimes the old people, or only the women, but more generally leaving an exhausted fraction of the population to bury the dead and renew the life of the community. The phenomenon was therefore not unfamiliar to the colonists, and they accepted it as an ineradicable condition of communal existence. Many remedial measures were taken to abate the severity of disaster,[33] but on the whole, the colonists were far more agitated about the social causes of loss than about disease itself.

The other great primary cause of elimination has evoked much controversy. In brief, it may be designated as the "homicidal theory" of loss, and its best-known

31. Archivo General de la Nación (Mexico City), *Ramo de historia,* Vol. XIV. "Providencia singular del Señor Moya y peste en Mexico 1575." 2½ MS. fols. (eighteenth-century copy). *PNE,* IV, 137; VI, 258–259. Peñafiel, ed., "Anales de Tecamachalco," *Colección de documentos para la historia mexicana,* V, 66–67. *Annales de . . . Chimalpahin,* pp. 288–291. Dávila Padilla, *Historia . . . Santiago de México,* pp. 516–518.

32. T. F. Troels-Lund, *Gesundheit und Krankheit in der Anschauung alter Zeiten* (Leipzig, 1901), pp. 217 ff.

33. Such remedial measures were the moderation of tribute, private philanthropies, the foundation of hospitals, and the institution of certain forms of government relief. See C. Pérez Bustamante, *Los Origenes del gobierno virreinal en las Indias españolas, Don Antonio de Mendoza, primer virrey de la Nueva España (1535–1550)* (Santiago de Compostela, 1928), pp. 108–109 (Anales de la universidad de Santiago, III).

publicist was the Dominican Bishop of Chiapas, fray Bartolomé de las Casas. The title of Las Casas' famous tract, *Breve relación de la destrucción de las Indias occidentales,*[34] is an epitome of the homicidal theory, which attempts to assign all losses of population to direct action—to the bestial cruelty of the Spanish colonists, and their systematic slaughter of enormous masses of the Indian population. Torture and overwork and massacre were the chief instruments of mass homicide, with the result that the *Breve relación* is a catalogue of horrors, containing no mention of disease. Las Casas' attention was devoted mainly to conditions in the Antilles, where, in his opinion, in 1552, of three million Indians on Española at the time of the Discovery, only two hundred remained alive. Las Casas felt that the situation was less incriminating in Mexico,[35] but he insisted that between 1518 and 1530, four millions had been slaughtered there, and in 1519, thirty thousands were massacred in Cholula alone. Two facts should be kept in mind. Las Casas never experienced the fury of any of the great epidemics. In 1520–21, he was engaged in the foundation of the ill-starred colony of the Knights of the Golden Spur on the Pearl Coast of Venezuela, while in 1531, he resided in Española and in Nicaragua.[36] In addition, the bulk of the humanitarian literature he issued in order to secure legislative reforms was written before the development of statistical knowledge regarding the Indies. Las Casas may have witnessed isolated incidents in which the Spaniards behaved cruelly, and he knew of many more through hearsay, but at no time could he have had access to accurate accounts of population loss, for the simple reason that no such accounts existed.[37]

The homicidal theory nevertheless bears some relation to a reality that we may reconstruct from other sources. As we have seen, torture, overwork, and murder were the means employed by the Spaniards, in Las Casas' theory, to destroy the Indian populations. In this form, it was a massive and undifferentiated theory, which assigned effects of an unknown magnitude to direct, malevolent action. The encomendero lashed his Indians to death, buried them alive, loaded their bodies to the breaking point, or else he murdered them with knife and gun. Las Casas admitted no indirect causes that might lie beyond the control of the indicted party. Later in the century, however, it is of the greatest interest to behold this blunt doctrine analyzed, refined, and made accurately descriptive in the hands of civil servants, whose commissions probably derived in part from the agitation aroused in Spain by Las Casas' writings.

The treatment of the question by the learned and intelligent Auditor, Alonso de

34. Simpson has provided an admirable study of the history of this remarkable work in *Encomienda,* pp. 1–18. The following edition of the tract is used here: B. de las Casas, *Breve relación de la destrucción de las Indias occidentales* (London, 1812).

35. B. de las Casas, *Colección de las obras del venerable obispo de Chiapa, Don Bartolomé de las Casas* (Paris, 1822), I, 198. J. A. Llorente, ed.

36. Simpson, *Encomienda,* p. 142.

37. See p. 33.

Zorita,[38] is worth close attention. In general, Zorita interpreted excessive mortality as a function of economic extortion. For the concept of direct homicide, he substituted a far richer social interpretation. Thus he catalogued the examples of extravagant forced labor conducive to a high death rate. Among these were the great public works; an excessive rate of tribute; heavy labor in the mines, in personal services, in the cultivation of certain crops, such as cacao and sugar-cane; and in military duty. Zorita even assigned pestilence to these various causes, and he was perhaps not far from the mark. For instance, reform legislation upon forced labor (the Nuevas Leyes) preceded the longest recess from epidemic during the century, from 1546 to 1573.

It will be noticed, however, that the homicidal theory, whether in its absolute, or in its relative and differentiated form, always was proffered by individuals or groups who were pro-Indian and anti-encomendero—a party, in short, closely affiliated with the humanitarian (and anti-feudatory) tendencies prevalent in Court circles. But it is not enough merely to have declared that population was eliminated by direct action and inhumane economic treatment, that is, to restate the case of the special pleaders of the sixteenth century. The precise ways in which cause and effect were enmeshed have not yet been described, nor have we an adequate concept of the actual kinds of loss, or even of their effective significance.

So far we have discussed high mortality only, avoiding carefully the use of any terms that might refer to depopulation. In the strict sense, depopulation may be taken to signify a failure in the fertility of a people. Elimination by disease, massacre, or the ravages of war is not synonymous with depopulation. When we speak of depopulation, we refer to processes affecting the rate of replacement of the population, in short, to declining human fertility.

No evidence of a quantitative character is available for the birth rate in sixteenth-century Mexico. It may perhaps be inferred, from the graph presented in Fig. 7, that the alternation of epidemic loss and recovery followed in a rhythm that displays dwindling powers of recovery. The great epidemic of 1545 merely checked the viability of the race, a viability manifested in the recovery before 1576. Following the second great epidemic, the indices of recovery are not in evidence. An acceleration of all the processes of elimination was under way, to be sure, but these processes, taken by themselves, do not materially affect the fertility of the survivors.

In gross outline, it becomes apparent that in addition to the obvious check or

38. A. de Zorita, "Historia de la Nueva España," *Colección de libros y documentos referentes á la historia de América,* IX (Madrid, 1909); Zorita, "Breve y sumaria relación de los señores y maneras y diferencias que habia de ellos en la Nueva España," *NCDHM,* III (1891). Zorita composed his historical writings in Spain, during his old age, between 1567 and 1585, after ten years' residence in New Spain (1556–66). On our problem, others shared his views: Motolinia, *Memoriales,* pp. 17–28; Mendieta, *Historia eclesiástica indiana,* p. 519.

hindrance to increase—a high incidence of epidemic disease that is possibly related to homicidal forms of economic exploitation—other determinants worked towards depopulation. Such causes are of two distinct kinds; those deriving from the dislocation of Indian culture, with attendant cultural shock, and those deriving from the reorientation of Indian culture—into the channels of a Christian society, an absolute State, and a mercantile economy. Both were powerful agents for depopulation, acting in rather different ways.

The effects of reorientation are fairly obvious. It should be emphasized that such effects occurred, not directly because of the greed and ill-will of the colonists, but as part of the price of any cultural reorganization, however benevolent in intention.

We must look to the Indians themselves for some account of the effects of reorientation. About 1580, after the great epidemic losses, the Crown was sufficiently concerned to inquire through its agents what interpretation the natives themselves placed upon the fact of their decline. The answers are recorded in the *Relaciones geográficas,* and although the full series has not been published, the available documents of this class yield most interesting clues to the problem. In these cosmographic questionnaires, it was asked of the natives in each community why the Indian race displayed greater longevity in antiquity. The answers came from many regions, and they display surprising acuity. Their general drift pertains to the superiority of indigenous culture over that of the Europeans. The ancient ways are always portrayed as more austere and less luxurious. Nearly all the declarants who pronounced upon the matter asserted that the Indians took less food in antiquity, and therefore enjoyed better health.[39] The taking of much salt and hot food were particularly blamed. Only one settlement claimed that the diet did not differ as to quantity.[40] The ancient restrictions upon alcoholic beverages, the practice of ceremonial warfare with its limited mortality, and the observance of the ancient pieties are also very frequently catalogued among the reasons for the superior health of the Indians before the Conquest.[41] In many communities it was significantly reported that general hygiene and medication were much better in antiquity. The Indians especially approved the pre-Conquest costume, which involved fewer clothes and greater immunity to weather. They also noted that their ancestors had been more addicted to bathing; that they slept upon hard beds; that their herb-doctors were

39. *PNE,* IV: Mitlantongo, 80; Ocelotepec, 141; Chichicapa, 116. *PNE,* V: Tetela del Volcan, 145; Coatzingo, 94. *PNE,* VI: Zumpango del Rio, 315; Tasco, 265; Oztoman, 111; Coatepec de Guerrero, 119; Tetela del Rio, 135. The Indians' statements have recently been confirmed by a study of pre-Conquest disease: S. F. Cook, "The Incidence and Significance of Disease among the Aztecs and Related Tribes," *Hispanic American Historical Review,* XXXVI (1946), 320–335.

40. Mexicatzinco, *PNE,* VI, 196.

41. Alcoholic restriction: *PNE,* VI, 16–17, 29, 37, 57, 91, 111, 147, 163, 227. Ancient warfare: *PNE,* IV, 80, 141; *PNE,* VI, 84. Ancient piety: *PNE,* IV, 132–133, 236; *PNE,* V, 171.

better than the colonial practitioners; and that the European custom of bloodletting was harmful. Finally, the ancient cleanly method of disposing of the dead by cremation was preferred to the Christian burial enforced by the whites.[42] An allusion to the deleterious effects of a mercantile economy dependent upon transportation by human carriers is contained in the numerous assertions that the Indians were formerly more healthy and long-lived because they travelled less.[43] Finally, direct reference to the central problems of fertility and the sex-ratio between males and females is carried by the many protests against the abolition of polygamy and against the practice of youthful marriages enforced by the Christians. Here the Indians touched upon the heart of the problem: the most delicate mechanisms of the culture, its rituals and customs of procreation, had been tampered with by the whites. The complaints are registered from all the main areas of New Spain, and they are among the few verbal expressions from Indian sources attesting to the essential lesions effected by the reorientation[44] of Indian life into a colonial pattern.

As to losses deriving from the dislocation of Indian culture, no quantitative measure of any kind is suggested by the texts. But one set of replies from Indian informants, contained in the *Relaciones geográficas* cited above, bears upon the question, and it yields an important clue. It was supposed by the Indians that their reduced longevity was partly to be explained by the amount of work they were doing. A peculiar difference of opinion was expressed: in some communities, the view was advanced that the Indians did *less* work in antiquity than in colonial life, and in others, it was stated that the Indians did *more* work in antiquity and therefore lived longer. The number of communities in which the latter view was voiced is double the number of those in which the Indians were represented as doing less work before the Conquest.[45] The prevalent opinion in 1580 was therefore that the Indians were not working so hard as before the Conquest.

A sixteenth-century text explicitly mentions this situation. In 1545, a colonist writing to the Emperor said that great orderliness had prevailed in Motecuzoma's time: "Each man followed his calling. . . . There were inspectors . . . and now all

42. *PNE*, IV, 249; *PNE*, VI, 57, 84, 243–244, 258–259.

43. *PNE*, V, 82, 94, 110; *PNE*, VI, 265.

44. Late marriages in antiquity: *PNE*, IV, 102, 116, 141; *PNE*, V, 6, 129; *PNE*, VI, 84, 91, 135. Polygamous habits: *PNE*, VI, 196; Paso y Troncoso, comp., "Papeles de Nueva España," MS, Vol. VIII, Library of the Museo Nacional, Mexico City (Cocochol, New Galicia).

45. The Indians did less work before the Conquest: Guaxolotitlan, *PNE*, IV, 200; Miahuatlan, *PNE*, IV, 291–292; Chilapa, *PNE*, V, 179; Mexicatzinco, *PNE*, VI, 196; Tasco, *PNE*, VI, 265; Tetela del Volcan, *PNE*, VI, 286. The Indians did more work before the Conquest: Mitlantongo, *PNE*, IV, 80; Chichicapa, *PNE*, IV, 116; Ocelotepec, *PNE*, IV, 141; Axacuba, *PNE*, VI, 16–17; Coatepec Chalco, *PNE*, VI, 57; Chicualoapa, *PNE*, VI, 84; Ichcateopan, *PNE*, VI, 91; Oztoman, *PNE*, VI, 111; Coatepec Guerrero, *PNE*, VI, 119; Tetela del Rio, *PNE*, VI, 135; Teloloapan, *PNE*, VI, 147; Atitalaquia, *PNE*, VI, 202; Tequesistlan, *PNE*, VI, 227; Zumpango del Rio, *PNE*, VI, 315.

are vagabonds and idlers."[46] The white settlers naturally shared this official opinion. But it may be pointed out that their allegations did not always benefit their interests. To assever that the Indians were not working hard enough was needed to undermine the pro-Indian, humanitarian legislation on forced labor. The tax-collector, however, took it to signify that the tribute-burden was inadequate. The encomendero, in turn, knew that increase in the tribute-burden entailed some decrease in his own profit from Indian labor.

The most articulate opinion upon this question came from the pen of the learned and experienced Alonso de Zorita. He pointed out, after 1565, that the Europeans were mistaken in believing that the Indians were not working hard. But most of their work was being done for Europeans, and very little work was being done by the Indians for themselves. Hence it was perfectly true that the work of self-sustenance done by Indians was less in colonial times and more in antiquity; in the total labor-burden, however, the Indians were giving most of their time to the service of the whites.[47]

To return to the Indians' own views upon the matter, it is to be emphasized that any proper interpretation of the proposition that the Indians worked harder in antiquity depends upon the meaning of the term, "work," to Indians. Their allegations make sense only when "work" is interpreted as "occupation," that is, as the entire routine of a ritual life that includes subsistence activities. To the pre-Conquest highland Indians, few differences were apparent between the work of producing ceremonial, and the ceremonial of doing work. All communal activities were ritual in character, and the year was filled with an intricate succession of ceremonial occasions, among which subsistence activities played a cardinal role.[48] But in colonial life, when physical labor without ceremonial adornment was forced on the Indians, they became, so to speak, psychologically unemployed. In the absence of ceremonial, a dissipated indolence between moments of forced economic labor was inevitable. What would have been "leisure" to a modern community was complete absence of "occupation" to the Indians, only partly filled by the ritual and service of the church. Thus an extravagant economic exploitation may quite rightly have been regarded by the Indians as insufficient "work." An unoccupied leisure, filled with idling, drunkenness, and a minor ritual obligation to the church, would also be regarded as insufficient. In brief, the European secularization of all labor was antithetic to the Indian concept of "work." For the pre-Conquest Indian, all work was ultimately a

46. Gerónimo López to His Majesty, Feb. 25, 1545. *Epistolario,* IV, 169–170, "cada uno hiciese su oficio . . . e había veedores . . . Agora . . . todos son vagamundos, holgazanes."

47. Zorita, "Breve y sumaria relación," *NCDHM,* III, 171–173. Zorita was pro-Indian, pro-Mendicant, and anti-encomendero. Cf. *ibid.,* p. 212.

48. See Chap. IV, pp. 157–158.

ritual: for the European, work was almost exclusively a profane necessity, and to the Indians, the metamorphosis of work from ritual into an unadorned necessity must have been among the most disturbing and revolutionary aspects of their contact with Europeans.

Now the ritual life of Indian culture, with its rich and intricate forms of esthetic experience, may have been far from ideal. It was punctuated by human sacrifice and by rites of great cruelty. Yet its psychic values must have been more satisfying to Indians than the drab and incomprehensible life of partial labor for economic ends imposed by the Spaniards. The Mendicant missionaries realized these deficiencies in colonial life, and sought to compensate for them with an abundant ceremonial which was unusual even by contemporary European standards. In an admirable chapter, Robert Ricard commented upon the extraordinary frequency and complexity of the ceremonial instituted by Mendicants. Sumptuous decorations filled the churches for the many important festivals; each community prepared musical offerings of voices and instruments; pilgrimages were encouraged to holy sites; each week processions, public dances, and theatrical performances of religious character were arranged; the needs of organized sociability were supplied by the intricate system of the sodalities, or *cofradías,* in each settlement. All these ceremonial activities, Ricard implies, were continuous, occupying the various groups and classes during the entire year, replacing the elaborate pre-Conquest calendar, and bringing Christianity a little closer to the Indians.[49] Yet all this could be true only for the great Mendicant communities, in which friars were constantly resident, always available to supervise and encourage the new festivities. Where there were no friars, and where the secular clergy held control, little of the substitute or surrogate ceremonial could be supplied. In effect, a majority of the Indian population of Mexico was not provided with such relief from labor.

Hence it is reasonable to suggest that the Indians of Mexico were psychologically unemployed during the first century following the Conquest. Their situation in the sixteenth century is closely comparable to that of the natives of Polynesia and Melanesia and other island groups of the Pacific during the nineteenth century. The dislocation and reorientation of an antecedent culture entail a decrease in the rate of replacement among the bearers of that culture. An observable depopulation of the area is apparent. As the reorientation and dislocation of Indian life went on, numerous symptoms of a state of shock among the affected peoples became evident. These symptoms usually took the form either of violently destructive action, or of a lowered vitality and will to survive.

49. R. Ricard, *La "Conquête spirituelle" du Mexique* (Paris, 1933), chaps. iv, v.

Systematic abortion and infanticide, as well as mass suicides, were reported from several areas.[50] In Michoacan, for instance, a certain sorcerer was said to have induced crowds of bewitched Indians to kill themselves. Alonso de Zorita knew of many cases of Indian suicide to escape the payment of an impossible tribute, and he also cited the numerous abortions and the general refusal to procreate among the Mixe and Chontal Indians. In western Mexico as well, Lebrón de Quiñones found that the Indian women had been ordered not to conceive, that many refrained from intercourse, and that abortion was regularly practised, to ensure the rapid disappearance of the tribe. These are perhaps no more than isolated and sporadic instances, but they bespeak a general disintegration of the vital forces of the Indian race that also took much less radical forms. Drunkenness, for example, became alarmingly common, as reported by the Indian informants of 1579–81, and it appears to have been the drunkenness of despair and frustration.[51]

The history of the many Indian revolts during the century may also be construed as a phenomenon of cultural shock. Such revolts were severely punished, and the rate of elimination in certain areas may reasonably be attributed to Spanish reprisals. The uprisings were especially common at the periphery of the colony.[52] The most famous of these border revolts was the so-called "Mixton" war of 1541. It originated in western Mexico, in the province of Tepic, and rapidly spread towards central and southern Mexico. The Indians meant to break Spanish control of New Spain by a strategy of violent raids. Viceroy Mendoza himself commanded an expedition to quell the revolt, and in the process, large Indian groups were eradicated. Smaller disturbances broke out in Oaxaca during 1547–48, and again in 1550. In northwestern Mexico they recurred periodically, as in 1560 among the Zacatecas Indians of the Llerena-Sombrerete region.

Hence all approaches to the problem appear to yield the same answer: increased elimination and decreased replacement are the results of colonization, constantly reducing the spread and density of the native populations. The narrowing phases of recovery suggest that the Indian race still possessed certain powers of recuperation, if indeed these moments of apparent recovery are not the result of intensive urban reconcentration. The net losses, however, between 1520 and 1600 clearly indicate de-

50. Grijalva, *Crónica de la orden de N. P. S. Agustín*, p. 217. Zorita, "Breve y sumaria relación," *NCDHM*, III, 192, 195. Lebrón de Quiñones, "Visita a Colima, 1551–1554," MS (modern copy by F. del Paso y Troncoso) in Library, Museo Nacional, Mexico City.

51. *PNE*, VI, 16–17, 29, 37, 57, 91, 111, 147, 163, 227. Zorita, "Breve y sumaria relación," *NCDHM*, III, 173.

52. Pérez Bustamante, . . . *Don Antonio de Mendoza*, pp. 73–85, 110–111, appendices IX, X. *Documentos sobre Nueva Galicia*, MS copy, F. del Paso y Troncoso, in the Museo Nacional, Mexico City. See also López de Velasco, *Geografía*, p. 276, regarding an analogous revolt in Culiacan, and *Epistolario*, II, 32, for a minor revolt in the region of Cuscotitlan in 1531.

population. At every point the two processes of increased elimination and decreased replacement are closely related. It is hard to believe that great epidemic losses are not registered in some decreases of the birth-rate, for an epidemic reducing the numbers of young women involves losses in fecundity which cannot immediately be recovered. In any case, depopulation seems to be the general secular trend, and accelerated elimination is a regional tendency. These are hypotheses. We lack quantitative knowledge of birth-rate and sex-ratio; of the influence of monogamy upon the birth-rate; and of the psychological consequences of culture contact. But it remains important to relate these factors in historical life, however poorly quantified they may be, to the building operations that chiefly concern us.

The initial problem remains. How may the chiastic relationship between population movement and general cultural activity be resolved? A striking disharmony among the factors of historical life is implied, a disharmony that violates the accepted notion of historical happening as an integrally harmonious process. It is not infrequently assumed that history contains ages of "decline," in which all the forms of existence appear uniformly and consistently decadent. It is a common belief, again, that ascendant cultures or epochs contain no phases of disintegration, and that all the strands of happening lie neatly parallel rather than inextricably tangled and uneven. Yet every moment in history is obviously at once a process of building and unbuilding; decay and integration are simultaneous processes, and rarely are they to be witnessed more clearly at work than in America in the sixteenth century. For as colonial life assumed its characteristic forms, the Indian cultures disintegrated. It is not simply a matter of displacement, in which one existing culture edged another out of being. Colonial life in the sixteenth century was a *tertium quid,* an unprecedented phenomenon of shock, resulting in a cultural pattern whose future stability remained imponderable. Hence none of the durable forms of colonial life took shape until after the opposition of Indian and European cultures had developed problems to which the solutions were desperately needed.

In the first place, an attempt should be made to place the great losses of population in their proper perspective, from the point of view of the white colonists of the period. It is beyond question that epidemic disease was the most efficient single cause of loss, and all authorities referred to it as such, without, however, revealing any sense of defeat or any lessening of their intention to remain in the country. The imperatives of colonial action were never weakened. It should perhaps be recalled that larger human groups react to disease somewhat as do individuals. From a state of well-being and normal activity, the organism is thrown into a condition of lowered vitality and limited effort. Normal affairs cease, the perspective alters, values change. A diseased state becomes normal, until recovery, when the organism is once again capable of full activity. The readjustment seems slow, and yet, after normal tempo has been resumed, little sense of loss survives. The disease appears only as a vaguely terrible interlude, as an interruption few of whose consequences were permanently registered. A sense of continuity between the broken phases of healthy life is gradually asserted, and the memory of sufferings through tedious weeks, months, or years is ultimately effaced.

Then again, widespread disease has the valuable effect of heightening the social conscience of the members of the community. Differences, factions, strife, and discontent evaporate when the agglomeration is at grips with a common danger. All the symbols and rituals of social experience are affirmed with new vehemence. The religious behavior of the crowds suddenly assumes new and ecstatic forms of singular extravagance, as with the flagellant cults of fourteenth-century Europe and sixteenth-century Mexico.[53] And after the cleansing scourge, the community emerges diminished and weary, but with many problems resolved by the fact of having gained distance from them.

It is true that neither pestilence nor depopulation held the terrors of novelty for Spaniards of the sixteenth century. With epidemic disease they were fully familiar, and population loss at home in Spain had frequently troubled many alert minds. An ample literature grew upon the theme of depopulation, concerned mainly with its economic effects and cures.[54] The great difference is, that whereas very little happened in Spain to remedy the evil, in American colonies, extraordinary efforts were made to concentrate and stabilize the surviving population, and to remedy or reform the chief causes of loss.

The nature of the relationship between these remedial efforts and the decline of population may provide the answer to our central problem. In general, the most suggestive implication of the material presented here concerns the *actual rate* of diminution. It was clearly not an unremitting process. A great population at the time of the Conquest was reduced by 1600 to a fraction of its former size, but the intermediary stages did not compose a steady decrease. On the contrary, the encomienda lists reveal that abrupt decline alternated with a rapid recovery, and that the processes of recovery were at first thorough enough to offset the crippling effect of the great losses.

53. *Annales de . . . Chimalpahin*, p. 301. In 1583, on Good Friday, "les religieux dominicains et les Espagnols firent de nouveau une procession; on célébra la passion de Notre-Seigneur Jésus-Christ, et l'on fit un enterrement magnifique après avoir exposé toutes les souffrances de N.-S. Dieu dans la passion. Jamais il ne s'était fait pareille chose dans les diverses églises de Mexico." This is the first recorded performance of the sufferings of the Passion in America, in a form which has since assumed full representation in the Penitente cult of New Mexico.

54. See R. Gonnard, *Histoire des doctrines de la population* (Paris, 1923), pp. 98–101.

Of some significance should be the fact that the moments of sharp decline coincided with the most active campaigns of legislative reform and material construction. In the decade of the 1540's, so afflicted by the pestilence of 1545, we find vigorous agitation for a reasonable tribute, to be based upon accurate geographical and statistical knowledge. Private philanthropy assumed sizeable proportions; the foundation of hospitals proceeded apace, and the great reform of the decade was, of course, the incomplete but humane revision of the tenure of encomienda proposed by the Nuevas Leyes.[55] During the decade of the 1570's again, the great epidemic of 1576 seems to be the nucleus of another constellation of legislative and judiciary reforms,[56] such as the court of appeals for Indian litigation (*Juzgado de indios*), and the later creation of the Court of Congregation, designed to concentrate and stabilize the surviving native populations.

Thus, population decline and the positive definition of colonial life appear to be functionally related. Institutional improvement and a great material production were the alternating phases of a humane colonial policy, animated by the Crown's inflexible sense of obligation to the humanity of America, and stimulated by repeated disaster.

Now that the magnitude, nature, and social significance of the great population losses have been established, the question arises whether any correlation can be made between the decline of the Indian race and the building activity of the colonists. The greatest volume of construction work is seen among the settlements of the Mendicant Orders. The study of their rhythms of production will serve as an index to the cultural problem implicit in all colonial building activity.

At the beginning, one self-evident proposition may be stated. The fact that many new urban centers were created by the Mendicants implies the progressive human denudation of the countryside. It has already been pointed out that Table *B* represents urban populations, and yields no direct clue to the density of scattered and rural settlement. But it may be inferred that an increase in urban concentration reduced the "protective isolation" of aboriginal living. This, however, was a short-term result. Urbanization may have promoted immediate contagion, but in the long run, it also diminished the chances of contamination among townspeople adequately supplied with drinking water and shelter.

To establish quantitative measures is equally difficult for another phase of Mendicant urbanization. The friars had at their disposal the pre-Conquest guilds of specialized building laborers. To utilize such reservoirs of labor involved mass dis-

55. See p. 16.

56. Simpson, "Studies," *Iberoamericana,* XIII (1938), 22–23; VII (1934), 29–129.

placements and transplantations analogous to those of the military enterprise. We know, for example, that Tlaxcalan military auxiliaries were settled in northern Mexico and in Central America during the sixteenth century. Skilled artisans were also shifted to the frontiers, as when, about 1574, Indians from Tepeaca built the mining structures in Oaxaca.[57] A constant flow of trained Indian laborers moved from the capital to the provinces, and Indians from the outlying regions were sent to the center for training in European crafts. Within a given area, moreover, considerable movement from one form of enterprise to another was constantly under way. A spectacular example appears from the experience of the Dominicans in southern Mexico. When mines were discovered in Oaxaca, their service immediately drew off the whole laboring population previously engaged in building the church and convento.[58]

Hence building activity within the frame of urbanization may have entailed immediate population losses, and the work itself was conducive to many shifts of population, both to and from the sites of construction. But the functional relationship between long-term building campaigns and long-term population trends can be clarified only by an examination of the rhythm of production maintained by the Mendicants. It is necessary first to distinguish among the Orders.

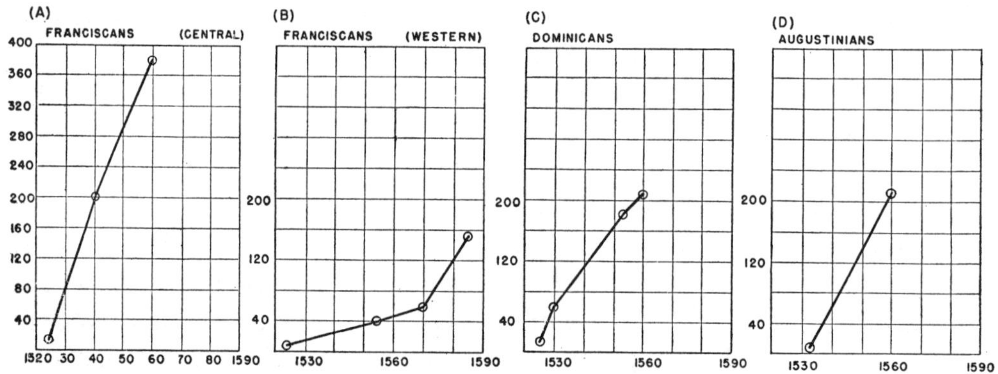

11. Mendicant population. A. Franciscans (Santo Evangelio) B. Franciscans (SS. Pedro y Pablo) C. Dominicans D. Augustinians

The chief factors concerned in the rhythm of production are the territorial scope and priorities enjoyed by the Order in question, the numbers of effective missionaries (Fig. *11a,b*), and the relative homogeneity of the laboring population. The Franciscans, who spread across the continent, to work among unconverted and newly-discovered tribes, suffered at first from serious deficiencies of numbers. A

57. "Códice Mendieta I," *NCDHM*, IV, 212.

58. F. de Burgoa, *Geográfica descripción* (Mexico, 1934), I, 24–25, 45–46, 96; II, 52–53.

multitude of variant solutions to the problem of building had to be devised for the many different cultural environments. It may be expected, therefore, that the Franciscan oeuvre was slower of attainment and more variegated than that of the rival Orders. Beginning in 1524 with a staff of but twelve friars, the Franciscans immediately spread over vast territories, undertaking the initial labors of conversion. Their first foundations were provisional and impermanent constructions. In 1529, nine establishments were in existence, but they lacked durable churches.[59] A remarkable letter written in 1529 by fray Pedro de Gante, to his Flemish brethren, alludes boastfully to immense churches, two and three hundred feet in length—this testimony may be read as the effort to recruit new helpers by a man faced with immense tasks.[60] During this decade, before 1530, friars were also sent to Michoacan.[61] Rarely can permanent Mendicant building enterprise in New Spain be identified before 1530. During the 1530's, the Franciscans increased the number of their foundations to twenty, of which five or six were in Michoacan.[62] By 1538, over-expansion had occurred, and Franciscan activity was in danger of coming to a standstill for want of friars. But by 1541, Jacobo de Testera returned from Europe with one hundred fifty new recruits.[63] During the 1540's, accordingly, the friars undertook to replace the primitive, temporary constructions of the first evangelizations by more durable and imposing edifices.[64]

By 1560, the number of Franciscan foundations rose from twenty to an extravagant number, more than eighty. Over fifty were in existence before 1555.[65] Hence some thirty establishments were founded in five years. The situation proved unmanageable, and in the 1560's, the friars swiftly unloaded their settlements, transferring them to the rival Orders, or exchanging the valuable sites for communities held by their rivals but useful to the Franciscan pattern of deployment. In 1568 alone, seven or eight establishments went by the board, and by 1569, the Order retained but fifty-three foundations in New Spain, exclusive of Yucatan and Guatemala.[66] Concurrently with their geographical contraction, the friars met difficulties in completing edifices already begun. Between 1567 and 1570, when fray Miguel Navarro was Provincial of

59. T. Motolinia, "Historia de los indios," *CDHM*, I, 101. Mendieta, *Historia eclesiástica indiana*, p. 601.

60. García Icazbalceta, *Bibliografía mexicana*, p. 395. Cf. Chap. III, n. 64, and Chap. VII, n. 29.

61. I. F. de Espinosa, *Crónica de la provincia franciscana de los apostoles San Pedro y San Pablo de Michoacán* (Mexico, 1899, p. 96. N. Leon, ed.). The six whose names are known were Martín de Jesús alias de la Coruña; Angel de Saucedo alias Angel de Valencia; Jerónimo de la Cruz; Juan Vadiano or de la Vadilla; Juan de Padilla; and Miguel de Bononia, or Bolonia, a Fleming. Their mission to Michoacan occurred about 1525.

62. P. de la P. C. Beaumont, *Crónica de Michoacán* (Mexico, 1932), II, 157.

63. Motolinia, *op. cit.*, p. 136.

64. *Ibid.*, p. 68. ". . . los templos que primero se hicieron pequeños y no bien hechos, se van enmendando y haciendo grandes." Written *ca.* 1540.

65. *Ibid.*, p. 255. Spain, Ministerio de fomento, *Cartas de Indias* (Madrid, 1877), pp. 141–142.

66. Mendieta, *Historia eclesiástica indiana*, p. 353. "Códice franciscano," *NCDHM*, II, 1–2.

the Order, much attention was devoted to the proper architectural conduct of the monastic buildings in the various foundations. Whenever necessary, the plans were reduced to a more modest scale; new edifices arose in the important sites, and enterprises in settlements not needing large buildings were discontinued.[67] By 1583, however, the total number of Franciscan establishments in the metropolitan province of the Santo Evangelio had risen again to 68, of which 38 were in the Archbishopric of Mexico, and thirty in the Bishopric of Tlaxcala (i.e., Puebla). In addition, the Order controlled the western province of SS. Pedro y Pablo, comprising 48 foundations in Michoacan and Jalisco, and the custodies of Zacatecas, with ten missions, and Tampico, with seven.[68]

Thus the history of the Franciscan diaspora was one of searching for a proper relation among number of missions (Figs. *12*, *13*), number of friars (Fig. *11a,b*), and scale of establishment (Table *A*). Extravagant experiments were undertaken, but the guiding desire was to achieve a suitably ascetic, yet serviceable formula. As we shall see, this ethical ideal and the practice were forever at variance.

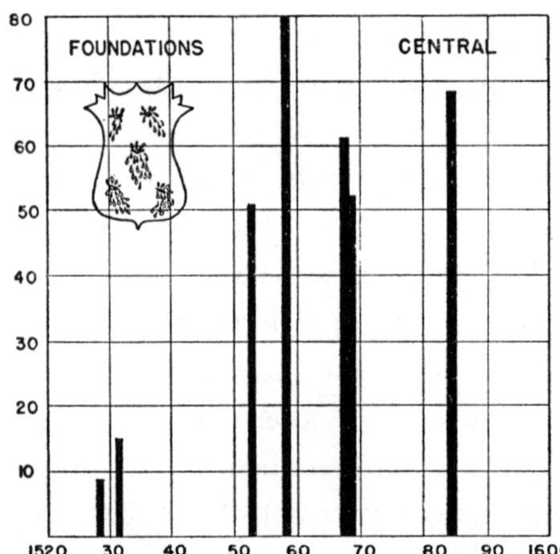

12. Franciscan expansion by number of active foundations (Provincia del Santo Evangelio)

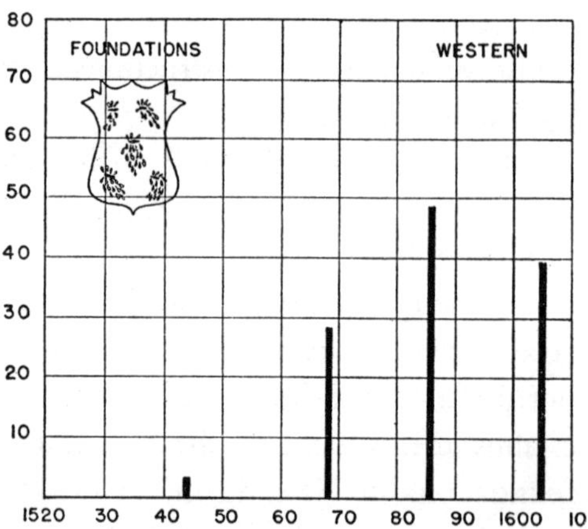

13. Franciscan expansion by number of active foundations (Provincia SS. Pedro y Pablo)

In the western province (SS. Pedro y Pablo) of Michoacan and Jalisco, which separated from the mother province in 1555,[69] a more regular pattern of behavior is

67. "Códice Mendieta I," *NCDHM*, IV, 79–80. Mendieta, *op. cit.*, p. 542. Miguel Navarro improved the "edificios de iglesias y casas, porque apenas hay alguna buena en que su diligencia y cuidado no haya tenido parte en la comenzar, proseguir ó acabar."

68. *Relación breve y verdadera de algunas cosas de las muchas que sucedieron al padre fray Alonso Ponce en las provincias de la Nueva España* (Madrid, 1873), I, 85–87, 517.

69. A. Tello, *Libro segundo de la Crónica miscelanea . . . de la santa provincia de Xalisco* (Guadalajara, 1891), pp. 5–6.

to be noted (Fig. *13*). Evangelization began among the Tarasca Indians of the Michoacan lake district as early as 1525.[70] Originally staffed by but six friars, the region contained few missions before 1545.[71] By 1553, the custodia was worked by some forty friars, presumably recent arrivals in Michoacan.[72] Their missionary activity spread far, and by 1569, the province contained some 28 establishments, of which fourteen were in New Galicia.[73] The decade of the 1580's shows intense activity in New Galicia (Jalisco), when 135 friars were engaged in the conduct of 48 missions, 25 in New Galicia, and 23 in Michoacan.[74] In 1606, New Galicia separated from the Michoacan province as the Provincia de Santiago. At that moment, its missions numbered 39.[75] In New Galicia as in New Mexico, the newly defined frontier mission of the Franciscans encouraged them to proceed with the foundation of new establishments long after the rival Orders had ceased activity among unconverted peoples. New Galicia, and for that matter, Michoacan, were always among the peripheral areas for Franciscan activity. They did not cease to be frontier regions for the Franciscans until the end of the colonial era. Hence the Franciscans found a far more durable mission in the west than at the center, where their activity was forced to contract after the initial campaigns of evangelization and urban concentration. In the west, they transferred their urban mission to peoples of nomadic habits, whereas in the center, their vocation had been among highly civilized tribes. The Christianization of nomads is not achieved within a generation or two, and the long usefulness of the Franciscans at the frontier must be regarded in terms of their capacities as frontier agents, as in New Mexico.

The Dominicans, the second Mendicant Order to arrive in Mexico (1526), began their operations with twelve friars. By 1530, some fifty workers were available, and only three missions had been founded.[76] This rate of expansion was sluggish, compared with the other Orders (Fig. *14*), but it is to be remembered that the Dominican provincial, Domingo de Betanzos (*obit* 1549), originally planned to have but twelve conventos in the province at best. Each house was to accommodate thirty friars. Although the plan never was realized, the Dominicans always discriminated carefully between *conventos principales* (Yanhuitlan) and mere *casas* (Cuilapan).[77] With their great southern province in Guatemala and Oaxaca, and the mother house

70. Espinosa, *Crónica . . . de Michoacán*, p. 96.
71. *Epistolario*, IV, 189.
72. *Epistolario*, VII, 240.
73. "Códice franciscano," *NCDHM*, II, 166–168.
74. *Relación . . . Ponce*, I, 517.
75. A. de la Rea, *Crónica de la orden de N. serafico P. S. Francisco, provincia de San Pedro y San Pablo de Mechoacán en la Nueva España* (Mexico, 1643), p. 77b. Mendoza, *Fragmentos*, pp. 155–228, gives the list of dated foundations.
76. Dávila Padilla, *Historia . . . Santiago de México*, p. 50. J. B. Méndez, "Crónica de la provincia de Santiago de Mexico del orden de predicadores," MS (coll. F. Gómez de Orozco in 1941). G. Gillow, *Apuntes históricos* (Mexico, 1889), p. 22. Torquemada, *. . . Monarchia indiana*, III, 40. Mendieta, *Historia eclesiástica indiana*, p. 363.
77. Dávila Padilla, *op. cit.*, p. 48. Méndez, *op. cit.*, fol. 139.

some one hundred fifty miles distant in Mexico City, the Dominicans were forced in practice to establish conventos as if they were inns, one day's journey apart on the road to Guatemala.[78] Many had the size and magnificence of conventos principales, but were accounted merely as casas.

We have little information about the quantity of Dominican work in the 1530's. That it was considerable may be judged from the style of several establishments in the Valley of Mexico. In the chapter meeting of 1541, a resolution passed that future undertakings should be modest.[79] Later in the century, about 1550, the great building campaigns in southern Mexico are recorded in the chapter meeting minutes by the decision to enlarge some establishments.[80] By 1559, some forty foundations were staffed by 210 friars. In January 1564, of forty-eight foundations, building had been completed at only three.[81] The Dominicans acquired some more sites from the Franciscans in 1570, but undertook few new conversions.[82]

About 1583, the Dominicans responded to the anti-Mendicant pressures then current in New Spain by ordering all edifices in progress to be completed as soon as possible, in a moderate style of building.[83] This decision brought to a temporary halt the long campaign of sumptuous construction under way since the mid-century.

In brief, the Dominicans rarely attempted a mission among tribes of low civilization. The exception is found in their Chinantec evangelization,[84] but on the whole, their work was confined to fertile and densely populated districts in which many close-set establishments could be built. Elsewhere, unnecessary competition with other Orders was avoided. At the very end of the century, their undisputed control of southern Mexico permitted them the foundation of several new establishments, with the result that in 1596, of fifty-nine houses, thirty-seven were in southern Mexico alone.[85]

The career of the Augustinians began late, in 1533. Within a year after their arrival, four foundations were staffed by seven friars.[86] About a score of friars came to reinforce the first group before 1537, and the number of convents rose to seven.[87] By the beginning of the 1540's, sixteen establishments functioned. Operating, there-

78. Dávila Padilla, *op. cit.*, pp. 48, 365. Cf. T. Gage, *The English-American, a New Survey of the West Indies, 1648* (London, 1928), A. P. Newton, ed.

79. *CDIAI*, V (1886), 463 (document of 1569): "Ordenose . . . que los conventos que se edificassen, que fuessen muy humildes . . ."

80. *CDIAI*, V, 467: ". . . ampliaronse . . . algunos monasterios en la provincia."

81. Ricard, *La "Conquête spirituelle" du Mexique*, p. 211.

82. *CDIAI*, V, 469. Vetancurt, *Chrónica, Teatro*, Pt. IV, p. 26.

83. M. Cuevas, *Historia de la iglesia en México*, II, 168.

84. B. Bevan, *The Chinantec* (Mexico, 1938) (Instituto panamericano de geografía e historia, Publicación 24), pp. 47–64.

85. Mendieta, *Historia eclesiástica indiana*, p. 546. Dávila Padilla, *op. cit.*, pp. 64–65.

86. Grijalva, *Crónica de la orden de N. P. S. Agustín*, pp. 64, 66.

87. *Ibid.*, pp. 58, 59, 64. Basalenque, *Historia . . . Michoacán*, p. 3a. Escobar, *Americana thebaida*, p. 244.

fore, with very narrow facilities in men, the Augustinians achieved rapid, consistent expansion (Fig. *15*), centered mainly in the present State of Morelos, about sixty miles from the capital. Few of these early establishments were given imposing monumental form until 1543 or thereabouts, when the friars undertook to build permanent edifices.[88] In the same decade, the number of foundations was doubled, mainly in

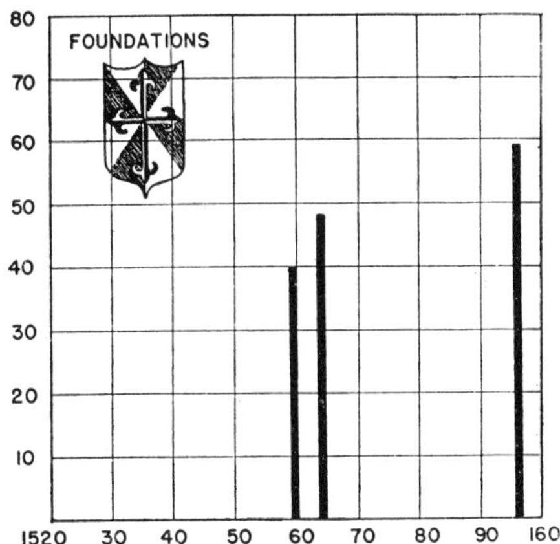

14. Dominican expansion by number of active foundations

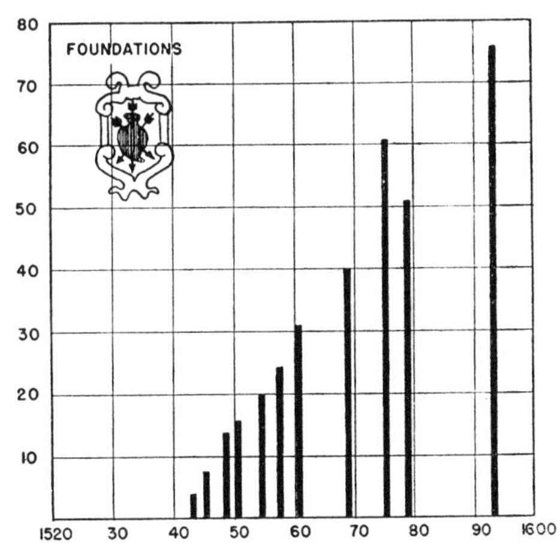

15. Augustinian expansion by number of active foundations

Hidalgo, and thirty-one establishments were in existence by 1551.[89] In the mid-sixties, the number was again doubled by penetration in Michoacan, rising well over sixty, when, like the Franciscans, the friars experienced the difficulties of over-expansion, and abandoned several sites in the *tierra caliente* between 1566 and 1569. This contraction, under the provincialate of fray Diego de Vertavillo, is closely analogous to the Franciscans' pruning or tidying of their region at the same time. Not only were useless sites abandoned, but building activity went forward with great vigor in many surviving establishments.[90] Well before this period, however, the Augustinians had faced accusations that they were building too sumptuously. The complaints about this extravagance appear as early as 1554.[91]

The tide of complaint came from civilians and secular clergy; directed not only at the Augustinians, but also against the other Mendicant Orders. In the 1570's,

88. Grijalva, *op. cit.*, p. 221. After 1543, the friars "pusieron sus conatos en edificar algunas Yglesias y conventos."

89. See J. Román, *Repúblicas de Indias idolatrías y gobierno en México y Perú antes de la conquista* (Colección de libros raros o curiosos que tratan de América, XIV, XV), II, 233 ff.

90. Grijalva, *op. cit.*, p. 387. Basalenque, *op. cit.*, p. 100a. Escobar, *op. cit.*, p. 137.

91. *Epistolario*, VII, 248–249. Lebrón de Quiñones to His Majesty.

anti-Mendicant opposition rose to such a pitch that all Orders underwent contraction, suffering the secularization of some of their most valuable communities. The Augustinians, however, resumed activity after 1580. Working assiduously in Michoacan, the friars made many new foundations and initiated an ambitious campaign of terminal construction that continued well into the seventeenth century.[92] In 1595, the Augustinians held seventy-six establishments in Mexico, Michoacan, and Jalisco.

Given these brief ordinal biographies, we may now tabulate for the relationships between the rate of expansion, the increase in the number of friars, the rate of building, and the rate of change in the population. Table *C* and Fig. *16* are perhaps inexact as to specific quantities, but they will indicate relative magnitudes and rates of change with reasonable accuracy.

If the numerical increase of conventual foundations through the century be plotted, it must be recalled that this increase pertains only to territorial expansion by the Mendicants. It does not refer to the rate of construction, excepting in a limited sense. Nearly every act of foundation implies a campaign of urban settlement and provisional construction. But building of permanent edifices came later in the history of the individual settlement, with some economic affluence. The rhythm of production may therefore be said to shift from the temporary buildings of the periods of expansion, to the campaigns of permanent construction in periods of consolidation. Rapid territorial expansion was achieved by all Orders until 1570. The rate of increase thereafter in the central areas of New Spain declined, ceasing towards the end of the century. After 1585, the processes of secularization arrested fresh missions (exception: the Augustinians in Michoacan) in the central areas, but vigorous campaigns of foundation continued at the periphery of the colony, in New Galicia and in New Mexico. These marginal expansions are not recorded in the graphs.

Some explanation of Table *C*, displaying building campaigns, is in order. The texts do not permit the individual building campaigns to be identified more closely than by the decade in which each occurred. Where a short campaign bridged the boundary between two decades, the campaign is tabulated as pertaining to the one decade in which most of its work may be assumed to have been done. If, however, a campaign lasted between fifteen and twenty years, it is scored for both decades. Hence, in the same decade, short campaigns and long ones are scored with equal values. But it is generally true that only the important operations were mentioned by the chroniclers or in the documents. Very brief or superficial campaigns of repair or enlargement did not usually enter the record. Brief campaigns, as at Epazoyucan, were intensive if they were mentioned, and long campaigns usually were dilatory.

92. Basalenque, *op. cit.*, p. 115a. Mendieta, *op. cit.*, p. 546. P. de Vera, "Relación hecha en la provincia de Mechoacan en el año de 1603," *CDIHE*, C (1891), 459–502.

The record is by no means adequate for the building history of all Mendicant establishments. Of *ca.* 270 foundations among all Orders and in all New Spain (excepting Yucatan and Chiapas), the documents yield reliable information concerning only 220, or 81.5 per cent. Again, the building record for each of these foundations is surely incomplete, although we may believe that a substantial number of the principal operations was recorded. Each of the units in Table *C*, then, refers to an important building operation at one of the Mendicant foundations, and it is sustained in most instances by textual evidence (summarized in the Appendix). In a very few cases, the style of part of a building now in existence can be securely dated, even in the absence of texts. Where this is possible, the fact is entered as a separate campaign in the appropriate place (e.g., Atotonilco el Grande, convento, 1540–50), but only if the evidence is strong. On the whole, there is no reason to believe that the summation of these single campaigns in the accompanying graphs (Fig. *16*) does not represent objective relationships, within an approximately correct order of magnitude.

The most striking general inference from these graphs concerns the relationship of building activity to other factors. Building activity, expressed in terms of the number of campaigns per decade, fluctuated rapidly. Where the activity of all Orders is concerned (Fig. *16g*), the volume of building rose to a peak in the decade 1570–80, thereafter subsiding to a minimum in the seventeenth century. The other factors showing the rate of geographical expansion and the growth of personnel (Fig. *11*), progressed steadily as the century advanced, attaining a plateau from which no striking decrease was evident. Therefore we may assume that building activity, initially conditional upon expansion and personnel, was affected by further processes as well; and that its fluctuating volume responded to influences which have not yet been clearly defined.

The remarkable decrease in volume of building activity after 1570–80 reflects, among other things, the pressure of secularization upon the Mendicants. This pressure has already been subjected to preliminary analysis: Mendicant privileges were seriously curtailed during the last quarter of the sixteenth century, and the friars' freedom of action was greatly restricted. But the processes of secularization cannot be made to account for the temporary diminutions of building activity occurring before 1570, as among the Franciscans between 1540 and 1560, or among the Dominicans between 1540 and 1550.

These temporary diminutions may be explained in part by invoking the concept of saturation. New expansion provoked new building, until saturation had been reached. A saturated area was one completely equipped with necessary buildings. In fact, the great decline in building activity after 1580 implies the relative saturation of

TABLE C

Franciscan Santo Evangelio	1520–30	1530–40	1540–50	1550–60	1560–70	1570–80	1580–90	1590–1600	1600–10	1610–20
Acatzingo					x	x	x			
Alfajayucan					x	x	x			
Amozoc							x			
Apam							x			
Atlancatepec						x				
Atlixco			x		x					
Calimaya				x						
Calpan			x							
Calpulalpan							x		x	
Chiauhtla (Texcoco)						x				
Cholula, S. Gabriel		x		x		x			x	
Churubusco		x								
Coatepec Chalco	x	x								
Coatlinchan						x				
Cuautinchan					x	x				
Cuautitlan		x								
Cuernavaca		x		x						
Ecatepec						x				
Huamantla							x			
Huaquechula		x		x						
Huejotzingo		x	x	x	x				x	
Hueytlalpan			x						x	
Huichapan							x			
Ixtacamaxtitlan					x					
Jalapa (Vera Cruz)		x				x				
Jilotepec								x		
Mexico	x		x	x			x	x		
Milpa Alta		x								
Nativitas		x								
Pachuca								x	x	x
Puebla		x			x	x				
Quecholac				x						
S. Felipe Cuixtlan			x							
Tacuba					x					
Tecali						x				
Tecamachalco			x	x						
Tecomitl						x				
Tehuacan						x	x			
Teotihuacan						x				
Teotitlan del Camino				x						
Tepeaca		x	x	x	x			x		
Tepeapulco		x		x						
Tepeji del Rio					x					
Tepetitlan						x				
Tepeyango					x					
Texcoco	x					x				
Tlahuac	x			x	x					
Tlahuelilpa					x					
Tlalmanalco		x		x			x			
Tlalnepantla							x			
Tlaquiltenango			x							
Tlatelolco		x							x	
Tlaxcala	x	x						x		
Tochimilco			x		x					
Totimehuacan							x			
Tula		x	x	x						
Tulancingo		x				x				
Tultitlan					x	x				
Veracruz										x
Xichu							x			
Xiutepec						x				
Xochimilco		x	x		x		x	x		
Zacatlan				x	x			x		
Zempoala						x				
Zinacantepec					x					

Recorded Building Activity

Franciscan Michoacan	1520–30	1530–40	1540–50	1550–60	1560–70	1570–80	1580–90	1590–1600	1600–10	1610–20
Acambaro		x								
Apaseo						x				
Celaya							x			
Chamacuero					x					
Charapan						x				
Chocandiro							x			
Erongaricuaro					x					
Morelia			x				x			
Patzcuaro				x		x				
Periban				x						
Purenchequaro							x			
Queretaro				x						
San Felipe					x					
S. Miguel Allende									x	
Tajimaroa					x				x	
Tancitaro						x				
Tarecuato			x							
Tarimbaro							x			
Toliman							x			
Tzintzuntzan		x						x		
Uruapan					x					
Zacapu			x				x			
Zitacuaro						x				

Recorded Building Activity

Franciscan Jalisco	1520–30	1530–40	1540–50	1550–60	1560–70	1570–80	1580–90	1590–1600	1600–10	1610–20
Acaponeta									x	
Agua del Venado									x	
Ahuacatlan				x						
Ajijic		x								
Amacueca			x			x				
Atoyac					x					
Autlan			x							
Chalchihuites									x	
Chapala			x							
Cocula						x				
Colima				x	x		x			
Durango									x	
Etzatlan		x								
Guadalajara		x	x						x	
Huaynamota						x				
Jala				x				x		
Jalisco			x							
Juchipila			x							
Nombre de Dios					x					
Poncitlan			x							
Sayula						x				
Sentispac						x				
Tamazula							x			
Techaluta						x				
Teul		x								
Tlajomulco						x	x			
Tuxpa							x			
Zacoalco					x			x		
Zapotitlan							x			
Zapotlan		x								

Augustinian	*Recorded Building Activity*									
	1520–30	1530–40	1540–50	1550–60	1560–70	1570–80	1580–90	1590–1600	1600–10	1610–20
Acatlan				x						
Acolman			x	x	x					
Actopan				x						
Ajuchitlan				x						
Alcozauca						x				
Atlatlauca						x				
Atlixco										x
Atlixtac							x			
Atotonilco el Grande			x				x			
Ayotzingo			x							
Chapantongo						x				
Chapulhuacan			x							
Charo				x					x	
Chiautla				x						
Chietla					x					x
Chilapa		x								
Copandaro					x					
Cuitzeo				x				x	x	x
Culhuacan						x				
Epazoyucan				x	x					
Huango				x						
Huatlatlauca					x					
Huejutla					x					
Ixmiquilpan				x						
Jacona					x				x	
Jonacatepec					x					
Lolotla		x								
Malinalco			x		x					
Metztitlan			x	x						
Mexico			x	x	x	x	x			
Molango			x							
Morelia				x					x	x
Oaxaca							x			
Ocotlan (New Galicia)						x				
Ocuilan			x		x					
Ocuituco		x								
Pahuatlan					x					
Panuco				x						
Parangaricutiro									x	
Patzcuaro						x				
Puebla						x	x			
Pungarabato				x						
San Felipe									x	
Singuilucan			x							
Tacambaro		x	x		x					
Tantoyuca					x					
Tezontepec				x						
Tingambato									x	
Tiripitio		x	x						x	
Tlanchinol					x					
Tlapa						x				
Tlayacapan				x	x					
Tlazazalco				x						
Tonala						x				
Totolapan		x	x							
Tzirosto						x		x		
Ucareo				x					x	
Undameo								x		
Xochicoatlan						x				
Yecapixtla			x							
Yuriria				x	x					
Zacatecas						x				x
Zacualpa Mines								x		
Zacualpan Amilpas				x						
Zacualtipan						x				

Dominican	*Recorded Building Activity*									
	1520–30	1530–40	1540–50	1550–60	1560–70	1570–80	1580–90	1590–1600	1600–10	1610–20
Achiutla					x	x				
Almoloyas							x			
Amecameca		x	x	x						
Atzcapotzalco					x	x				
Chila					x					
Chimalhuacan Chalco		x		x						
Coatepec Chalco (see OFM list)										
Coixtlahuaca						x				
Coyoacan		x			x		x			
Cuilapan				x	x	x				
Etla						x		x		
Hueyapan						x				
Huitzo							x			
Mexico	x	x		x	x	x				
Miahuatlan					x					
Nejapa					x					
Oaxaca		x				x		x	x	x
Oaxtepec					x	x				
Ocotlan					x					
Puebla					x			x		
San Angel									x	
Tacubaya					x			x		
Tehuantepec				x						
Tenango Chalco						x				
Tepetlaoztoc		x		x						
Teposcolula			x			x				
Tepoztlan						x	x			
Tetela del Volcan						x				
Tilantongo						x				
Tlacochahuaya							x			
Tlahuac (see OFM list)										
Tlaquiltenango (see OFM list)										
Tlaxiaco				x						
Tonala				x						
Villa Alta				x						
Xaltepec				x						
Yanhuitlan				x	x	x				
Yautepec					x					

New Spain with monastic buildings. In earlier periods expansion was not continuous; it alternated with campaigns of construction tending towards saturation. Expansion entailed the diffusion of the energies of the friars; construction involved their concentration. The two processes could occasionally be conducted simultaneously, but Mendicant policy in all Orders tended to devote the best effort in a given decade either to territorial expansion or to construction.

For both these influences, the pressure of secularization and the approach to saturation, we have no quantitative measures. The documents fail to tell us how many campaigns of building were broken off because of anti-Mendicant opposition, and they also fail to give the abundance of dates needed for determining saturation.

One quantitative approach to the problem of fluctuating building volume remains. If building activity is conditional upon one factor more than any other, that factor is the supply of labor. From the record of population movements during the sixteenth century, a partial correlation between building and labor supply can now be attempted. Nearly all significant changes in the volume of building activity occur in the vicinity of the great epidemics, *ca.* 1545 and *ca.* 1576. In the Franciscan province of the Santo Evangelio (Fig. *16a*), the decade of the 1540's shows a striking decrease after unparalleled activity. At the frontier, on the other hand, in Jalisco (Fig. *16c*), activity decreased in the 1550's. Total Franciscan building (Fig. *16d*) fell off in the 1540's (the quantities are governed by the dominant metropolitan province). The Augustinians attained the peak of their activity in the decade following the great plague of 1545 (Fig. *16e*); the Dominicans accelerated their program steadily in the years between epidemics, from 1540 to 1580 (Fig. *16f*).

Thus the decade of the great epidemic of 1545 coincides in all instances with critical moments in the volume of building. For the Franciscans, a slump or trough is evident; for the Augustinians, the epidemic preceded a decade of extravagant building; and for the Dominicans, the decade was one of minimal activity followed by great undertakings. In all cases, the decade of the epidemic was followed by increased production, reaching maximum at different periods in each Order. In general, the Franciscan production followed closely the fluctuations of population. The Augustinian rhythm of production was far more rapid than the Franciscan, and the friars would seem to have disregarded the epidemic elimination of their labor supply. The Dominicans, finally, like the Franciscans, were governed by the movements of population, reducing their efforts in times of epidemic disease. The summation of these various ordinal rhythms (Fig. *16g*) reveals interesting properties: if saturation was reached in the decade of the 1570's, the approach to that state was made in a series of steps, with alternating phases of increase and stability.

One more remark should be made about depopulation. It will readily be seen that depopulation has among its consequences an advanced rate of saturation. If a fixed number of monuments serves dwindling populations, a state of monumental surplus may even be attained. In Mexico, reduced production by all Mendicant agencies after 1580 was surely stimulated by the fact of dwindling population. This connection between production and population may throw some light upon the peculiar Augustinian increase of volume before 1550 (Fig. *16e*): a great campaign was presumably planned to accommodate immense populations of which but a part remained by 1580.

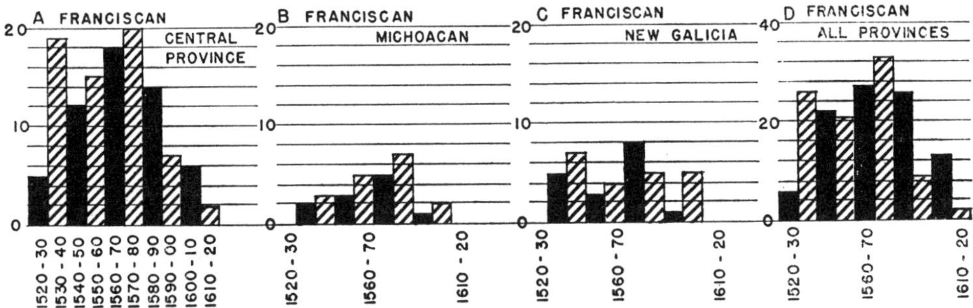

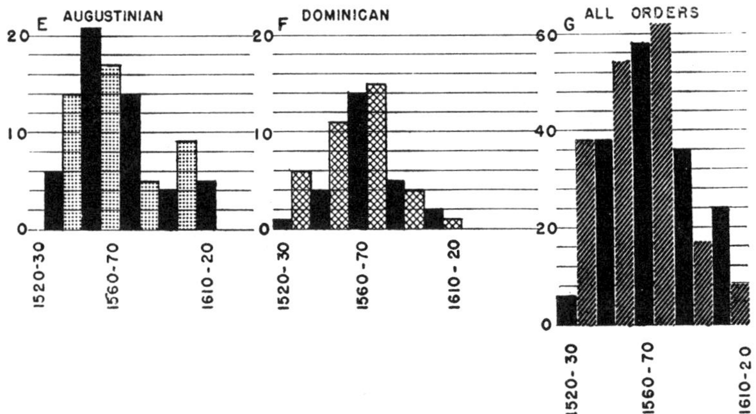

16. Amount of construction by Orders. A. Franciscan (Santo Evangelio) B. Franciscan (SS. Pedro y Pablo) C. Franciscan (New Galicia) D. Franciscan (all provinces) E. Augustinian F. Dominican G. Summary (all Orders and provinces)

That the friars were intimately aware of the problems invoked by epidemic losses is recorded in their own statements. Thus fray Alonso de la Vera Cruz: the purpose of Augustinian church-building was "in order that the Indians might forget their past labors, and their gentile tradition, in the splendor of building, the richness of churches, the solemnity of festivals, and in the divine cult."[93]

On the other hand, the great epidemics had the immediate consequence of bringing many building operations to a halt. Following the epidemic of 1576, for instance, all operations in Texcoco province were arrested by governmental decree in 1580–81.[94] And as we have already seen, the epidemics gave rise to social legislation favoring the Indians. A report from the cabildo of Mexico City to the Viceroy in 1581 is of particular interest in this context. The cabildo recommended that because of their high rate of mortality, the Indians needed to be carefully managed, assisted, and comforted.[95]

Every available line of evidence returns us to the correlation between decline and the building activity of the religious orders. This activity does not mean simply the building of churches; it signifies the layout and construction of entire settlements according to rudimentary concepts of regional planning. The greatest number of urban projects was in progress at the time of the most severe losses of population. Was such activity a cause, or an effect of decline in number? The correct answer depends upon how we assess the intentions of the building friars. It is certain that the friars regarded a well regulated community life as essential to the health of the inhabitants. Such a community life could develop only in well planned, well built towns.

The urbanizing work of the Mendicants was both cause and effect, disease and cure, reason and consequence, at least in part, for the high mortality suffered by the Indians. The heavy burden of labor, and the unhygienic conditions of work in new and improperly equipped settlements gave epidemic disease a rich harvest. And yet the same work, continued through and beyond the epoch of contagion, helped to protect and shelter the town-dwellers from new incursions.

As with other significant fragments of colonial life, the construction of any one of the buildings studied in this book is a process enmeshed in most intricate relationships. It has been demonstrated that no building could be achieved in Mexico without prior urbanization of the participants. To urbanize the Indian populations was to dislocate and destroy the patterns of indigenous culture. Such cultural extirpation, in turn, brought about the biological decrease of the Indian race. Hence the architecture that is the subject of this study was built at the expense of one of the great historical

93. Grijalva, *Crónica de la orden de N. P. S. Augustín*, p. 221, "para que los Indios, con la gloria delos edificios, con las riquezas de los templos, con la solemnidad de las fiestas, y cō el culto diuino, se oluidassen del trabajo passado, y de la flor de su gentilidad."

94. Mexico (City) Cabildo, *Actas de cabildo de la ciudad de México*, VIII (1893), 475: ". . . que las dichas obras y edificios cesen por algun tiempo hasta que se vea el subceso de la enfermedad y los indios se puedan reformar."

95. *AC*, VIII, 488: ". . . la general mortandad de los yndios . . . no a sido la menor parte para la caida o rruina desta tierra por donde parece . . . que pide gran atencion e advertencia que los yndios que quedan sean muy mirados e rregalados e rrelevados."

configurations of human society. Each building, and each colonial artifact was nourished by the destruction of a culture, and the decline of a race.

The artistic activity of the sixteenth century in New Spain therefore enters a special category. A distinction may be drawn between works of art which affirm an unbroken cultural tradition upon its own soil, and those works of art that stem from the destruction of a culture. The recipient of the new art, in the latter instance, receives it under coercion, and thereby forfeits the social bond with his own past.

II

URBANISM

Postquam Religiosi non sine magno labore per mōtes & deserta dissipatos Indos congregauerunt & ad vitae societatem conuocauerunt mores & instituta vitae rerum familiarum ac domesticarum rationem illis sollicite tradiderunt. Primum autem, locorum futuris aedificiis viis & itineribus metatio condecēs facta est: necnon agrorum distributio ex praescriptio Regiae maiestatis & senatus facta est.

D. Valadés, *Rhetorica christiana* (Perugia, 1579), pp. 109–110.

THE foundation of innumerable towns was the exceptional privilege and duty of the early colonists in Mexico. The traits of this program of urban foundation have no exact counterparts elsewhere in the history of Spanish colonization. Beginning with the first advance into the country, all authorities engaged in a steady, unsystematic, and prolific campaign of urban creation. The paths of the conquistadores, of the missionaries, the bishops and priests and civilian settlers were lined with hundreds of settlements founded before 1580; within the generation following the Conquest, the Spaniards had caused to be built in New Spain all the essential physical elements needed to house colonial society. These included an impregnable metropolitan center; a wide-meshed net of provincial cities for the residence of white colonists; a diversified industrial equipment of mining and manufacturing towns; new urban housing for millions of Indian settlers; and provisional accommodations for transient and nomadic tribes at the periphery of the colony. The towns varied from a few families to the city of sixty thousand inhabitants. Some were intended to fulfil strategic needs; others were trade-route settlements; and still others satisfied the need for segregating Indians from white settlers.

The colonization of Peru followed another course altogether. In Peru, an entire generation elapsed before the campaign of systematic urbanization began under Viceroy Toledo. The Christianization of the Quechua Indians was not achieved until the mid-seventeenth century. In Peru, the initial colonization lacked a dominant urban policy. But in Mexico, urbanization was concomitant with initial colonization. The reasons for this capital difference are extremely elusive. The fact of ten or twelve years' difference between the two Conquests implies profound differences in the philosophic orientation of the two campaigns of colonization. Mexico was initially colonized during a decade of humanist ascendancy in Spain; Peru was conquered in a decade of anti-humanist reaction. The Crown, in Cortés' time, was concerned for the spiritual welfare of new subjects: in Pizarro's day, the Crown relaxed its controls over new colonizations. Peru was less accessible; its geography was more difficult; its peoples showed more resistance.[1]

Whatever the reasons may be for this cardinal difference between the colonizations of Mexico and Peru, it is obvious that *immediate* post-Conquest urbanization was not an integral part of Spanish Crown policy in colonial matters. Intensive urbanization was first achieved, not by the State, but by the agencies of the church as a corollary of conversion. Hence, those colonial expansions in which the Church took little part were colonizations initially lacking any remarkable campaign of urbanization. The Mexican towns of the sixteenth century are a phenomenon unparalleled elsewhere in the history of colonial Latin America. Their study as a problem in architectural production deserves to be conducted with care.

Early in 1522, Cortés took the decision to rebuild Tenochtitlan as the metropolitan center of the colony. The issue was whether or not to place the capital city upon an island, and the decision followed upon much debate and difference of opinion. The arguments against settling upon the island were numerous and convincing. It was low-lying, marshy, and constantly subjected to disastrous floods. It had the reputation of being unhealthful, a reputation hardly improved by the devastation of the Conquest, when the besiegers destroyed the city by filling its canals with the debris of buildings, to allow the maneuvers of cavalry. It was incapable of sustaining any agrarian or stock-raising activity, in the absence of pastures, fields, and springs. The problem of water-supply needed solution by expensive artificial means. It communicated with the mainland over causeways, and the colonists felt that these causeways, with their easily invested bridges, would be dominated by the Indians of the mainland rather than by the island Europeans. In short, some thought the site was a trap, incapable of resisting siege, and peculiarly vulnerable in its provisioning and water-supply.

These fears concerning the island kept recurring during the sixteenth century; they worried the municipal governors until long after the consolidation of the colony. Cortés himself at first did not wish to settle there.[2] In 1521 he said the city must be de-

1. Kubler, "The Quechua in the Colonial World," *Handbook of South American Indians,* II, 331–410. The characters of the two leaders differed radically. Cortés was the master of indirection and subtle persuasion. He was strategically competent to suppress factionalism among his men. His actions were governed by the wish to secure unity and coherence of colonial government. Pizarro, on the other hand, was unable to control factionalism, perhaps because of the fabulous immediate rewards in precious metal, peculiar to Peru but lacking in Mexico. Also his illiteracy, and consequent dependence upon unscrupulous and powerful personalities, prevented him from achieving a purposeful and unified colonial policy.

2. *Archivo mexicano. Documentos para la historia de México* (Mexico, 1852–53), I, 97, 235; II, 100–101;

populated and transferred, and that any Indians seeking to resettle there were to be hanged. Cortés persisted in this intention until November of 1521, so that between November, 1521, and January, 1522, he changed his mind and gave orders for the rebuilding of Tenochtitlan. In Cortés' words, "as the city was so renowned and was so important, it seemed well to us to rebuild it." What motives inspired this abrupt change of intention?

Three interlocking sets of considerations were involved. They concerned the economic capacities of the site, its strategic properties, and its traditional or historic prestige ("renown and importance"). Everyone, including Cortés, agreed about the economic defects of Tenochtitlan. From the urbanist's point of view, no site could be more disadvantageous: marshy, unhealthful, and separated from its subsistence activities by a costly water-gap in the continuity of transportation. On the other hand, the alleged strategic defects of the site were interpreted in terms of party and faction. Although Cortés' companions wished to settle in Coyoacan, Tacuba, or Texcoco, i.e., on the mainland, Cortés believed that it was as strong a site for Europeans as for Indians. If Aztec Tenochtitlan could resist European arms and powerful Indian allies during a siege of four months, Europeans upon the same site would be impregnable. A further consideration played in Cortés' calculations. He was accused in 1529 of settling upon Tenochtitlan in the desire to make himself strong;[3] there can be no doubt that the selection of Tenochtitlan afforded a situation where Cortés could secure himself not only against future Indian attack, but also against the factional disturbances among his own European followers. In other words, Cortés probably envisaged a situation in which great weaknesses could be the result of too rapid a dispersal of the conquerors. Upon a mainland site, they would have been less constrained by their common fear of Indian attack than on the island capital. Herded together under conditions they regarded as dangerous, these unruly men were unassailable; but dispersed, they could become the victims of their scattered numbers and their disagreements.

Thus Tenochtitlan had positive strategic values, which were reinforced by the appeal to tradition and prestige. The triumph of Christians over Saracens in Spain had long been manifested in the European occupancy of Moorish towns: Christianity has perhaps always sought to identify itself with the ruins of preceding civilizations in the relationship of new spirit occupying old forms. In Tenochtitlan, the motives for reoccupation are perhaps identical with those of the resettlement of Granada or Cordova in the *Reconquista* of Spain. Furthermore, not to have reoccupied Tenochtit-

J. M. Marroqui, *La Ciudad de México* (Mexico, 1900–1903), I, 21–23; F. Cortés, *Letters of Cortés* (New York, London, 1908), II, 135–136, F. A. MacNutt, ed. and tr.; H. R. Wagner, *The Rise of Fernando Cortés* (Los Angeles, 1944), p. 395 (Documents and Narratives Concerning the Discovery and Conquest of Latin America, new ser., III).

3. *Archivo mexicano. Documentos*, I, 60–62.

lan would have been to leave its ruins as a monument to Aztec grandeur, and as a source of Indian nostalgia for a lost Golden Age. By occupying Tenochtitlan, the Europeans not only destroyed its pre-Conquest appearance, but also they identified themselves with its tradition as a political and governmental center. It is interesting to note, in this connection, how slowly the name Tenochtitlan disappeared from use. It was not until the mid-century that it atrophied in official documents.[4]

Early in 1522, then, the rebuilding of the island city was begun. By May 15, work was sufficiently advanced for Cortés to refer to the city as "already very beautiful," but there is no evidence that he took up residence with his followers until the summer of 1523.[5] The gigantic scale of the undertaking struck many observers. Immense numbers of Indian artisans, under the direction of Ixtlilxochitl of Texcoco, and the *cihuacoatl* (war-priest) of Tenochtitlan, whose name is given as Tlacotzin, were drafted for the work.[6] If Ixtlilxochitl is to be believed, nearly the whole laboring population of the Valley of Mexico was brought to work. The seventh of the ten "plagues" of Mexico listed by Motolinia is worth quoting: "In the building of the great city of Mexico, more people worked during the first years than upon the Temple of Jerusalem . . . the crowds of laborers were so thick that one could hardly move in the wide streets and causeways. Many died from being crushed by beams, or falling from high places, or in tearing down old buildings for new ones. . . . The laborers carry everything on their backs; they drag great stones and beams with ropes; and in the absence of skill but abundance of hands, four hundred men are used to move the stone or beam for which only one hundred are necessary. It is their custom, when moving materials, that the crowds sing and shout, and these voices continued by night and day, with the great fervor of building the city in the early years."[7]

There can be no doubt that the island community housed between fifty and a hundred thousand people in the period 1522–50. Therefore, it was the largest city in the Spanish world, and it outranked many European capitals in size. In 1516, for

4. Kubler, "The Name 'Tenochtitlán,' " *Tlalocan,* I (1944), 376–377.

5. Cortés, *Letters,* II, 135–136; Wagner, *Rise of . . . Cortés,* p. 396.

6. Cortés, *Letters,* II, 200–202; M. Orozco y Berra, *Historia antigua y de la conquista de México* (Mexico, 1880), IV, 662; F. de A. Ixtlilxochitl, *Obras históricas* (Mexico, 1891–92), II, 55. A. Chavero, ed. In pre-Conquest society, the *cihuacoatl* was analogous to a viceroy, and was appointed by the Aztec ruler to discharge administrative and judicial functions, as well as to regulate the cult of the goddess Cihuacoatl. See M. M. Moreno, *La organización política y social de los Aztecas* (Mexico, 1931), pp. 66–70.

7. Motolinia, *Memoriales,* p. 24: "La séptima plaga fué la edificacion de la gran ciudad de México, en la cual los primeros años andaba más gente que en la edificacion del templo de Jerusalem . . . apenas podia hombre romper por algunas calles y calzadas, aunque son bien anchas; y en las obras á unos tomaban las vigas, y otros caian de alto, sobre otros caian los edificios que deshacian en una parte para hacer en otras . . . Todos los materiales traen á cuestas: las vigas y piedras grandes traen arrastrando con sogas; y como les faltaba el ingenio é abundaba la gente, la piedra ó viga que habian menester cient hombres, traianla cuatrocientos, y es su costumbre que acarreando los materiales, como van muchos, van cantando y dando voces; y estas voces apenas cesaban de noche ni de dia, por el grande hervor con que edificaban la ciudad los primeros años."

instance, Toledo contained but eighteen thousand settlers, and Seville fifteen thousand.[8] Ixtlilxochitl says of Tenochtitlan that one hundred forty thousand dwellings were built in the 1520's; this figure, put in writing about 1610, is probably too great. In 1555, however, Robert Tomson reported three hundred thousand Indians living among fifteen hundred families of Europeans. The significant fact is that no sixteenth-century source indicates a metropolitan population less than one hundred thousand.[9] The size of parts of the city is given by the census of 1569, reported in 1571. At this moment, Mexico City consisted of four central parishes, with two Indian parishes at the western and northern periphery of the island (Fig. 17). The Cathedral parish housed the government and the wealthier colonists; the parish of S. Catarina contained some Spanish laborers, merchants, and artisans. Subordinate to it were two Indian wards (*barrios*) housing several thousand Indian tributaries. The parish of Veracruz, founded in 1568, sheltered poor Europeans and mixed breeds, as well as about six thousand Indian tributaries. The parish of San Pablo, finally, was a middle-class neighborhood of merchants and artisans. The two peripheral parishes, San Jose and Santiago, were entirely Indian. By official census, *ca.* 1570, the European population cannot have been much less than seventeen hundred whites or white-associated householders, and the Indian population cannot have been under eighty or ninety thousand persons.[10]

That this great population was unstable should be obvious. In the decade of the 1530's, the cabildo observed that the city was shifting to the west side of the island, leaving the eastern shores vacant, and the effort was thereupon made to attract settlers by generous grants in that district. At the same time, the authorities were disturbed by the exodus to Peru. Emigration began as early as 1532, and in 1534, it was noted that ten to thirty Spaniards were leaving New Spain daily. Hence there was movement to and from New Spain; the metropolitan population was constantly changing; and like any metropolis, it was from the beginning a clearing-house for many kinds of enterprise.[11]

8. F. Colón, *Descripción y cosmografía de España* (Madrid, 1908–18), I, 136, 294.

9. Ixtlilxochitl, *Obras históricas,* II, 55; R. Tomson, *An Englishman and the Mexican Inquisition, 1556–60* (Mexico, 1927). G. R. G. Conway, ed. Hakluyt's *Voyages* (ed. 1810), III, 549. Henry Hawks in 1572 asserted there were 50,000 households (i.e., families). López de Velasco, *Geografía* (Madrid, 1894), p. 189, estimated in 1574 "3,000 vecinos espanoles entre encomenderos, mercaderes, mineros y oficiales mecánicos," living among more than 30,000 households of Indians. Taking each *vecino* as five persons, this gives 165,000 people at least. The smallest sixteenth-century estimate is given by F. Hernández *ca.* 1570, as 20,000 Indian families, or 100,000 Indians. *De antiquitatibus Novae Hispaniae* . . . facs. ed. (Mexico, 1926), p. 4.

10. Cf. A. Vázquez de Espinosa, "Compendium . . . of the West Indies," *Smithsonian Miscellaneous Collections,* CII (1942), 156. In 1628 the city contained "over 15,000 Spanish residents (i.e., 3,000 families) and over 80,000 Indians," including Tlatelolco and the *chinampa* districts. Later growth of the city is discussed by N. S. Hayner, "Mexico City: Its Growth and Configuration," *American Journal of Sociology,* L (1945), 295–304.

11. *AC,* III, 52–53, September 1533. *AC,* II, 179; III, 89. ". . . se despueble la tierra por las nuevas del peru. . . ."

17. Mexico City, plan of the *traza* and parishes, *ca.* 1570

18. Puebla, aerial view

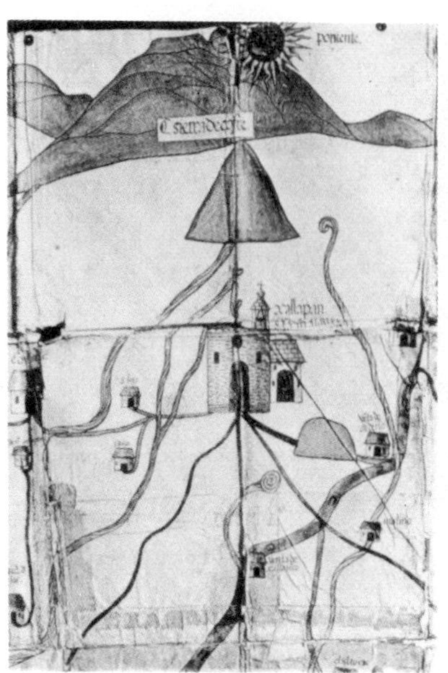

19. Jalapa (Veracruz), plan in 1580. Detail

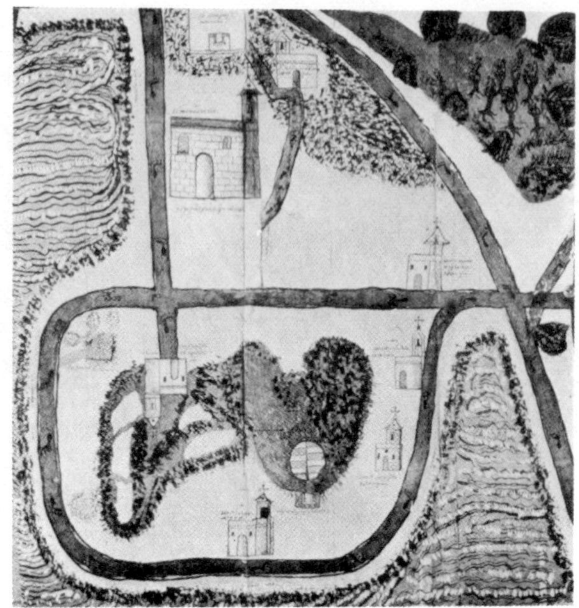

20. Chimalhuacan Atenco (Valley of Mexico), plan in 1579

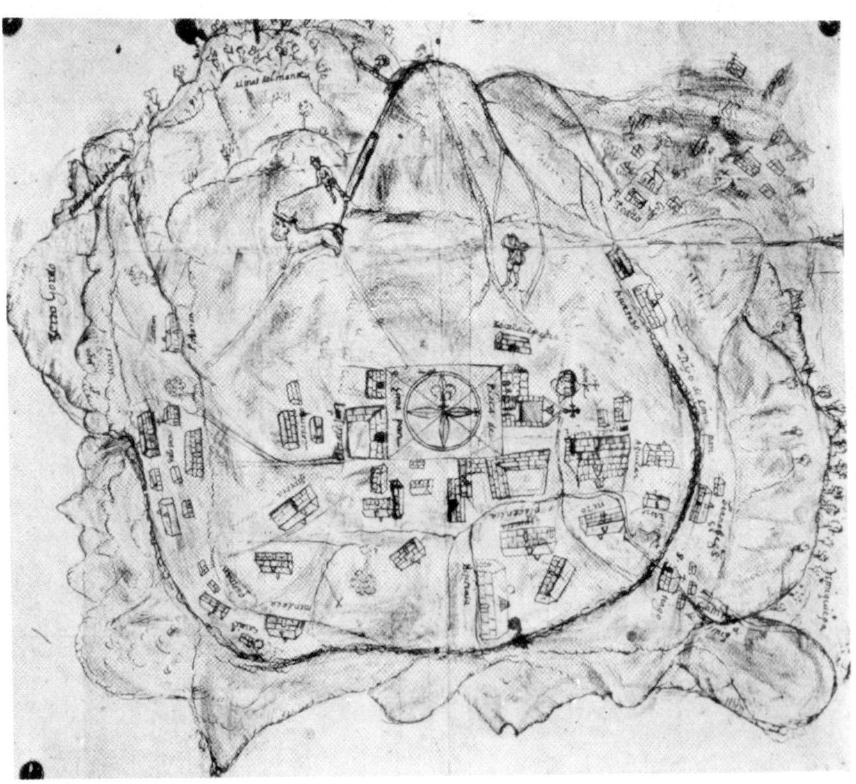

21. Zimapan, plan in 1579

When and by whose hand the central parts of Mexico City took their present striking form remains unclear. According to the testimony of early settlers, the famous *traza,* or master plan, had not been established in 1523. At that time, however, cardinal thoroughfares had been laid out: the present Calle de Tacuba, the present Avenida Madero, the street to Ixtapalapa, and two roads leading from the eastern part of the town to the western marketplace,[12] one to the south, apparently crossing the Ixtapalapa causeway, and the other passing north and skirting the Dominican establishment.[13] It has been suggested, furthermore, that the traza was only a record of titles, rather than a manuscript plan regulating the future growth of the city.[14]

Nevertheless, in connection with the assignment of municipal lands in 1524, the *medidor,* or surveyor of the city, was called upon. It is difficult to conceive that this official could discuss land-titles without reference to some preëxisting graphic record, or without entering them upon such a record. Other notices pertaining to the traza leave little doubt concerning its reality as an actual graphic plan of the city. In 1530, upon the appointment of the *alarife,* the cabildo gave him the custody of the traza and of the measures used in the allocation of lots and gardens. These measures were standard rods, made of wood (see pp. 159–160), and we may believe that the traza was also a physical object, a drawing in which all land grants and streets were entered to scale.[15]

Hence it will be assumed that the traza was in effect a drawing, a master-plan; that it recorded the primitive form and regulated the future growth of the city; and that it was drawn up not earlier than 1523, and not later than 1524. Furthermore, we possess the name of one of its authors. Alonso García Bravo, who served Cortés as the builder of a provisional fortress at Veracruz, claimed credit for the metropolitan traza in 1561, and in the document setting forth this claim, García admitted that he was assisted by another Spaniard, who was a good surveyor (*muy buen jumétrico*).[16]

As we have seen, no traza existed in 1523, when the city had been reoccupied for over a year, so that two conclusions are forced upon our attention. The armature or network of the arterial thoroughfares of the city was already in existence, before the

12. This western marketplace was called the *tianguiz* de Juan Velásquez; named for an Indian headman, it was situated beyond the traza proper, upon the site of what was later to be the Convento de S. Isabel, bounded on the east by the site of the Hospital de Terceros, and on the west by the late sixteenth-century Alameda. L. González Obregón, *Época colonial. México viejo* (Paris, Mexico, 1900), p. 370.

13. "Documentos inéditos, relativos á Hernán Cortés y su familia," *Publ. AGN,* XXVII (Mexico, 1935), 308, 310. Luis de la Torre. Testimony confirmed by Sebastian de Grijalva, p. 310. As late as 1550, the course of such important streets as the modern Calle de la Moneda, along the north side of the National Palace, was still uncertain. (See p. 195, n. 19.)

14. M. Toussaint, *Planos de la ciudad de México: siglos XVI y XVII* (Mexico, 1938), p. 193.

15. *AC,* I (1524), 4. *AC,* I, 114, 117, 121. E.g., on January 4, 1527 (p. 114), the officers of the cabildo ". . . mandaron que se pregone en esta Cibdad que todos los que tienen solares en ella . . . muestren los titulos de ellos para que se asyenten en la traza. . . ." Later on the cabildo ordered "maese martin" to assume office, "e luego los dichos diputados le dieron y entregaron la traza de la cibdad y medidas de solares y huertas." *AC,* II (March 31, 1530), 45. See also pp. 49, 53.

16. Icaza, *Conquistadores y pobladores,* I, 55; Toussaint, *Planos,* pp. 21–22; Wagner, *Rise of . . Cortés,* p. 396.

preparation of the traza; and Alonso García Bravo cannot have established his master-plan before 1524 or the end of 1523. In other words, the *trazador* modified or regulated a preëstablished pattern, but he did not create it. This preëstablished pattern, following the reoccupation and before the creation of the traza, probably followed the main arteries and house-blocks of the Aztec city.[17]

The Spanish traza recorded the nucleus of European settlement upon the island. It defined a square area at the center of the island within which rigorous municipal control prevailed. This central area differed from the remainder of the island in that the portions lying outside it were subject to no urban plan. The Indian parishes were casual, dense agglomerations of huts and shelters; they served as a reservoir of labor for the proud, orderly Spanish city. In 1541, the Indian sections of the city were built in such disorderly fashion that it was difficult to circulate in them, whether by foot or on horseback.[18] The only solution, at first, was for Europeans to buy up many small tracts from the Indians, and thus to expand their metropolitan holdings. Later on, in 1571, a separate traza was prepared for the Indian section at the order of the Viceroy.[19] It pertained only to the resettlement of the Indian artisans living in the area between the causeways of San Francisco and Tacuba; and the project was inspired by a strategic desire to clear the western approaches to the city. The island therefore contained several subordinate municipalities. One was the European town; another was Santiago Tlatelolco, with its own plaza, *tecpan,* and Indian government; and others were the Indian barrios or wards.

It was in reference to the Spanish nucleus, controlled by the traza of Alonso García Bravo, that Cortés wrote to Charles V in 1524 that within five years it would be the finest city in the world.[20] The words of the Anonymous Conqueror, written in 1530, appear to bear out the prediction. The unknown soldier rhapsodized over the handsome squares and the fine, solid buildings of which not even Spanish cities could boast.[21] Such buildings, however, did not extend beyond a restricted central area, defined by the following streets: on the east, the Calle de la Santísima;[22] on the south,

17. For contrary opinion, see D. Stanislawski, "The Origin and Spread of the Grid-Pattern Town," *Geographical Review,* XXXVI (1946), 105–120.

18. Cervantes de Salazar, *México en 1554,* pp. 137, 279. From the height of Chapultepec, in 1554, Alfaro beheld the Spanish town, surrounded on all sides by Indian huts, arranged without order ("colocadas sin órden"), and interrupted by fields, pastures, and orchards. *AC,* IV, 249 (1541): "Los yndios tienen sus casas cercadas y puestas de arte que la cibdad no se puede andar libremente a pie ni a caballo por donde ellos biben." Cf. *AC,* V, 354 (1543).

19. *AC,* VII, 517 (1571). Mendieta, *Historia eclesiástica indiana,* pp. 182, 421. This author mentions Tlatelolco as a "barrio por sí de la ciudad de México." It received no orderly plan until the rule of Viceroy Revillagigedo. L. Alamán, *Disertaciones sobre la historia de la república megicana* (Mexico, 1844–49), II, 198–200.

20. Cortés, *Letters,* II, 202–203.

21. M. H. Saville, ed. and tr., *Narrative of Some Things of New Spain . . . by the Anonymous Conqueror, a Companion of Hernán Cortés* (New York, 1917), p. 74 (Documents and Narratives Concerning the Discovery and Conquest of Latin America, I).

22. The later church under the advocacy of the Santísima Trinidad originally lay beyond the eastern limit of the traza (*AC,* I, 226, ed. n. 66).

the Calle de San Gerónimo or San Miguel; on the north, the Dominican establishment; and on the west, the Calle S. Isabel.[23] Within this great square, the traza included about fourteen streets, intersecting one another at right angles to form a gridiron plan with rectangular blocks (Fig. 17). Four great main avenues converged upon the central plaza, where the Cathedral and the government buildings were situated. The entire plan was therefore extremely regular: a writer in the early seventeenth century compared it to a checkerboard:

> De sus soberbias calles la realeza
> A las del ajedrez bien comparadas,
> Cuadra á cuadra, y aun caudra pieza á pieza.[24]

Between 1550 and 1575 various English visitors commented with amazement upon the regularity of the city. Robert Tomson, writing in 1555, remarked: "The said Citie of Mexico hath the streetes made very broad, and right, that a man being in the high place, at the one ende of the street, may see at the least a good mile forward. . . ." John Chilton, whose impressions were gained in 1568–70, wrote that the city had "good and costly houses . . . builded all of lime and stone, and seuen steets in length, and seuen in breadth, with riuers running thorow euery second street, by which they bring their prouision in canoas." But the most detailed description of the appearance of the early city came from the pen of Cervantes de Salazar, the professor of rhetoric in the newly founded University of Mexico. Writing in 1554, he caused a European visitor to exclaim upon the regularity and beauty of the central plaza, and upon the fact that the Calle de Tacuba was so wide and straight, with the houses accurately and uniformly lined, and all of uniform height, in order that they might not overshadow one another.[25]

Great regularity of appearance, then, was the quality that elicited comment. It was achieved less by conscious design than by the fact that all construction was rapid, under the control of strict municipal legislation and enforcement. The porticoes (*portales,* Figs. 82, 83) surrounding the main plaza were city property, but they were built by private citizens, according to strictly regulated dimensions. Portales that did not conform were torn down. Uniformity was the result.[26]

23. Alamán, *Disertaciones,* II, 198–200. *Diccionario universal de historia y de geografía* (Mexico, 1853–55), V, 608–609, places the northern boundary in the center of the territory occupied by the Dominican establishment, on the strength of remarks in *AC,* I (Aug. 12, 1527), 139.

24. B. de Valbuena, *Grandeza mexicana* (Mexico, 1604), chap. ii; cf. Alamán, *Disertaciones,* II, 273.

25. Hakluyt, *Voyages,* III, 539 (Robert Tomson), 542 (John Chilton). Cervantes de Salazar, *México en 1554,* pp. 89, 95. In the sixteenth century, the main plaza was far smaller than the present Zócalo (Figs. 63, 64). It was about two-thirds filled with temporary buildings, such as the Parián market, and the residences in what today is the northeast corner of the Zócalo. Even then, however, it was regular in plan. (See Alamán, *Disertaciones,* II, 232–260; Cervantes de Salazar, *op. cit.,* note by García Icazbalceta, p. 169.)

26. *AC,* I, 8: in 1524 each householder with property facing the plaza was allowed to build portales twenty-one feet deep. *AC,* V, 16: the portales were municipal property rather than property of the owner of the house

The straightness and uniformity of the street façades were likewise controlled by municipal legislation and enforcement. Any individual to whom the *cabildo* awarded land was engaged to respect the building lines on the streets; the façade of his house was to be built of masonry; and he was to provide a stone curb on the street. No city lot might be used for any purpose other than residence, without the permission of the cabildo. These conditions, as we learn from the minutes of the municipal council, were explicitly stated as early as 1536.[27] But similar conditions had been enforced for several years. In 1531, for example, a member of the council declared his opinion that the looks of the city would be forfeited unless the streets were made to continue straight,[28] and in 1532, the council ordered that façades not conforming to the street line must be torn down. Interestingly enough, the first recorded offender in this respect was Cortés himself, for whom houses were being built which encroached upon the public streets.[29]

This program of esthetic unification accompanied a thoroughgoing program of municipal legislation concerning hygiene and public utilities. The installation and maintenance of the water supply for man and beast was a municipal responsibility; stringent regulations surrounded the use of water, which often was piped into individual houses. The law forbade householders to dispose of garbage and sewage through the ducts supplying the houses.[30] The cleaning and repair of the streets under official supervision, on the other hand, was the owners' responsibility; gutters had to be kept up, and in certain districts, these gutters were vaulted over, with grilles at intervals.[31] The paving of the streets was also the citizens' responsibility, subject to certain municipal restrictions. Periodically, the cabildo ordered the paving of substantial districts.[32] The paving of all streets within the limits of the traza was finished about 1558; the main streets, such as the Calle de Tacuba, had been paved since 1547. These streets were fourteen *varas* wide;[33] in the sixteenth century, they alternated with canals, of which many survived from before the Conquest. The canals were most useful in supplying the city; the Indians from the mainland could bring their produce by boat directly to the marketplaces and houses. Their width was less than that of the streets; one of the largest (Figs. 63, 64) ran just south of the National Palace, fifteen

to which they were attached. *AC*, IV, 193: portales torn down in 1539–40.

27. *AC*, IV, 44 ff., 126, 345.

28. *AC*, II, 102 (May 5, 1531). Diego Hernández de Proaño asserted "que le paresce que para conserbar la buena traza de la cibdad ques que las calles bayan derechas. . . ."

29. *AC*, II, 191 (August, 1532). Gil González de Benavides and Juan Cano were the directly responsible parties.

30. *AC*, IV, 67 (January, 1537), 79.

31. *AC*, IV, 77, 93 (March, 1537), 124. The supervisors were the *almotacenes*, appointed annually by the cabildo.

32. *AC*, V, 176, 235; *AC*, III, 10 (1532); cf. Viceroy Mendoza, "Relación, apuntamientos y mandados que . . . di al señor D. Luis de Velasco" [1550], *CDIHE*, XXVI (1855), 296 f.

33. *Ca.* 11.75 m.: the Mexican vára is equal to .838 m. Francisco Hernández noted *ca.* 1570 that their length was fifteen hundred paces, and their width fifty paces. *De Antiquitatibus*, p. 4.

feet wide and about six feet deep, with the water-level three feet below the street.[34]

Municipal supervision extended to many other activities. Policing was provided by the city, and a curfew rang each night between nine and half-past, whereupon no one was to appear abroad with arms, and all miscreants were arrested. In addition, the cabildo regarded as its responsibility the maintenance of the slaughterhouse and meat-markets, the granary, the University buildings, all fountains, bridges, causeways, sewers, water-conduits, and public squares.[35]

Mexico City was unique among the great cities of the sixteenth-century world, in that it was an unfortified metropolis, occupying a plan that shows close affinities to the ideal town plan of Italian architectural theory (see pages 98–99). As we might expect, however, its occupants were deeply worried about its defensibility. At best the Spaniards were few; in 1574, in New Spain, about seven thousand European men faced three million five hundred thousand Indians, and under such conditions, the feeling of security never prevailed. In Mexico City itself, a preoccupation with defense remained strong throughout the century. No decade in the early history of the capital was without its alarms over various dangers, within and without the city. In 1524, for example, the encomenderos were forbidden to leave the city to go among their Indians, for fear of weakening the city's guard.[36] This was during the epoch of great construction activities; the city swarmed with Indian laborers, and no adequate citadel provided for the defense of the white colony. Cortés speaks of this situation in the Fourth Letter, on October 15, 1524; he states that the Europeans were unable to settle in great numbers upon the island until the completion of a suitable fortress.[37] This edifice, the *atarazanas,* or fortified docks (Fig. 89) was symbolically important to the security of the colonists (pp. 207–209).

During the decade of the 1520's this primary fear of Indian attack was reinforced and complicated by fears of another order among the colonists. The civil government, with its factions and inner disturbances, was torn by strife and competition. One consequence was the production of an astonishing number of fortified dwellings. Each citizen sought to build himself an impregnable fortress. The description of these curious dwellings is contained in the documents pertaining to the official investigation (*residencia*) of Cortés' administration of the affairs of the colony. The residencia was held in 1529, and at that time, in addition to the atarazanas, Cortés had built a government palace, crenelated and fortified at the corners with towers, and provided with two ranges of embrasures for artillery. Situated upon the site of the present

34. Vetancurt, *Chrónica, Tratado,* p. 1; A. de Alcedo, *Diccionario geográfico-histórico de las Indias occidentales ó América* (Madrid, 1786–89), III, 166; A. de Zorita, "Historia de la Nueva España," *Colección de libros y documentos referentes á la historia de América,* IX (1909), 178. Cf. Marroqui, *La Ciudad de México,* I, 141 ff.

35. *AC,* III, 78; IV, 70 (curfew).

36. *AC,* I, 12 (May 26, 1524).

37. Cortés, *Letters,* II, 202–203.

Palacio Nacional, this edifice was alleged by Cortés' detractors to have served his designs against the European colonists. Nearby, moreover, a powerful civilian, Pedro de Alvarado, had built an even larger fortified dwelling, to cover the approaches to Cortés' building, with thicker walls and loopholes for archers in addition to embrasures.

Many other persons were permitted, and it was even said that they were ordered by Cortés, to build houses with towers, supposedly for the defense of the land. At least nine of these are mentioned, and the imputation is always that Cortés encouraged these projects in defense of his own interests within the various factional disputes, to the detriment of Crown interests.[38]

In 1528, the perennial worry of the citizens over possible Indian attacks gave rise to a peculiar project. The plan was to line the western exits from the city with houses so densely built that they might form a *casa-muro,* or wall of houses. With this purpose in mind, the cabildo granted many lots along the *calzadas* (causeways) to Tacuba and Tlatelolco, overlooking the shapeless Indian settlements between the highways. A typical grant fell to Rodrigo de Baeza on February 28; he gained a lot on the road to Tlatelolco on condition that he build a *casa fuerte* of masonry which should serve to fortify the city.[39] The notion of fortifying the city with houses, however, quickly fell into discredit. Few grants appear after 1528, and in 1535, Viceroy Mendoza examined the traza, and ordered that nothing more be built along the calzada to Tacuba, for fear that the row of houses thus created and already in existence might serve the enemy as a fortress.[40]

Thoughts of fortifying the city, or at least of preparing it for defense against hypothetical Indian attacks, again preoccupied the cabildo in 1537. At the command of the Viceroy, it was resolved to remove all Indian dwellings from within gunshot of the city's edges. When the transfer of the Indians had been completed, their whole district was to be leveled and used as a neutral zone. To guard against isolation from the mainland, the cabildo further decided to provide stout bridges at the entrances to the city. The atarazanas were to be transferred to the western side of the island, in the vicinity of the end of the Calle de Tacuba, since no attack could be expected from the eastern approaches. Nothing was done until in 1541, the outbreak of the Mixton war in the western provinces again threw the colonists into panic. The cabildo requested the Viceroy to order immediate fortification of the city for protection of its women and children. The viceregal palace (then at the northeast corner of the *plaza mayor*) and Cortés' house were to be used as refuges. Nothing had been done about the Indian suburbs at the western fringe of the island, and it was still felt that they constituted a

38. *Archivo mexicano. Documentos,* I, 18, 47, 90, 92, 111, 120, 143, 227, 257, 411; II, 33, 97, 130, 173.

39. *AC,* I, 161, 175, 177, 180, 185.

40. *AC,* III, 132–133.

threat.[41] During the 1540's, agitation of this kind continued steadily in the cabildo, until in 1545, a reasonable plan was established. Since the great strategic weakness of the city was its island site, the decision was taken to build up permanent land between the Atzcapotzalco and Tacuba causeways, thus gaining a permanent exit on securely held ground.[42] In the 1550's the threatening attitude of the large Negro colony in the capital aroused fears; the cabildo was requested to build a fortress and repair the brigantines (the ships used by Cortés thirty years earlier).[43] On the whole, the fears of the colonists were exaggerated. The city never was attacked by Indians, and its greatest danger arose from the hostilities among the colonists themselves. In fact, the Indian parish at the western shore of the island was given a traza, or master-plan in 1571, with the approval of the cabildo, and under the direction of the Viceroy.[44] Nothing had been done about securing the permanent exit from the city, although it was still rumored in 1572 that the Indians knew a way to flood the city and bring about its downfall.[45]

Other plans for making the city strong were constantly under discussion. In 1554, the new cathedral was to be the center of a fortress-area in the main plaza. At the entrances to the plaza great towers would guard the approach to the heart of the city, and plans to this effect were sent to the Council of the Indies by Archbishop Montúfar.[46] In the 1560's another project of the same kind came forth. One of the main canals entering the plaza was to be extended all about the viceregal palace (then just purchased from Martin Cortés), in order to form a moat fifteen feet wide and nine feet deep, with drawbridges and cleared approaches. The estimates of the cost of such an undertaking, however, were formidable, and nothing came of the idea.[47] Such projects were probably conceived in view of the Chichimec hostilities along the "silver frontier" of Zacatecas. The mining rush began in 1546, and by 1551, Chichimec depredations were so serious that the viceregal government was obliged to provide a system of defensive towns and posts along the northern frontier.[48] It was not until the end of the century that the colonists could rest in peace from their fear of the northern nomads.

Hence, Mexico City possessed a superficial military aspect about 1554. Cervantes de Salazar, for instance, remarked with disapproval that the houses resembled for-

41. *AC*, IV, 98–99, 246–247.
42. *AC*, V, 88; *cf.* 294.
43. *AC*, VI, 275.
44. See n. 19.
45. Henry Hawks, Hakluyt, *Voyages*, III, 549.
46. *Epistolario*, VII, 307.
47. Zorita, *op. cit.*, IX, 178; *Epistolario*, IX, 218–219. Both Arciniega and Ginés de Tala were consulted; the estimate of cost ranged between 200,000 pesos and 300,000 ducados.
48. G. de Las Casas, "Noticia de los chichimecas y justicia de la guerra que se les ha hecho por los españoles," *Quellen zur Kulturgeschichte des präkolumbischen Amerika* (Stuttgart, 1936), pp. 127–181. H. Trimborn, ed. P. W. Powell, "Presidios and Towns on the Silver Frontier of New Spain, 1550–80," *Hispanic American Historical Review*, XXIV (1944), 179–200. Cf. *Relación . . . Ponce*, I, 222–223, on attacks at Xichu in 1586.

tresses, and that this mode of building was fitting only for the beginnings of the city, "cum cingi muris et turribus muniri civitas non posset." It was not until the last quarter of the century that the early edifices were rebuilt, and that this military appearance of the city was effaced. By 1579, a Mendicant visitor declared that the houses were not fortified. Then, as today, Mexico City was an open, unfortified town. It contained dwellings, public buildings, and an antiquated military dock. To visitors from Europe, the phenomenon of a great and unfortified city was a source of amazement. Friar Thomas Gage (1625) records his impression in admirable language, "all arms are forgotten, and the Spaniards live so secure from enemies that there is neither gate, wall, bulwark, platform, tower, armoury, ammunition, or ordnance to secure and defend the city from a domestic or foreign enemy. . . ." Thus Mexico City emerged as the first great modern city of America, a seat of government and industry, without fortifications, undefended, and open to commerce and travel.[49] Whether through indolence or lack of genuine interest, its inhabitants never achieved their grandiose plans for its defense; that they did not is to their credit. The early fortified residences had disappeared by 1580, and excepting for the atarazanas, nothing of military character ever again obscured the clear outlines of the ideal Renaissance city planned by Alonso García Bravo.

Many other early towns for European occupancy were founded by Fernando Cortés, and their locations were strategically determined. Old Veracruz, founded in 1519, had streets and squares, fortifications and public buildings, all laid out upon previously unbroken ground.[50] On the plateau, Segura de la Frontera was founded in 1520, and Cortés retired to it after the disastrous retreat from Tenochtitlan late in June of that year.[51] It was then a large Indian hill town, called Tepeaca, and Cortés gave it merely the legal status of a Spanish municipality. No durable buildings arose, but Cortés installed a town government patterned upon the Spanish model. In following years Segura rapidly declined, and it was nearly abandoned in 1527,[52] probably because its population had been sent to Antequera, the modern Oaxaca.[53] Cortés founded another strategic settlement on the Mije-Zapotec border in southern Mexico about 1526, to maintain peace among the warring tribes of the region. This town, the Villa Alta de San Ildefonso, he settled with Náhuatl-speaking Indians who were non-

49. Cervantes de Salazar, *México en 1554*, p. 88. Valadés, *Rhetórica christiana*, pp. 167–168. Gage, *The English-American*, pp. 81–82.

50. B. Diáz del Castillo, *The True History of the Conquest of Mexico* (New York, 1927), pp. 91–92, 99–100. M. Keatinge, tr. (Argonaut ser., III–IV); Orozco y Berra, *Historia antigua*, IV, 149–150. The present town was founded in 1599, by Viceroy Monterrey. Cf. W. Krickeberg, "Die Totonaken," *Baessler-Archiv*, VII (1918–22), 15.

51. Cortés, *Letters*, I, 308; G. R. G. Conway, ed., *La Noche triste, documentos* (Mexico, 1943), p. 87.

52. *Epistolario*, I, 121. Not long afterwards the town was moved to another site, which it occupies today.

53. J. Galindo y Villa, "Algo sobre los Zapotecas," *Anales del museo nacional de México*, época 2, II (1905), 232. Cortés, *Letters*, II, 163.

partisan, and with Spaniards paid from Crown funds to reside there.[54] The town of Nejapa was likewise established, about 1560, as a garrison between the hostile Mije and Chontal Indians.[55] Other instances in the north and west testify to the strategic concern of the colonists throughout the century.[56]

Trading towns were even more commonly founded. Uruapan, a Franciscan missionary foundation in the bishopric of Michoacan, lies at an intermediate level between the hot lowlands of the Rio Balsas drainage, and the highland plateaus of the Rio Lerma. Constant traffic flowed through the passes above which Uruapan is located, and the settlement has always had a vivid commercial life.[57] A like situation exists on the East Coast, where the function of Veracruz has never changed, although the city occupied several distinct sites. It was always a commercial seaport, populated by mercantile classes, and elaborately fortified.[58]

It is a fact of capital importance that throughout Hispanic America, no inland towns were effectively fortified. Peripheral walls appear only in the seaports, as at Cartagena, Havana, Santo Domingo, Acapulco, or Old Panama.[59] During the sixteenth century, nevertheless, it was often suggested that inland towns be fortified. The history of these suggestions for the capital has already been recapitulated. Motolinia insisted in 1540, and again in 1555, but without success, that Puebla be fortified.[60] Thus Friar Thomas Gage, who visited Mexico in 1625, could write of Oaxaca that "this city, as all the rest of America (except the sea towns), lieth open without walls, bulwarks, forts, towers, or any castle, ordnance, or ammunition to defend it." But he noted that at the Dominican establishment, then being built, the walls were thick enough for carts and teams to be driven with loads of building material upon their width.[61] Where inland towns were concerned, military architecture found expression only in religious construction, with churches capable of serving as forts. In the opinion of the Second Audiencia, writing to the King in the 1530's for more friars, the conventual establishments alone were thought a sufficient fortification for the colony.[62] Thus we find many monastic establishments located upon the main roads. The various highways from the capital to Veracruz were bordered by Franciscan houses:

54. Dávila Padilla, *Historia . . . Santiago de México*, p. 548.

55. Burgoa, *Geográfica descripción*, II, 234.

56. Powell, "Presidios," *Hispanic American Historical Review*, XXIV (1944), 179–200.

57. M. Sorre, "Mexique, Amérique centrale," *Géographie universelle*, XIV (Paris, 1928), 49–51. Justino Fernández, *Uruapán* (Mexico, 1936). Rea, *Crónica de la orden de N. serafico P. S. Francisco*, pp. 41–42. Fray Juan de San Miguel ". . . fundo el Pueblo . . . repartiendo la poblaçon en sus calles, plaças, y varrios, con la mejor disposicion que pudiera la Aristrocacia de Roma . . . todo el pueblo parece vn Pais Flamenco . . . se ha cõseruado el Pueblo en su primera fundación, que fue mas de mil fuegos."

58. López de Velasco, *Geografía*, pp. 212–213. *Relación . . . Ponce*, I, 189–190. See n. 50.

59. D. Angulo Iñíguez, *Bautista Antonelli; las fortificaciones americanas del siglo XVI* (Madrid, 1942).

60. Motolinia, *Historia de los indios de la Nueva España*, *CDHM*, I, 231–235.

61. Gage, *The English-American*, pp. 120, 121.

62. R. Aguayo Spencer, ed., *Don Vasco de Quiroga; documentos*, p. 25: ". . . los Conventos de Religiosos son, como lo ha descubierto la experiencia, las ciudadelas, las murallas, y los castillos para este Reino."

Atlancatepec; Calpan; Calpulalpan; Otumba; and so on.[63] Between Mexico and Oaxaca, the Dominicans founded houses one day's journey apart, such as Chimalhuacan Chalco, Amecameca, Puebla, and on down into Oaxaca at Yanhuitlan, Nochistlan, Etla, and Oaxaca.[64] Finally, on the road from Mexico to the northern mines, various Franciscan and Dominican establishments were situated: San Felipe in Michoacan, on the wagon road to the mines of Zacatecas, as well as Queretaro, S. Pedro Toliman, Apaseo, and Celaya.[65]

Other strategic objectives were sometimes manifest in the situation of the early monastic foundations. At Atlixco, the peculiar position of the Franciscan establishment may be explained by its relation to the springs that fed the city which was founded much later in 1574.[66] The important Franciscan house at Chalco Atenco, furthermore, served the large southeastern lake port, whence travelers took boats to reach the capital.[67]

Many new towns served several functions equally well. Valladolid (now Morelia) in Michoacan was founded in 1541 for trade, and to protect communications with the frontier upon the occasion of the Mixton war.[68] The layout of the city was entrusted, not to professionals, as in Mexico City or Puebla, but to distinguished citizens: Juan de Alvarado, Juan de Villaseñor, and Luis de León Romano. The site of an Indian settlement, named Guayangareo, was chosen for its beauty and amenity; and the original settlers numbered sixty white families, with nine religious to administer to their spiritual needs. The municipal lands were defined as extending one league in every direction from the church (i.e., a circle of land roughly six miles in diameter). The royal intention was that these lands should serve the future expansion of the city, and that they should contain commons and pastures. It was further ordered that at the center of the city a plaza be established. Labor was to be recruited from among the unconverted Indians roaming the region, after they had been reduced to urban order and brought to conversion. Morelia, or Valladolid, grew, however, very slowly. In 1586, the settlement housed only about one hundred European families, in adobe dwellings and a few masonry houses. Some Tarascan and Mexican Indians were also resident.[69]

A natural growth accompanying these foundations was the separation of Indian

63. Atlancatepec, Vetancurt, *Chrónica, Teatro,* Pt. IV, p. 86. Calpan, *Relación . . . Ponce,* I, 155; Calpulalpan, "Códice franciscano," *NCDHM,* II, 12; Otumba, on the *camino real de los carros, Relación . . . Ponce,* I, 112.

64. Dávila Padilla, *Historia . . . Santiago de México,* p. 365, designates them as "casas del camino (que las tenemos en proporció, de suerte que desde Mexico ay à cada jornada casa de Nuestra Orden)." See also Burgoa, *Geográfica descripción,* I, 383.

65. See *Relación . . . Ponce,* I, 535–536.

66. Vetancurt, *Chrónica, Teatro,* Pt. IV, p. 73.

67. "Códice franciscano," *NCDHM,* II, 11.

68. Beaumont, *Crónica de Michoacán,* III, 41. According to the terms of the deed of foundation, the purpose of the town was "para el seguro y resguardo de los caminos que cruzan de unas poblaciones a otras, e puedan pasar y caminar las gentes libremente por ellos, evitándoles los riesgos y peligros que, en parajes despoblados como ese, está cometiendo la gente bárbara que anda desparramada por las quebradas e montes de esa tierra. . . ."

69. *Relación . . . Ponce,* I, 531.

and European areas of settlement within the same urban agglomeration.[70] The process has already been noted in Mexico City, where the unplanned, impermanently housed Indian groups were assigned to the western and northern edges of the European colony. Whites were forbidden to live there. At Antequera (now Oaxaca de Juarez), the proposal came in 1552 that an Indian settlement be segregated in such fashion as to have entrances and exits distinct from those of the Spanish town. Another arrangement of more spontaneous character was the Indian town located away from the city, but serving as a reservoir of labor for public and private works.[71] Near Mexico City, Coyoacan provided thousands of laborers for the reconstruction after 1521, and as far afield as Oaxtepec, sixty miles distant, the entire population labored in the quarries for the stone needed in the capital.

An imagined need for total racial segregation found expression very early in the history of New Spain. Its object was to protect Indians from white exploitation, rather than to protect whites from contact with Indians. As such, it was a pro-Indian policy, without biological implications, promoted by Mendicants who wished no interference from civilians and secular clergy in their labors of conversion. Thus Puebla de los Angeles was founded in 1531 by order of the Audiencia in the densely populated provinces of Cholula, Tlaxcala, and Tepeaca.[72] It was established for the sole use of white settlers, at the instigation of the Franciscan missionaries. The chosen site was remote from the important road between Mexico City and Veracruz, and it later became necessary to shift the road to pass through the new town. A vague tradition reports the presence of an Indian town named Cuetlaxcohuapan on or near the site, but it was not important enough to affect the Spanish layout. The initial settlement on April 16, 1531, was directed by Franciscans. About forty civilians had been attracted to the project, and the first houses arose on the east bank of the San Francisco River. A few months later, the settlers moved across the river, thereby defining the modern urban center of Puebla. Indian labor erected the first buildings. They were located according to a traza or survey laid out by one Alonso Martín Pérez, who was also in charge of allotting the plots to the settlers. This first phase of urbanization was provisional, consisting of little more than rude huts. The population soon doubled and promised to increase at such a rate that a new traza was evolved in

70. Mexico: Alamán, *Disertaciones*, II, 199–201. Oaxaca: Puga, *Cedulario*, II, 184.

71. Coyoacan: "Documentos . . . Cortés," *Publ. AGN*, XXVII, 343–351. Oaxtepec: Cuevas, *Documentos inéditos*, p. 45. *Epistolario*, III, 2. According to the documents made available in Puga, *Cedulario*, I, 258–259, Cortés was drafting labor from as far away as Otumba and Tepeapulco in 1532.

72. Motolinia, "Historia de los indios de la Nueva España," *CDHM*, I, 231–235. M. F. Echeverría y Veytia, *Historia de la fundación de la ciudad de la Puebla de los Angeles* (Puebla, 1931), *passim*. F. Peréz Salazar, "La Fundación de la ciudad de Puebla," *Boletín de la sociedad mexicana de geografía y estadística*, época 5, XIV (1929), 99, offers the interesting but unproven suggestion that the second Audiencia initiated the program of founding *pueblos de españoles*, in order to satisfy the demands of those whites who had received no encomiendas.

1532, in consultation between an envoy from the Audiencia and the Franciscan guardians of various missions in the province. Construction according to the new survey progressed during 1533 and 1534. This second plan controls the present appearance of the city (Fig. 18). It is a rectilinear and rectangular gridiron of blocks, separated by streets 14½ yards wide. A main axis crossed at right angles with a secondary axis. Each block measured 200 by 100 yards, with the long side lying on the main, or east-west axis. Eight lots to the block each had a frontage of 50 yards.[73] Twenty-one such blocks formed the east-west extension of the city, and as many again in the north-south direction, giving total dimensions of 4½ by 2½ kilometers, or an area of 11.25 km^2. The corners of the blocks faced the cardinal points at such an angle that the prevailing winds might not sweep the length of the city. The central plaza measured 217 by 128 yards, framed by wooden colonnaded portals in the sixteenth century. A monumental fountain was erected in the eastern section of the plaza in 1557, leaving the remainder clear for bullfights and other spectacles. The necessary bridges connecting the two halves of the city were built in 1555. Fine communal lands (*ejidos*) surrounded the settlement, and there were large produce gardens on unoccupied allotments within the city itself. This history may be typical for the larger urban creations reserved by white colonists: first came the act of foundation, accompanied by a provisional plan, which was soon displaced by more authoritative proposals. The monumental aspect of the city, and its permanent utilities were not achieved until after the middle of the century. It was a slow process, but it was constantly controlled by farsighted planning.

All told, about thirty such towns for Europeans, known in order of their physical size or political importance as *ciudades* or *villas,* were built before 1574,[74] and their populations ranged from a few families to five hundred or more. The lesser agglomerations of this class obviously entailed little effort. In 1569, for instance, Guadalajara was inhabited by only fifty Spanish families, while as late as 1605, the city consisted of one-story adobe shelters, laid out on a gridiron of twenty streets. The Cathedral then in use was built of adobe, and the Audiencia of New Galicia was housed in the only two-story structure.[75]

It is to be emphasized that the foundation of these towns for Europeans was in no sense a haphazard enterprise. The sites were chosen with the greatest care, and according to a general plan of dispersion. Cortés revealed in the Fourth Letter his

73. A total of about 3,350 lots was available, capable of accommodating a population of that many families. In 1574, however, the city sheltered but 500 Spanish settlers (i.e., heads of families), 500 negroes, and 3,000 Indians. López de Velasco, *Geografía,* pp. 208–209.

74. López de Velasco, *op. cit., passim.*

75. "Informe . . . cabildo de Guadalajara," *CDHM,* II (1866), 504. Escobar, *Descripción geográfica,* pp. 44–45.

strong sense for regional planning. He believed in 1524 that there was no need for another large city so near to the capital as Tepeaca. He therefore directed the European householders of that town to remove to Oaxaca,[76] where they settled anew upon the site of the present city of Oaxaca. Not only Cortés, but the later administrators of Mexico City felt strongly on the point. In 1533, for example, the members of the municipal council strongly opposed the foundation of Santa Fe, near the city, and objected to the existence of Puebla.[77] Both settlements, they thought, threatened the supremacy of the capital. It should be pointed out, however, that the people whose interests were concentrated in the capital were sensitive to the great defects of its site. Cortés was attacked for not having settled the capital upon the mainland, and this kind of criticism of the capital's situation continued through the century (see p. 79). On the other hand, some civilians believed strongly that the Europeans should not scatter too far apart in small settlements, and in 1532, Luis de Castilla, a powerful citizen, gave voice to this opinion.[78]

The populations of the various European settlements about 1580 immediately reveal how carefully this policy was observed. Mexico City far outclassed all other settlements with 1,699 European settlers, or nineteen per cent of the white population of New Spain. The other cities of New Spain, insofar as their white populations are concerned, can scarcely rank as towns.[79] Interesting is the number of Europeans settled in mining towns; the diffusion of Europeans in mining enterprises was, however, achieved only after 1546, with the discovery of mineral resources.

Immensely more numerous than Spanish towns were the settlements created or revived exclusively for Indian use. They usually appeared among dense populations in food-growing regions, or near the mines, and in areas possessing the climate for sugar or for silk culture. The friars of the three Mendicant Orders controlled this activity until the last third of the century; they were originally given almost unlimited powers in dealing with the Indian populations. Hence the most numerous towns were missionary towns. The Franciscans operated in central and western Mexico; the Dominicans were active in the south (Oaxaca and Chiapas), and the Augustinians

76. Cortés, *Letters,* II, 163. Cortés' action, however, did not destroy the value of Tepeaca as a strategic settlement. In 1625, the town still preserved its reputation as a "frontier town, to secure the Spaniards, that came from St. John de Ulhua to Mexico, against the Culiacans and people of Tepeacao" (Gage, *The English-American,* p. 44). The English Dominican is alluding to the status of the town in the time of the conquest. Both the church and the Rollo, however, carry out the motif of the march fortress. An interpretation of 1791 interprets the church as designed for a "resistencia ofensiva" (Archivo General de la Nación, *Ramo Padrones,* MS, Vol. XXXVIII). M. Toussaint reports that a minuscule doorway in the convento gives access to a subterranean passage connecting the cloister and the Rollo. *Paseos coloniales* (Mexico, 1939), p. 128.

77. *AC,* III, 42.

78. Pérez Salazar, "Fundación . . . Puebla," *Boletín de la sociedad mexicana de geografía y estadística,* época 5, XIV, 111–112; quoting Castilla: "para que los yndios fuesen xristianos y la tierra estuviese mas segura que avia de aver muchos monasterios y pocos pueblos porque los españoles estubiesen mas juntos y no tan derramados en tantos pueblos."

79. Cf. López de Velasco, *Geografía.*

settled in Michoacan and in the mountains of the state of Hidalgo (Maps 1–5). The extensive production of urban equipment began as early as the 'twenties. Much later, many Indian towns were laid out by civilian authorities and by the secular clergy, but their work followed a technique of settlement invented by the Mendicants. In any case, most authorities recognized the need for Indian urbanization, which is one of the few aspects of colonial policy where the civil administration, the secular clergy, and the regular clergy agreed, in theory if not always in practice.[80]

The Mendicants did not agree, however, among themselves about town-planning. Their paternalistic attitude towards the Indians underwent several changes. In 1550 the friars urged the Crown to allow the grouping of Indians in loose villages like Spanish peasants.[81] The Mendicants thereby resumed, at least in intention, a kind of social experiment that had already been explored unsuccessfully in several efforts among the Indian populations of the Antilles.[82]

In specific policy, Domingo de Betanzos, the great Dominican apostle, differed from his colleagues in thinking that the plans devised for Indian benefit ultimately redounded to their disadvantage.[83] By this he meant that it was precisely in dense settlements that epidemic disease struck most heavily. On the other hand, certain Franciscans complained that the failures of the colonial enterprise were largely owing to inadequate urbanization.[84] Others, in the seventeenth century, both among the regular and secular clergy, attributed these failures to excessive town-life.[85] The supporters of intensive urbanization valued the moral effects of close daily contact with the Christian ritual, but its opponents argued that changes of habitat damaged the health and impeded the agricultural production of the Indians. Neither faction was entirely right, for the correct solution to the problem was always dependent upon local conditions. In practice, some areas were too heavily urbanized for economic benefit, and others were too thinly settled for the moral advantages of town life to accrue to the inhabitants. Disease took a heavy toll in the towns and cities, as we know from the encomienda populations (Table *B*). The proportional

80. The secular clergy not infrequently refused to collaborate (L. B. Simpson, *Many Mexicos* [New York, 1941], p. 96), while the Indians opposed the resettlement program for reasons implicit in the agricultural technology of the time (R. Ricard, *La "Conquête spirituelle" du Mexique* [Paris, 1933], p. 171).

81. Cuevas, *Documentos inéditos,* p. 166.

82. L. Hanke, *The First Social Experiments in America* (Cambridge, 1935) (Harvard Historical Monographs, V), pp. 40–71.

83. Dávila Padilla, *Historia . . . Santiago de México,* pp. 102–103.

84. Mendieta, *Historia eclesiástica indiana,* p. 496. Compare the opinion of the Augustinian prior of Tlachinolticpac, in the mountains of the present state of Hidalgo, about 1569, ". . . esta este pueblo diuidido en pueblos tan pequeños, porque la fragosidad y aspereza de la tierra no çufre menos, ni permite hazer mayores congregaçiones de pueblos." *PNE,* III, 135.

85. Writing about 1603, Fray Diego Basalenque looked upon the congregation of Indians into urban groups as the major cause for the drop in population. *Historia . . . Michoacán,* pp. 116b, 117a. Bishop Alonso de la Mota y Escobar felt likewise about conditions in the bishopric of Puebla. "Memoriales del obispo de Tlaxcala (1608–24)," MS copy (47 fols.) by F. del Paso y Troncoso, in the Museo Nacional, Mexico City, fol. 31 ro.

magnitude of such losses, however, is difficult to estimate. It is worth noting at least, that in the Bishopric of Tlaxcala, more large Indian cities existed than in the other dioceses, and reference to Figure 9 will show that Tlaxcala, of the four great bishoprics, participated least in the process of recovery between 1546 and 1575.

The process of founding Indian towns seems everywhere to have followed the same general pattern. Father Beaumont, who had access to the Mendicant archives in the eighteenth century, transmitted a detailed account of the formation of a Franciscan missionary town at Acambaro in 1526.[86] The friars' first gesture, after choosing the site, was to erect a cross. The streets were then laid out by simple surveying methods. On the level ground south of the Rio Toluca, upon an area about six thousand feet long in a north-south direction, and about twenty-four hundred feet wide from east to west, ten streets were plotted, five running north and south, and intersecting at right angles with five east-west streets. The center of this grid became the site of the church; the area north of the church was assigned to the Otomi settlers, and the southern half to the Tarascans.

The construction of a provisional chapel preceded the distribution of lots for the houses and gardens of the settlers. The four hundred families of Indians obeyed twelve chiefs; each of these *caciques* was assigned a lot about three hundred feet wide; he in turn assigned each of the families in his care a lot or *solar* about one hundred and fifty feet wide.

The municipal officers (a governor, two alcaldes, and one fiscal) were then elected, and the residence for the friars was built. In 1527, the water supply of the town was improved by bringing a conduit from the mountains of Ucareo. A network of surrounding villages was established, to stabilize the agricultural production of the area. Such were the villages of S. Mateo de Tocuaro and San Juan de Apaseo. The houses were built allegedly in 1528, and the permanent friars' residence was finished, or so we are told, in 1532. As a final touch, in 1535 (?), a separate community was set up for the five thousand alien Chichimec Indians on the opposite bank of the Lerma River, and connecting with Acambaro by a bridge. It is to be observed how this program alternates the ceremonial and practical responsibilities of foundation. Religious and civilian construction spell each other in a regular rhythm. In this case, the missionary program provides a rudimentary example of regional planning: to create the Christian community the friars built not only a church, but a functioning

86. Ricard, *La "Conquête spirituelle" du Mexique,* pp. 169 ff., who accepts the documents in Beaumont, *Crónica de Michoacán,* II, 298–306. The date is questionable: a peculiar Indian lawsuit is involved, in which certain Indian rights were presented as dependent upon long occupancy of the site. The process, however, is like that described by Remesal as occurring in Chiapas and Guatemala after 1548. A. de Remesal, *Historia general de las Indias occidentales* (2d ed. Guatemala, 1932), II, 244, 246 (Biblioteca "Goathemala" de la sociedad de geografía e historia, IV–V).

urban nucleus, with its dependent settlements, and an agricultural and industrial activity commensurate to the population of the area.

Similar activity is recorded for southern Mexico near the mid-century. About 1549, the Dominicans in Chiapas began to build new towns. Their activity is well described by Remesal. After a master plan had been laid out, a church suitable to the size of the population was built. Next door was the curate's residence, and both faced upon a plaza. Opposite the church buildings were the *casa de regimiento,* the prison, and the *mesón* (or *casa de comunidad*) for travelers. The remainder of the town was laid out in regular and oriented squares. Then, with the simple methods of Indian construction, the houses were built, each in a few hours, the whole town taking form in a few days.[87] Where more ambitious constructions were involved, the Indians were persuaded first to plant crops near the proposed site, then to build, and to move into their new homes at harvest-time, with many festivals and dances, "para hacerles olvidar las moradas antiguas."

Frequently, however, the friars encountered difficulties in the selection of a desirable site.[88] At Huejotzingo the pre-Conquest site of the town was unhealthful. The community had already been evangelized, when in 1529 it was decided to remove the entire community of forty thousand households to another settlement. Similar difficulties are recorded for Tecamachalco, moved after 1541; Tepeaca, moved in 1543; and Tehuacan, moved *ca.* 1580. At Guadalajara, the Franciscans had a difficult time; between 1543 and 1550, four separate changes of site were made, until the final relationships to the diverse Indian population of many tribes, and the hygienic proprieties of the emplacement were achieved. At Cuilapan in Oaxaca, the Dominicans likewise began their original campaign in an old village of which the site proved unsatisfactory. In 1555 the entire community moved a few miles to its present site, in spite of the fact that a religious establishment had already been built in the older settlement. Sometimes the Indians of a town refused the friars the particular plot of land desired for a church; at Yuriria, fray Diego de Chávez (Fig. 30) was frustrated at first, *ca.* 1550, by the reluctance of the wife of one of the principal Indians to move her home from the spot that Chávez had selected. He was forced to begin work, of which the traces still remain, at some distance from the village. When the owner of the more desirable plot changed his mind, Chávez broke off operations, and began anew at the present site of the Augustinian church.

87. Remesal, *op. cit.,* II, 244, 246.

88. R. García Granados and L. McGregor, *Huejotzingo, la ciudad y el convento franciscano* (Mexico, 1934) (Monográfias históricas mexicanos, II), p. 30. See *PNE,* V, 24 (Tecamachalco). *PNE,* V, 18, 23 (Tepeaca). Simpson, "Studies," *Iberoamericana,* XIII, 82–83; Mendoza, *Fragmentos,* p. 6 (Guadalajara). Burgoa, *Geografica descripción,* I, 398; *idem, Palestra historial* (Mexico, 1934) (*Publ. AGN,* XXIV), pp. 94–95 (Cuilapan). On Yuriria: Escobar, *Americana thebaida,* p. 564; Basalenque, *Historia . . . Michoacán,* p. 56a. Teposcolula: Murillo, *Iglesias de México,* VI, by Toussaint, 17.

Occasionally, when the friars wished to remove an entire settlement to a new site of their own choosing, they were restrained by viceregal order, as at Teposcolula *ca.* 1550, where the proposed site was uneven and humid, if convenient to the new monastic buildings. Elsewhere, inter-ordinal difficulties delayed the processes of resettlement. For instance, the Franciscans attempted to settle in Amecameca in 1534–37, where they were housed by the chief. In a neighboring village, however, his younger brother welcomed and encouraged the Dominicans from Chimalhuacan Chalco. The Dominicans managed to persuade the dominant Indian group that they were less ragged and crippled; more respectable a group of missionaries than the Franciscans, with the result that Amecameca became a Dominican site.[89]

Thus a noticeable lag often occurred between the initial conversion, with its church-building activities, and the definitive program of urban reformation. This lag was common in fairly central areas with large native populations.[90] For instance, the initial conversion at Cuautinchan in 1527–28 was followed by urban regrouping and planning only in 1558, when Mendieta was dispatched to counter a Dominican attempt to force the field away from Franciscan control. At Tecali the same process may be observed. Before 1554 the town was in disorder, and its reformation followed the initial conversion only after many years' delay.

It would be most misleading not to mention the many towns founded without any signs of rational and preconceived planning.[91] Their number was great, both among Mendicant and secular jurisdictions. In an important Franciscan settlement, for example, at Jalapa (Veracruz), the urban center was *ca.* 1580 merely a church (Fig. 19). A few dwellings stood nearby, but the greater part of the parish was scattered throughout the mountains, in the vicinity of the fields. Similar conditions prevailed at the mines of Sultepec, at Hueypoxtla, at Tezcatepec, Atitalaquia, and in the region of Teotihuacan, to name but a few settlements for which we have the record. At Sultepec, heavy depopulation had made it seem not worthwhile to urbanize the area; and at Atitalaquia, the Indians preferred isolated living. Occasionally, when the friars wished to urbanize a population upon the banks of a substantial body of water, the gridiron plan, with its rigorous centralization and radial extension,

89. Amecameca: *Annales . . . de Chimalpahin*, pp. 231–232, 233–235.

90. Cuautinchan: "Relación . . . Quautinchán," *NCDHM*, I, 70–91. Mendieta, *Historia eclesiástica indiana*, p. 344. Tecali: Torquemada, . . . *Monarchia indiana*, III, 317.

91. Jalapa: *PNE*, V, 99–102. Jalapa in 1580 was "algo junto, la mayor parte del, y por las quebradas y sin horden ay alguna parte del: estan darramados en esta forma porque estan en sus casas entre sus sementeras como es general en toda la *Nueua España*." The "town" itself had no streets, "no tiene calles." Sultepec, *PNE*, VII, 9; Atitalaquia, *PNE*, VI, 202; Hueypoxtla, *PNE*, VI, 27; Tezcatepec, *PNE*, VI, 32; Teotihuacan, *PNE*, VI, 220. Chimalhuacan Atenco: *PNE*, VI, 67. "Este . . . pueblo no esta traçado ni asentado por calles y plaça por que, como esta dicho, su asiento es orilla de la laguna. . . ." Jacona: Basalenque, *Historia . . . Michoacán*, pp. 78b–79a. Fray Sebastian de Trasierra OSA preferred "utilidad del rio, y assi todo lo demas se fundò à riberas del . . ." to the usual "policia de calles, y plaças." Zimapan, *PNE*, VI, 3.

proved unworkable. Such was the case at Chimalhuacan Atenco, on the shores of Lake Texcoco, where the settlement was controlled by the Texcoco road and by the lake shore (Fig. 20). In consequence, no effort was made to establish a clearly defined plaza, or any streets. In Michoacan, the foundation of Jacona presented similar problems. Situated after 1555 upon the banks of a river, the town was the center of a cereal-growing area. The founder's desire to utilize the river to best advantage, made it impossible to build a dense cluster of streets and houses about a centrally located church and plaza. The great rainfall in the region, moreover, produced such deep mud in the streets that the church was located upon a slight elevation at the edge of the town. The remainder of the settlement hugged the river bank in a long strip of houses. One of the clearest representations of such fluvial towns is given in a map of *ca.* 1579, representing the mining settlement at Zimapan, where Europeans first settled about 1575, and the houses follow the course of the little river (Fig. 21). In general, it may be said that wherever small regional populations did not favor the expenditure of much labor upon planning and urban concentration, the settlements tended to scattered, diffuse, and disorderly arrangement.

The greater part of the actual work of urbanization had already been achieved when the famous urban statutes were devised in the last third of the century.[92] Spanish towns obeyed laws quite distinct from those for the foundation of Indian settlements. Two separate campaigns of legislation are involved. The first comprised the regulations devised about 1573, and pertained chiefly to the physical layout of the Spanish towns. A later body of statutes (the *Recopilación*) concerning Indian towns was formulated after 1600, and it deals more with economic and administrative problems.

The laws of 1573 for Spanish towns merit some discussion: they are probably based upon Mendicant experience, and certain prescriptions can be understood only in the light of an abstract, standard emplacement. The legislators had in mind a generic site swept only by easterly winds.[93] New towns were to be located, if inland, to the east or west of hills and mountains, apparently in order that they might be spared the force of the assumed winds. Another provision urged that inland towns be swept only by north and south winds. Coastal towns were not to have open water

92. Spain, laws, statutes, etc. *Recopilación de leyes de los reinos de las Indias* (5th ed. Madrid, 1841), Bk. IV, *titulo* vii; F. Gómez de Orozco, "Las leyes de Indias," *Investigaciones históricas,* I (1939), 134–139. Z. Nuttall, "Royal Ordinances Concerning the Laying Out of New Towns," *Hispanic American Historical Review,* IV (1921), 743–753. *Recopilación de leyes,* Bk. VI.

93. Sixteenth-century theory concerning winds was as much magical as hygienic; many of its recommendations were drawn deductively from Aristotelian postulates (see J. de Acosta, *Historia natural y moral de las Indias* [Mexico, 1940], pp. 135–164, E. O'Gorman, ed.); perhaps also from Vitruvian prescriptions (K. Lehmann-Hartleben, "The Impact of Ancient City Planning on European Architecture," *Journal of the American Society of Architectural Historians,* III, no. 1–2 [1943], 29).

south or west of the settlement.[94] Under certain circumstances, it was a practical regulation, for if the prevailing winds are southeasterly, as on the Gulf Coast, constant offshore winds would hinder the approach of sailing vessels to ports with channels leading into the wind. It was also the law to lay out riparian settlements upon the east banks of rivers, in order that humors, infections, and mists might be swept away from rather than into the towns.

Urban legislation for Indian settlements came only at the end of the century, perhaps as a result of severe population losses through disease and cultural shock.[95] The legislation was enacted when the Mendicant Orders had not only already achieved the bulk of their program, but had even been compelled to withdraw from the active missionary life of the colony.[96] To replace the Mendicants, Viceroy Monterrey created the Court of Congregation[97] and entrusted it with the urbanizing activity previously confided to the friars. The statutes of 1600 were intended to implement the Court's work, but they are no more than legislative expressions of the practical solutions of the Mendicants.[98] Almost exact identities may be detected between the process at Acambaro, and the routine of settlement enacted by secular authorities early in the seventeenth century. L. B. Simpson has reconstructed the events at Tlanchinol in the state of Hidalgo.[99] Numerous dispersed farmers were transferred to four separate villages. Tlanchinol itself was laid out in eleven wards, each with its own community house and chapel. The project was completed within eight months, by 1605. The speed of action is remarkable, but the processes of concentration and articulation are precisely those of the friars. Thus the legal apparatus, whether it pertained to *pueblos de españoles* or to *pueblos de indios,* was but the crystallization of many experiments undertaken by the various classes of colonists. These, in descending order of effectiveness, were the friars, the civil bureaucracy, the secular clergy, the second-generation encomenderos, and the *conquistadores* themselves.

Self-evident as it may be that American urban experiments were initially free from strict legislative control, it does not follow that these experiments were free or spontaneous inventions. On the contrary, they may be shown to follow from earlier

94. *Recopilación de leyes,* pp. 104–108. The passage about coastal towns depends directly upon Vitruvius.

95. See pp. 42, 46.

96. Writing in the decade 1610–20, Remesal complained that the failure of the Crown to entrust urbanization to the Mendicants in the new campaign after 1595 had incurred grievous errors, the loss of a million Indians in New Spain, and a useless expense of 300,000 ducats in salaries to civil servants. (Remesal, *Historia . . . Indias,* II, 246–247.)

97. Simpson, *Many Mexicos,* p. 96.

98. "Códice Mendieta, II," *NCDHM,* V, 96–98. The Franciscans suggested about 1589 that anyone wishing to found Indian towns should choose the site, and then "al cabo del año . . . echar luego el cordel y trazar las calles, dejando en el medio el sitio de la iglesia, y delante de ella la plaza, y después . . . Hecha la traza del pueblo por sus calles y solares . . . se debe repartir en barrios. . . ." The Indians were to build their own houses first, by communal labor in groups of twenty and one hundred workers, and only then were they to proceed to the building of the church.

99. Simpson, *Many Mexicos,* p. 101.

habits of European urban theory and practice. To establish those habits, and to determine firm historical connections is often difficult, particularly where interferences from Indian urbanism may be suspected.

Fortunately, many drawings of Mexican town plans, made about 1580, have survived. Executed by Indian artists, they are often fairly accurate documents, forming part of the great cosmographic project undertaken by the advisers of Philip II. Officials in villages, towns, and cities in every part of the Spanish world were required to answer an elaborate questionnaire concerning local history, geography, botany, zoölogy, and vital statistics. The answers were compiled by informants of many kinds, often including Indian sources. Maps and plans often accompanied the reports.[100]

An excellent plan of Cholula was drawn in 1581 (Fig. 22), probably by an Indian craftsman, since the roads and certain buildings are designated by words in Aztec language (e.g., *ohtli,* road). The plaza occupies the intersection of roads from Puebla, Mexico, Tlaxcala, and Atlixco. Various government buildings and the church, with its great walled courtyard, surround the plaza. The distribution of the house blocks accurately records relationships that prevail today, although the linear distances are greatly contracted. The layout is extremely regular, and the administrative divisions of the town (barrios) are clearly marked, each with its chapel on or near a pre-Conquest pyramidal platform.

In southern Mexico, Texupa and Nochistlan in the Mixteca Alta, likewise display an extraordinary, schematic checkerboard plan. At Texupa (Fig. 23) the main axis ran north and south. It defined thirty-nine blocks, each with eight house symbols. Although the plaza is not shown, it certainly stood near the church where the roads converge, and where a flowering garden is indicated. At the time of this drawing (1579) the town sheltered only seven hundred fifty persons, the remnants of a district population numbering about twelve thousand at the time of the Conquest. At Nochistlan, some 720 families lived on the gridiron of 110 blocks (Fig. 24). The church, with a geometric frieze, faces on a plaza near which three substantial buildings are sketched.

In the same series an excellent drawing of Chicualoapa in the Valley of Mexico,

100. See Bibliographical Note, pp. 434–436. G. de Rojas, "Descripción de Cholula," *Revista mexicana de estudios históricos,* I (1927), Apendice, pp. 158–170. Texupa: *PNE,* IV, 53. Nochistlan: *PNE,* IV, 206. Chicualoapa: *PNE,* VI, 81. "Este pueblo esta asentado èn pueblo formado, traçado por sus calles y plaça; los yndios . . . biben en pulicia y congregaçion," 1579. Coatepec Chalco: *PNE,* VI, 47, 63. "Este . . . traçado en la forma y manera que estan traçados los pueblos de españoles," 1579. The houses of the Indians were built "con alto y baxos, corredores, puerta y ventanas, portadas de piedra de canteria y encalados con pinturas de colores." Huejutla: *PNE,* VI, 190. "En este pueblo no ay fortaleza ni casa fuerte si no es el monesterio." The same text contradicts the drawing (pp. 186–187), "no ay calles concertados." An absolute gridiron plan was impossible because of the broken topography of the town. Tenango del Valle: *PNE,* VII, 1.

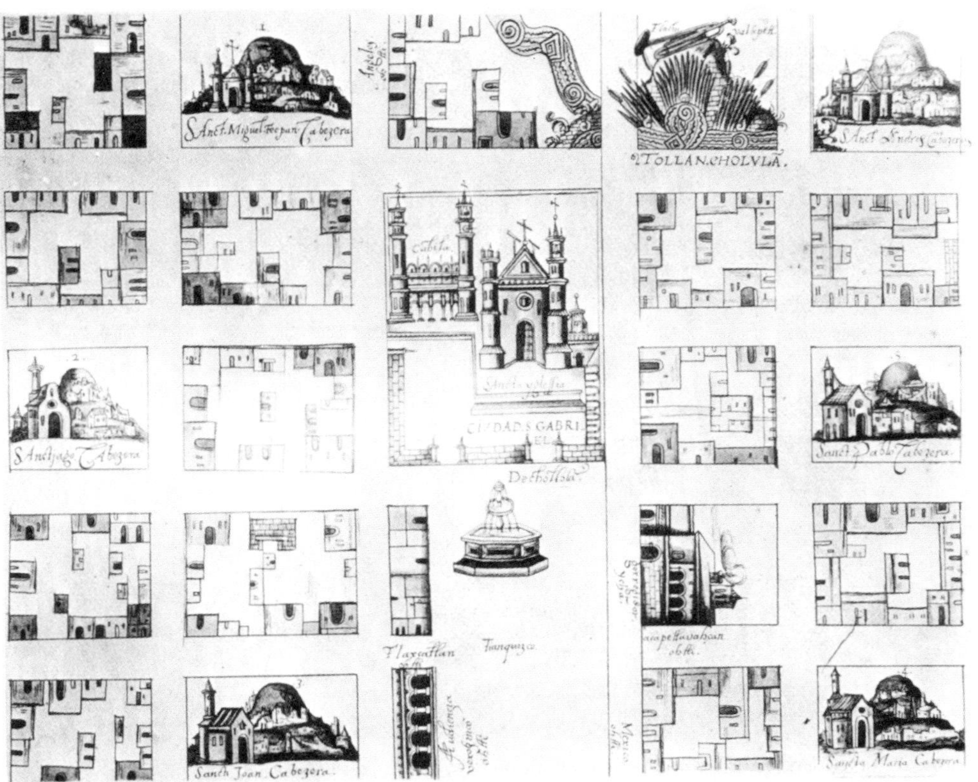

22. Cholula, plan in 1580

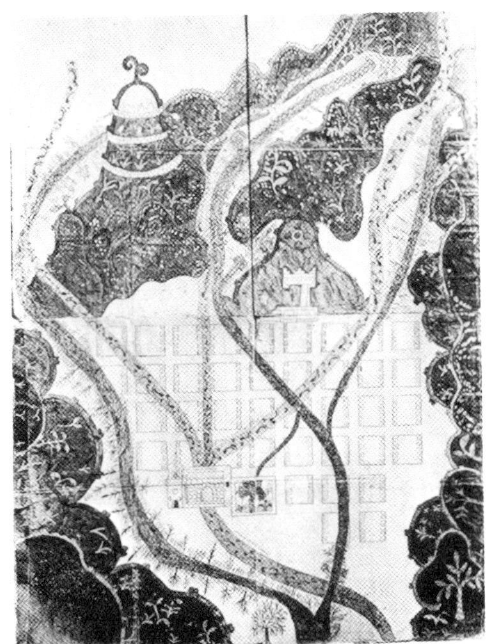

23. Texupa (State of Oaxaca), plan in 1579

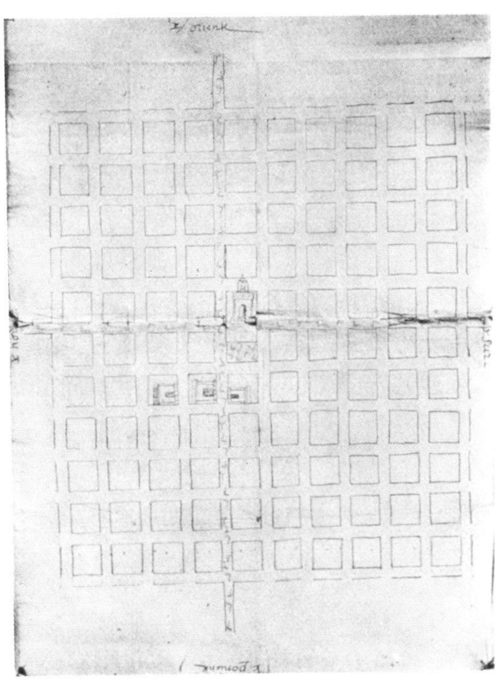

24. Nochistlan (State of Oaxaca), plan in 1581

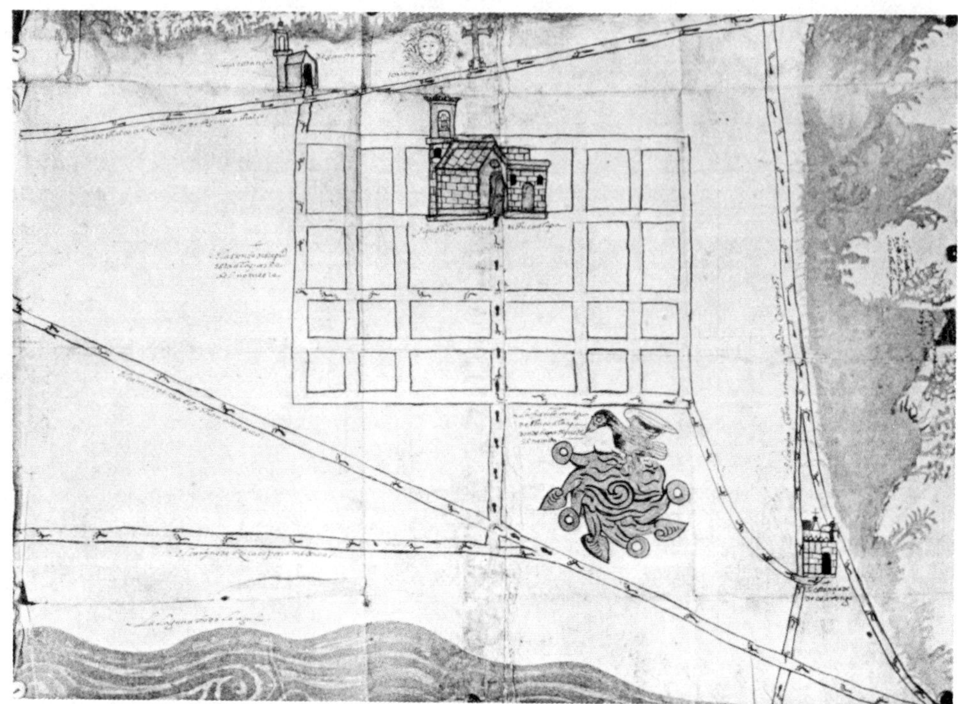

25. Chicualoapa (Valley of Mexico), plan in 1579

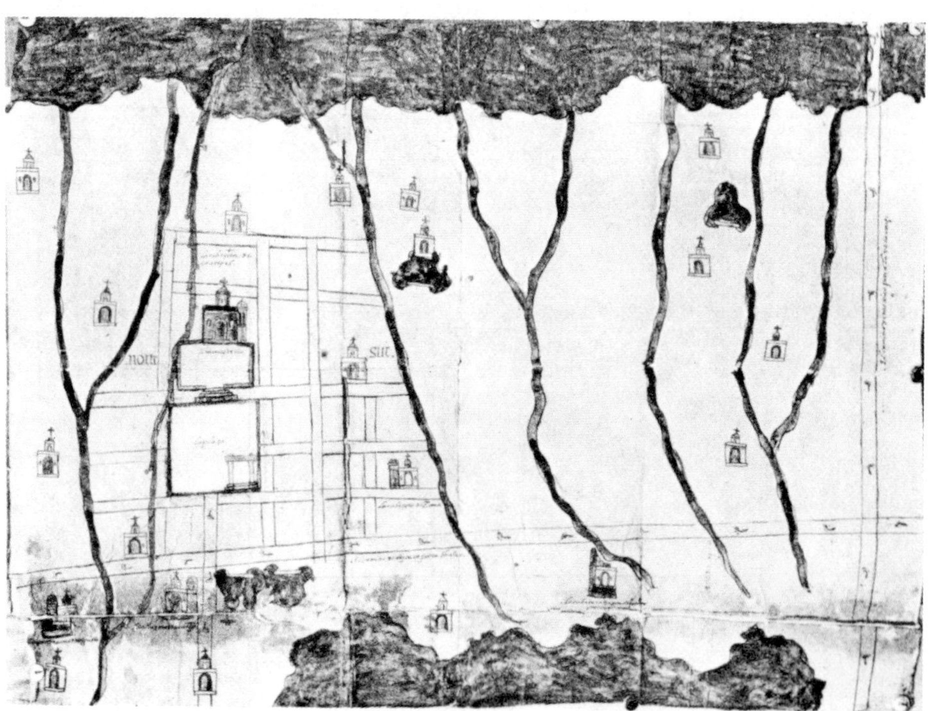

26. Coatepec Chalco (Valley of Mexico), plan in 1579

made about 1579, shows the relation of the settlement to three important highways (Fig. 25). The plaza is twice as long as wide, with its main axis running north and south. The text speaks of many two-storied stone houses, although the lime for mortar had to be brought from a site twelve leagues distant. Not far from Chicualoapa, seven hundred families inhabited Coatepec Chalco, on the eastern shore of Lake Texcoco. Here again the highway bypassed the town, bounded and traversed by several streams (Fig. 26). A gallows stood in the plaza, and the church dominated many subsidiary chapels in neighboring villages and ranches, as well as within the town itself. A large number of building craftsmen resided in Coatepec, and the houses were fairly pretentious.

A relationship of great importance is shown with unusual clarity at Huejutla in the mountains of Hidalgo (Fig. 27). The only fortified element is the church, which dominates the entire agglomeration. The courtyard seems to have encroached upon what would be the plaza in other towns of this class, while the square itself is indicated in the lower right hand corner (*tianguis*, marketplace). It was a small town which had suffered great losses, so that in 1580 it sheltered but fifty persons. Tenango del Valle, on the other hand, accommodated some 440 families. It stood west of Mexico City, in the neighboring valley of Toluca. Its plan gives a detailed account of all the normal features of the larger sixteenth-century towns (Fig. 28). The text asserts that the layout was patterned upon that of Mexico City. The church, the courtyard, the public buildings all face upon a rectangular plaza of which the length is twice the width. The buildings around its periphery are monumentally conceived and symmetrically disposed. Three smaller, ancillary villages appear northwest of the town.

Among the urban forms represented in these various drawings,[101] several dominant traits emerge. The houses were distributed upon a gridiron plan developed from two main axes intersecting at right angles. At their intersection a large public square of symmetrical proportions lies among public buildings of uniform and monumental style. The square might or might not be fortified, but its eastern range was usually occupied by a church of massive and military aspect. No peripheral fortifications protected the settlement; its approaches were distinguished only by the regularity and order of the house blocks. Within the town, there were subdivisions by precinct or ward (barrio),[102] and each of these subdivisions was likely to have its own chapel. As a whole, then, the town looked quite unlike coeval European towns. Each of the forms

101. Many towns recorded by these drawings do not display the regular forms of the preceding examples. The map for Cuzcatlan (*PNE*, V, 46) shows only the barest urban essentials—church, fountain, and gallows. Compare Jalapa de la Veracruz (*PNE*, V, 99) and Xonotla (*PNE*, V, 127). The text indicates that Tetela (*PNE*, V, 145) possessed a regular plan, but the drawing reveals casual urban forms: a plaza with three zones of wooded dwelling acres containing huts. In general, however, the plans show orderly form, and spontaneous house-groups are the exception (see p. 90).

102. See R. Redfield, *Tepoztlan, a Mexican Village* (Chicago, 1930).

just listed, however, had its morphological antecedents, sometimes in practice, sometimes in theory.

The gridiron plan cannot be said to have any critical significance. Felix de Verneilh pointed out long ago that it is a generic urban solution, independently achieved by many peoples.[103] It demanded a limited kind of forethought, and it often represented an evasion of more complex problems. Its medieval uses, as Lavedan has shown,[104] did not involve a renaissance of the Roman *castrum* layout,[105] but rather the regularization of certain rectilinear plans of an almost spontaneous sort. Such medieval checkerboards, however, were usually enveloped by fortifications, and they often lacked the plaza which characterizes the towns under discussion here.[106] In general, from the ancient cities of the Mediterranean world to the industrial towns of North America, the gridiron plan was a standard form, often latent, sometimes dominant. Pre-Conquest American examples are not unlikely.[107] In Mexico, the colonial checkerboard may represent less an invention or major departure, than a repetition of the system used before the Conquest on both continents.

Extremely unusual was the Mexican habit of fortifying the church, while leaving the city open to attack on all sides. The object was to fortify the nucleus rather than the periphery. All avenues led to the church, surrounded by a vast courtyard and crenelated walls. The churches were occasionally used as fortified refuges from which a strategic defense, whether against outside enemies or a rebellious town, could be maintained.[108]

In Spain, nothing like the fortified, single-nave church, situated within an unfortified town, can be identified. It is necessary here to distinguish between church-building and church-position. The church-type itself can be traced to Peninsular antecedents without difficulty (see pp. 232–238). But the urban position of the church has no Peninsular precedent. The concept of the open and unfortified town, containing but

103. F. de Verneilh, "Architecture civile au moyen âge," *Annales archéologiques*, VI (1847), 71–88. See also K. Lehmann-Hartleben, "Städtebau Italiens und des römischen Reiches," *Paulys Real-Encyclopädie der classischen Altertumswissenschaft* (Stuttgart, 1894–19–), II Reihe, 6 halbband, cols. 2016–2124, G. Wissowa, ed.; and "The Impact of Ancient City Planning," *Journal of the American Society of Architectural Historians*, III, nos. 1–2 (1943), 23–24. A diffusionist point of view is expressed by D. Stanislawski, "The Origin and Spread of the Grid-Pattern Town," *Geographical Review*, XXXVI (1946), 105–120.

104. P. Lavedan, *Histoire de l'architecture urbaine* (Paris, 1926), pp. 292–293, 407.

105. Although literary descriptions of the *castrum romanum* (Polybius, Vegetius) were known to the scholars of the Italian Renaissance (W. B. Dinsmoor, "The Literary Remains of Sebastiano Serlio," *Art Bulletin*, XXIV [1942], 83–91), no exact knowledge of its form became common until the archaeological revelations of the nineteenth century. Cf., however, p. 99 on Santa Fe near Granada.

106. I shall return in a moment to the question of the unfortified towns of medieval France. Exceptional cases of the public square in medieval towns are treated by Lavedan, *op. cit.*, pp. 340–366, 446.

107. See the pre-Conquest plan for a section of Tenochtitlan, the "Plano en papel de maguey," in the National Museum of Mexico. Toussaint, *Planos*, pp. 49–74. Contrast Stanislawski, "Early Spanish Town Planning in the New World," *Geographical Review*, XXXVII (1947), 98.

108. A. Tello, *Libro segundo de la crónica . . . de Xalisco*, pp. 308–309; *PNE, passim;* Murillo, *Iglesias de México*, VI, by Toussaint, 58; Ricard, *La "Conquête spirituelle" du Mexique*, p. 198.

one strong defensive position in the fabric of the church, invokes an altogether different historical perspective from that of the single-nave, fortified church itself. Isolated from its urban context, the Mexican fortress-church is easily filiated with Peninsular churches of the same type (Yuste, Ovila, or Armedilla); but the combination of church and town must be traced to other sources.

The pattern of the unwalled town with fortified church has analogies in medieval Mendicant practice. In all Europe there is but one area, in southwestern France, where it was common.[109] Along the Mediterranean coast, from Roussillon to Provence, fortress churches had long been built, first to afford defense against the sea and land attacks of the Saracens, then to counter the Catalan and Aragonese invasions of the twelfth century.[110] It was here also, in the Albigeois, the Toulousain, and in Gascony that the Albigensian heresy flourished in the second half of the twelfth century. The members of the sect of the Cathari insisted that the Savior's life was not a sacrifice nor an expiation, but a pedagogical mission. As successors to the Manichaeans, their universe was dual, and they rejected the Sacraments.[111] In 1208 a papal legate was murdered and the Albigensian crusade was organized, to extirpate the heresy. By 1229, when peace could be established, the countryside had been laid waste. The population had been decimated, the towns were in ruins, and the feudal society of the brilliant court of Toulouse had been destroyed. The political control of the area rested in the hands of the Capetian dynasty of northern France.[112]

The year 1229 marks two further events of great importance. The feudal representatives of the French king were given authority to found new, *unfortified* towns. Throughout southwestern France, hundreds of these arose during the thirteenth century, simple villages and towns in which the only fortified refuge was the church.[113] The other event was the organization of the Inquisition at Toulouse, under the auspices of the Dominican Order. By this act the Mendicant Orders, later including the Franciscans and Augustinians, became dominant in the religious affairs of the pacified region. Enjoying royal and papal support, the friars came to have far greater authority than the secular clergy.[114] The reconstruction of the devastated provinces was undertaken by the Mendicants, collaborating with the French Crown.

109. The resemblance was first noted by Toussaint, "La Catedral de México," in Murillo, *Iglesias de México,* II, 8. Writing of Tepeaca, Sr. Toussaint pointed out, ". . . no puede dejar de evocar, aunque no tenga con ellas sino semejanzas de finalidad, las iglesias fortificadas del mediodía de Francia, las de Albi o Carcassonne." Their functional identity was also mentioned in passing by L. Gillet, "L'art dans l'Amérique latine," *Histoire de l'art* (Paris, 1905–29), VIII, Pt. III, 1026. A. Michel, ed.

110. R. Rey, *Les Vieilles églises fortifiées du midi de la France* (Paris, 1925), pp. 89–126.

111. J. Guiraud, "Albigeois," *Dictionnaire d'histoire et de géographie ecclésiastiques* (Paris, 1912), I, col. 1621 ff. A. Baudrillart, ed.

112. R. Rey, *L'Art gothique du midi de la France* (Paris, 1934), pp. 35–84.

113. Lavedan, *Histoire de l'architecture urbaine,* pp. 290–291.

114. Heimbucher, *Die Orden und Kongregationen der Katholischen Kirche,* I, 476–479. E. Maire, "Dominicains," *Dictionnaire pratique des connaissances religieuses* (Paris, 1925–28), II, col. 916. J. Bricout, ed.

It is to be recalled that the Mendicant vocation was an urban mission from the beginning, in contrast to the older monastic predilection for rural retreat and hermetic solitude, as among the Cistercians.[115] The resultant form of the thirteenth-century *ville neuve,* then, is the open town containing a fortified church,[116] produced under direct or indirect Mendicant supervision. Economy and the magnitude of the resettlement program necessitated the frequent use of a simple gridiron plan, with a single-nave church, usually built of brick, and heavily fortified. The system was provisional and improvised, composed of inherited elements, and constituting a solution *faute de mieux* rather than a planned, deliberate reform.

The typological analogies between these events of the thirteenth century and those of the sixteenth century in Mexico are obvious. The Mendicant Orders, in Mexico as in France, served as the instruments of royal rule over newly conquered territories. The Mendicants enjoyed far greater authority than the secular clergy, and their building activity was an urban activity, in agreement with their vocation and in consequence of the great destruction of cities during a military campaign. The specific architectural forms are analogous: both in France and in Mexico the standard church is a single-nave, rib-vaulted structure of massive proportions. Even specific measurements are strikingly similar.[117] The use of brick is common to both areas, for reasons of general expediency. In both, the church is a fortified, defensive enclosure within a town which otherwise lies completely open to attack.

It is difficult to establish firm historical links between the two campaigns, separated as they are by three centuries. But it is not impossible that the Mendicants, when faced with the great task in America, recalled their earlier experience under similar conditions in France.

Too little attention has been paid to the large number of Mendicants of southwestern French extraction who participated in the initial evangelization of Mexico. Their most eminent representative was Jean Focher (also Faucher, and Fucher), a Franciscan of Aquitanian origin, who had held the title of Doctor in the Sorbonne, where he taught Alonso de la Vera Cruz. The date of his arrival in New Spain is not certain: he died in 1572 or 1573, and we have from his pen an *Itinerarium Catholicum* published at Seville in 1574. Arnaud de Bassac, or fray Arnaldo de Basaccio, was another Aquitanian, constantly in touch with the Indians. He professed Latin grammar to Indian pupils in the famous Colegio de Santa Cruz in Tlatelolco, gave

115. H. Vogels, *Lexikon für Theologie und Kirche* (Freiburg, 1930–38), II, col. 306.

116. Rey, *L'Art gothique,* pp. 140–169.

117. At Najac, a single-aisled church with four bays and rib vaults resting upon corbels, each bay is 11.5 m. square, while the height of the nave to the keystone is 17 m., and the total length (interior) is 46 m. Rey, *op. cit.,* p. 45. At Huejotzingo, each of the bays is about 13.5 m. square, the height to the keystone 22.98 m., and the total inner length 60 m. The ratio in both cases approximates 2 : 3 : 8.

instruction at San José de los Naturales, translated the Gospel into Nahuatl, and taught music in Cuautitlan and elsewhere. Jacobo de Testera, the Franciscan who contrived a method of ideographic notation for Indian use, was a native of Bayonne; he arrived in New Spain in 1529, and it was suspected that he never relaxed his loyalty to the French Crown: as *comisario general* in 1543, he was accused of encouraging rebellion against Spaniards on account of the war between Francis I and Charles V. Other friars of southwest French origins were Juan Badiano (Badillo), who was sent to Michoacan in 1525 with the Franciscan mission; he is perhaps the same friar who, later on, accompanied Nuño de Guzmán and baptized the chief of Poncitlan. And in 1531, a fray Juan de Vadia, working with Antonio de Segovia, converted the provinces of Tonala, Tlajomulco, Ocotlan, Amaxac, and the entire Caxcana country. Mendieta briefly mentions an Aquitanian Franciscan, Juan de la Cruz. Finally, the great linguist, Maturino Gilberti (born 1498) was a member of the Aquitanian province of the Franciscan Order.[118]

Thus we can establish a substantial number of French friars working in Mexico during the primitive epoch of evangelization. That there were others whose names are unknown is suggested by the famous letters of 1532, addressed by Martín de Valencia and Bishop Zumárraga to the general chapter of the regular Observance held in Toulouse, pleading for missionaries to work in the Indies. About 1541, fray Jacobo de Testera, whom we already know as a native of Bayonne, returned to Mexico with a contingent of one hundred fifty new friars, whom he had probably recruited, at least in part, from his home country of southwestern France. It should be emphasized, that no French friar in Mexico can be unmistakably associated with any building operation. Still, as we shall see, the identification of early missionaries with specific buildings is technically difficult in all but a few cases.

Rather different associations arise from the problem of the rectangular plaza, at the central intersection of the main axes, framed by colonnades and public buildings, and constituting a monumental urban center. Its most imposing manifestation was realized in Mexico City. An exact knowledge of the plaza mayor of Mexico City can be gained from the scholarly dialogues by Cervantes de Salazar, written in 1554, and from drawings made in the 'fifties and 'sixties (Figs. 63, 64), showing the symmetrical, harmonious, and monumental appearance of the square.[119] Public plazas

118. Focher: Ricard, *La "Conquête spirituelle" du Mexique*, pp. 21–22, 76. A. Génin, *Les Français au Mexique*, p. 74. Basaccio: Alamán, *Disertaciones*, II, 158; Génin, *op. cit.*, p. 87; Ricard, *op. cit.*, p. 77; Mendieta, *Historia eclesiástica indiana*, p. 414. Testera: *AC*, IV, 349; Ricard, *op. cit.*, p. 70; Génin, *op. cit.*, p. 75; H. Harrisse, *Bibliotheca americana vetustissima* (New York, 1866), pp. 98, 168, 177, 186, 244. Vadia: Beaumont, *Crónica de Michoacán*, II, 107, 196, 216; Torquemada, . . . *Monarchia indiana*, III, 598; Mendieta, *op. cit.*, p. 378. Juan de la Cruz: *ibid.* Maturino Gilberti: Ricard, *op. cit.*, pp. 78–79; Génin, *op. cit.*, p. 97.

119. Cervantes de Salazar, *México en 1554*. D. Angulo Iñíguez, *Planos de monumentos arquitectónicos de América y Filipinas existentes en el archivo de Indias* (Seville, 1933–39), pls. 2A–2D, 2E–2H.

of this character do not occur in the medieval towns of Europe. As Lavedan has pointed out, the monumental concept of the plaza is anti-medieval.[120] In the Middle Ages, such open spaces grew as markets, near the junction of old and new city quarters, or as gradual excrescences upon traffic arteries, ultimately culminating, but rarely beginning as the specialized square. Thus in Spanish towns: in the sixteenth century the great plaza of Salamanca was an irregular, unplanned void within the urban solid.[121] The Mexican plazas, on the other hand, are unprecedented in general European practice, but for a very few exceptions. Their form is suggested, not in coeval European towns, but in Italian theory of the fifteenth and sixteenth centuries,[122] where the relation between open spaces and house blocks was an object of constant study in the ideal urban layouts, by such men as Leone Battista Alberti, Antonio Averlino Filarete, and the author of the urban reveries of the *Hypnerotomachia Poliphili.*

Alberti was the most lucid exponent of these speculations. The problems of architecture were so to speak re-invented by him, in the sense that building is conceived as a civic activity in which each house, each detail, should be phrased in the terms of both social use and esthetic unity. Alberti insisted that the ideal city should have open squares where the children might play, and where their nurses might set a competitive standard of cleanliness. Such squares were to be framed by loggias and colonnades in which the old people might supervise the young, sun themselves, and set an example of virtue. Alberti also prescribed the proportions of the plaza; it was to be twice as long as wide, with colonnades scaled to the over-all dimensions. At the center of the city, the municipal buildings were to overlook such a plaza. Throughout all streets and squares, a uniform style was to govern all construction; streets were to be of one width; cornices and moldings were to be continuous and uniform; and above all, the plaza was to be symmetrically and harmoniously adorned.

One should not disregard the fact that Alberti's thought systematized certain sporadic landmarks in Italian civic art prior to this time,[123] as at Cremona or Piacenza in the fourteenth century, where the square is monumentally adorned, or at St. Mark's Square in Venice in the fifteenth century. But on the whole, Italian cities of the late fifteenth and early sixteenth centuries reveal a concept of planning that is essentially medieval. This is true even at Pienza,[124] one of the few urban creations of the day,

120. Lavedan, *Histoire de l'architecture urbaine,* p. 446.

121. O. Jürgens, *Spanische Städte* (Hamburg, 1926), p. 85. (Hamburgische univ. Abhandlungen aus dem Gebiet der Auslandskunde, XXIII [Reihe B, XIII]).

122. O. Stein, *Die Architekturtheoretiker der italienischen Renaissance* (Karlsruhe, 1914). A. Blunt, *Artistic Theory in Italy, 1450–1600* (Oxford, 1940). L. B. Alberti, *De re aedificatoria libri decem* (Strassburg, 1541). P. H. Michel, *La pensée de L. B. Alberti* (Paris, 1930). The first Spanish edition appeared in 1582. A. A. Filarete, . . . *Tractat über die Baukunst* (Wien, 1896). W. von Oettingen, ed. (Quellenschriften für Kunstgeschichte, N. F. III). *Hypnerotomachia Poliphili* (Venice, 1499).

123. Blunt, *op. cit.,* p. 8. See also P. Zucker, *Entwicklung des Stadtbildes; die Stadt als Form* (Munich-Berlin, 1929), pp. 25–32.

124. F. Bargagli-Petrucci, *Pienza, Montalcino e la*

where the quattrocento buildings occupy a dense, irregular medieval layout. Spanish civic art was even more static. The plaza is a normal form in very old Spanish cities, but even in the sixteenth century, it remains small and irregular.[125] The one exception, in which the traces of contact with Italian urban theory are recalled, is the remarkable castrum built by Ferdinand and Isabella at the siege of Granada in 1491. In consequence of a fire, and in anticipation of a prolonged siege, the Catholic Kings built a camp called Santa Fe. It was a fortified rectangle, intersected by the crossing of two perpendicular axes, and approached by four cardinal gates. The entire accommodation was built in eighty days.[126] But the undertaking reveals the influence of Vegetius or Polybius more than that of the Renaissance theorists whose work we are discussing. The fact of its fortification relates Santa Fe more closely to the Roman castrum than to the ideal Italian city as projected by Alberti or Filarete.

Elsewhere in Spain, Italian theories did not become effective until after the middle of the century.[127] Thus the expansion of Madrid after it became the royal residence in 1561 was left utterly to chance. The Italianate appearance of parts of Seville was not realized until after 1550. The rebuilding of Valladolid was the work of the men of the seventeenth century. Italian travelers to Spain, such as Guicciardini, the Florentine ambassador in 1512–13, commented on the squalid, disorderly aspect of Spanish cities.[128] In short, it is difficult to avoid the impression that Europe was saturated with cities; the possibilities of realizing the theoretical program were limited by the abundance of inherited urban material. Hence it would appear that the Spaniards in Mexico, working with an extremely plastic human material, and under no obligation to preserve the monuments of an old culture, were able to implement Italian theory with extensive practice.[129]

Once again, it is difficult to establish more than tenuous historical connections between the events. A manuscript of the treatise by Filarete, incorporating some

Val d'Orcia Senese (Bergamo, 1911) (*Italia artistica,* LXIII). S. J. C. Brinton, *Francesco di Giorgio Martini of Siena* (London, 1934), p. 103.

125. Zucker, *op. cit.*, p. 21.

126. See Peter Martyr of Anghiera, *Opus epistolarum* (Amsterdam, 1670), p. 51. Lib. IV, epist. XCI. "Sulco interea urbs signatur, urbem namque, etsi parvo capacem, jubent appellari. Quadringentorum passuum in longitudine, trecentorum vero duodecim in latitudine, exstruitur moenibus, pinnis, propugnaculis fossisque ac validis turribus minitis, quadrata orthogonia fere signatur, *platea in medio sinitur* [italics mine]. Ab illa quatuor in singulis lateribus portae relictae circumspiciuntur . . . tanta ferbuit operis diligentia, ut intra octogesimum diem coepta perficerentur." See also Francisco Bermúdez de Pedraza, *Antiguedad y excelencias de Granada* (Madrid, 1608), p. 73.

127. Jürgens, *Spanische Städte*, p. 8 (Madrid), pp. 60 ff. (Seville), pp. 75–76 (Valladolid).

128. A. M. Fabié y Escudero, ed. *Viajes por España* (Madrid, 1879), p. 196 (Libros de antaño, VIII).

129. After having composed the present chapter, the writer learned of the excellent article by Rafael Altamira, "La Décentralisation législative dans le régime colonial espagnol," *Bulletin of the International Committee of Historical Sciences*, XI (1939), in which, on p. 186, he wrote as follows, in 1938: "Il faut bien dire que le plan classique de la cité coloniale est tout à fait particulier à celle-ci, et qu'il répresentait alors une nouveauté profonde à l'égard de l'irrégularité urbaine des anciennes villes espagnoles."

aspects of Alberti's thought, was written in the fifteenth century for the house of Aragon, and found its way to a Jeronymite monastery near Valencia about 1513.[130] The Jeronymites obeyed an Augustinian monastic rule, and it is not impossible that the manuscript should have circulated among persons connected with the evangelization of America. In any case, many well-born Spaniards of the generations about 1500 were educated in Italy, where they became acquainted with the Italian theories about civic art. By 1554, Italianate ideas concerning town-planning circulated freely in Mexico, with the publication in Mexico City of the dialogue by Francisco Cervantes de Salazar, entitled *Mexicus interior*. Its language reveals an intimate familiarity with the concepts of modular composition, canonical proportions, uniform street-façades, and monumental public squares. Cervantes was beyond doubt well read in contemporary Italian literature about architecture, but the peculiar implication of the *Mexicus interior* is that all propositions of Italianate theory were in practice, as physical realities, when Cervantes wrote.[131] It would be an excessive refinement of criticism to suggest that Cervantes described an ideal rather than an actual city. The *Mexicus interior* is not a delicate suggestion to the Mexicans to improve their urban appearance; it is an expression of astonishment at what was unique among the great cities of the world in the sixteenth century.

A major problem of relationship to Indian urban practice remains to be mentioned. The Mexican colonial solution is composed of elements that had already been anticipated in pre-Conquest Indian cities. Cortés and the conquistadores spoke with amazement of the great towns they overcame in their march upon Mexico. They were naturally anxious to enhance the splendor of their own achievement, by comparisons to the great cities of Spain. For the Anonymous Conqueror, Tlaxcala resembled Granada in some ways, Segovia in others. Cholula recalled Valladolid, and Huejotzingo evoked Burgos.[132] In fact, Indian urbanism contained a wide variety of civic plans. For example, a whole state, the "republic" of Tlaxcala, had been fortified. When pinched off from coastal resources by the Aztecs of the Valley of Mexico, the people surrounded their boundaries with high walls, many miles long, with ravelins, redoubts, and permanent garrisons, in order to undergo a permanent siege.[133] Other settlements were fortified peripherally. A large town like Huaquechula[134] huddled entirely, like Carcassonne or Avila, within crenelated city walls and heavily defended entrances. And in the Valley of Mexico, many Indian towns were unfortified, but at

130. R. Dohme, "Filarete's Traktat von der Architektur," *Jahrbuch der königlich preussischen Kunstsammlungen*, I (1880), p. 228. Oettingen has shown that the Valencian version was written *ca.* 1470–90. Filarete, *Tractat*, p. 12.

131. Cervantes de Salazar, *México en 1554*, pp. 97, 107.

132. Saville, ed., *Narrative . . . by the Anonymous Conqueror*, p. 55.

133. D. Muñoz Camargo, *Historia de Tlaxcala* (Mexico, 1892), p. 21. F. S. Clavigero, *The History of Mexico* (Philadelphia, 1817), II, 147. C. Cullen, tr. Cf. Wagner, *Rise of Cortés*, p. 151.

134. Cortés, *Letters*, I, 314.

their center a fortified temple enclosure stood upon the intersection of axial thoroughfares (Fig. 29). Motolinia described them admirably:[135] "In the whole land we find that the Indians had a large square court in the best part of the town; about a crossbowshot from corner to corner, in the large cities and provincial capitals; and in the smaller

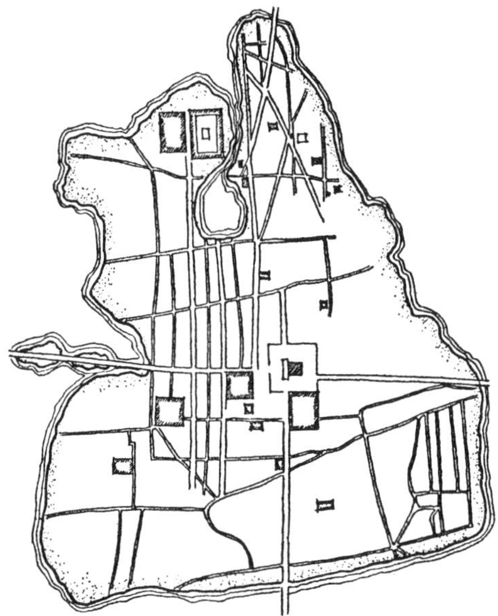

29. Tenochtitlan, reconstruction of the plan

towns, about a bowshot. The smaller the town, the smaller the court. They walled it about, leaving entrances to the streets and highways, which all led to the Devil's courtyard. In order to distinguish the temples, they laid out very straight highways, and one or two leagues in length. It was much to see from the temple tops how the people came from all the lesser towns along the straight roads to the courtyard."[136]

135. Motolinia, *Memoriales,* pp. 82–83: "En toda esta tierra hallamos que en lo mejor del pueblo hacian un gran patio cuadrado, cerca de un tiro de ballesta de esquina á esquina, en los grandes pueblos y cabecera de provincia, y en los menores pueblos obra de un tiro de arco, y en los menores, menor patio; y este cercábanle de pared, guardando sus puertas á las calles y caminos principales, que todos los hacian que fuesen á dar al patio del demonio; y por honrar más los templos, sacaban los caminos por cordel, muy derecho, de una y de dos leguas, que era cosa de ver desde lo alto cómo venian de todos los menores pueblos y barrios todos los caminos derechos al patio." Cf. I. Alcocer, *Apuntes sobre la antigua Mexico-Tenochtitlán* (Tacubaya, 1935) (Instituto panamericano de geografía e historia, Publicación 14), map after p. 15.

136. On the other hand, it is interesting to observe that in 1529, when Cortés was required in the *residencia* to justify the destruction of Tenochtitlan, many of his supporters came forth with declarations that the Indians had no urban science, and that the destruction of Tenochtitlan was necessary to make it habitable for Europeans. Alonso de Villanueva declared, "forzado se había de destruir porque los yndios no tienen en sus pueblos traza que satisfaga a la manera de nuestra España." In a sense, this was literally true. Martin Vázquez held that "los naturales thienen poco rrespeto a calles e pueblos muy desconcertados." *CDIAI,* XXVII (1877), Pt. I, 504, II, 165.

This was the case at Tenochtitlan. Four wide boulevards led to the walled temple precinct, with its fortified gateways. The temple enclosure itself stood among monumental palaces and public buildings.[137] In a northern section another great square, the marketplace of Tlatelolco, brought thousands of merchants together within a colonnaded enclosure.[138] The affinities to Italian theory are striking.

After the Conquest, the form of the Indian towns may have affected and conditioned the Spanish layouts. Mexico City still reveals the form of the Aztec capital. Many central streets follow the pattern of otherwise obliterated Indian canals. Likewise at Texcoco: the spacious ruins of the dwelling of Nezahualcoyotl survived as late as 1582. The plaza of modern Texcoco occupies the site of the largest patio of this residence, where the ball court of the Indian town was located. Thus colonial Texcoco drifted in among the ruins of the old city, and the modern reticulated appearance of the town may derive from a pre-Conquest plan.[139] In other words, the Indian civic armature was found to be highly suitable, and more easily adaptable than contemporary European models, even though individual Indian buildings, with their peculiar terraced structure and permeable materials, were useless to the white settlers.

The urban foundations of the sixteenth century in Mexico are relevant not only to the history of Spanish colonization, but to the history of urban forms in general. It may well be that the Mexican program constitutes one of the most important chapters of civic art in Occidental history. It enjoyed dimensions not often encountered in Europe: the dimensions of free experiment, surging expansion, and unlimited resources. There is nothing to compare with it either after the Roman Empire or before the industrial creations of the nineteenth century. Hence, in spite of the great economic disintegration of the Mexican town in recent years, and the inescapable squalor of its physical appearance, it offers urban forms that not merely absorbed the greater part of colonial energies, but also anticipated many of the normal solutions of later European practice.

137. Toussaint, *Planos.*

138. Diáz del Castillo, *True History,* Bk. I, chap. viii, 176–177.

139. J. B. Pomar, "Relación de Texcoco," *NCDHM,* III, 68. Often enough, however, a pre-Conquest settlement was totally unsuitable, as an Huaquechula, where the friars had to create rational order ("pulicia"). See Cervantes de Salazar, *Crónica de la Nueva España,* p. 539.

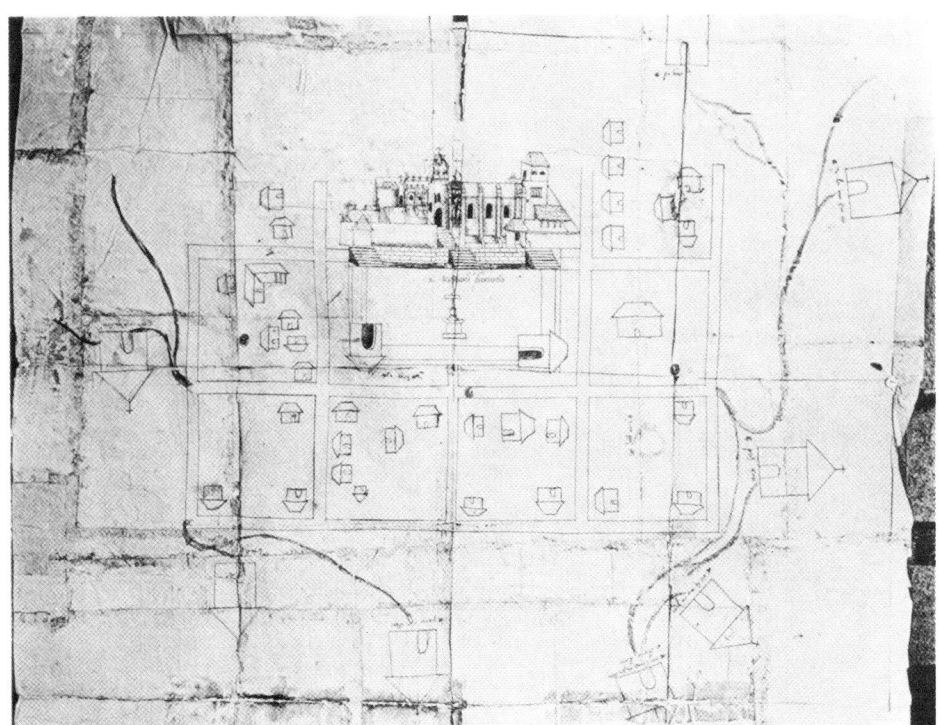

27. Huejutla (State of Hidalgo), plan in 1580

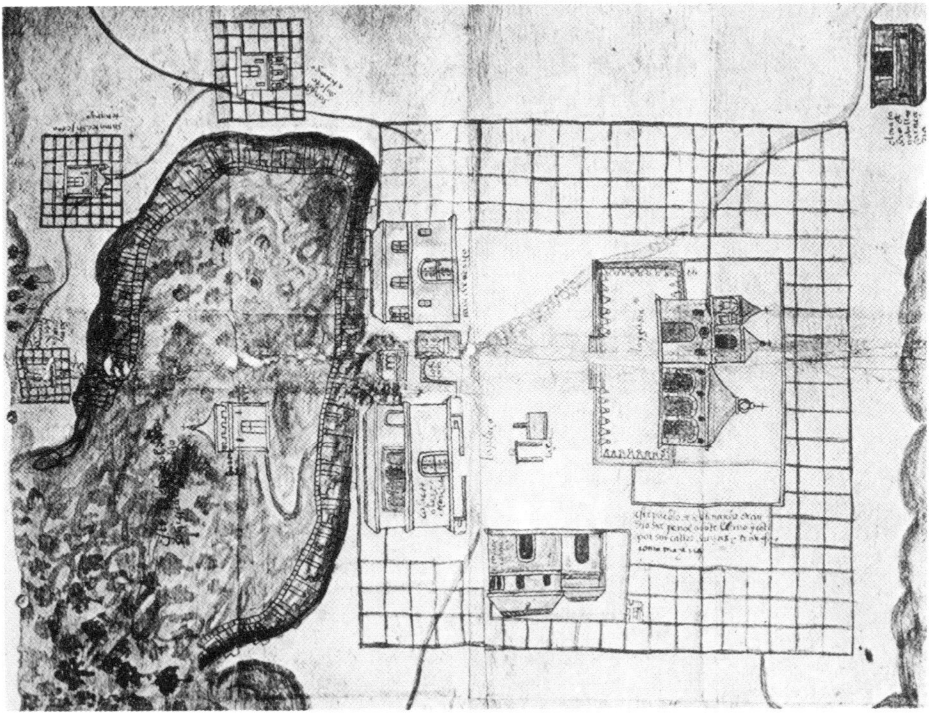

28. Tenango del Valle (State of Mexico), plan in 1582

30. Fray Diego de Chávez

31. Fray Pedro de Gante, portrait in the Museo Nacional de Historia

33. The Franciscans in Michoacan

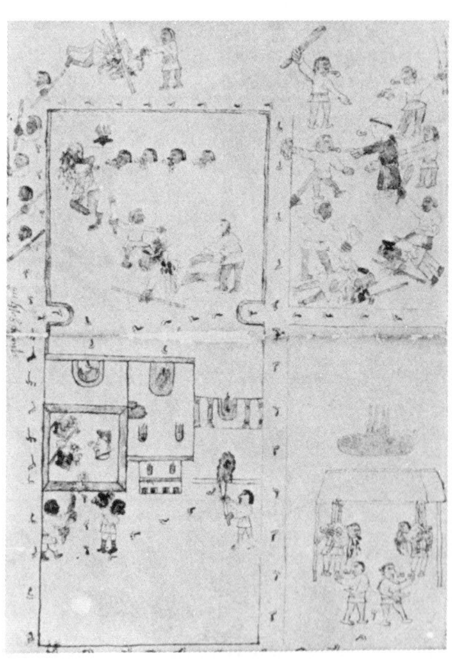

34. Indians in revolt at Ixtacmaxtitlan

III

DESIGN AND SUPERVISION

En lo que toca á edificios de monasterios y obras públicas, ha habido grandes yerros, porque ni en las trazas ni en las demás se hacia lo que convenia, por no tener quien los entendiese ni supiese dar órden en ello. . . .

Viceroy Mendoza, 1550 (*Instrucciones,* I, 46).

WHEN the transmission of architectural knowledge from one area to another happens in large part by graphic means, whether in printed matter or in manuscript materials, that fact is of major consequence for the correct interpretation of the transmitted architecture. For example, any detailed understanding of the Renaissance architecture of western Europe is impossible without knowledge of the literary continuum from Vitruvius to Alberti, Vignola, and their later editors and commentators. It may be observed, furthermore, when an architectural style is heavily dependent upon literary transmission of its methods and techniques, that the architecture tends towards internal conformity, that norms and canons prevail within rigorous standards of taste, and that free departures from the established repertory forms are relatively infrequent. Ultimately, however, as in the nineteenth century and at the present time, the proliferation of many separate and mutually exclusive literary canons of architectural style conduces to their collective cancellation. The theorists and practitioners revert to fundamental studies, and reconsider architectural design in terms of human needs and uses.

In sixteenth-century Mexico, there is no need to speak seriously of any substantial literary transmission of architectural knowledge. Architectural books did not circulate until after the middle of the century, when much of the need for abundant building of all kinds had been satisfied. The *túmulo imperial* (Fig. 442) by Arciniega, built in 1559–60, was the first edifice in Mexico of integral Renaissance form.[1] The earliest reference to a classicizing canon of architectural composition occurs in the dialogue, *Mexicus interior,* composed by Francisco Cervantes de Salazar in 1554, in which Vitruvian properties of proportion were admired in the columns of the edifice then used as the *palacio real* (Figs. 66, 67), at the corner of Tacuba and the

1. See pp. 332, 409, 467.

Empedradillo (see Chap. V, n. 5). The earliest reference we have to the presence of an architectural book in Mexico occurs in an inquisitorial listing of the library of one Pedro Cuadrado of Mexico City, who had in his possession, about 1569, a "libro de *Arquitectura* intitulado Vitrubio."[2] In 1577 a bookseller named Juan Fajardo returned to Mexico from a journey of three years in Spain with a large collection of books, perhaps including architectural publications.[3] In 1584, finally, among a shipment of forty cases of books sent to the dealer Diego Navarro Maldonado in Mexico from Medina del Campo, four folio copies of an edition of the "Arquitectura de Vitruvio" arrived, as well as four copies of a quarto edition of the "Arquitectura de Alberto [sc. Leone Battista Alberti]" and two copies of a folio edition of the "Architectura de Serlio."[4] It will be recalled, of course, that architectural books had been printed in Europe for only a century before this date. Alberti's *De re aedificatoria,* published at Florence in 1485, was the first printed treatise on building. Vitruvius was first printed at Rome in 1486; and Sebastiano Serlio's *Regole generali di architettura* was first published at Venice in 1537.[5] Outside Italy therefore, no substantial reliance upon a printed literary tradition was possible during the fifteenth century, and the appearance of Renaissance architecture in Spain, France, and northern Europe cannot be established until fairly advanced dates in the sixteenth century.

It is well known that Diego de Sagredo wrote a Vitruvian commentary entitled *Medidas del romano,* published at Toledo in 1526,[6] but Vitruvian studies at that time were a grafting of questionable survival value upon the hybrid stock of Spanish style. In 1565 Villalpando's translation of Books III and IV of Serlio appeared in Spain, and it was not before the seventeenth century that the printed transmission of architectural knowledge amounted to much.[7] Since the literary tradition was slow in acquiring weight in Spain, no rigorous adherence to the canon of classicizing taste may be supposed in America until after the middle of the sixteenth century.

Yet the formation of standards based upon literary texts can be established prior to the dated appearance of the books in America. Arciniega's túmulo imperial was a

2. [F. Fernández del Castillo], ed., *Libros y libreros en el siglo XVI* (Mexico, 1914), p. 479 (*Publ. AGN,* VI). Although the listing enumerates the forbidden books in Cuadrado's possession, there is no indication that the Vitruvius, like the other volumes on the list, was to be confiscated. It is likely that since the document also (*ibid.,* p. 493) implies that Tlaquiltenango was still a Franciscan convento, and since Hueychiapa is mentioned as a convento still in existence (see Appendix, p. 480), the document may antedate 1570 by a small interval.

3. J. T. Medina, *La Imprenta en México* (Santiago de Chile, 1908–12), I, ccxix–ccxx.

4. Fernández del Castillo, ed., *Libros y libreros,* pp. 263 ff.

5. W. B. Dinsmoor, "The Literary Remains of Sebastiano Serlio," *Art Bulletin,* XXIV (1942), 55–91, 115–154, gives an admirable survey of the state of the literary tradition of Renaissance building in the fifteenth and sixteenth centuries.

6. F. J. Sánchez-Cantón, *Fuentes literarias para la historia del arte español* (Madrid, 1923–41) (Spain. Junta para ampliación de estudios y investigaciones científicas. Centro de estudios históricos [Obras]), I, 7–8.

7. See M. Menéndez y Pelayo, *Historia de las ideas estéticas en España* (Santander, 1940), II, chap. xi.

Renaissance building designed by an architect whose skilful knowledge of classicizing form can have been secured only from books, since he arrived in America in 1545, aged about seventeen.[8] Internal evidence makes it almost certain that Arciniega had access to Serlio's methods of proportional design for classicizing forms. It is tempting to suppose that Arciniega knew Cervantes de Salazar, the humanist professor of rhetoric in Mexico, in whose writing a knowledge of classicizing architecture is revealed.[9]

It is occasionally suggested that the illustrations of non-architectural books served to inspire the designs of Mexican builders,[10] specially among friars whose technical training was deficient. Yet where any measure of canonical correctness is present in the design of a building, such as the façade of Tecali (Fig. 370), an accurate knowledge of modulation must be supposed. For it is asking too much both of xylographic or engraved illustration, and of the designers, to produce correct form from the diminutive indications of book-size graphic material. Book illustrations occasionally served the purposes of painters and sculptors. Builders, however, cannot proceed with approximate or unclear methods of composition. Exact knowledge is required, and in the case of classicizing form, the exact knowledge contained in architectural treatises is indispensable.

It has occasionally been supposed that the splendid examples of sixteenth-century architecture in Mexico were built according to plans and drawings prepared in Spain and obeyed in Mexico. In the first place, however, European builders of the time nowhere placed such reliance upon architectural drawings. Few of the standard conventions of architectural drawing were then in existence, and these were meant to afford only the most general notion of *parti* and plan. Accurate, graphic prevision of construction details was impossible in the sixteenth century. In the second place, the vast official documentation for the colony contains almost no reference to drawings prepared in Spain for American use. In the seventeenth century, it is true, one doubtful case is reported. Bishop Palafox, in the mid-seventeenth century, asserted that the plan for Puebla Cathedral had been sent from Spain between 1551 and 1555.[11] Internal evidence nevertheless makes it extremely improbable that any such plan, if sent, was ever followed (see p. 308). Very few other drawings for Mexican buildings were unquestionably prepared in Spain. In 1612, Viceroy Guadalcazar sent Philip III an elevation sketch for Mexico Cathedral, prepared in Mexico by Alonso Pérez de

8. Cuevas, *Historia de la iglesia en México*, III, 66.

9. Cervantes de Salazar, *México en 1554*, p. 97. See Fig. 442.

10. J. McAndrew and M. Toussaint, "Tecali, Zacatlán, and the 'Renacimiento Purista' in Mexico," *Art Bulletin*, XXIV (1942), 323.

11. D. Angulo Iníguez, "Las Catedrales mejicanas del siglo XVI," *Boletín de la real academia de la historia*, CXIII (1943), 165.

Castañeda. In 1615, the King returned another, alternate elevation sketch (*montea*), incorporating corrections to the original proposal offered by Juan Gómez de Mora, with the request that a suitable plan be devised to accommodate the changes in elevation.[12] In this instance, however, an initial project, prepared in Mexico, was merely amended in Spain. The initiative for the design did not come from the Peninsula. Concerning another recorded instance of direct graphic transmission from Spain we are very poorly documented. In his testament, Fernando Cortés mentioned briefly a plan sent by him from Spain in 1547, to be followed in the building of his favorite foundation, the Hospital de Nuestra Señora de la Concepción.[13] It is reasonable to believe that this traza was no more than a verbal sketch of the general dispositions (Fig. 97), to conform to current hospital design on the Peninsula. Cortés observed, in the testament, that the plans for the *capilla mayor* of the hospital church had been prepared in Mexico and were elaborated in a wooden model by Pedro Vázquez, whom he designates as *jumétrico,* or surveyor.[14] Where such specific partis were concerned, then, designers were available in Mexico, however unprofessional their antecedent training may have been. And Cortés' own instructions concerning the layout of the hospital would appear to pertain more to the general program for the buildings than to their actual design.

Still, it should not be imagined that early Mexican building was conducted in the absence of all graphic preparation. On the contrary, abundant records survive of the use of drawings prepared in Mexico by resident craftsmen. On December 15, 1554, for example, Archbishop Montúfar wrote to the Council of the Indies that it had been decided to follow the model of the Cathedral of Seville in the building of the new metropolitan cathedral, and that a plan (traza) to this effect was being sent for His Majesty's inspection.[15] The plan evidently accounted for maintaining the older structure intact during the future operations, and must have recorded a fair amount of detail. There can be no question that, whatever its character, it was prepared in Mexico, and that it resulted from decisions taken in Mexico, rather than under orders from the royal court.

12. I. Sariñana y Cuenca, *Noticiá breve de la solemne, deseada, ultima dedicación del templo metropolitano de México* (Mexico, 1668), fol. 6 ro.

13. Alaman, *Disertaciones,* II, Appendix II, 106.

14. *Ibid.* "Item mando, que la obra del hospital de Nuestra Señora de la Concepcion, que yo mando hacer en la ciudad de Mégico, en la Nueva-España, se acabe á mi costa, segun y de la manera que está trazada; e la capilla mayor de la iglesia de él, se acabe conforme á la muestra de madera que está hecha é hizo Pedro Vazquez Jumétrico, é á la traza que dijere el escrito que yo envié á la Nueva-España este presente año de mil é quinientos é cuarenta y siete. . . ."

15. *Epistolario,* VII, 307; A. M. Carreño, ed., *Un desconocido cedulario del siglo XVI* (Mexico, 1944), *passim.* Murillo, *Iglesias de México,* II, by Toussaint, 16; R. Ricard, *Études et documents pour l'histoire missionnaire de l'Espagne et du Portugal* (Louvain, Paris [1931]) (Collection de la section scientifique de l'Aucam, no. 1), p. 78. Among the men then available in Mexico who could have prepared this plan, we may name Gregorio de Saldaña, Alonso Franco, or Toribio de Alcaraz, among others.

Leaving aside for the moment the question of the famous traza or city plan for Mexico-Tenochtitlan, which is mentioned so often in the early records of the municipal cabildo before 1530 (see pp. 73–74), we read of many architectural drawings in sixteenth-century documents. In 1567 two were prepared for the cabildo, probably by the municipal alarife, Miguel Martínez, to illustrate the plan for the building of the proposed public granary.[16] What must have been a detailed plan, displaying all the public lands (ejidos) of the city was commissioned by the city from Antonio de Contreras in 1573, in an order qualifying it as a *pintura.* The finished work was perhaps not unlike the famous *Plano en papel de maguey.*[17] Many other trazas and pinturas are recorded in the minutes of the municipal council. In 1574 the councillors were ordered to consult with the alarife, then Claudio de Arciniega, upon the merits of a traza which had been prepared for the new town hall building.[18] Litigation over titles and boundaries not infrequently necessitated the preparation of detailed plans, as in 1576, when Arciniega was requested to draw up the proper boundaries in a case where the property-line between a tile-factory and certain public lands was in dispute.[19] In 1581, the alarife, Francisco de Ojeda, was ordered to draw plans for proposed shops with their upper stories. A *planta* and pintura were duly submitted, and the buildings were completed before February in 1582.[20]

Whether such numerous and detailed graphic preparations governed other kinds of buildings than those sponsored by the metropolitan council is not known. The records of the regular clergy rarely mention drawings, and their silence upon this point leads one to suspect that graphic preparation for building enterprises was far less important with them than among the city fathers, whose acts were all accountable and subject to strict revision. In general, the custom of preparing detailed plans was common only for the capital,[21] and it is obvious that conditions there differed vastly from those in rural districts. Most of the plans noted in the council minutes pertained to property-boundaries. The rapid growth and crowded space of the city made accurate graphic prevision far more necessary than elsewhere. When detailed building plans are called for, as with the shops designed by Francisco de Ojeda, an important factor of city revenue is at stake, and it may be supposed that the plans pertained more to the economic yield from the property than to its structure and design. In any case, the

16. *AC,* VII, 367.

17. *AC,* VIII, 62; Toussaint, etc., *Planos,* pp. 55–84.

18. *AC,* VIII, 136.

19. *Ibid.,* p. 238.

20. *AC,* VIII, 519–520. ". . . Mandaron quel alarife de la cibdad haga una planta donde ponga todo el citio del dicho lienzo e trace e señale que tantas tiendas se pueden hazer consus trastiendas y altos que sirvan para dormitorios de los moradores dellas. . . ." See also *ibid.,* pp. 523, 544, 560.

21. The single exception, to the writer's knowledge, was the *traza* for the Franciscan foundation at Chietla, sent in 1550 to Mexico City for the inspection of Viceroy Mendoza. "Mandamientos del virrey . . . Mendoza," *Boletín del archivo general de la nación,* X (1939), 269.

practice of graphic prevision was current in Mexico quite early: what we do not know is the extent to which drawings were used by builders operating outside the capital.

Certainly the Mendicant and clerical builders often had specific Spanish models in mind. We have seen that an early plan for the Cathedral in Mexico was based upon the cathedral in Seville (p. 106). Escobar tells us that when Father San Román secured permission in 1544 to build the new Augustinian church in Mexico City, he had it in mind to follow "la moda y traza del que tienen los Reverendos Padres Geronimos de Salamanca."[22] In 1585, again, when the Dominicans had occasion to build the Colegio San Luis in Puebla, they patterned it quite literally, even to the defects of claustral proportion, upon San Gregorio in Valladolid.[23] Between 1558 and 1571, the Dominicans rebuilt their metropolitan church. A seventeenth-century chronicler tells us that the plan was the same as that of Nuestra Señora de Atocha in Madrid.[24] Actually, however, this writer may have indulged in hyperbole, for he also relates that the façade was comparable to that of the Escorial. Yet the present plan of the church, which follows the outlines of the sixteenth-century edifice, is not unlike certain church plans of the early sixteenth century in Spain. We shall return to these filiations later (p. 286).

Thus it is sure that a literary transmission of architectural designs was rare in Mexico before the abundant importation of books in the third quarter of the century. But local craftsmen were capable of preparing plans and elevations long before this, so that there was no express need for designs to be brought from Europe. More important than any direct literary or graphic transmission, then, are the memories of admired buildings in Spain, informing the wishes and desires of the ecclesiastical *entrepreneurs* in Mexico. That these memories were vague and inexact, unsupported by working measurements, will later be shown.

In such a situation, where the initial builders are reliant entirely upon their antecedent training and a casual knowledge of matters of construction, it may be expected that their style will display wide divergences, both internally and with respect to contemporary European architecture. The absence of a firm literary or graphic transmission helps to account, in Mexico as in Spain, for the rich non-conformities of sixteenth-century building. And as Mexico is more distant than Spain in space and in culture from Italy, the source of normative Renaissance style, so may it be expected that variants and free inventions will be particularly abundant in the colony.

22. Escobar, *Americana thebaida*, p. 262. See also Basalenque, *Historia . . . Michoacan*, p. 28b, and Grijalva, *Crónica de la orden de N. P. S. Augustín*, pp. 211–212, as well as F. Gómez de Orozco, "Monasterios de la orden de San Agustín en Nueva España en el siglo XVI," *Revista mexicana de estudios históricos*, I (1927), 46.

23. Dávila Padilla, *Historia . . . Santiago de México*, p. 571; Vetancurt, *Chrónica, Tratado*, p. 54.

24. H. Ojea, *Libro tercero de la historia religiosa de la provincia de México* (Mexico, 1897), p. 10.

For more than a full generation after the fall of Tenochtitlan in 1521, no competent professional architect[25] was available in New Spain. Toward the middle of the sixteenth century, the highest authorities of Church and State complained of the lack of proper personnel. Their remarks are of considerable interest, because at that time the vast architectural production of the sixteenth century in Mexico was well beyond the initial stage. By 1550, in effect, many complex acquisitions of European art had been transmitted to America, with an immediacy unmatched by any other colonial effort in modern history.

The texts of the period reflect an attitude of frustration. Zumárraga, writing to Philip II in 1547, complained that there was no master of sufficient competence to whom might be confided the enterprise of laying the foundations for the new cathedral in Mexico City.[26] In 1550, Viceroy Mendoza, one of the most able administrators whom the Spanish Crown sent to America, wrote likewise, in the instructions to his successor in office. No one was available in New Spain who understood construction or knew how to supervise work. Great errors therefore had been committed in the erection of monastic establishments and public works.[27] Again, Archbishop Montúfar complained to the Council of the Indies in 1555, asking that a competent master be sent to work on the cathedral, since there was none at hand in Mexico.[28]

The problem of personnel was not so hopeless as the prelates and the Viceroy implied. If there were no architects trained in design, a few professional European builders in Mexico were capable of preparing architectural plans before 1551, such as those sent to the Council of the Indies by the ecclesiastical cabildo of the City of Mexico. The plans (now lost) were for the new cathedral; they were based upon the Cathedral of Seville, providing for the construction of a seven-naved edifice.[29] But since Archbishop Montúfar by implication rejected these plans in 1555, they cannot have been adequate. Another clue to an architectural personality is offered by Viceroy Mendoza. In the *Instrucción* of 1550 he speaks of one Toribio de Alcaraz, implying that he was knowledgeable in building matters, and that he had often traveled on tours of inspection at the Viceroy's request, examining the conduct of various opera-

25. The term *architectus* was used in Spain shortly after 1516, referring to Pedro de Gumiel. See V. Lampérez y Romea, *Historia de la arquitectura cristiana española en la edad media* (2d ed. Madrid, 1930), I, 32. Indeed, the term "architect" is correctly defined as "one who plans buildings as opposed to one who executes them, and furthermore one who plans with a view to aesthetically as well as functionally satisfactory results, as opposed to one who concerns himself only with the technical requirements of building. . . ." N. Pevsner, "The Term 'Architect' in the Middle Ages," *Speculum*, XVII (1942), 549. To satisfy this Renaissance and modern definition of the term. Claudio de Arciniega may be adduced as the first architect with an identifiable oeuvre in Mexico. See pp. 121–123.

26. Cuevas, *Documentos inéditos*, p. 140. ". . . No bastarían todos los diezmos, ni veo maestro de tanta suficiencia a quien se puede fiar semejante obra."

27. *Instrucciones que los vireyes*, I, 46.

28. *Epistolario*, VIII, 33. ". . . Mándenos enviar la traza que fuere servido y algún buen maestro que acá no le hay."

29. *Epistolario*, VI, 63. Also Ricard, *Études*, p. 78. Carreño, ed., *Un desconocido cedulario . . .*, *passim*.

tions, such as monastic establishments, bridges, and public buildings. At the time, Alcaraz was in Veracruz. It is reasonable to infer that, whatever the inspector's capacity, Mendoza did not esteem him competent enough for more practical purposes.[30]

There are other indications that a colony of European building craftsmen was resident in Mexico City well before 1550. The Augustinian missionaries at Tiripitio, in the bishopric of Michoacan, were engaged after 1537 in the construction of a large church and monastery. The Indians of the area, who had been ignorant of building skills, were taught the arts of stonecutting and joinery by Spanish craftsmen. These were brought to Tiripitio by the missionaries for that specific purpose.[31] The Augustinians then reversed the process, sending Indians to Mexico for training. They were placed in apprenticeship to masters practising those particular crafts of which the mission had need.[32]

The identification of these masters is far from hopeless. The most likely candidate, of course, is the Portuguese mason, Diego Díaz of Lisbon.[33] His activity in New Spain began about 1526–27, and in an autobiographical notice composed about 1547, he recorded the claim that he had taught all the Indian masons of Mexico their trade. During the rule of the Second Audiencia (1531–35) he was *maestro de obras* for the capital, and he says that during this period, many Spaniards and Indians had profited from his knowledge. It is not unlikely that the many traces of Manueline ornament may be attributed to his teaching in sixteenth-century Mexico. His own work is attested by signature and the date 1535 upon an *ajimez* window formerly situated at a corner of the east range of the Hospital de Jesús in Mexico City (see p. 221).

Other men very probably responsible for the training of Indian craftsmen were Rodrigo Pontesillas and a man designated as "maestre martin." These two are mentioned here because in 1530 they were characterized as the best building craftsmen in

30. *Instrucciones que los vireyes . . .*, I, 47. "V. Sa. mande buscar dos ó tres personas que sean buenos oficiales, y déles salarios en quitas, y vacaciones y corregimientos para que anden por toda la tierra visitando las obras y enmendando los defectos que son muchos. . . . Toribio de Alcaraz, que estaba en el puerto cuando V. Sa. vino, lo ha hecho muy bien muchas veces, así en los monasterios y puentes, como en los demás edificios, pueda ser uno de ellos." An autobiographical notice, recorded about 1547, when the question of the new distribution of encomiendas was uppermost in every white civilian's mind, mentions his arrival in New Spain about 1544, and that his profession had been and still was that of "Maestro mayor de obras de cantería, y en el dicho ofiçio está presto a seruir a Su Magestad, ofreçiéndose en qué." Thus his services to Mendoza probably were rendered after 1547. Icaza, *Conquistadores y pobladores*, II, 140. See H. E. Wethey, "The Problem of Toribio de Alcaraz," *Gazette des Beaux-Arts*, XXXI (1947), 165–174.

31. Basalenque, *Historia . . . Michoacán*, p. 20b. "En lo que mas se aventajaron, fue en la canteria, y samblaje, porque como para estas dos cosas, que eran necessarias para la Iglesia, y Convento, se escogieron buenos oficiales Españoles de que ya avia abundancia en la tierra, enseñarōles bien, y salieron tan eminentes, que ellos por si hazian muchas obras."

32. Grijalva, *Crónica de la orden de N. P. S. Augustín*, pp. 222–223.

33. Icaza, *Conquistadores y pobladores*, II, 310. ". . . Á veynte años que pasó a esta Nueua Spaña . . . todos los yndios que al presente son offiçiales de cantería, lo son por su yndustria. . . ." *Ibid.*, p. 157. ". . . de su arte se an aprouechado muchos spañoles e naturales." Alamán, *Disertaciones*, II, 85–86.

the city.[34] Rodrigo Pontesillas' name first appeared in the municipal records in 1527, when he submitted a bid for the construction of the water-conduit from Churubusco, and on April 14, 1527, he was appointed *maestro mayor* for the city. His death, however, occurred before May 6, 1532, so that he could have influenced Indian masons only during ten years at the most, and from 1524 at the latest, since that is the date of his first recorded appearance in the city. "Maese Martin" is more shadowy, and the name may refer either to Cristóbal Martín or to Martín de Sepúlveda. Of Cristóbal Martín we know that he was paid an annual salary in 1524 for his services to the city in matters of construction, but in May of 1525, the municipal minutes note that he was suffering an illness and would henceforth be paid only half his usual salary as maestro de obras. Since his name does not reappear as "Cristóbal Martín" in the town records, it is more plausible to identify "maestre martin," who does reappear, as Martín de Sepúlveda. He was the maestro de obras appointed by Cortés shortly after the fall of Tenochtitlan, and he directed the construction of many important works. Among them were the primitive cathedral (Figs. *210–214*), the *casas reales* (Figs. 66, 67) on the site of the present Monte de Piedad, and the early water supply of the city. His presence in Mexico City was considered indispensable, so that he was forbidden to participate in any of the later campaigns of conquest following the capture of Tenochtitlan. In the fulfilment of his duties, Sepúlveda must have directed very large numbers of Indian workmen, for no other laboring population was available.

The titles of maestro de obras and alarife de la ciudad were interchangeable during the sixteenth century, and signified the incumbent of an appointment in the power of the municipal councillors. The salary varied between fifty and two hundred pesos per annum,[35] and the official was responsible for the technical supervision of all public works in the city, such as the building and repair of roads and bridges, the maintenance of the water-supply, and the construction of such edifices as municipal shops, slaughterhouses, granaries, public colonnades and civic buildings such as the town hall, and the regulation of property-lines between land grants within the city limits. In all his undertakings the alarife was subject to the approval of another official, the *obrero mayor*.[36] This personage was not a technical expert, but the equivalent of a commissioner of public works, and he was appointed from among the number of the town councillors. The initiative for new undertakings was in the obrero mayor's

34. *AC*, II, 49. ". . . los mejores oficiales que ay en la cibdad es un potencillas y maestre martin. . . ." Pontesillas: *AC*, I, 128, 129, 166. *AC*, II, 178. *AC*, I, 17. On August 19, 1524, Pontesillas asked to be made a citizen and be awarded a plot of land in the city. Thus he cannot be numbered among the first European settlers of Mexico. The conquistadores did not need to petition for citizenship. Pontesillas probably arrived in Mexico early in 1524. Cristóbal Martín: *AC*, I, 27, 42, 59, 63. Martin de Sepúlveda: Icaza, *Conquistadores y pobladores*, I, 134–135, gives an account of his life written by his widow about 1547.

35. The term alarife designates one experienced in the auxiliary arts of construction. Rodrigo de Pontesillas received fifty pesos *ca.* 1530 (*AC*, I, 129); Miguel Martínez was paid two hundred pesos between 1563 and 1573 (*AC*, VII, 232).

36. *AC*, X, 159.

hands, and he exercised much control over the allocation of Indian labor reserved for municipal needs. But the alarife de la ciudad contributed the technical knowledge to all municipal building enterprises. There is even some evidence that the allocation of Indian labor actually passed into the hands of the alarife about 1549, when Antonio García Saldaña was in office.[37] Hence, it is probably among the official alarifes that we may search for those European building craftsmen who were in direct contact with Indian labor, and in a position to impart technical instruction.

Among the names in this list of municipal architects, Sepúlveda, Cristóbal Martín, and Rodrigo Pontesillas are already known. Three other men, occupying the office before 1550, may be mentioned in connection with their possible influence upon the Indian building craftsmen. Of Alonso García, it is not clear whether he was the same individual as the soldier named Alonso García Bravo, whom Cortés designated as a "muy buen jumétrico," and who was entrusted with the important task of laying out the streets of Tenochtitlan in 1522. Alonso García Bravo had already taken part in the building of old Veracruz, and it is known that he later moved to Oaxaca and became an encomendero.[38] It is not unlikely that this conquistador was maestro de obras of the city between 1524 or 1525 and 1527. If a homonym is involved, the fact is of little consequence to the present discussion. In any case, Alonso García, the maestro de obras, was engaged in 1524 in directing the construction of the town hall (*obras de las casas de concejo*). In 1527 it was ordered that no house might be built on any city land unsurveyed by the maestro. In that same year, moreover, García competed unsuccessfully against his successor, Pontesillas, in offering bids for the construction of the Churubusco conduit, and it was in April that Pontesillas displaced García as maestro de obras. The brief accounts of these events in the municipal minutes reflect much strategic maneuvering among the interested parties for what was in all probability a highly coveted and influential public position, carrying much authority over land assignments within the city.

Juan de Entrambasaguas, an illiterate mason, first appeared upon the record of the cabildo in September 1527, when he received payment for quarrying the stone needed in the building of a public fountain.[39] In connection with this fountain, incidentally, it was specified that the duty of the alarife, then Rodrigo Pontesillas, was to supervise the labor of the Indians and the mixing of the mortar. Entrambasaguas' appointment as alarife was recorded on November 8, 1531. During his term of office, we find him supervising various enterprises. At the jail there was the question of replacing some wooden columns with stone ones in 1532; and in May, a similar problem arose with the

37. *AC*, V, 204, 260–261.

38. Toussaint, etc., *Planos*, p. 21. *AC*, I, 16, 23, 40, 58, 77, 108. *AC*, I, 117, 128, 129.

39. *AC*, I, 146; II, 48, 142, 165–166; III, 36; IV, 83, 99–101.

portico of the town hall, where a defective stone was being used in the colonnade. Another commission given Entrambasaguas was to design an inn on the road to Veracruz, near the Cofre de Perote. Entrambasaguas established only the plan in 1537; the actual construction was directed by one Juan de León. Finally, in 1537, he was entrusted with the task of building some two-storied shops on the site of the slaughterhouse.

Juan Franco (died 1554) held the office of alarife for fourteen years, longer than any other incumbent in the sixteenth century.[40] He belonged to the carpenters' craft, and we first encounter his name in the municipal records in 1538, as the recipient of an urban land grant (solar). He was appointed maestro mayor by the council on September 14, 1540, and during his long term, he was associated with no important building enterprises, other than the building of a corral for the city in 1542, and the widening of a bridge. We do learn, however, that he disposed of the labor of the Indians of the town of Ixtapalapa, the municipal encomienda, and that in 1543 he served as paymaster, dispensing municipal funds among these Indian laborers.

TABLE D

MAESTROS DE OBRAS OR ALARIFES DE LA CIUDAD DE MÉXICO

Martin de Sepúlveda	after 1521–?	Icaza, *Conquistadores y pobladores,* I, 134–135
Cristóbal Martin	?–1525	*AC,* I, 27
Alonso García	1525–27	*AC,* II, 40, 77, 108, 117
Rodrigo Pontesillas	1527–31	*AC,* I, 129
Juan de Entramabasaguas	1531–40	*AC,* II, 142–143
Juan Franco	1540–54	*AC,* IV, 211
Antonio García Saldana	1554–55	*AC,* VI, 147
Claudio de Arciniega	1555–63	Cuevas, *Historia de la iglesia en México,* III, 66; Cervantes de Salazar, *Crónica de la Nueva España,* p. 321
Antonio García Saldana	?1563–65	*AC,* VII, 232
Miguel Martínez	1565–73	*AC,* VII, 232
Diego de Arteaga	1573	*AC,* VIII, 46
Francisco Espino	1573	*AC,* VIII, 73
Claudio de Arciniega	1573–78	*AC,* VIII, 120, 315
Cristóbal Carballo	1578–81	*AC,* VIII, 315
Juan Francisco de Hojeda	1581–84	*AC,* VIII, 473
Pedro Ortiz de Orive	1584–?	*AC,* VIII, 666
Juan Francisco de Hojeda	?–1590	*AC,* X, 2
Cristóbal Carballo	1590–92	*AC,* X, 16
Juan Fernández Peraleda	1592–93	*AC,* X, 178
Rodrigo Alonso	1593–94	*AC,* XI, 79–81
Cristóbal Carballo	1595–?	*AC,* XIII, 111, 240, 258

40. *AC,* IV, 148; VII, 147; IV, 154, 256–287, 266, 345, 349. It is perhaps significant that Juan Franco's autobiographical notice, composed about 1547, makes no mention either of his profession or of his office. This suggests that other building craftsmen of the time may be hidden behind the blank indications of Icaza, *Conquistadores y pobladores,* II, 115.

On the whole, the municipal minutes do not indicate that the alarifes were prolific builders. Their main duties were to attend to maintenance, repair, and supervision. Only occasionally were they called upon to provide design or supervise new construction. But these men wielded political authority, and they were in touch with Indian labor. Therefore they are relevant to the present task of identifying the men under whom Indians might have learned European building trades.

Little is known about other European building craftsmen active in private undertakings. We have the name of Luis de la Torre, who advised Cortés about 1523 on the building of the new palace (*casas nuevas*) on the east side of the plaza mayor (Figs. 71–72). Torre laid out the plan with the help of one Juan Rodríguez, who was either a plasterer or bricklayer. In 1530, two masons were granted citizenship, Pedro Vázquez (whom we have met as the model-maker for Cortés, see p. 106) and another Portuguese, Jaime Trias. Of these men, nothing further is known. Jorge de Xexas, employed by the council as a bricklayer in 1524, is likewise obscure, although it seems that in 1525 he subscribed to the anti-Cortés faction. Still another plasterer and bricklayer, Juan de Santa Ana, was a property-owner in 1526. Carpenters were relatively numerous. We have seen that Juan Franco, the alarife, was a carpenter: other lesser-known figures of the trade were Diego Ramírez, Martin Pérez, and Juan de Larios, all property-owners in 1526. These few names exhaust the record of civilians who were professionally engaged in building activities prior to 1550.[41]

Now to what extent did such men guide the extensive building campaigns throughout the rest of New Spain? Their influence must have been manifested through one or both of two channels: direct participation in construction or the training of Indian workmen. Direct participation of civilians elsewhere than in Mexico City or Puebla is rarely recorded. Only two cases come to notice: the Spanish craftsmen brought to Tiripitio by the Augustinians after 1537 (see p. 152), and the Spanish artisans sent to New Galicia in the 1530's, to assist fray Juan de Padilla (OFM)

41. Rodríguez: "Documentos . . . Cortés," *Publ. AGN*, XXVII (1935), 307–308, 321, 325. Trias: *AC*, II, 64, 65. Xexas: *AC*, I, 31, 40, 47, 54. Santa Ana: *AC*, I, 74. Carpenters: *AC*, I, 29, 39, 47, 64, 80. Sawyers: see pp. 295–296. In 1540, Francisco de Chaves, a *maestro de cantería* from Azpeitia, contracted to go to Mexico to build for Zumárraga. See Angulo, "Catedrales mejicanas," *Boletín de la real academia de la historia*, CXIII, 149. His arrival has not been established, and no one answering his description was listed in the compilations of 1546–47.

Little is known of the later history of the numerous builders and masons who were active in Santo Domingo after 1510. Their movements should be traced closely. See F. A. de Icaza, comp., "Miscelanea histórica," *Revista mexicana de estudios históricos*, II (1928), Apéndice, 38–39, and Miguel Solá, *Historia del arte hispano-americano* (Barcelona [1935]), p. 22. (Colección Labor. Seccion IV; Artes plásticas, no. 371–372). See M. S. Noel, *Teoría histórica de la arquitectura virreinal* (Buenos Aires, 1932), p. 115. J.-B. Delawarde, "Les premiers Monuments chrétiens du Nouveau Monde," *Journal de la société des américanistes de Paris*, nouvelle sér., XXX (1938), 209–212. T. T. Waterman, "The Gothic Architecture of Santo Domingo," *Bulletin of the Pan American Union*, LXXVII (1943), 312–325. E. W. Palm of Ciudad Trujillo has in press a definitive work entitled "Los Monumentos arquitectónicos coloniales de la Española."

in his labors among the Indians at Zapotlan.[42] In fact, the Indians themselves insisted that the white civilians never participated. An interesting letter, written by some Indian chiefs to the King in 1570, categorically states that no Spaniard had ever assisted in the building of churches and government edifices. All the religious and civil buildings were the work solely of Indians.[43]

In another sense, an organized movement existed to keep Europeans from participating in architectural activities outside the capital. The Franciscan missionaries were particularly insistent upon preventing any Europeans other than themselves from mingling with the Indian communities. The friars were at one time accused of wishing to convert New Spain into a huge monastery,[44] and there is reason to believe that some of the principal figures in the Franciscan Order conspired in 1529 to prohibit entirely the further immigration of civilians.[45] By implication, the hermetic enterprise of the friars excluded European skilled labor. Any white driven by imperatives other than those of the Mendicants was *persona non grata*.[46]

That the white artisans should have extended any generous instruction to Indians beyond that which has been mentioned, seems as improbable as that they participated intimately in widespread building. There are indications that the whites were, on the contrary, reluctant to give any such instruction for fear of increasing economic competition. Motolinia relates that the Spaniards were extremely careful to guard trade processes from the Indians, without great success.[47] The formation of trade guilds later in the century, such as that of the painters and gilders, organized in 1557, with an administrative staff, inspections and examinations, surely represents to some extent the effort of white craftsmen to maintain control over a market invaded by Indian competitors.[48]

If it is necessary to deprecate the role of professional architects and skilled white labor in the "croisade monumentale," in the "fièvre architecturale"[49] that possessed

42. Mendoza, *Fragmentos*, pp. 23–27.

43. "Carta de los señores y principales," *NCDHM*, IV, 129.

44. See the angry report by Archbishop Montúfar, of May 15, 1556. [A. de Montúfar] *Descripción del arzobispado de México hecha en 1570*, pp. 421–456. L. García Pimentel, ed.

45. J. F. Ramírez, "Noticias de la vida y escritos de fray Toribio de Motolinia," *CDHM*, I, li.

46. Mendieta, *Historia eclesiástica indiana*, p. 501.

47. Motolinia, "Historia de los indios de la Nueva España," *CDHM*, I, p. 213. H. B. Parkes, *A History of Mexico* (Boston, 1938), pp. 92–93.

48. M. Toussaint, *La Pintura en México durante el siglo XVI* (Mexico, 1936), pp. 39–40. (Enciclopedia ilustrada mexicana, II.) Viceroy Mendoza reports that he organized Indian trades to some extent during his term of office. "Yo he procurado que haya oficiales indios de todos oficios en esta república, é así viene á haber gran cantidad dellos. Estos tales oficiales se manda que no usen los oficios si no estuvieren examinados conforme á lo que en las repúblicas Despaña se hace; é porque las ordenanzas que se han hecho vienen á decir quel oficial que se hubiere de examinar sepa enteramente todo el oficio en perficion, y que si dejare de saber alguna cosa, que no pueda tener tiendas, sino que tenga amo como aprendiz por excluirlos de todo; y siempre he proveido que particularmente examinen los indios y españoles en aquellas cosas que salen bien, é de aquello les den título é permitan que tengan tiendas porque haya mas oficiales y no haya tanta carestía." *Instrucciones que los vireyes* . . ., I, 35–36. The regulations are metropolitan and restrictive in character, implicitly unfavorable to Indians. See pp. 364–365.

49. Gillet, "L'Art dans l'Amérique latine," *His-*

New Spain, to whom shall the technical direction be attributed? There is overwhelming reason to believe that it was integrally assumed by the members of the Mendicant Orders, Franciscans, Augustinians, and Dominicans.

Before 1550, there were certainly at least seventy-five major monastic establishments in existence, founded with some architectural pretensions by the missionaries of the three Orders (Fig. *16*). We have already discussed the methods employed by the various rules. It is not to be thought that the construction of a church and monastery was the sole objective of the missionary enterprise. On the contrary, its monumental phase was merely a tangible expression of the enormous labors of the "spiritual conquest." Both Franciscans and Augustinians, and later the Dominicans, were chiefly concerned, in the material aspect of their labors, with establishing proper settlements for their charges. Thus the Franciscan fray Juan de San Miguel in Michoacan (*obit* 1555), in the role of culture-donor: his concern was with every aspect of communal existence, choosing an urban site, laying out the plan of the streets, squares, and buildings, establishing the administrative machinery, and introducing the practice of mechanical arts.[50] The Augustinians left the most complete record of their urban foundations; the technique was like that of the Franciscans. The Dominicans of Oaxaca assumed similar responsibilities. At Cuilapan, for instance, the population was induced after 1555 to move to a site more amply provided with water, and fray Domingo de Aguiñaga himself participated in the manual labor of constructing the conduits.[51] In all three Orders, such operations went forward in the absence of outside financial support.

Within the Mendicant Orders, the incidence of formal and practical building knowledge is difficult to determine. With one questionable exception, nothing is known about the pre-colonial architectural activity of the friars whose names are associated with building enterprises in America. The exception is fray Martín de Valencia (*obit* 1534). Mendieta says he built several establishments in Spain before his arrival in Mexico aged over fifty.[52]

toire de l'art, VIII, 1023. Gillet's article remains a useful survey of Latin American art, though marred by gross generalities, such as the insistence that colonial art contains no regional variety, but is an "art de gouvernement" throughout the hemisphere. Elsewhere an analogical method conduces to the comparison of viceregal America with Ptolemaic Egypt, or Africa in the time of St. Augustine.

50. Rea, *Crónica de la orden de N. serafico P. S. Francisco*, p. 39: ". . . lo primero que hizo . . . fue, fundar los Pueblos, y Ciudades, diuidiéndolas en calles, plaças, y edificios, escogiendo el sitio, y cielos . . . Instruyòlo en el modo que auia de obseruar en su gouierno, componiendo sus Republicas, trayendo de todos oficios para que los aprendiessen; y assi salieron los Tarascos grãdes oficiales." See also Beaumont, *Crónica de Michoacán*, II, 136; F. de la Maza, *San Miguel de Allende* (Mexico, 1939), pp. 25–30.

51. Burgoa, *Geográfica descripción*, I, 398 ff. Among the Dominicans, however, a sharp distinction was drawn between *religiosos legos* and *religiosos de coro*. The latter were dedicated to study, meditation, and preaching, while the lay brothers were entrusted with temporal affairs and the tasks of administration. One consequence was that the most learned members of the Order took no part in material concerns such as building. Dávila Padilla, *Historia . . . Santiago de México*, pp. 196–197.

52. Mendieta, *Historia eclesiástica indiana*, p. 573. The buildings in Spain are: S. María del Berrogal, near

His residence in America was filled with administrative duties. Elected first Custodian of the Mexican Province of the Holy Gospel in 1524, he served as guardian of the new establishment in Oaxaca (1529), following a year as guardian at Tlaxcala. Motolinia says fray Martín built the monastic establishment in Tlaxcala, but it is difficult to fit such responsibilities among his other duties. Thus, although he participated in the first evangelical labors (Xochimilco, Coyoacan, Cuitlahuac) in 1524, it is excessive to identify him as the technically competent person who must have stood at the head of the pretentious undertaking at Tlaxcala (Figs. *157*, 164).[53]

Authentic builders among the friars, to present knowledge, were few. Fray Juan de Alameda, OFM (*obit* 1570) is probably one of them. He arrived in Mexico with Zumárraga in 1528. It was he who moved an alleged forty thousand inhabitants of Huejotzingo from the unhealthful ravines to their present location in 1529. He also laid out the town and built a convento. The present fabric at Huejotzingo (Fig. *142*) is not certainly his work, although building operations were surely in progress during April of 1529.[54] His town-planning activity was continued at Tula, where he was guardian in 1539. At Huaquechula (Fig. 197), also, where he is buried, he built the church after 1533, and before 1570 when he died.

Another active builder was fray Francisco de Tembleque, OFM, an autodidact, according to Mendieta.[55] He built the aqueduct from Zempoala to Otumba, which carried water for forty-five kilometers over a system of 156 arches of imposing proportions (Fig. 100). The work lasted from *ca.* 1541 to *ca.* 1557, and Tembleque was the only European involved in the enterprise, conceiving and executing it himself. In 1564, Tembleque was consulted by the metropolitan council upon its water supply.

Fray Diego de Chávez (Fig. 30) is the only monastic architect of this period for whom a coherent, sequential record is available.[56] Born of a powerful family in Badajoz, he came to Mexico as a boy (before 1535), and was nurtured in the household of his uncle, Pedro de Alvarado. He took the Augustinian habit in Mexico City in 1535, and next appears at the mission of Tiripitio in Michoacan, during 1537. It will be remembered that important works were in progress at Tiripitio from 1538 until

Belvis, before 1516; S. Onofre de la Lapa, and N. S. de Monteceli del Hoyo. See Madoz, *Diccionario . . .*, IV (1846), 149, on Belvis (convento now in ruins); and X (1847), 73, on S. Onofre de la Lapa.

53. *Ibid.*, pp. 242, 540–543, 586, 598. Motolinia, "Historia de los indios de la Nueva España," *CDHM*, I, 158. Motolinia was resident in Tlaxcala in 1540, writing his memoirs, according to Mendieta, *op. cit.*, p. 298.

54. *Ibid.*, p. 654. Torquemada, . . . *Monarchia indiana*, III, 478, is the source of the usual attribution of Huejotzingo. Motolinia, "Historia de los indios de la Nueva España," *CDHM*, I, 119–120.

55. Mendieta, *op. cit.*, p. 697. Ricard, *La "Conquête spirituelle" du Mexique*, pp. 176–177, gives a full account and bibliography. See also *AC*, VII, 209, 289; *Catálogo . . . Hidalgo*, II, 236.

56. Grijalva, *Crónica de la orden de N. P. S. Augustín*, pp. 448–450; J. González de la Puente, "Primera parte de la choronica augustiniana de Mechoacan," *Colección de documentos inéditos y raros para la historia eclesiástica mexicana, pub. por . . . F. Plancarte y Navarrete* (Cuernavaca. 1907), pp. 33, 249, 254–255. Basalenque, *op. cit.*, pp. 20–21, 56, 59b, 61b. Escobar, *Americana thebaida*, pp. 156, 286, 291–292.

1548. The young friar probably learned with the Indians, from the Spanish craftsmen brought to the site. His architectural activity is first documented at Tacambaro in 1538, where he participated in the laying of the cornerstone for the church. After the completion of the campaign at Tiripitio, fray Diego went to Yuriria in Michoacan, *ca.* 1550. Chávez is specifically named as the maestro mayor and architect. He built a provisional structure at first, and then vacillated between two sites, laying foundations at both of them. His final choice rested on the earlier site (Fig. *118*), and work was pushed nearly to completion. He later returned to Tiripitio *ca.* 1562 and completed an unfinished doorway. Elected bishop of Michoacan in 1572, he died before assuming office, and remained legendary for his choleric temper and for the "Escorial" he claimed to have built at Yuriria.

In addition to these few men, the texts often attribute a technical activity to personalities who cannot be described as professionals in any sense of the term. Their attitude towards architecture can best be designated as that of the "good householder." They were solicitous for the orderly operation of an establishment,[57] probably gifted with mechanical ability, and more often than not, engaged in projecting, organizing, and realizing with their own hands the needed constructions and improvements. At the same time they maintained an intense activity in other fields of effort. Such was the missionary in remote parts, doing a single-handed task of indoctrination, town planning, building, engineering and general education, in an area of several days' travel from one end to the other. But the "good householder" cannot be credited, even where his participation is manifest, with the great monastic structures which texts often attribute to him.[58] Such enterprises must have been executed by trained persons whose names have been lost.[59] In any case, the versatile, effective friar was the normal type of missionary during this period; he was trained by circumstances, and the pattern that he created survived long after the restriction of Mendicant authority in New Spain.[60]

Events occurring at Acambaro, allegedly between 1529 and 1532, are typical of such activity. Fray Antonio Bermul, OFM, organized the water supply, and his companion, fray Juan Lazo y Quemada, collaborated in laying out the town, in which a rectory and a hospital were built.[61] Fray Pedro de Pila, OFM, is typical too:

57. Certain encomenderos should be included in this class. The work at Tiripitio was pushed almost to the point of encumbrance by Juan de Alvarado, and a full account of the role of the Las Casas family in the work at Yanhuitlan is available. See Escobar, *op. cit.*, chaps. xii–xiii; *Códice de Yanhuitlán, passim.*

58. e.g., fray Juan de Sevilla, OSA, at Atotonilco el Grande. See *Catálogo . . . Hidalgo*, I, 141–147.

59. One theoretical possibility is that generalized projects and instructions were part of the missionary's equipment. If so, none of it has survived.

60. This pattern recurs again and again during the colonial history of Latin America. The Franciscans in New Mexico (1610–80) and the Jesuits of Paraguay (1610–1767) are examples.

61. Ricard, *La "Conquête spirituelle" du Mexique*, pp. 169–170. The date assigned to the event is improbably early. The friars are not recorded elsewhere. The entire story is recorded only in an Indian petition which suggests fabrications. And yet the events are typical of authentic process elsewhere. Beaumont is the only source for the story. See p. 87.

"very competent in all affairs, and especially in government . . . he built the church anew, so sumptuously and solemnly, with so extensive a convento, that it is among the best in the realm . . . he laid the first foundations and completed the last details, without owing anything to the Doric or Corinthian styles. . . ."[62]

Many others can be mentioned,[63] among them, fray Martín de la Coruña at Tzintzuntzan in 1526, fray Juan de San Miguel at Uruapan; fray Jorge de Avila, OSA, at Totolapan, after 1534; Juan de Sevilla and fray Antonio de Roa, OSA, in the Sierra Alta of Metztitlan, after 1537; fray Simón de Bruselas, OFM, at Amacueca, after 1547; and fray Antonio de Cuéllar, OFM, at Etzatlan, after 1538. The necessities of making a habitable settlement were their teachers.

Finally there should be mentioned those individuals whose function was that of entrepreneurs, without active participation in the processes of design and construction. Fray Martín de Valencia may perhaps be included here. Other figures of great importance in Mendicant society are certainly of this class. Such was fray Pedro de Gante, OFM (Fig. 31), credited with the "erection" of one hundred to five hundred churches in the Valley of Mexico alone.[64] The "erection of a church" probably signifies the gathering of a congregation; it is certain that such numbers of durable edifices are out of the question, even during Gante's fifty years' residence in Mexico.

Though Gante was described by his somewhat younger contemporary Mendieta as being "muy ingenioso para todas las buenas artes y oficios," the arts of construction are not specifically mentioned. García Icazbalceta, furthermore, has doubted his competence in the mechanical arts.[65] Gante was active at Texcoco in the pre-Apostolic period until 1526–27[66] but permanent construction is not recorded there until 1527.[67] Mendieta further credits Gante with the initiative of building San José de los Naturales in Mexico City.[68] It was brought to completion during his lifetime, but final proof is lacking that Gante himself was the technical director of this extraordinary structure (see p. 329).

62. Rea, *Crónica de la orden de N. serafico P. S. Francisco*, pp. 92b–94: "muy capaz en todas materias, y tan particular en la del gobierno . . . hizo de nueuo la Yglesia tã sumptuosa, y graue, cõ cõuento tã estendido, que es de lo mejor del Reyno, abriendo desde el primer cimiẽto, basta poner el vltimo capital, sin deuer nada al Dorico, ni al Chorinto . . ."

63. See Appendix, according to community, for the activities of these men.

64. Mendieta, *op. cit.*, pp. 608–609; Vetancurt, *Chrónica, Teatro*, Pt. IV, p. 26. The problem of how much actual building was achieved by Gante is most difficult. Fray Pedro wrote in June, 1529, to his brethren in Flanders, with the object of recruiting more enthusiastic helpers, as follows, "Ego, . . . in hac provincia de Mexico, . . . meis laboribus, Deo cooperante, ultra centum domos Deo dicatas struxi, templa videlicet et sacella; quorum quaedam sunt templa magnificentissima nec minus divino cultui accommoda magnitudine tricentorum pedum, et alia ducentorum." Were these remarks merely the propaganda of an enterprise desperately in need of more help? García Icazbalceta, *Bibliografía mexicana del siglo XVI*, p. 399.

65. Mendieta, *loc. cit.*, J. García Icazbalceta, *Obras* (Mexico, 1896–99), III, 27 (*Biblioteca de autores mexicanos. Historiadores*, III).

66. Mendieta, *op. cit.*, p. 606, gives 1524. García Icazbalceta, *Bibliografía mexicana*, p. 399, correctly indicates 1526–27.

67. Mendieta, *op. cit.*, p. 262.

68. *Ibid.*, p. 608. García Icazbalceta, *Obras*, II, 20–21.

Motolinia's enterprise is attested by Vetancurt, who places him in Puebla about 1530.[69] He shows us the historian choosing the site for the Franciscan rectory and initiating its construction. Mendieta, however, attributes the actual work to fray García de Cisneros. In any case, Motolinia was in charge of the administration of the new foundation. It is worth noting that Motolinia was guardian at Huejotzingo in 1529, where he probably sanctioned and observed the labors of fray Juan de Alameda. He may also have built the first church at Atlixco, but no source indicates that he had practical charge of the work. Motolinia's writing is adorned with detailed descriptions of floral decorations, pageantry, and the precious arts; nowhere in his historical works or letters are there passages that reveal an exceptional interest in architecture.

Fray Mendieta himself may be regarded as a capable entrepreneur.[70] In 1558, four years after his arrival in Mexico, he was appointed guardian of Cuautinchan, where he laid out the town and is said to have "built" the rectory. His writings show some interest in architectural description, but he never claimed to have participated in construction.

From the mass of names associated with the colonization of New Spain, a bare handful can be characterized as genuine builders. None of the men active in the first generation, to the mid-century, was a competent professional. And yet, the style and technique of American building were firmly established before 1550. Later arrivals of European professionals signify simply the refinement of an existing formula of construction, or else the orientation of the cathedral fabrics towards an Herreran severity. No interpretation of sixteenth-century Mexican architecture can be attempted, therefore, without a careful assessment of the work prior to 1550 (see Chapters VI–VII). The most salient and singular aspect of that work is its amateur character. It is ironic that the greatest and most demanding task of architecture in late Renaissance history escaped so completely from the control of professional theory. Instead, it was achieved by amateurs and handymen in Mendicant habits, building with plenitude and raw vigor. In the provinces and in the capital, a wide divergence appeared between "architecture" and plain building. Wherever there was building, Mendicant friars were likely to be. That it should have been otherwise is unthinkable; the complexity and magnitude of the task could not have been undertaken by any other than the missionary. He alone, among sixteenth-century colonists, commanded the understanding of Indian society and the affection of its members, without which no solution to the endless problems of improvised construction would have been possible.

69. Vetancurt, *Chrónica, Teatro,* Pt. IV, p. 48. Mendieta, *op. cit.,* p. 622. J. F. Ramírez, "Noticias," *CDHM,* I, li, cxv.

70. *"Relación de . . . Quauhtinchán," NCDHM,* I, 70–91; Vetancurt, *op. cit.,* pp. 28–29. Torquemada, . . . *Monarchia indiana,* III, 161, attributes some activity as a painter to Jerónimo Mendieta, at Xochimilco. See Toussaint, *Pintura,* p. 12.

If it is true that no distinguished architectural designers came to Mexico before 1550, that European building craftsmen in civilian life were few, that their activity was confined to the capital, and that the missionaries were in effective charge of nearly all building operations away from the metropolis, many significant changes within this pattern may be detected in the years immediately after the mid-century.

Most striking is the appearance of distinguished civilian talent, foreshadowed in 1550 by the viceregal recommendation of Toribio de Alcaraz. The most remarkable civilian architect of the epoch was Claudio de Arciniega. More enigmatic is the contribution of the well-known Francisco Becerra. Many other civilians appear briefly, but Arciniega and Becerra were the outstanding figures of the second half of the century.

Upon Arciniega, a monograph remains to be written. Born *ca.* 1527,[71] his presence in New Spain is first attested about 1545. Ten years later, by his own statement, he was *maestro mayor de las obras de cantería* in Mexico City, and sufficiently influential to be consulted upon the question of rebuilding Puebla Cathedral in 1555.[72] The designation as maestro mayor refers to his newly-awarded post as *alarife de la ciudad.* The salient fact is that Arciniega came to America at an age well under twenty. Nothing of his life in Spain is known; his training as a designer was probably secured in Mexico, and he is therefore the first architect schooled in design solely in America. That his education was based upon printed books brought to Mexico before 1559 is proved by the remarkable structure designed for the obsequies of the Emperor Charles V in 1559. Known as the túmulo imperial (Fig. *442*), it displays a style of canonical correctness,[73] at least insofar as its design depends upon Serlio's method of modulation. The extraordinary property of the túmulo is the fact that it is exactly contemporary, as to style, with the Mannerist tendencies of mid-sixteenth-century Italy.[74] In 1563 the Audiencia requested his opinion upon the cost of the conversion of the casas nuevas into a fortress.[75] During the 1560's, Arciniega gave various opinions for the cabildo, in the course of discharging public offices, such as that of maestro de obras and inspector of aqueducts.[76] About 1560–63 Arciniega built the handsome

71. Angulo, "Catedrales mejicanas," *Boletín de la real academia de la historia,* CXIII, 158. See M. Toussaint, ed., *Proceso y denuncias contra Simón Pereyns* (Mexico, 1938), p. 21 (Documentos para la historia del arte en México. Suplemento al no 2 de *Anales del instituto de investigaciones estéticas*), where Arciniega declared his age in 1568 as over forty.

72. Cuevas, *Historia de la iglesia en México,* III, 66–67.

73. F. Cervantes de Salazar, *Túmulo imperial de la gran ciudad de México, impreso . . . en 1560* (facs. ed. Mexico, 1939), 1b. The unique surviving copy has but half the plate preserved.

74. The Mannerist disparity between load and support was indicated by McAndrew and Toussaint, "Tecali," *Art Bulletin,* XXIV, 322, who, in a study of rare perception, suggested that the entire "Purista" movement in Mexico centers about Claudio de Arciniega. McAndrew, however (*ibid.,* p. 324), assigns a greater influence to Claudio's truncated plan for the metropolitan Cathedral than to the túmulo. The túmulo, however, stood complete in 1560; its forms were seen by vast multitudes, and the monument was built perhaps mainly for Indian edification.

75. *Epistolario,* IX, 218–219.

76. *AC,* VIII, 64, 72.

reservoir attributed to him by Cervantes de Salazar.[77] Nothing actually survives today, although a stenographic rendering (Fig. 32) may be seen in a rude drawing of the Codex Aubin. In 1573–78, he served again as alarife de la ciudad, occupying the office for five years, during which he provided plans for the building of the new *ayuntamiento,* and surveyed various outlying municipal lands. Although he never returned to fill the office of alarife, he later advised the city, in 1590–92, upon projects concerning the jail and municipal shops or markets, during a period in which he was designated with the grandiose title of *maestro mayor por su magestad en toda esta nueva españa.*[78]

32. Mexico City, the *caja de agua*

The problem of Arciniega's exact contributions to the design of the two great cathedrals in Puebla and Mexico is still unsolved. Manuel Toussaint has correctly supposed that both edifices owe much to Arciniega. In the 1580's Claudio received a high annual salary from the metropolitan cathedral chapter for his services. The payment for 1584, it might be noted, came to 827 pesos, and was but one year's salary. This sum was about eight times as great as the payments made to the municipal maestro de obras. And a document of 1619 specifically mentions Claudio as the author of the plan of the cathedral edifice then in construction. Claudio's participation in the Puebla enterprise, moreover, is suggested by the fact that he was asked for an opinion in 1555, and by the close resemblances between the plans of the two great cathedrals.[79]

Arciniega's death may be supposed to have occurred before 1593, for in that year his office as maestro mayor was assumed by Diego de Aguilera.[80]

The great significance of Arciniega's œuvre resides in the fact that it was the first work in Mexico to be composed according to the strict rule of formal order in Renaissance architecture. With him, an effective director of form appears upon the Mexican scene, a civilian professional trained in Mexico, whose designs in the metropolis profoundly affected the habits and manners of design among monastic amateurs. After Arciniega, the friars were held often without their knowledge, in the tight web of classicizing design that he threw about the abundant variety and experimental eclecticism of previous Mexican building. Arciniega taught no radically new

77. Cervantes de Salazar, *Crónica de la Nueva España,* p. 321. Cervantes says that Arciniegas was then *maestro mayor de las obras de México,* assisting the obrero mayor of the day, Don Fernando de Portugal. According to the municipal minutes, Fernando de Portugal was appointed obrero mayor in August 1557 (*AC,* VI, 300), serving until the beginning of 1563 (*AC,* VII, 97). During part or the whole of this period, then, Claudio served as maestro mayor for the city, probably between two separate terms occupied by Antonio Garcia Saldaña (*AC,* VII, 128). This first term of service by Claudio is, apparently, not registered in the cabildo minutes.

78. *AC,* VIII, 136, 139; IX, 5, 24, 26; XI, 40, 43 (1593).

79. Murillo, *Iglesias de México,* II, by Toussaint, 21; VI, by Toussaint, 58–59. *AC,* VIII, 79. Cuevas, *Historia de la iglesia en México,* III, 51, 551–552.

80. H. Berlin, "Artifices de la catedral de México," *Anales del instituto de investigaciones estéticas,* III (1944), 25. Angulo, "Catedrales mejicanas," *Boletín de la real academia de la historia,* CXIII, 158.

structural devices or technological methods; he simply mediated the Renaissance language of form, with a fidelity and correctness that were soon lost among the rural adaptations by Mendicant builders.[81]

With Francisco Becerra,[82] on the other hand, Mexico had access for a few years (1573–80) to the services of an architect trained in Spain. Born in Trujillo in the mid-century, he grew up in the classicizing circle of Alonso Berruguete, and before coming to America in 1573, constructed buildings in Trujillo as well as minor work at the monastery of Guadalupe. In Mexico he was most closely associated with the design of Puebla Cathedral after 1575, and must be given credit for laying the foundations. Other than Puebla Cathedral, it is very difficult to accept for Becerra any further Mexican work. He has been given credit for the choir of San Francisco, Puebla, and the conventos of Santo Domingo, San Agustín, and the Colegio San Luis, all in Puebla. Other attributions are the rebuilding of Santo Domingo in Mexico, as well as the churches in Totimehuacan, Cuautinchan, Tlalnepantla, Cuitlahuac, Tepoztlan, and in other towns of the Marquesate. All these attributions are based upon Becerra's own claims, presented in an official petition or *informe de servicios.* Few can stand in their present form. An examination of the history of these various churches will reveal that Becerra had nothing to do with them beyond possibly giving counsel in matters of execution and decoration:

Puebla, San Francisco; church finished before 1570 (Fig. *133*)
Puebla, Santo Domingo; entire establishment built *ca.* 1590–1602
Puebla, Colegio San Luis; construction begun 1558 and incomplete in 1585
Puebla, San Agustín; convento unfinished in 1585, and church not begun until several years after 1579
Mexico, Santo Domingo; principal campaign 1558–71 (Fig. *203*)
Totimehuacan, San Francisco; church and convento unfinished in 1585
Cuautinchan, S. Juan Bautista; begun 1569 and finished *ca.* 1593 (Fig. 191)
Tlalnepantla, Corpus Christi; church in construction 1586–87
Cuitlahuac, San Pedro; church after 1587 and before 1596; convento in existence before 1587 (Fig. 336)
Tepoztlan, Natividad de N. Sra.; in construction between 1580 and 1588

Nowhere are the attributions confirmed by other documents; in none of the published records pertaining to these establishments is Becerra's name mentioned. Of the entire list, only the Colegio San Luis in Puebla, Totimehuacan, and Cuautinchan

81. McAndrew and Toussaint, "Tecali," *Art Bulletin,* XXIV, 311–325.

82. E. Llaguno y Amírola, *Noticias de los arquitectos y arquitectura de España* (Madrid, 1829), III, 56–58. Angulo, "Catedrales mejicanas," *Boletín de la real academia de la historia,* CXIII, 166. E. Marco Dorta, "Arquitectura colonial: Francisco Becerra," *Archivo español de arte,* no. 55 (Jan. 1943), 7–15. On Becerra in Peru, see E. Harth-Terré, in *El Comercio,* Lima (Jan. 1, 1945), p. 19.

show clear signs of having been in construction during Becerra's residence in New Spain (1573–80). It remains possible, nevertheless, that Becerra was brought into consultation by many institutions desiring to build, and that this advisory relationship is the basis of Becerra's sweeping claims. Becerra's architectural activity is firmly proved only for Puebla Cathedral and in the Viceroyalty of Peru after 1581. It may be pointed out that in Mexico, execution is the criterion of authorship. The peculiar conditions of the organization of labor, and the nature of Mexican building technology would have made it difficult for an itinerant European, unschooled in the problems of Mexican recruitment, to be significant in execution elsewhere than among European populations. Successful building among Indian groups remained the prerogative of the Mendicant clergy throughout the century. The close resemblances between the cathedrals in Mexico and Puebla, may, furthermore, be accounted for by the fact that Becerra had no close knowledge of Mexican building conditions. By patterning his Puebla design upon that of the capital, Becerra could benefit from Arciniega's experience, and avoid the pitfall of attempting design for which no labor had ever been trained. Indeed it is reasonable, even within the unequivocal documents supporting Becerra's authorship, to give Arciniega a hidden and unacknowledged share in the design of Puebla Cathedral, a share which Arciniega would himself perhaps have been reluctant to acknowledge.

Thus the effectiveness of any architect in Mexico must be gauged in the terms of his familiarity with Indian labor. An architect unfamiliar with the conditions of colonial labor was an architect whose work could never come to realization. On the other hand, Becerra, coming from a family closely associated with the great names of Spanish building and sculpture, must have brought to Mexico a standard of taste and a knowledge of the theory of design which were avidly solicited by the craftsmen long resident in the colony. The grandson of Hernán González de Lara, Berruguete's heir, must have enjoyed prestige in the new, busy cities of New Spain.

Juan Miguel Aguero, like Becerra, found provisional employment in Mexico between 1572 and 1585. He made the model for the Cathedral in Mexico, following Arciniega's plan. Later on, about 1585, he moved to Yucatan, where he collaborated with Gregorio de la Torre upon the building of Merida Cathedral. An inscription there records his participation as late as 1598.[83] One puzzling bit of information contributed by Llaguno pertains to Aguero's activity upon the fortifications of Havana in 1574; if this is true, either the commentators are in error, or else Aguero moved about rapidly from one part of the colonial world to another.

83. Angulo, *op. cit.*, pp. 152–159; Cuevas, *Historia de la iglesia en México*, III, 50, 551; Llaguno y Amírola, *Noticias*, III, 67; J. García Preciat, "Catedral de Mérida," *Archivo español de arte y arqueología*, no. 31 (1935), 81.

Other civilian architects and builders of the second half of the century are harder to identify. Among the municipal alarifes, Claudio de Arciniega has already been discussed. Antonio García de Saldana,[84] a native of Seville, whose activity in Mexico spans the period from his arrival, in 1532, to about 1573, functioned mainly as a technician, building installations for the mines, such as *yngenios para fundar metal y batanes,* and as a surveyor. Early in his Mexican career (1551–52) he supervised Indian slave labor for the metropolitan cabildo. He was described in 1564 as being very old and sick. After each of his terms as alarife for the city, it is interesting to note that he was replaced by men of known architectural capacities, first by Arciniega, and then, in 1565, by Miguel Martínez.[85]

Since Martínez is not mentioned in Icaza's biographical dictionary, compiled mainly in 1546–47, we may assume that he first arrived in Mexico after that date. During his term as alarife, lasting eight years (1565–73) his record was not very abundant. Known as a carpenter and mason, he built the platform and the canopy in 1566 for the Corpus Christi festival. In 1572 again, he executed the pageant architecture for the plaza mayor in connection with the festival of S. Hipólito. Among his duties was the building of the aqueduct from Chapultepec where his work was not satisfactory and elicited complaints. In 1567, incidentally, he prepared plans for a municipal granary. We also find him serving upon the commission that met in 1570, together with Ginés Tala, to advise upon the laying of the cathedral foundations. He last appears in 1588, with fourteen children, petitioning a grant from the Viceroy.

In the last quarter of the century, the office of alarife was occupied by a number of men of whom little or nothing can be determined. Their work was trifling, consisting of odd tasks of supervision, and it may indeed safely be said that during this epoch the office no longer had the importance attached to it earlier in the century. Cristóbal Carballo was thrice alarife (1578–81, 1590–92, and after 1595), and during these years, the only work for which he received special compensation from the city was for the extraction of stone from the Rio Santiago,[86] in 1583. A contemporary called him incompetent excepting as the *empedrador* (paver). Of the other men functioning as alarifes, even less can be said.

Striking, however, is the number of professional building experts who were resident in Mexico and discharging no public office. Their names are preserved, but it is often impossible to identify them by more than a casual mention. Such were Francisco Gudiel, Diego de Zamora, Pedro de Oñate, Joanes de Enberes (Antwerp), and Pedro Donato, named in 1564 as consultants in the affair of the water-supply from

84. Icaza, *Conquistadores y pobladores*, II, 85. *AC*, VI, 25, 44; VII, 169. See also *AC*, VI, 147, 173; VII, 128, 232; VII, 14.

85. *AC*, VII, 232, 277, 288, 365, 367, 384; VIII, 25, 32, 46, 51. Alamán, *Disertaciones*, I, Appendix, 148; Angulo, *op. cit.*, p. 151.

86. *AC*, VIII, 315; X, 16; XI, 74; XIII, 111, 240, 258. See also *AC*, VIII, 631.

Churubusco.[87] In 1565, a similar commission examined the broken arches of the Santa Fe aqueduct; among the names appear Rodrigo de la Puente, a *maeso de albañileria e cantería* who later was given the contract for the conduit from Santa Fe to Chapultepec, in 1574;[88] Juan de Vega, in Mexico since 1543–44, whither he came after having been in Florida with Hernando de Soto;[89] and one Diego Hernández.

More distinguished were such men as the enigmatic Ginés Tala, or Talaya.[90] We first hear of him in 1563, in connection with the conversion of the casas nuevas into a fortress, at a time when he was employed by the Dominicans as the maestro de obras of their vast new mother-house in the capital. This enterprise was characterized at the time as the greatest in the Indies. He also participated in the technical commission summoned in 1570 to advise upon the laying of the foundations of the cathedral. Because of his connection with the Dominican Order, it is not at all unlikely that Ginés de Tala was one of the *grandes arquitectos* mentioned by Burgoa as having been imported to Mexico from Spain and Italy. Tala disappears from our view after 1593, when he gave counsel for the arcades of the Chapultepec aqueduct.

Other men of the period were Melchior Dávila, whose death was distinguished by a fall from the scaffolds of the old cathedral, where he was in charge of the repairs in 1584.[91] Dávila designed the fortifications erected at the time of the Chichimec uprising (1561); we also know him as the director of the construction of the University upon the pre-Conquest Volador site in 1584.

Not at all uncommon during the latter part of the sixteenth century was the qualification of a man as "architect." Diego de Aguilera[92] was thus characterized, as "maestro en el arte de cantería y architectura." Unfortunately his work is difficult to identify. In 1591 he gave an opinion in his capacity as "arquitecto" for the Chapultepec aqueduct; three years later he enjoyed the office of Familiar of the Inquisition, and he is known to have consulted with Arciniega upon the rebuilding of the municipal prison. Finally, in 1599, we find him as maestro mayor at the cathedral, and as the author of a *modelo y planta* for the oft-ruined church of San Hipólito at the western edge of the capital.

Another individual of shadowy achievement was Rodrigo Alonso de Anis, *maestro de geometría y architectura,* of whom we know nothing at present beyond the fact that he threw suspicion upon the competence of the alarife, Cristóbal Carballo, in

87. *AC,* VII, 209–210. Arciniega and Martínez also appeared among these consultants.

88. *AC,* VIII, 96–97.

89. Icaza, *Conquistadores y pobladores,* II, 311.

90. *Epistolario,* IX, 218–219 (Ledesma to His Majesty). Angulo, *op. cit.,* p. 151. Murillo, *Iglesias de México,* II, by Toussaint, 19. Cuevas, *Documentos inéditos,* pp. 183, 184. Burgoa, *Geográfica descripción,* II, 2–3. *AC,* XI, 143–144. Berlin, *op. cit.,* p. 20.

91. Llaguno y Amírola, *Noticias,* III, 71; Toussaint, *Paseos coloniales,* p. 14; *Codex Aubin, histoire de la nation mexicaine . . . reproduction du codex de 1576* (Paris, 1893), pp. 125–126. Alamán, *Disertaciones,* II, 216–222.

92. *AC,* X, 54; XI, 43; XII, 91: XIII, 363, 372, 374.

1593.[93] Martín Casillas, on the other hand, is known to have participated in two great enterprises: in 1585 he was employed at the metropolitan cathedral, presumably under Melchior Dávila; thereafter he appears in Guadalajara, as the maestro mayor of the cathedral in construction there.[94]

One exotic, finally, may be noted among the civilian architects and builders of the second half of the century. An Englishman named Miles Philips was long captive in New Spain, and during his term of exile, supervised the Indian workmen who were building San Agustín in the capital in 1572. During the process, he learned Nahuatl and became an admirer of his Indian charges.[95]

The number of identifiable Mendicant builders increased enormously in the latter part of the century. But the appearance of many civilian architects, with a high order of professional training, set a standard for the friars to which they had never been held during the formative and most significant years of the initial colonization. In the foregoing enumeration of these civilian experts, however, there are certain extremely shadowy figures, of whom the mention comes to us only in the Mendicant chronicles.

For example, at Coyoacan, although the building of the church was assigned by a historian of the Dominican Order to fray Ambrosio de Santa Maria, the presence of certain *architectos,* presumably of civilian status, is mentioned. Who they were is difficult to say, although it may be supposed that Ginés de Tala was often asked to function in some such capacity.[96] Among the Augustinians, likewise, an unknown maestro, Pedro del Toro, is mentioned as active at Yuriria. At Cuitzeo, the curious master mentioned in the inscription of the façade stands behind the usually accredited designer, fray Francisco de Villafuerte. Basalenque mentions the fact that the establishments at Cuitzeo and Copandaro were both based upon the designs by a "mismo official de México."[97] Such functions, of giving behind-the-scenes advice and counsel were perhaps not infrequently discharged by Francisco Becerra or Toribio de Alcaraz. An enigmatic case is met at Acolman, where, about 1558, the capital at one side of the chancel arch bears an inscription with the legend, "Mo Palomira fissome." No other record pertaining to this man has been found, and it is an open question whether he was an ornamental sculptor or a responsible building designer.

Thus it is not infrequent that behind the friars to whom great building operations have been attributed, there hovers the shadow of a civilian technician. Unfor-

93. *AC,* XI, 62, 68, 74.

94. M. A. de la Mota Padilla, *Historia de la conquista de la provincia de la Nueva-Galicia* (Mexico, 1870 [1871–72]), p. 209; Cuevas, *Historia de la iglesia en México,* III, 77; "Informe al rey por el cabildo eclesiástico de Guadalajara," *CDHM,* II, 506; Angulo, *op. cit.,* p. 168.

95. Hakluyt, *Voyages,* III, 572.

96. A. Franco y Ortega, *Segunda parte de la historia de la provincia de Santiago de México* (Mexico, 1900), pp. 62–63. Fr. S. Martínez, ed.

97. Basalenque, *Historia . . . Michoacán,* p. 86b.

tunately, the stylistic indications offered in such instances are too meager for us to unravel the authorship of the designs, but the situation is no more perplexing than in the case of many great buildings in Renaissance Italy, where the documents are far more abundant.

Among the Mendicant builders, the incidence of formal architectural education, low everywhere in Europe at the same period, remained very rare in Mexico. The civilian, Francisco Becerra, we know as the son of the son of a builder, but of no others can we ascertain such a background of training. Often, however, the friars learned building by taking an exemplary part in the humble tasks of construction. Such was the case with fray Juan de Gaona at Xochimilco, before 1550, when he labored as a hod-carrier and ditch-digger among the Indian *macehuales*.[98] Architectural education, then, among the Mendicants, remained highly informal, guided by no theory other than that which could be assimilated from reading and from experienced men in civilian and monastic life. The new quantum that must not be overlooked, however, is the presence in Mexico after 1550 of men bearing an academic, book-formed standard of classicizing taste in architecture. The indirect effects of Arciniega or Becerra upon monastic building are demonstrably great.

In the Augustinian Order, the grand entrepreneur was fray Alonso de la Vera Cruz (*obit* 1584). Enjoying great authority at the court of Philip II, he discharged many responsibilities and founded at least twelve establishments. As a notable bibliophile, he may be supposed to have brought architectural books to New Spain among the sixty cases of volumes he imported from the Peninsula.[99]

Perhaps the most prolific Augustinian builder of the third quarter of the century was fray Juan Bautista de Moya (*obit* 1567, *aet.* 63). He learned the craft as a workman and alarife in 1552 on the construction crew in Valladolid (Morelia), and the Bishop of Michoacan, Juan de Medina Rincón (1572–88 *sed.*) awarded him unstinted praise as an architect, saying that he "compitió y aun excedió en la Arquitectura a Meliágenes y Demócrates."[100] Traces of his work perhaps survive at Ajuchitlan and Pungarabato.

The work of fray Andrés de Mata (*obit* 1574) was less diffuse and more ambitious. He is credited with the construction of the great edifices at Actopan (Fig. 166)

98. Mendieta, *Historia eclesiástica indiana*, p. 691.

99. Escobar, *Americana thebaida*, p. 340; Basalenque, *op. cit.*, pp. 35b, 40b. Cf. García Icazbalceta, *Obras*, III, 46.

100. Escobar, *op. cit.*, pp. 483, 526. See also González de la Puente, ". . . Chorónica augustiniana," *Colección de documentos . . . pub. por . . . F. Plancarte y Navarrete*, p. 190. Medina Rincón's classical allusions are interesting. "Democrates" is surely the architect of Alexandria, Dinocrates, mentioned by Vitruvius (Prologue, Lib. 2) and by Plutarch (in *Vita Alexandri*); "Meleagenes" is surely Metagenes, also mentioned by Vitruvius as builder of the Temple at Ephesus, and as the inventor of an ingenious system for moving stone. Medina Rincón's misspelling of the names may be traced through Jeronimo Román (*Repúblicas del mundo* [Salamanca, 1595], II, 65b), who wrote before 1575; to C. de Villalón, *Ingeniosa comparación entre lo antiguo y lo presente* (Madrid, 1898), pp. 147–148. M. Serrano y Sanz, ed. (Sociedad de bibliófilos españoles. Libros publicados, 33), and to Filarete, *Tractat*, p. 76.

and Ixmiquilpan (Fig. *122*). Nothing is known of his training or of his possible advisers in design.[101] About fray Juan de Utrera, on the other hand, we have certain details. His activities as an organizer of highly efficient building techniques are recorded. Stationed at Ucareo between 1550 and 1564, he came originally to New Spain as a civilian, and took the habit in 1539.[102]

Another such founder-builder was fray Juan Cruzate (*obit* 1575), associated with the enterprises at Jonacatepec (Fig. 305) and at Zacualpan Amilpas (Fig. 300). He was also prior at Malinalco, where, however, his building activity has not been identified.[103]

One peculiarity of Augustinian building, especially in Michoacan, was the length of time needed for construction. Few of the great establishments were completed in one campaign of construction. The work usually stretched out over several generations, often attaining completion only at advanced dates in the seventeenth century. For many friars, therefore, additions, fragments, and repairs of existing fabrics constitute the list of their credited works. Such was strikingly the case with fray Gerónimo de la Magdalena (*obit* 1614, over seventy). Parts of his work may be named at Cuitzeo, Copandaro, Jacona, and Yuriria, but in no case can he be assigned the integral design of an entire establishment brought to completion under his direction. Magdalena twice visited Rome; with Arciniega he may be designated as a native architect, for he came to New Spain as a boy from Cordova, and presumably acquired all his knowledge of building in America.[104] A similar career fell to the lot of fray Francisco de Villafuerte; he was the director of work at Cuitzeo and in Patzcuaro in the second half of the sixteenth century, but he cannot be credited with integral accomplishment.[105]

On the whole, it may be said of the Augustinian architects that, apart from the primitive, barrel-vaulted cloisters of the 1530's, their epoch of great activity did not begin until several years later than the major Franciscan campaign. It coincided, as we have seen, with a period of depopulation, during which the recruitment of labor was more difficult than in the initial years. The settlements taken up by the Augustinians were usually the lesser centers of urban life, which had earlier been appropriated by the Franciscans. The net character of their building activity, if slower in achievement, was certainly more ambitious. Some concern with technical and stylistic

101. Grijalva, *Crónica de la orden de N. P. S. Agustín*, pp. 440–441.

102. G. Kubler, "Ucareo and the Escorial," *Anales del instituto de investigaciones estéticas*, II (1942), 5–12.

103. F. Gómez de Orozco, "Monasterios," *Revista mexicana de estudios históricos*, I, 46; Toussaint, *Proceso*, p. 27.

104. Basalenque, *Historia . . . Michoacán*, pp. 152b–154a; Escobar, *Americana thebaida*, pp. 666–671; J. G. Romero, *Noticias para formar la historia y la estadística del obispado de Michoacán* (Mexico, 1862), p. 128.

105. Escobar, *op. cit.*, p. 667.

refinement was manifested; at Ucareo the Augustinians were preoccupied with the more efficient use of a restricted supply of labor. At Epazoyucan (Fig. 167), they had to build feverishly, on the other hand, to counter the rising tide of secular opposition to monastic building. In the northeastern provinces, however, the Augustinians enjoyed the uncontested use of large native populations, together with geographical remoteness from civilian interference. On the whole, then, population loss, prior preemption of desirable settlements by other Orders, and civilian interference with monastic building were the unfavorable factors to be accounted in the architectural program of the Augustinians. These disadvantages, however, stimulated the structural and stylistic perceptions of the architects.

The Dominican friars in New Spain proper to whom building activities have been credited were few. It has already been noted that the highly spiritual and intellectual vocation of the Dominicans inhibited many of their most able men from mechanical or technical duties. Occasionally a friar contrived to incorporate architecture among his intellectual pursuits. Such was the case with fray Domingo de Aguiñaga (*obit* 1597, *aet. ca.* eighty-seven). A friend of S. Ignatius Loyola in Spain, Aguiñaga was distinguished within the Order for his wide readings in history, mathematics, geography, architecture, and other useful arts. Not only did he discharge many high offices, but he founded and supervised the construction of the mission town of Cuilapan, in Oaxaca province, after 1555. He also negotiated for the construction of the Colegio de San Luis, endowed in Puebla by Luis de León Romano.[106] At Cuilapan the actual maestro de obras was a lay brother named Antonio Barboso (*obit* 1608). Portuguese by origin, he arrived in America about 1541, and associated himself with the Dominicans in 1548. His trade was the carpenter's, but his colleagues designated him as "mui ingeniosso en el arte de la . . . architectura." He was also active at Chilapa, and probably was associated with the great enterprise at Yanhuitlan.[107]

Another distinguished Dominican builder, fray Juan de la Cruz (*obit* 1597), originally came from Trujillo in Estremadura. He took orders in Mexico in 1537, and built three conventos, Coyoacan, Izucar, and Tetela. Other edifices in which he had a hand were at Ahuehuetlan, the convento de la Piedad in the capital, and at Atlixica. These last-named and poorly identified works occupied his old age.[108]

An advanced knowledge of architectural theory was attributed to fray Alberto Garnica (died 1597) by his contemporaries. Garnica developed a profitable sugar mill at Coahuixtla de las Amilpas, presumably near Cuautla. He was educated at San

106. Burgoa, *Geográfica descripción*, I, 398, 403. *Códice de Yanhuitlán*, pp. 23–24. Dávila Padilla, *Historia . . . Santiago de México*, pp. 480, 573. Franco, . . . *Historia . . . Santiago de México*, pp. 127–128. Ojea, . . . *Historia religiosa*, pp. 42–43.

107. Burgoa, *op. cit.*, II, 405. Franco, *op. cit.*, pp. 209–212.

108. *Ibid.*, pp. 129–130. Ojea, *op. cit.*, p. 44.

Pablo in Valladolid, after a long career as a soldier in Italy. Nothing exact, however, is known concerning his specific architectural activities.[109] Fray Francisco Marin, who worked many years in the Mixteca region, had architectural knowledge, and is reputed to have planned churches and municipal buildings in the communities under his care. Again, as with so many monastic architects, none of his works has been identified.[110] At Chimalhuacan, however, we are told that a fray Miguel de Zamora (died 1564) laid on the water supply, and that he was competent in matters of architecture.[111]

This brief list nearly exhausts the catalogue of Dominicans credited with building activities. The number is impressively smaller than with the Augustinians. The ordinal prejudice against manual occupations may be recalled in this connection. It is also significant that the Dominicans achieved the greatest part of their missionary labors in the isolated and populous Mixteca of southern Mexico, remote from any competition with other Orders. A profitable mission economy based upon the culture of silk and nopal also enabled them to hire the necessary technical experts for their constructions. In short, the Dominicans of New Spain were rarely compelled to recruit building talent from within their own ranks. Father Burgoa, the seventeenth-century chronicler, constantly speaks with pride of the secular professionals imported from Europe for the great building enterprises in southern Mexico, with an ostentation that is never found among the chroniclers of the other Orders. Unfortunately, these civilian professionals are not clearly identified, although we have already supposed that Ginés de Tala was among their number.

The chroniclers of the Dominican province of Chiapas, which belongs stylistically to Central America more than to New Spain, give us the names of several architects who learned their craft in the Order. Unlike the Dominicans of Oaxaca, the friars of Chiapas and Guatemala relied after 1550, when activity began, upon their own personnel for all architectural undertakings.[112] The same may be said of the Dominicans working in the Sierra region of eastern Oaxaca. In the vicinity of the Villa Alta, among the Chinantec tribespeople, the Dominicans were "total" missionaries.[113]

Among the Dominicans, the most active friars in architectural matters are to be found in the province of Chiapas. Elsewhere we have indications that the Dominicans

109. Franco, *op. cit.*, p. 126. Ojea, *op. cit.*, pp. 39–40.

110. Ricard, *La "Conquête spirituelle" du Mexique*, p. 136. Dávila Padilla, *op. cit.*, pp. 241–242, 303b.

111. *Ibid.*, pp. 472, 477.

112. Remesal, *Historia . . . Indias*, II, 247. "Pero quien dirá lo mucho que trabajaron y padecieron los padres de esta sagrada religión en asentar los pueblos, edificar las casas, hacer las iglesias, y todo lo demas necesario para una república? Ellos eran los que tiraban los cordeles, median las calles, daban sitio a las casas, trazaban las iglesias, procuraban los materiales, y sin ser oficiales de arquitectura, salián maestros aventajadísimos de edificar. Cortaban los haces de caña por sus manos, formaban los adobes, labraban los maderos, asentaban los labrillos, encendian el horno de cal, y a ningun ejercicio por bajo que fuese se dejaban de acomodar."

113. B. Bevan, *The Chinantec* (Mexico, 1939).

tended to employ secular talent, and it was only in Central America that the friars themselves undertook technical responsibility. Thus fray Vicente de Santa Maria is reported as having taught his colleagues the use of proportioned design, and methods of structural computation, before his death in 1565.[114] In the same province fray Melchor de los Reyes also seems to have served as an indispensable technical consultant, to whose influence we may perhaps assign the great massiveness of Central American construction (Fig. 220).[115]

Franciscan builders after the mid-century are even rarer than Dominican practitioners of the craft. Whereas nearly every Augustinian prior initiated or supervised some campaign of construction at his post, the Franciscans undertook little new work. The situation demands some explanation. In the first place, the Franciscan chroniclers made little show of their brethren's accomplishments. Yet Torquemada, whom we shall see as a builder, would be expected to rehearse the ordinal achievement in some detail. More significant is the fact that the Franciscans ceased to maintain an expanding mission enterprise in the densely populated areas of New Spain. The great work there was accomplished before 1560, and it was done with dispatch and finality. Their sprawling extension over central, southern, and western Mexico made them the first target of the campaign to secularize the missions. Extremely sensitive to criticism, the friars early withdrew their pretensions to many important sites in the mountains of Hidalgo, ceding them to the Augustinians. The same process took place systematically in Michoacan, and Morelos. It is also to be noted that the Franciscans began earlier than all other ecclesiastical organizations with an effective campaign of peripheral colonization. They appear before 1550 in northern Mexico, and by the end of the century, their first envoys took up the long labor in New Mexico.

Hence it is rare that we find important new Franciscan enterprises under way. At Tzintzuntzan, however, the church and convento (Fig. 461) were rebuilt from the foundations about 1590, under the supervision of fray Pedro de Pila (*obit ca.* 1597). He was responsible for the design, and had also achieved the rebuilding of the church at Zacapu about 1586.[116]

Another such builder was fray Francisco de Gamboa, who arrived in New Spain in 1568 as a civilian in the suite of Viceroy Enríquez. It was he who, in 1603–4, tore down the decaying fabric of Santiago Tlatelolco, who built the bell-tower for San José de los Naturales in the capital, and rebuilt San Francisco in Mexico between 1590 and 1602.[117]

114. Remesal, *op. cit.*, p. 438.

115. *Ibid.*, p. 329. See pp. 271, 282.

116. Rea, *Crónica de la orden de N. serafico P. S. Francisco*, pp. 92b–94, 50a,b. Torquemada, . . . *Monarchia indiana*, III, 375.

117. *Ibid.*, III, 581. Vetancurt, *Chrónica, Teatro*, Pt. IV, pp. 40–41.

Fray Juan de Torquemada himself followed Gamboa at Tlatelolco. Modestly implying that he was but an amateur, he writes that he laid out the plan of the new church (Fig. 120), and directed the labor of the Indians who worked upon its construction.[118] No other work by Torquemada is attested.

In the western provinces, finally, we find two Franciscans supervising construction. At Amacueca in Jalisco, during the third quarter of the century, fray Simón de Bruselas rebuilt the convento and a large masonry church which had been destroyed by an earthquake.[119] And at Zacapu, the strange humanist and Erasmian, fray Jacopo Daciano, perhaps a Dane, undertook the building of a church probably anterior to the rebuilding by fray Pedro de Pila, *ca.* 1586.[120]

This meager record for the Franciscans indicates the durability of their first constructions, and the modesty of their appetite for sumptuous enterprises after the great period in the decades near the middle of the century.

In conclusion, one example of Franciscan influence upon the training of Indian architects may be observed in western Mexico. At Tlajomulco, in New Galicia, an Indian architect named Francisco Gerónimo participated in the construction of a three-aisled basilica, presumably of the type of Tecali or Zacatlan de las Manzanas. In his profession he was active between 1567 and 1598. He is the only Indian architect recorded in the period.[121] The profession of builder-designer, like that of the clergy, was apparently not opened by the Europeans to their Indian charges.

118. Torquemada, *op. cit.*, III, 212.

119. Mendoza, *Fragmentos*, p. 88.

120. Mendieta, *Historia eclesiástica indiana*, p. 450. Vetancurt, *Chrónica, Menologio*, p. 116.

121. Tello, *Libro segundo de la crónica . . . de Xalisco*, p. 689. Mendoza, *op. cit.*, pp. 179, 183.

IV

LABOR, MATERIALS, AND TECHNIQUES

Asentados, pues, los indios en sus nuevas poblaciones, se comenzaron a edificar las iglesias y casas de los religiosos, y dentro de siete u ocho años, estaban muchas dellas acabadas y tejadas, y tan buenas como en muchos pueblos de España.

Remesal, *Historia . . . Indias,* II, 247.

THE problem of recruiting the vast quantities of Indian labor needed for the architectural enterprise of sixteenth-century Mexico was solved by a variety of methods. Their relation to one another was successive, as with progressive stages yielding a final and definitive solution. However productive of administrative and practical abuses these stages may have been, they reflect the desire of the Crown to achieve a humane and melioristic treatment of the Indian population, under the stimulus of serious population disasters. In brief, we have the following: to 1550, more or less, the use of unpaid labor, recruited by various methods; the use of forced wage labor after 1550, recruited by draft; and finally, in the last quarter of the century, the tentative creation of a reservoir of voluntary wage labor. These stages, of course, overlap one another generously.[1]

The role played by slavery was negligible, although it has often been overestimated. For the purposes of this work, slavery may be defined as the institution whereby human beings are owned and negotiated as property without voice in the transaction. That such a slave class existed in Mexico cannot be denied, but it was formally abolished in 1569, in consequence of the movement for emancipation that had been under way since 1530. The practical abolition of Indian slavery was virtually completed by 1561 in New Spain. Indeed, in 1555, Motolinia estimated that but a thousand Indian slaves remained to be manumitted. For that matter, the class had never been very numerous. Fewer than four thousand cases of slavery were handled during the period 1551–61 in the Audiencia of Mexico and peripheral provinces. This figure, however, probably represents but a part of the slave population that was emancipated, for the records deal only with cases upon which individual review was necessary, and the

1. See S. A. Zavala, *New Viewpoints on the Spanish Colonization of America* (Philadelphia, 1943), pp. 93–103; L. B. Simpson, "Studies," *Iberoamericana,* XIII (1938), 7.

total number of emancipations was certainly much larger.[2] During the brief period in which Indian slavery existed, the slaves were recruited by a variety of means. Prisoners of war were distributed as slaves among the victorious soldiers. Many of these were captured during the campaigns to subdue Indian rebellions. Indian slaves were also introduced into Christian colonial society through barter with tribes among whom enslavement was practiced. The Spanish colonist might also acquire slaves by accepting them in partial payment of tribute obligations. Finally, criminals were condemned to slavery. Hence the class was recruited from among the peripheral, rebellious, or criminal elements of colonial Indian society, and slavery was a method of social punishment.

There is little evidence that Indian slaves participated significantly in building operations, as did the Moors of the Reconquest in Spain. In 1551–52, Indian slave labor was used in paving the streets of the capital. After 1569, it is true, we find Chichimec slaves working on the Cathedral of Mexico, but this was an exceptional case. Negro slaves, on the other hand, were highly valued, especially those who possessed some knowledge of building techniques. In 1538, for example, Bishop Zumárraga imported three Negro sawyers for the building of the primitive Cathedral of Mexico.[3]

If slavery was a marginal and residual institution of negligible viability, how then was Indian labor recruited? The basic device was *repartimiento,* or the fiduciary assignment of the labor of a specified number of Indians for a limited period to a designated beneficiary or trustee. If the trustee were granted Indians for his lifetime or longer, the grant was called encomienda. Short-term grants for specific tasks were sometimes called *cuatequil,* or draft labor, as in pre-Conquest life. The institution of repartimiento underwent several important changes during the sixteenth century; in 1549, direct levies of unlicensed labor from repartimiento Indians were forbidden. But whether the Indians were liable for tribute in kind or in money, after the abolition of direct labor-levies, they continued to give, however indirectly, of their labor to the colonists. During the early Colonial period, the lifetime trusts thus established were often feudatory in tendency. It often happened that the Church, or an institution, or a social group was assigned a repartimiento in encomienda.[4]

No title to land was ever conveyed by the assignment of repartimiento. The beneficiary, or trustee, had right merely to the use of the labor of the Indians in question, whether in tribute (in money or in kind), or in the form of direct levies of labor (personal services) until 1549. In return for these benefits, the encomendero con-

2. Zavala, *op. cit.,* pp. 49–68; Simpson, *Many Mexicos,* pp. 60–61. *Idem,* "Studies," *Iberoamericana,* XVI (1940), *passim; idem, Encomienda,* p. 270.

3. *AC,* VI [1862?], 25, 44, 66. Zavala, *New Viewpoints,* p. 66. Cuevas, *Historia de la iglesia en México,* I, 250–251. See pp. 295–296.

4. Simpson, *Encomienda,* p. 92; Pérez Bustamante, . . . *Don Antonio de Mendoza,* pp. 88 ff. Simpson, "Studies," *Iberoamericana,* XIII, 5.

tracted to provide certain facilities to the Indians in his trust. At the beginning of the colonial era, Cortés drew up specific regulations upon the tenure of encomienda. Dated in 1526, these regulations provided that the Indians were to receive religious instruction, in return for their donations of food, labor, and services. The encomendero agreed to suppress idolatry and to build churches within six months after receiving the trust: to build and inhabit a house (Fig. 77) on his encomienda within eighteen months: to bring his wife to the encomienda, or to marry within eighteen months after award. The male children of the chiefs were to be delivered to monastic establishments for religious instruction, but in the absence of monastic foundations, this instruction was to be given by paid teachers. In any case, the encomendero was to maintain a resident priest among his Indians, whether singly or in coöperation with other encomenderos. Cortés further provided that the Indians should receive annual pay amounting to a half-peso gold for their services, and that the Indians have thirty days' repose between turns of service. No contributions in gold were to be made to the encomendero, nor could women and children be alienated from their communities. Finally, the colonist's title to the encomienda was proved by eight years' residence, and his tenure was limited to two generations, whereupon the encomienda was either reassigned, or it escheated to the Crown.[5] Encomienda regulations changed later, especially as to tenure and the perception of tribute, but their fundamental sense remained the same: the use of Indian labor continued to be assigned to provisional trustees. Encomienda never had any other legal meaning.

Within the institution of repartimiento, however, two radically distinct categories of labor-performance by Indians may be distinguished. On the one hand, we must reckon with services voluntarily performed, and on the other, with services performed under compulsion. In recent years, writers have tended to underrate or neglect the volume and character of voluntary donations of labor by Indians. These voluntary contributions were secured by moral persuasion; they were achieved, in all likelihood, only by the earliest Mendicant missionaries working in humility and with devotion among Indian populations. To achieve the voluntary donation of Indian services was the ideal pattern set for themselves by the friars. That they frequently failed to achieve it is obvious, but the truth remains that voluntary donation of labor was the ideal pattern to which Mendicant activity adhered or at least approximated.

Thus the missionary who was beginning his work in a settlement, had no means of coercion, and no outside support immediately at hand, other than the antecedent fact of the Conquest. Later on, of course, when his labors became institutionalized, and he could call upon the various agencies of enforcement, such as the encomendero, the corregidor, or the clergy, he forfeited the peculiar moral dominion he had earlier

5. *CDIAI*, XXVI (1876), 135–148, 163–170; *CDIU*, IX (1895), 368–399.

enjoyed. Such was the case at Ocuituco in 1534–36, where the Augustinians forced the Indians to labor, thereby entering the abhorred class of civilian colonist-extortioners.[6] But at first, the missionary went barefoot among the Indians, clad only in a coarse, tattered frock, sleeping on mats, taking the same food as the Indians, and accepting the hard conditions of their physical life in a manner unique among all classes of colonists (Fig. 33).[7] It is only partly true that Mendicant records themselves are the sole sources for verifying these feats of moral persuasion; conclusive proof for them is found in the building record itself, where a few dozen friars, working single-handed during the first years of the Mexican conversion, achieved an astonishing work of building, and alone gained the unquestioned loyalty and affection of large Indian groups.

L. B. Simpson somewhat obscured the situation by remarking that "the method used in obtaining labor for the erection of a monastery differed in no essential way from that used in the operation of a mine or the cultivation of a plantation."[8] This holds true only for the relatively advanced date at which the short-term repartimiento (cuatequil) was the generalized solution to all labor problems, and it does not bear upon the period of primitive construction before 1540 or 1542, when the New Laws were framed. Then, on the contrary, Indian labor was performed at the moral behest of a missionary. In a great town, such as Huejotzingo, the initial evangelization and campaign of construction came to pass without encomienda to the Franciscans, which was awarded at first only to conquistadores and civilian settlers. Simpson's earliest document bearing upon repartimiento granted for religious construction pertains to activity at Oaxaca in 1539. Other labor grants for religious construction occurred after 1551, when the burden of the initial campaign had already been borne by the Indians.[9] For example, a repartimiento was given the Dominicans for the construction of a monastery at Izucar in 1551. Furthermore, Father Beaumont categorically denied the use of paid labor in the earliest campaigns of construction. He wrote, "Neither in these days, nor for many years later, were the Indians paid for their work on the churches. Each town built its own, and even on the works of Mexico, many other towns helped in the beginning without pay. In the conventual establishments all who worked and built were fed. . . ."[10] Thus Father Beaumont was particularly anxious to clear his Mendicant predecessors of the charges of having shared in the onerous

6. Genaro García, "El Clero de México," *Documentos inéditos ó muy raros para la historia de México* (Mexico, 1907), XV, 83.

7. Beaumont, *Crónica de Michoacán*, II, 138.

8. Simpson, "Studies," *Iberoamericana*, XIII, 5.

9. *Ibid.*, p. 84.

10. Beaumont, *op. cit.*, II, 105: ". . . en aquellos tiempos, ni muchos años después, no se les pagaba a los indios, lo que trabajaban en los edificios de las iglesias, sino que cada pueblo hacía la suya, y aún a las obras de México, ayudaron otros muchos pueblos a los principios sin paga, y cuando mucho daban de comer en los monasterios a los que en ellos trabajaban, y los edificaban. . . ."

system of paid repartimiento labor,[11] and preferred to have them understood as participating in the system of unpaid labor, which he described as voluntary, at least insofar as Indian contribution was concerned. The process is further documented for Michoacan, where during the 1520's, the missionaries worked single-handed in scattered communities without government support. At that time, the Tarasca Indians lived either in family groups or in small farming settlements.[12] Among them, the first Franciscans built "iglesias pajizas" and "habitaciones pobres" (Fig. 33). In such instances the relation of the missionary to the community was one in which the missionary at first merely took up residence, barely touching the life of the community, then gradually exercising more penetrating influence, until finally, its total resources might be mobilized for the purposes of conversion and Christian polity. Similar cases are abundantly reported from New Galicia, where accounts of the initial conversions are far more detailed than for the more central areas. At Cutzalan, for example, in the district of Lake Chapala, where fray Martín de Jesús preached, he began by persuading the Indians to destroy idols, and dissuading them from polygamy. He then built a provisional chapel, and induced the chief to accept baptism. By his example the rest of the tribe was brought to baptism. With the assistance of the converted chiefs, a new settlement and church were built at Ajijic in 1531, and other congregations were established at Tomatlan and Tecolotlan. In the entire precedure, no record of repartimiento or paid labor is to be found.[13]

Indian donation of labor became more and more rare as the century progressed, and as building plans became more pretentious. When labor abuses were generally common and notorious, any Indian offer to donate labor or material met with suspicion from the viceregal government, as in 1576, when the Indians of Culhuacan, who donated lime for the convento then being built, were investigated at the Viceroy's order, to determine whether or not any coercion were involved.[14]

With the decay of their primitive apostolic fervor, and the increase in scale and pretentiousness of their building, the Mendicants rapidly became exploiters of Indian labor (Fig. 34), recruiting it by the legal devices current among other classes of colonists. As institutions, the Orders became the beneficiaries of encomienda grants, with the usual facilities for compelling the Indians to provide labor. Thus the Governor

11. Contrast Simpson, "Studies," *Iberoamericana,* XIII, 28, "In the early days encomiendas were allotted to priests and religious organizations [for building churches and convents], but the encomiendas were removed from them by the New Laws (1542) and thereafter physical tasks were supposed to be performed either by paid repartimiento or by free labor."

12. Beaumont, *op. cit.,* II, 136–137. ". . . se congregaban en familias, o se agregaban a las que vivían de asiento en rancherías."

13. *Ibid.,* II, 218. It may be that the adhesion of the chiefs was secured by compulsion, for military force was brought into the area under the notorious Nuño de Guzmán.

14. S. A. Zavala and M. Castelo, *Fuentes para la historia del trabajo en Nueva España* (Mexico, 1939–41), I, 77.

at first, and later the Audiencia or the Viceroy, might assign a town or group of towns in repartimiento to one of the Orders, for the specific purpose of building a church and monastery. In 1541, Viceroy Mendoza assigned the tribute of Texcoco to the Augustinians for the specific purpose of building their new church in Mexico City. Not only was Texcoco expected to provide tribute in money and in kind, but also the necessary laborers, to be paid at the customary rate of two reales daily for a six-day week.[15] The Indians did not provide the labor of their free will; they were compelled by repartimiento to labor, and repartimiento specified their rate of pay. In other words, the Augustinians profited from wage labor recruited by compulsory draft. This repartimiento continued for three years, when it was replaced by an annual money-tribute of three thousand pesos. To raise the tribute, the Indians had to work, although it was no longer specified that the work should be for any particular enterprise.

In another case, the Audiencia (*ca.* 1534) relieved the town of Ocuituco of one-third its tribute obligations, so that the inhabitants might assist the Augustinians in building their church. Actually, the friars abused their privilege, and in planning not only a sumptuous church but a convento as well, so heavily taxed the labor capacity of the village that rebellion broke out. To enforce their will, the friars took justice into their own hands, building prisons for recalcitrant workmen. In 1536, accordingly, the site was assigned to Bishop Zumárraga; the Augustinians were expelled; and a curate was placed in charge.[16]

Other institutions likewise profited from repartimiento. The secular clergy was particularly dependent upon paid draft labor for the accomplishment of its building enterprises. In 1555, the Cathedral of Mexico became a petitioner for the renewal of encomienda grants, not only for the prosecution of the cathedral fabric, but also for the repair of the archepiscopal palace.[17]

The building of cities was performed by labor recruited through encomienda. In Mexico City, for example, before 1529, Cortés assigned several towns to the cabildo, expropriating private grantees in the process; of these towns only one, Ixtapalapa (cf. Fig. 43), remained in the city's trust after the mid-century.[18]

15. Grijalva, *Crónica de la orden de N. P. S. Augustín*, pp. 159, 211–212.

16. G. García, "El Clero," *Documentos inéditos ó muy raros para la historia de México*, XV, 83–86; Cuevas, *Historia de la iglesia en México*, I, 360–361.

17. Motolinia to Charles V, 1555 (in Simpson, *Encomienda*, p. 263; also *CDIAI*, XX [1873], 175–213): "The central church of Mexico, which is the metropolitan, is very poor, old and patched, for it was built flimsily twenty-nine years ago. It is just that your Majesty order it rebuilt and aid it, as of all the churches of New Spain it is the head, Mother and Mistress. So your Majesty should order this church, as well as the other cathedrals, to be given each a town (in encomienda) as they had before, for there will be no encomienda so well employed in all New Spain. They have great need of these towns to repair, roof, clean, and adorn the churches and houses of the bishops, as all are very poor and in debt. Here shoemakers and blacksmiths have encomiendas, but churches have much greater need of them, for they have no rents [sc. income], or what they have is very little."

18. *Archivo mexicano*, I, 62, 235, 262: "D. Fernando [Cortés] señaló por propios desta cibdad cinco

In the early epoch, therefore, until *ca.* 1540, labor was recruited through encomienda. It fell, however, upon the beneficiaries of repartimiento labor to pay their drafted workmen at fixed rates. Here serious obstacles arose. Money was not minted in Mexico until 1535, and after its introduction, so many abuses characterized its use that the Indian populations were the uncomprehending victims of the novel money economy. At first, in 1535, only silver was minted, in pesos, reales, and half-reales. In 1542, Viceroy Mendoza caused two hundred thousand pesos in copper coin to be minted. The Indians then threw the money in the lake of Texcoco because it seemed to them a thing of little value. Even silver coins were held in low esteem, because of their small size.[19] Hence the financing of construction was beset by perplexing problems. Among the Mendicants, cash subsidies were occasionally provided. The Franciscans, for example, received four hundred ducats in cash from the Crown for the building of their establishment at Morelia in the 1580's (Fig. 78); other royal grants of cash were awarded the Dominicans in Puebla and Oaxaca; and the Augustinians enjoyed a viceregal *ayuda de costa* (grant-in-aid) for the building of the great establishment at Yuriria (Fig. *118*).[20]

With or without cash financing, nevertheless, the various agencies engaged in building met troubles with payment. These defects worked to the Indians' disadvantage. The colonists often withheld payment, or failed to discount for labor in the perception of annual tribute. These topics form the substance of many royal orders in the 1530's;[21] a notorious case was that of the city of Mexico, which failed in its payments to the many Indians contributing labor to the public works of the capital in 1552. Of course, the city itself had inadequate revenue. In 1538, the city commanded no funds from which to pay the salary of a building inspector, and this salary had to be met by the Crown from the income of certain corregimientos near the city.[22]

In general, anyone wishing to build in New Spain had to follow two sets of procedure. The first involved securing the assignment of labor through repartimiento. Without such an assignment, no one had access to laborers excepting in the insignificant market of free labor, composed of whites from the poorer classes of the colonists. The next step pertained to the payroll. Labor had to be paid for, but in a currency of

o seys pueblos [sc. Ixtapalapa, Churubusco, Mexicalzingo, Coyoacan, Tlahuac, Mixcoac]."

19. Beaumont, *Crónica de Michoacán*, II, 277. Prior to coinage, grains of cacao served as currency, "como . . . no había moneda de oro, plata, ni vellón, había cesado mucha parte de la contratación; por este motivo, andaban contando los pedazos de oro y plata para hacer las pagas . . . y . . . no podían pagar los indios los tributos, sino en bastimentos y ropa . . ." The minting was done by encomienda Indians from Xiquipilco in 1540; with the cancellation of the encomienda, the casa de moneda was obliged to suspend its minting operations. Puga, *Cedulario*, I, 360–367. *AC*, IV, 210.

20. *Relación . . . Ponce*, I, 531; Puga, *Cedulario*, II, 211; Basalenque, *Historia . . . Michoacán*, p. 56b.

21. e.g., Puga, *Cedulario*, I, 252–253 (Queen to Audiencia, March 20, 1532); II, 122, 225.

22. *Corregimiento* signifies the repartimiento of Indians assigned to the Crown. The Crown administered these Indians through officials designated as *corregidores*.

which the nature and validity were uncertain, and under circumstances in which the Indians were at the colonists' mercies.

The Indian communities, therefore, came under several conflicting labor-levies. Not infrequently, one community was awarded in encomienda to a private trustee, and at the same time, it fell within the jurisdiction of one of the Mendicant Orders. This happened at Huejotzingo between 1529 and 1532. The inhabitants, forty thousand in number, were summoned not only to build the church and the new town, but to provide and transport stone, wood, and lime for the residence of the Oidor Matienzo in Mexico, sixty miles away and across the mountains. In 1529, furthermore, Huejotzingo equipped Nuño de Guzmán's army for the expedition to western Mexico, and provided one thousand warriors.[23]

It has been pointed out elsewhere that the supply of Indian labor decreased steadily (Fig. 7) during the first half of the sixteenth century, mainly because of epidemic disease. Under encomienda, the distribution of Indian labor proved inequitable. There were not enough Indians to satisfy the labor needs of all the various classes of colonists, especially when the labor of large numbers was exclusively enjoyed by a few encomenderos. Beyond their humanitarian and anti-feudatory tendencies, the New Laws of 1542 had the effect, even in their compromised final state, of freeing large reserves of Indian labor from private control. The process was gradual: it will be recalled that with the expiration of encomienda, the Indians in trust reverted to the Crown, coming under the control of Crown officials designated as corregidores. A clear illustration of the effects of Crown incorporation appears in the history of the building of the sumptuous palace for Cortés in Mexico City during the 1530's. Construction began with labor drafted from towns which had not yet been declared *pueblos de realengo* (Crown properties). When their appropriation by the Crown occurred, much to Cortés' dissatisfaction, work upon the palace ceased. Later on, however, the Audiencia assigned a repartimiento, composed of workmen from Crown communities such as Chalco, Otumba, and Tepeapulco to the enterprise. The significant fact is that the workmen were made tributary to the Crown; their labor was assigned to Cortés for a limited period of time, and the men were to receive standard pay from Cortés. Thus the Marqués del Valle lost control over the full labor-potential of these communities, and his usufruct was limited to periods designated by civil authority.[24] As the process of Crown incorporation was achieved throughout Mexico, the Crown became the controlling trustee for the greater part of Indian labor.[25]

Pending the total incorporation of outstanding encomiendas, the Crown sought

23. García Granados and McGregor, *Huejotzingo*, pp. 82, 86–91.

24. Puga, *Cedulario*, I, 258–259 (Queen to Audiencia, March 20, 1532).

25. In New Spain there were 721 encomiendas in 1574 (López de Velasco, *Geografía*); by 1602, only 140 privately-held trusteeships survived (Zavala, *La Encomienda indiana*, pp. 173, 314).

to relieve the Indians' load by forbidding encomenderos to demand or accept labor in place of tribute. The enforcement of this legislation, achieved in 1549, signified the end of the encomienda as a mechanism for providing abundant labor. It still remained necessary, however, after the middle of the century, to coerce the Indian populations to systematic habits of work. The intention of the Crown was to create a system whereby all native labor would be performed voluntarily for wages. This plan fell far short of realization, but a compromise was instituted in the so-called cuatequil, or *corvée,* recruited from forced wage labor by a system of draft. Under this institution the Indians were compelled to serve at stated periods for standard pay on specified tasks. The administration of this draft labor was in the hands of specially appointed officials (*jueces repartidores*) who were to ensure that the draft labor was performed within reasonable distance from the laborer's place of residence, and that his term of service should not be more than one week at a time, for three or four weeks each year. With the cuatequil, the unqualified and unspecified labor exactions typical of encomienda came to an end.[26]

However greatly the condition of Indian labor improved under these legislative reforms after 1550, the workmen remained subject to many abuses difficult to control. In 1574, for example, the cuatequil administration was the subject of complaint by the Indians to the King. Skilled laborers suffered most. When an artisan's turn came to serve in draft labor, his services were paid at the common laborer's rate (one *tomin* daily), although in ordinary service, such artisans were accustomed to earning three and four times that sum. The difference between the wages of free labor and cuatequil labor was, of course, exploited by the Spaniards, who formed the practice of hiring out the skilled labor assigned to their service at whatever rates the artisan customarily earned upon the free labor market. In other cases, the beneficiary of a cuatequil assignment retained the laborers long after the completion of the task to which they had been assigned, hiring them out for his own profit.[27] The fault here lay with the jueces repartidores, for they were required to specify the pay and provide exact descriptions of the kind of task to which the draft labor was assigned. A typical case concerns the Hospital Real de los Indios in Mexico City in 1576. The juez repartidor for the province of Chalco specified the task as that of cutting and transporting five hundred roof beams to the edge of the lake ready for shipment to the capital. The

26. Zavala, *New Viewpoints,* pp. 85, 93, 95. The term *cuatequil* is the Nahuatl equivalent of the *mita* in Peru. It occurs rarely in sixteenth-century texts. Zavala, however, uses the term to distinguish Mexican draft labor from the Peruvian mita, and to distinguish draft labor from repartimiento. This latter distinction is perhaps unwarranted. Between repartimiento and cuatequil there are few if any differences: Simpson, *Many Mexicos,* p. 115, gives a definition for the juez de repartimiento which is indistinguishable from Zavala's definition of the juez repartidor. As Simpson has pointed out, repartimiento without encomienda is equivalent to state control of labor; encomienda implies feudal overlordship (Simpson, *Encomienda,* p. 92, n. 18).

27. "Códice Mendieta I," *NCDHM,* IV, 182–183; Zavala, *Fuentes,* II, 201, 233.

rate of pay and the number of Indians were fixed by the judge.[28] The probity of the cuatequil administration was in the hands of these officials: their collusion with other colonists was common.

Another cause for Indian complaint concerning the draft labor repartimiento arose because of their compulsion to labor away from their own homes. The jueces repartidores seem to have conceived the problems of labor distribution in a regional sense. In road building enterprises, this was inevitable.[29] It was also necessary in areas recently depopulated, where an insufficient labor-supply was available. Such was the case in the district of Tepeapulco in 1575, when the villagers of one town were compelled to work upon the churches in both of two neighboring settlements.[30]

Thus the administration of forced wage labor by the jueces repartidores was not unlike the Manpower Commission of modern wartime days, serving under emergency conditions for the rationing of a limited supply of labor. But the institution also embraced the functions of a Labor Relations Board designed in theory at least to protect the Indian workmen from extortion and exploitation. Indian complaints were heard and judged by a special court, the *juzgado de indios,* and direct appeals to the King and Viceroy are frequently recorded.[31] The weakness of the system lay in its venal administrators and in the lax agencies of enforcement.

As Zavala has pointed out, it was not until after 1600 that an abundant supply of voluntary Indian wage labor appeared in New Spain. Early seventeenth-century legislation substituted *comisarios de alquileres* for the jueces repartidores. They were empowered to assign Indian labor, but not without the consent of the laborer. Thus state control of Indian labor underwent restrictions tending to favor the Indian. Such dispositions, however, did not become really effective until after 1632.[32]

When Indian communities wished to undertake building operations for their own benefit, during the latter part of the sixteenth century, they called upon a local supply of voluntary building labor, within the administrative machinery of the repartimiento. In 1575, for instance, the Indians of Tlatelolco needed a more abundant water supply. Although the community could furnish the necessary labor, supervision, and materials for building a conduit from Chapultepec, no facilities for burning lime were available. The headmen, therefore, approached the Viceroy with the suggestion that the Municipal Council of Mexico City provide the lime. The city agreed, and

28. *Ibid.*, I, 59.

29. Simpson, "Studies," *Iberoamericana,* XIII, 25, for the viceregal repartimiento for roadbuilding in Tehuantepec province, 1542.

30. Zavala, *Fuentes,* I, 15–16. The inhabitants of Tlaltecaguan were compelled to build churches in Tepeapulco and in Apam, by the authorities at Tepeapulco.

31. Compare the sampling of cases handled by the juzgado de indios, presented by Simpson, "Studies," *Iberoamericana,* XIII, *passim.* See also "Códice Mendieta I," *NCDHM,* IV, 182.

32. Zavala, *New Viewpoints,* pp. 95–103.

three thousand pesos worth of lime was provided. The work was completed before September, 1582. It is a striking case of initiative coming, or so we may suppose, from the Indians.[33]

Zavala has also indicated that the system of debt-servitude was elaborated in New Spain during the seventeenth century. There are indications, however, that peonage, which is closely related to the emergence of voluntary wage labor, was fairly well-established as early as 1575. In essence, peonage is the device whereby the voluntary wage laborer is bound to his employer by substantial debts of money and goods advanced against his pay. In Puebla in 1575, we have the case of some quarryworkers who were receiving advances against future pay; the men had been in the service of one employer for twenty years. Again in Puebla, a skilful Indian mason employed by the Dominicans died in 1586, owing the considerable sum of twenty pesos drawn in advance.[34]

The relationship of these various devices of labor-recruitment to building activity is obvious. An apparently unlimited supply of labor during the first decades of colonization was used to realize a vast program of urban architectural activity. With the charting and diminution of the actual labor-supply, stringent state controls were devised, culminating in the cuatequil. But as the supply was reduced by disease, labor became more and more expensive. Substantial wage increases are reported in the last quarter of the century for draft laborers,[35] perhaps to compete with the growing class of voluntary wage workers. As the cost of labor rose, so did building activity diminish. It should not be forgotten, nevertheless, that a state of saturation had been reached by *ca.* 1580. At that time, the initial architectural needs of the colony had been satisfied. The great cathedral-building campaigns of the last quarter of the century utilized highly specialized, expensive Indian labor, but the building of the cathedrals cannot be compared as to scale or magnitude of operations with the vast missionary undertaking of the preceding generations.

The construction of a European building, such as a church or a house, requires a construction crew trained in many different kinds of skills. In sixteenth-century Mexico, the supply of such workmen was formed very slowly. Pre-Conquest construction was done mainly by the accumulation of large quantities of inert material, which could be assembled and shaped by relatively untrained labor. The temples were structurally simple enclosures upon immense platforms of solid material (Fig. 35). Houses and public buildings likewise consisted of solid platforms bearing simple trabeated shelters. Individuality was given by surface decoration, in painted and carved orna-

33. *AC,* VIII (1893), 181, 184; cf. 599.

34. See Simpson, "Studies," *Iberoamericana,* XIII, 78, 93; Zavala, *New Viewpoints,* pp. 48–49, 97–99; Dávila Padilla, *Historia . . . Santiago de México,* p. 83.

35. Zavala, *New Viewpoints,* pp. 93–103.

ment. Highly trained labor, therefore, was needed before the Conquest only for the decoration of buildings, where painters, stonecutters, plasterers, and wood-carvers enriched the surfaces. The structural program, which necessitated the piling of earth and simple post-and-lintel construction (Fig. 36), was achieved by large numbers of unskilled laborers, recruited by a system of communal draft not unlike the colonial cuatequil, to which indeed it gave origin.

The organization of early colonial construction crews, therefore, followed closely the pattern of pre-Conquest labor organization. The colonists had to utilize large quantities of unskilled Indian labor, and in its mobilization, they were forced to revive and implement certain pre-Conquest modes of civil and political authority. A critical relationship grew up between the colonists and the chiefs or headmen of Indian society. As we have seen, virtually all labor was secured under the fiduciary conditions of repartimiento. But to utilize Indian labor, the colonists had to be sure of the collaboration of the men who commanded Indian society. Whenever Indian labor was adapted to European uses, in quantities where social discipline was essential for the efficient use of the labor, it may be assumed that Indian chiefs and headmen were retained in power. Political, economic, military, or moral pressures secured the chiefs' collaboration. Some Indians participated in the colonial enterprise in order to retain their previous powers; others were bought, and still others were coerced. Some were reëducated, and, perhaps, morally persuaded into Christian service.

An illustration appears in the rebuilding of Mexico City. In 1522, Cortés found it necessary to reinstate several great Indian officials, and to endow them with specific powers, in order to proceed with the ambitious program of recreating the island capital. Thus one of Motecuzoma's war captains, the Cihuacoatl priest, named Juan Velásquez Tlacotzin, was assigned the lordship (señorío) of one of the four great districts of the city, the barrio of S. Antonio Abad (known before the Conquest as Xolloco and Acatlan). A son of Motecuzoma, Don Pedro Motecuzoma Tlacahuepan, was assigned the ward of San Sebastian (Atzacoalco), and other Indian nobles were likewise confirmed in large powers.[36] Don Fernando Ixtlilxochitl, lord of Texcoco, also applied his authority to the task. After accompanying Cortés to Honduras in 1524, he sought to prove his loyalty to Cortés, and his Christian piety by summoning his nobles to aid in building the primitive cathedral, and the Franciscan establishment. In these operations, Ixtlilxochitl is said to have labored with his own hands as an *albañil* (plasterer or bricklayer), and his nobles assisted in transporting stone, lime, and sand. Twenty thousand workmen from Texcoco (!) are alleged to have partici-

36. J. M. Marroqui, *La Ciudad de México* (Mexico, 1900–1903), I (1900), 25–26 (citing F. L. de Gómara, *Historia de las conquistas de Hernando Cortés* [Mexico, 1826], II, cap. 51). Cf. also Gage, *The English-American*, p. 80, obviously following Gómara.

pated under Ixtlilxochitl's orders.[37] Cortés obliged the Chalcas, the Xochimilcas, and the Tepanecas to bring lumber, earth, and other building materials for filling the marshes of the island, building houses, and laying out streets. Here again, it is inconceivable that such masses of labor can have been adapted without recreating in some measure the ranks and authorities of Indian society. Although they are not specifically mentioned, lords, chiefs, and headmen were surely induced by the colonists to mobilize the resources of labor at their disposal.[38]

The Mendicants also made use of Indian chiefs to exploit Indian labor. In the southern part of the Valley of Mexico, the Franciscans were powerfully aided in their endeavors by the services of a converted chief, called Don Francisco, of Tlahuac, of whom we are told that he built many churches.[39] Similarly in southern Mexico, the Dominicans received help from Cosijopi, a grandson of Motecuzoma, and the ruler of the Zapotecs. Taking the name Juan Cortés de Motecuzoma II at baptism, he remained a secret idolater, but ordered his people to work upon the building of the Dominican establishment in Tehuantepec.[40]

The early colonial institution of cuatequil likewise depended upon the collaboration of local chiefs. A case in point is recorded for Morelia, where in 1543, the Viceroy gave orders to recruit draft labor through the agency of local headmen and officials.[41]

Apart from empowering the traditional rulers of Indian society, the colonists also bestowed authority upon competent Indian craftsmen who lacked other civil prestige. By making an Indian an *alguacil,* the Spaniards enabled him to recruit construction gangs. Such was the case in 1576, when an Indian named Marcos Carpintero, in the metropolitan ward of San Juan, was entrusted with enlisting and assembling the workmen needed in Mexico City for the building of the monastery of Regina Coeli. The Indian was made responsible for the payroll and the welfare of the workmen in his charge.[42] Municipal works, however, remained under the supervision of the obrero mayor, whose immediate assistants might be Indian officials. The labor for public works, as we have seen, came from the municipal encomienda of Ixtapalapa, and in 1549, the encomienda furnished forty-six workmen, of whom two were chiefs, serving also upon occasion as carpenters.[43]

Without such alliances between the colonists and the headmen of Indian society, the labors of colonization would have been impossible.[44] The colonist working among

37. Ixtlilxochitl, *Obras históricas,* I, 435–436. Also cited by Vetancurt, *Chrónica, Teatro,* Pt. IV, p. 26.

38. D. Durán, *Historia de las Indias de Nueva-España y islas de Tierra Firme* (Mexico, 1867–80), II, 64.

39. Torquemada, . . . *Monarchia indiana,* III, 146. Tlahuac was originally Cuitlahuac.

40. Burgoa, *Geográfica descripción,* II, 378, 389; J. Galindo y Villa, "Algo sobre los Zapotecas y los edificios de Mitla," *Anales del museo nacional de México,* época 2, II (1905), 222, n. 35.

41. Simpson, "Studies," *Iberoamericana,* XIII, 28.

42. Zavala, *Fuentes,* I, 66.

43. *AC,* V (1862), 260–261.

44. It is interesting to observe that among mixed populations it was difficult to recruit labor. At Pahuatlan, for example, the Augustinians were unable to build any permanent edifices between 1552 and 1571,

the members of an alien culture is rarely able to manipulate its internal arrangements successfully. The best he can do is to exert pressure upon the total configuration, and thus bring about its internal deformation. Sustained pressure is sometimes best brought to bear upon non-democratic culture as a whole through the intermediary of its most responsible and authoritarian members. In Mexican society, the Conquest, fortunately for the Spaniards, induced relatively few phenomena of delayed resistance, as was later the case in Peru. With few exceptions, the headmen of Indian society proved tractable to European coercion and persuasion, and the work of colonization was realized in large part through their agency.

The internal organization of the Indian construction crews shows little change from pre-Conquest antecedents. Communal levies of labor, based upon the tribal or administrative divisions of Indian society, provided the framework of the organization. An admirably detailed record of the communal composition of the crew on one of the metropolitan undertakings in 1576 has been preserved. It pertains to the building of the tecpan (town hall) of the Indian community of Tlatelolco (Figs. 90–92), and provides an exact program, schedule, and chronology for an important civil edifice, of a type probably normative for all Indian communities in the colony.[45] In 1576, Tlatelolco was divided into six *parcialidades,* or districts, each with its subordinate barrios, or wards. In addition, the community included twenty nearby settlements, called *hermitas,* and five outlying hamlets, called *pueblos de visita.* It was the function of the Indian governor of Tlatelolco to summon the representatives of these various divisions together, to assign the work on the new casa de comunidad. The governor himself, named Miguel García, was appointed by the Viceroy. The document in question is composed as a running dialogue between the governor and the tribal representatives. The inhabitants of Tequipeuhquinepantla undertook to build the viceregal rooms; the Cohuateca were made responsible for the building of all inner partitions throughout the edifice; the men of Calpoltitlan were assigned the building of the upper stories, and so on. Three parcialidades were made responsible for the feeding of the workmen, and another parcialidad was entrusted with the planting and the care of the gardens. The building assignments show a relatively high degree of specialization. The men of Atzompan were entrusted with the water-conduits for the new building, and two other districts built nothing but the bathhouse.

A similar articulation of labor, by draft from communal groups, is also suggested by the sparse notices for Mendicant building. The *Códice franciscano* of 1569, for instance, mentions such an inter-communal division of labor in the building of the

because of the "floxedad y pereza de los naturales, . . ." composed of Otomies, Mexicans, and Tarascas. *PNE,* V, 280–281. The divided native command in the community may perhaps be blamed.

45. J. Fernández, ed., "Códice del tecpan de Tlaltelolco," *Investigaciones históricas,* I, no. 3 (1939), 243–264.

establishment at Zempoala, in the State of Hidalgo (Figs. 199, *241*), where the inhabitants of Zempoala, Zacuala, Tlaquilpa, and Tequipilpa collaborated in church building, although they were distinct communities held in different encomiendas.[46] And at Tlalnepantla (Fig. 317), near Mexico City, the participant communities in a similar enterprise recorded their labors in inscriptions distributed about the buildings.[47]

The procedure with regard to public works outside the towns is also recorded in the case of the building of a bridge near Ocuituco in 1576. At the Viceroy's order, the provincial *alcalde* (a European) was commissioned to survey the labor situation. In agreement with his recommendations the Viceroy ordered that all settlements and ranches in the neighborhood of the proposed bridge aid in its construction. Certain villages were ordered to provide the timbers for the scaffolding, delivered to a site where they might be picked up by ox-teams. The Spanish farmers of the region were required to provide the teams. Other Indian villages furnished the lime, while still others furnished their share of the crew of fifty laborers and twelve masons necessary for the work. Thus the undertaking was regionally distributed, so that the full load fell upon no single community. The Indians were held responsible for the contribution of materials and labor, and the more expensive equipment (ox-teams) was furnished by resident Europeans.[48]

Later on in the sixteenth century, the officers of the Court of Congregation followed the same method of communal levies in the building of many new towns. In the province of Tlanchinol, for instance, some two thousand people were congregated in a new settlement which was to have eleven wards. Each ward corresponded to one of the scattered communities brought together in the new congregation, and each ward was to have its own casa de comunidad and its own chapel, remaining a self-governing entity within the town as a whole. The men assembled by squads of ten, and each squad was assigned to particular tasks, such as clearing, carrying materials, and so on. Squads of women fed the workmen. The task of equipping the new town was completed in eight months, without interruption to planting or harvest. This late instance probably reflects closely the earlier organization for town-building activities developed by the Mendicants.[49]

The communal labor levy simplified the problem of recruitment. By its means, large labor gangs could be mobilized rapidly. But its great disadvantage resided in the fact that it was composed mainly of unskilled laborers. Its size for most enterprises, therefore, tended to become unwieldy, and immense gangs of men were needed for operations otherwise easily within the capacities of a few highly trained workers with

46. "Códice franciscano," *NCDHM*, II, 15. Vetancurt, *Chrónica, Teatro*, Pt. IV, pp. 4, 70.

47. See Appendix, p. 480. J. McAndrew has informed me of many such inscriptions at Tultitlan, near Cuautitlan. Compare the glyphs on the Arcos de Zempoala.

48. Zavala, *Fuentes*, I, 135–136.

49. See Simpson, *Many Mexicos*, p. 101.

adequate tools. In the building of the façade galleries of the palace of Cortés in Mexico City (Figs. 70–72), the repartimiento Indians of Coyoacan were engaged for twenty-seven years, from 1524 to 1551. During this period, four hundred Indians worked for two days to bring the stone for the staircase alone. Some 320 Indians were busied for four days merely in bringing to the city the eight stone bases for the gallery columns. On the building itself, 110 Indians worked daily all during 1532, and five carpenters were steadily employed to make the doors and windows for the edifice. Such extravagant outlays of labor are only partly explained by the absence of adequate numbers of draft animals: the retrograde technology and the deficient training of the workmen should be accounted.[50] It will be granted that the building of a great urban palace required diversified and highly finished workmanship which draft laborers were ill-equipped and indifferently disposed to provide.

Other undertakings required no specially skilled workmen. Such was the building of the great Ecatepec causeway, under the direction of Gerónimo de Zárate OFM, in four months at the beginning of the seventeenth century.[51] On this enterprise, two thousand workmen were continuously employed to build a wall some eighteen yards wide. Their main task was transporting an immense volume of earth. The building of the famous aqueduct to Otumba (Fig. 100), on the other hand, under the direction of Francisco de Tembleque OFM, lasted sixteen years. One section of its arcades took five years to build, during which Tembleque had the assistance of three to four hundred artisans and laborers. The construction of large arches required a certain skill; and the gathering of the materials required a great volume of unskilled labor. The undertaking was therefore costly both as to time and as to quantities of labor.[52]

In churchbuilding, large groups of workmen labored for long periods to achieve the intricate and diversified structures of religious architecture. In 1556, Archbishop Montúfar complained that the Indians were brought by the friars to work on the great monastic churches "in gangs of 500, 600, or 1,000, from a distance of four, six, or twelve leagues, without . . . any wages, or even a crust of bread."[53]

At Yanhuitlan (Fig. 171), in the 1570's, the Indians assigned to the cuatequil for the church numbered six thousand. These were divided in ten shifts of six hundred each,[54] which were charged with transporting stone, lime and water for the fabric. These numbers did not include the artisans who worked the stone, mixed the mortar, and assisted the European craftsmen who directed the enterprise. The Europeans'

50. "Documentos . . . Cortés," *Publ. AGN,* XXVII, 300–342. Many observers have noted the extravagant use of labor by modern employers throughout Latin America. The phenomenon has been related to class rigidity, under which a cheap labor is kept cheap by little education and by wasteful laboring methods.

51. Vetancurt, *Chrónica, Teatro,* Pt. IV, p. 74.

52. "Códice franciscano," *NCDHM,* II, 31–32; cf. Chap. VII, p. 298.

53. Simpson, *op. cit.,* p. 82.

54. Burgoa, *Geográfica descripción,* I, 193, 291–292; B. Cobo, "Dos cartas inéditas," *Revista histórica* [Lima], III (1928), 35, gives four hundred.

assistants, however, were selected from among the most competent workmen in the undifferentiated, unskilled laboring mass.

With distance from the capital, moreover, the size of construction crews increased. Small establishments, such as Etzatlan or Ajijic in New Galicia, required large gangs of workmen.[55] In thinly populated areas, these construction levies seriously depleted the labor reserves of the area in question. The skill of the workmen, furthermore, may be said to have been inversely proportional to their distance from the pre-Conquest centers of high culture.

It is generally true that organization was deficient within the laboring mass on an enterprise. Great numbers were relied upon, in the absence of careful planning, highly skilled labor, and internal organization. One of the consequences of amateur or defective supervision was an actual increase in the laboring load of the workmen. Errors of design and miscalculations often necessitated the expenditure of many times the effort that would have been needed under competent direction.[56] Thus in Michoacan, in 1561, the Augustinians were accused of having made the Indians rebuild unnecessarily many times over. In Guadalajara an absurd situation existed before 1547, where "in little more than a year there were two churches built and two demolished" by the Franciscan guardian of the establishment. In Oaxaca likewise, the Dominicans were accused of having wasted much effort on thoughtless rebuilding.[57] Without close supervision, the Indians were likely, moreover, to work shoddily. In Mexico City the Indian workmen, when not under inspection, were in the habit of mixing mortar with ashes instead of with lime, and in 1538, the situation called for a building inspector who should be specifically commissioned to supervise the mixing of mortar.[58]

During building operations, the laborers usually took up residence at the site. This was as much for the convenience of the encomendero as for the workmen. For example, Fernando Cortés built a compound in Mexico City near the Casas Nuevas, upon part of the site of the Plaza del Volador, to house his Indian workmen from Coyoacan.[59] The fixed domicile of the modern construction-worker was often impossible. A building-site resembled a camp of impermanent dwellings, swarming with the families of the workers, who disappeared after completion of the buildings. The temporary residence of the workers at the site still may be observed in modern Mexico.[60] The economic reason is obvious enough; for the wage-laborer whose only shelter is a wretched hut of impermanent construction, that shelter may be reproduced with little effort wherever the workman is employed. Of course, where a church was being

55. *PNE*, I, 135. At Etzatlan in 1554, the church was being built by one hundred men, and the trivial structure at Ajijic was the work of seventy-five men. Fig. 430 is surely a later edifice than the one implied here.

56. Cuevas, *Documentos inéditos*, p. 262.

57. Simpson, "Studies," *Iberoamericana*, XIII, 83; Burgoa, *op. cit.*, II, 201.

58. Puga, *Cedulario*, I, 413.

59. Alamán, *Disertaciones*, II, 214.

60. See G. Diamant, *The Days of Ofelia* (Boston, 1942), pp. 29–30.

built by the inhabitants of the town for whom the edifice was destined, the displacement from home to place of work might be so slight as to make it unnecessary for the workmen to change their domicile. Sometimes the white supervisors provided the workmen's nourishment. On the great monastic enterprises, a friar was appointed as *refitolero,* or commissary, as with fray Juan Bautista de Moya in 1552 at the building of the Augustinian establishment in Morelia.[61] And if the workmen came from any distance, they were given leave to return home at intervals. Fernando Cortés' Indians from Coyoacan, for instance, resided in Mexico City in the compound from Monday noon to Saturday noon, and returned weekly to their villages some miles to the south.[62] It is not unlikely that such building crews changed composition rapidly, being drafted from different parts of the community in each period of service.

The initial success of any colonial building campaign depends in part upon the state of building knowledge among the native peoples. If the initial campaign is successful, as it was in Mexico, one may postulate a high degree of building skill among the Indians, dependent in the main upon pre-Conquest traditions. A few colonists, however, tended to deprecate the architectural knowledge and ability of their Indian laborers (contrast pp. 155–157). Motolinia, for example, *ca.* 1540, wrote (perhaps in praise) that the Indians "no saben sino servir y trabajar. Todos saben labrar una pared, y hacer una casa, torcer un cordel, y todos los oficios que no requieren mucho arte."[63] The statement contains a confession: if the Indians were lacking more advanced techniques, they were at least equipped with basic skills, and for Spanish purposes, these basic skills were essential.

The real difficulty with Indian labor was discovered in the diversity of tribal traditions. The state of technical knowledge varied widely from tribe to tribe. In western Mexico, for example, the sparse villages possessed little tradition of monumental building such as the Spaniards found in the eastern and southern parts of New Spain.[64] In southern Mexico, on the other hand, among the Zapotecs and Mixtecs, the Dominicans discovered an abundant and docile supply of unskilled building labor, well accustomed to monumental undertakings.[65] But the lack of highly trained artisans prevented the construction of permanent establishments until well after the middle of the century.[66]

The real center of highly developed building skills was in the Valley of Mexico.

61. Escobar, *Americana thebaida,* p. 483.

62. "Documentos . . . Cortés," *Publ. AGN,* XXVII, 346.

63. Motolinia, "Historia de los indios de la Nueva España," *CDHM,* I, 76.

64. Grijalva, *Crónica de la orden de N. P. S. Agustín,* pp. 222–223.

65. Torquemada, . . . *Monarchia indiana,* III, 41. The Indians of southern Mexico were "mas dociles, y obedientes, que lo estàn los de esta Comarca de Mexico."

66. See Burgoa, *Geográfica descripción,* II, 207, on conditions at Juquila, in Oaxaca province.

Pomar, for instance, tells us that the education of the nobles of Texcoco was partly dedicated to learning such crafts as masonry and carpentry, painting, woodcarving, gem-cutting, and goldworking.[67] Near the capital, each village was likely to have its own masons, bricklayers, carpenters, lime-burners, and iron-workers, as at Coatepec Chalco in 1579.[68] As we have already learned, the rebuilding of Tenochtitlan in the 1520's was carried on by twenty thousand workmen from Texcoco, under the direction of Fernando Ixtlilxochitl, the ruler, who worked as albañil, supervising his tribesmen. Even his nobles are reputed to have shared in the work of transporting stone, lime, and sand for the building of the Franciscan establishment in the capital.[69] In 1540, according to Motolinia, virtually all the Indian masons in New Spain came from Tenochtitlan or from the province of Texcoco; they traveled throughout the land, working for daily wages, probably serving as foremen and as the leaven of skilled labor in the mass of local, unskilled workmen.[70] Their services were much sought after: in 1528, Cortés specified that masons from Texcoco and Otumba should build the casas nuevas in the capital.[71] Other competent craftsmen were found in Xochimilco: Ixtlilxochitl tells us that the Xochimilcas were "grandes maestros de obras de arquitectura y carpintería, y otras artes mecánicas."[72] Xochimilco ultimately became so important a center for skilled labor, that in the seventeenth century, the census and tax-lists of the community were registered by crafts rather than by wards or precincts, as was customary elsewhere in New Spain.[73]

The best laborers were concentrated in the vicinity of the capital, and the peripheral provinces were initially devoid of adequately trained craftsmen. For the colonists, it was essential to remove this differential. The diffusion of technical knowledge was achieved by two methods. Trained craftsmen, both Indian and European, were sent from the capital to the province; and Indians were sent from the provinces to be apprenticed to craftsmen in the capital. The Augustinians were particularly active in these operations. At Tiripitio, in 1537, they imported European master craftsmen, masons, and joiners. In the building of the church and convento (Fig. *158*), these masters not only directed building operations, but they consciously gave instruction until 1548, to such an extent that Tiripitio became the trade school for all Michoacan, sending its craftsmen far and wide, thus hastening its ultimate human impoverishment.[74] An analogous case among the Franciscans is that of Zapotlan (now Ciudad

67. J. B. Pomar, "Relación de Texcoco," *NCDHM*, III, 41.

68. *PNE*, VI, 63–65.

69. Ixtlilxochitl, *Obras históricas*, I, 435; cited by Vetancurt, *Chrónica, Teatro*, Pt. IV, p. 26. *Albañil* signifies plasterer or bricklayer.

70. Motolinia, *op. cit.*, p. 186. Vetancurt, *Chrónica, Teatro*, Pt. IV, p. 26.

71. A. de Valle-Arizpe, *El Palacio nacional de México* (Mexico, 1936), p. 28.

72. Ixtlilxochitl, *Obras históricas*, I, 455.

73. Vetancurt, *op. cit.*, pp. 56–57.

74. Escobar, *Americana thebaida*, pp. 77, 148; Basalenque, *Historia . . . Michoacán*, p. 20b.

Guzman) in Jalisco, where fray Juan de Padilla introduced three albañiles from Mexico in 1535. One of these men was later sent, *ca.* 1550, to nearby Zacoalco, to direct construction there, where the Indians were unacquainted even with the manufacture of adobes. Even nearer the metropolis, the techniques of masonry were sometimes not familiar to the Indians. Echeverría, writing in the eighteenth century, reported as follows: "The Indians were more skilful in building with wood than with masonry, for many of their houses, in the Mexican Empire as in the provinces of Tlaxcala, Cholula, and elsewhere, were of wood daubed with mud inside and outside and whitewashed."[75]

The Indians sent from the provinces to the capital were schooled at such centers as the great trade school affiliated with the Franciscan establishment in Mexico City. Located near the chapel of San José de los Naturales, the school was founded and directed by the remarkable lay brother, Pedro de Gante. In a set of rooms specially reserved for the purpose, he gave instruction to grown Indians in all the arts and crafts, in order to provide the artisans for the construction, ornamentation, and furnishing of churches.[76] Mendieta reports that at the school, the pupils were taught the use of metal tools, such as picks and mason's chisels (Figs. 38–40). They also learned to build the various kinds of arches, doors, windows, columns, and pilasters.

More effectively than by formal schooling, the Indians learned construction technique in practice. For example, the Indians first saw vaulted construction being erected in the earliest chapel of San Francisco in Mexico. When the scaffolds and centerings were removed, the Indians at first refused to risk walking underneath so novel a structure, but soon overcame their fear and built other vaults on their own initiative. Motolinia cites two small chapels in the *atrio* of San Francisco in Tlaxcala (see pp. 331–332) as the earliest examples of this new Indian activity (Figs. 253–256). Later on, if we are to believe Mendieta, a wave of enthusiasm for building churches swept over the evangelized populations in the late 1530's, and the Indians built abundantly, finishing many churches in a half-year or less, to have them ready before the arrival of the friars assigned to those posts.[77]

Sometimes the friars alone undertook to teach the Indians certain skills. Fray Juan de Alameda, for example, taught the Indians of Huejotzingo the principles of hydrostatics in connection with the urbanization of Huaquechula; later in the cen-

75. N. A. de Ornelas Mendoza y Valdivia, *Crónica de la provincia de Santiago de Xalisco* (Guadalajara, 1941), pp. 16–34; Mendoza, *Fragmentos,* pp. 23–27; Echeverría, *Historia . . . Puebla,* I, 295: "Los indios . . . eran más diestros en edificar de maderas que de mazonería, porque una gran parte de sus casas, tanto en el Imperio Mexicano, como en las provincias de Tlaxcala, Cholula y las demás eran de madera revocadas de lodo por dentro y fuera y blanqueadas."

76. See Ricard, *La "Conquête spirituelle" du Mexique,* p. 255; F. Ocaranza, *El imperial Colegio de indios de la Santa Cruz de Santiago Tlaltelolco* (Mexico, 1934), pp. 21–24. Mendieta, *Historia eclesiástica indiana,* pp. 407–410, 608. Torquemada, . . . *Monarchia indiana,* III, 211, reports having seen these rooms, where the smiths and painters learned their trade.

77. Mendieta, *op. cit.,* pp. 321–322, 410.

tury, in 1576, those specific Indians were needed by the civil authorities of Puebla because of their previous training.[78] But civilians were not without influence: an interesting case is found at Etla in Oaxaca at the end of the century. A Spanish carpenter named Sebastián García had been employed by the Dominicans to fashion and install an elaborate wooden ceiling on the church. When he died, shortly before 1595, the Indians were able to complete the last third of the intricate work he left unfinished.[79]

By 1575 the specialization of labor in certain regions was well established, and the Indian craftsmen enjoyed some legal protection. A case arose in Puebla in which the procurer for the Cathedral fabric attempted to alienate quarry workers who had been regularly employed by a private individual for twenty years. As wage earners, they were better off than under the supervision of the cathedral officers. A court decision finally supported the status of the workmen, decreeing that they should remain in their usual employment.[80] But it cannot be overlooked that within the guilds, the Indians were the victims of prejudicial treatment. The discrimination against them usually took the form of keeping them as apprentices. They were not allowed in the guilds to advance beyond the rank of journeyman.[81] The antagonism between Indian and European workmen in the same craft was natural: it arose because of the serious competition offered by Indians.[82] We have seen, of course, that the government occasionally bestowed civil rank and authority upon Indian overseers and supervisors. But these were trivial offices of limited tenure. Permanent appointments of greater responsibility were closed to Indian candidates. In 1552, the Indian practitioners of the oficios mecánicos were barred from holding office as corregidores, or administrators of Crown properties, for the reason that the rank and status (calidades) of the Spanish officials might thereby be lessened in the eyes of the Indians.[83] Thus possession of a craft or profession did not allow the Indian any great mobility within the society. His prestige, however high it might rise among his own people, remained small as to civilian status among white Spaniards.

So far in this chapter, we have accounted for Indian labor as to the methods of its recruitment, the organization of the building crews, and the training and skill of Indian workmen. All these problems, however, are preparatory to the central question. What sensibility did the Indian workmen bring to the work in hand? What were their esthetic preferences, what were their standards of taste, and what psychological adjustment did they develop in regard to the conqueror's style of building? Apart

78. Zavala, *Fuentes*, I, 138.

79. Burgoa, *Geográfica descripción*, II, 5. In 1941, the beds of the main members of this ceiling were still visible.

80. Zavala, *Fuentes*, I, 48–49.

81. Simpson, "Studies," *Iberoamericana*, XIII, 130. See J. F. del Barrio Lorenzot, *El Trabajo en México durante la época colonial. Ordenanzas de gremios de la Nueva España* (Mexico, 1920), *passim*.

82. See Motolinia, "Historia de los indios de la Nueva España," *CDHM*, I, 213.

83. Puga, *Cedulario*, II, 185–186.

from the primary evidence of the monuments (see Chaps. V–VIII and Conclusion), these questions may be approached through texts pertaining to contemporary Spanish judgments. Other texts yield the Indians' own attitude towards architectural labor.

Among the colonists, it is interesting to note that even the Indian's enemies, with few exceptions, praised his learning capacity, and the readiness with which he acquired the most exacting European skills. That the guilds would not admit Indians to the advanced ranks is a proof of the fears of competition aroused by Indian proficiency. The sources tend to agree upon the point: the Indians were highly gifted for the exercise of the arts, and we find the theme discussed in many different circles. In Sahagún, the artistic ability of the Indians is the subject of dispassionate ethnological observation. Bernal Díaz del Castillo and other chroniclers allude to the fact with astonishment and admiration. Finally, the pro-Indian propagandists, such as Las Casas, made of the Indians' artistic ability a cardinal point in their defense. Among the apologists, the artistic skill of the Indians was made into a telling argument in favor of the rationality and humanity of the native peoples of America. Thus Las Casas demonstrates the lucid intelligence, the valor, the physical beauty, sobriety, chastity, judgment, self-control, and social virtue of the Indian quite briefly. But the ensuing description of the material culture of the Indies takes twenty-two chapters, with extremely detailed accounts of cities, buildings, public works, agriculture, stock-raising, industries, arts and crafts, and commerce.[84]

It is perhaps characteristic of the Spaniard of the sixteenth century that he was willing to be impressed by the magnificence of exotic civilizations. We may recall Charles V's deep admiration for the monuments of Islamic culture in Granada; a similar respect or piety for alien achievements was also felt by his colonists in New Spain. They were anxious, perhaps, to aggrandize their own conquests by praising the splendor of the conquered civilization, but it cannot be denied that the men of Cortés' generation demanded and sought the opportunities for awestruck admiration of other cultures. Hence the texts with which we are occupied were written by men willing to admire, and by men whose colonial ambitions could not be achieved without the assistance of the Indian peoples.

On the other hand, one cannot escape the impression that the Indians of metropolitan Mexico were avid for technological experience, absorbing it much more rapidly than the civilian colonists were willing to allow. Mendieta compared the Indians to monkeys, imitating everything they saw the whites do in their workshops. In 1524 or 1525, the Indians surreptitiously copied a Spanish loom and learned all the processes connected with its use through observation.[85] They likewise copied the

84. Las Casas, *Apologética historia de las Indias* (Madrid, 1909) (Nueva biblioteca de autores españoles, XIII. Historiadores de Indias, I), pp. 158–163.

85. Mendieta, *Historia eclesiástica indiana*, p. 255.

goldworkers' techniques, and the skills of the makers of gilt leather, the saddlemakers, and so on, with disastrous effects upon the Europeans' monopoly of those manufactures.[86] In short, even the Indians' enemies were forced to take account of the lively, collected, and pertinacious understanding described by Motolinia. Such receptivity to new technological experience was, moreover, a fundamental trait of Aztec culture before the Conquest, as we know from the rapid and eclectic absorption of the techniques of other peoples by the Aztecs in the fifteenth century. Part of their political domination of Middle America was based upon the ease with which they learned and used the skills of other peoples.[87] That such rapid learning was a matter of pride among the Indians we learn from the remarkable Códice del Tecpan, of Tlatelolco. In that document, written *ca.* 1576, we find the whole costly enterprise (Figs. 90–92) interpreted by the Indians as one "a fin de que no os humillen los españoles."[88] In other words, Indian prestige could be maintained, even within the framework of colonial life, by excelling in the skills and undertakings of the conqueror.

But the Indians were not interested only in learning new techniques. Their interest in new techniques presupposes something else. It presupposes a vital interest in productive workmanship itself. The Indians were not concerned merely to earn a living by European industrial methods and practices. As we have seen, they did not comprehend, and they resented the European money economy. Therefore, their interest in working must be assigned other causes than economic ones. First we may discuss a number of sixteenth-century texts bearing upon Indian crafts. The most remarkable are the records collected by Bernardino de Sahagún.[89] Written in Nahuatl language, they are the Indians' own statements about their work. The craft processes are described in language of remarkable accuracy and richness, and they reveal the thorough interpenetration, in the Indian mind, of ritual and work. The exercise of any craft was governed by religious rites and invocations. Entire guilds of featherworkers, for example, were consecrated solely to the manufacture of the ornaments for Huitzilopochtli, and others were dedicated to the manufacture of garments for Motecuzoma. In other words, the workmen produced their wares for specific and consecrated purposes, rather than for the unidentified consumers of a public market. In pre-Conquest Indian society, it is generally true that all work was punctuated by ritual and festival occasions; and that work itself was ceremonially performed. In colonial life, however, the Spaniards do not seem to have comprehended

86. Motolinia, "Historia de los indios de la Nueva España," *CDHM,* I, 211–212.

87. See G. C. Vaillant, *Aztecs of Mexico* (Garden City, N. Y., 1941) (American Museum of Natural History. Science ser., II), pp. 139–168.

88. "Códice . . . Tlaltelolco," *Investigaciones históricas,* I, no. 3, 257.

89. Sahagún, *Einige Kapitel aus dem Geschichtswerk des Fray Bernardino de Sahagún* (Stuttgart, 1927), pp. 369–380. E. Seler, tr., C. Seler, ed.; Sahagún, *Historia . . . Nueva España,* II, 385–394.

that, for the Indian, no work was worth doing which was not infused by ceremonial symbolism. In Christian life, work and worship are separate concepts. Under Christian direction, the Indian was expected to do unadorned work for six days, divorced from all forms of ritual behavior. His daily devotions had nothing to do with his work, and labor itself, from being an exercise of piety, was degraded into physical toil without spiritual compensation.

Given his pre-Conquest antecedents, the Indian naturally attempted to redeem his labor by ceremonial performances. The process of compensation is recorded in the Códice del Tecpan. The detailed account of the construction of the public buildings of the community (Figs. 90–92), between 1576 and 1581, reveals the religious character of Indian communal enterprise. Using the symbols and expressions of Christianity, the Indians attempted to identify their work with religious behavior. Far more than in European documents of the same class, the Trinity is invoked as the patron of the undertaking; and the Christian God and Jesus Christ are repeatedly brought into discussion. The laying of the cornerstone was blessed by the resident friar, and the finished edifice was consecrated by the archbishop. At every stage of construction, religious observances were held.

The alien rituals and symbols, however, were an inadequate substitute for the rich texture of pre-Conquest ceremonial life. The attentive observer cannot fail to note in sixteenth-century Indian life many of the symptoms of a psychological unemployment to which allusion has already been made (pp. 48–49). Father Mendieta described it unequivocally in 1562, in a letter written in Toluca to the Comisario General of the Franciscans in New Spain:

> If you ask of a chief, a headman, or an old man in the town, how it happens that today, under the law of God, there is more drunkenness and other vices than in gentile days, and less shame in the young, he will gently say "Achquenin? At this I am horrified, and if you wish to know the reason, it is that in our heathen state, no one followed his own will, unless ordered to, and today, our great liberty does us much harm, for we are not obliged to fear or respect anyone."[90]

To respect or fear no one is an unbearable human condition. In the Códice del Tecpan, we find the effort to remedy the unreligious performance of labor in a curious and beautiful antiphonal chant: the governor and the caciques engaged in a dramatic

90. "Carta de Mendieta," *NCDHM,* I, 4–5: "Si preguntais al indio cacique, ó alcalde, ó principal, ó viejo del pueblo, que cómo en los tiempos de ahora debajo de la ley de Dios hay más borracheras y otros vicios que en su infidelidad, y más desvergüenza en los mozos, diraos muy lindamente: *achquenin?* como quien dice y lo declara después: de eso me espanto, y si lo quieres saber, no es otra cosa sino que en tiempo de la infidelidad nadie hacía su voluntad, sino lo que le era mandado, y ahora la mucha libertad nos hace mal, porque no estamos forzados á tener á nadie temor ni respeto."

recital of conflict and response over the undertaking; even the documentary record reveals the ceremonial conception of public work.

The tools of sixteenth-century Europe had not changed radically for many centuries. But to the Indians their use brought a great technological acceleration. The texts describe durable cutting implements, measuring tools, energy-saving hoists, pumps, and wheeled machinery. Some were devices yet undreamed by pre-Conquest Indian craftsmen, to whom metals were precious substances, and wheels were ceremonial forms (*temalacatl*) rather than instruments of work. Of all the elements of European technology, those involving the metal blade and the wheel most rapidly became functioning elements of Indian colonial culture. Their acceptance probably marks a critical moment in the acculturation of the Indian.

The pictorial atlas illustrated by Indians for Sahagún[91] shows that the common use of European hand-tools was established by the decade of the 1570's. Planes, chisels, plumb-lines, saws, axes, hatchets, and knives are seen in daily use, the last-named even in such ancient crafts as feather-working (Figs. 36–40). In these illustrations, the purpose was rather to record prevailing customs than to provide Indian instruction, so that we may accept these representations as documents for the familiar use of European hand-tools. Certain other texts[92] of the second half of the century also guarantee the use of these tools by large numbers of Indians. Other than in architecture, an idea of the variety of specialized metal instruments used before 1549 in New Spain may be gained from the inventory of the effects of Cortés prepared after his death. In this list we find anvils, smith's hammers, hoof-parers, rasps, pincers, chisels, and veterinarian surgical instruments; in short, an entire panoply of metal tools connected with the care of horses.[93]

A search of the great Nahuatl vocabulary by fray Alonso de Molina, furthermore, reveals the extent to which metal tools had been appropriated by Indians. Their names were transposed into Nahuatl equivalents, and in these word-lists, a striking number of specialized builder's tools appears.[94] These names are sometimes formed by adding the radical for metal to another name for the tool. The radical for metal is simply the word for copper (*tepuztli*); in the case of iron, we have *tliltic tepuztli,* or "black copper." Only occasionally does a European tool appear for which a suitable Nahuatl word did not already exist. It is, therefore, urgent to point out the important fact that some European tools were novel merely as to their specific form and material. Few

91. Sahagún, *Historia general,* V (atlas) (1905), 157 plates.

92. See F. del Paso y Troncoso, ed., *Códice Kingsborough* (Madrid, 1912); N. León, ed., *Códice Sierra* (Mexico, 1933); E. Boban, *Documents pour servir à l'histoire du Mexique. Atlas* (Paris, 1891).

93. "Documentos . . . Cortés," *Publ. AGN,* XXVII, 249.

94. A. de Molina, *Vocabulario de la lengua mexicana* (Leipzig, 1880). J. Platzmann, ed.

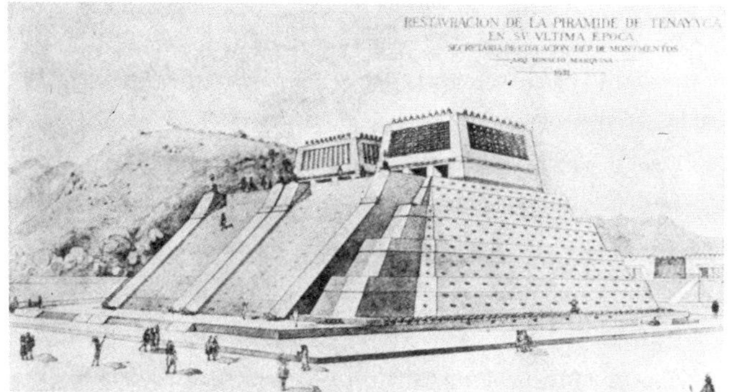

35. Tenayuca, reconstruction drawing of the pyramid

36. Indians building a chapel

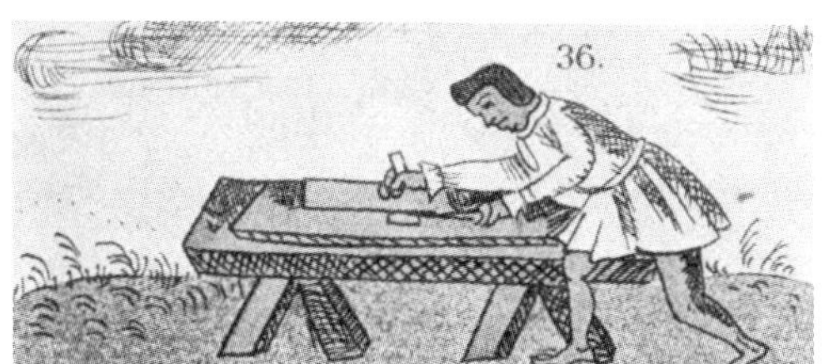

37. Indian carpenter planing a board

38. Indian sawyer, stonecutter, and mason

39. Indian mason using square and plumb

40. Indian stonemason

41. Spanish surveyor measuring a lot

42. Wheeled transportation of stone

43. Ixtapalapa, the acequia

44. Mexico City, pre-Conquest blocks used in the primitive Cathedral

45. Indian quarrying operations

46. Old Tehuacan, Franciscan church, north wall at sanctuary

47. Atlihuetzia, Franciscan church, from the southwest

48. Acatzingo, Franciscan church, sanctuary from the east

European tools were introduced for which the Indians did not already have the analogues in stone, wood, or some other material than metal. The proof is lexicological, in that Nahuatl already possessed words to describe the functions of the European tools. The Indian language lacked specific words with which to identify some new metals, such as steel ("hard black copper"), or the alloys, such as bronze.

On public works the Indians were supposed to be provided with tools by their employers. In 1555, the six thousand Indians assembled for the repair of the causeways leading to the capital were to be furnished by the municipal council with the necessary tools. This had been the custom under Motecuzoma as well, but in 1555, the cabildo objected to this provision, seeking to have the work done at less expense.[95] The objection is understandable, for the cost of tools during the sixteenth century was prohibitively high. In 1555, for instance, Archbishop Montúfar wrote the Council of the Indies that the rental of tools cost more in Mexico than their purchase in Spain.[96] Hence we may assume that the cases were not uncommon in which the Indian laborer was obliged to work without benefit of European tools. Unless he could provide them himself, his employer was unlikely to incur the cost of rental and the risk of loss. It is therefore likely that Indians manufactured more European-style tools than their employers provided. When labor was free, or nearly so, and tools were costly, the employer was not likely to economize labor and squander money on tools. Hence the appearance of European tools is all the more significant, in terms of an active Indian interest in their manufacture. Of course, certain tasks, such as fine woodwork or intricate stone cutting could not be achieved properly without metal tools, and for these the employer would have been more inclined to provide the necessary equipment. But in heavy manual operations, such as digging or piling earth and stone, the application of more labor was probably cheaper than the issue of metal picks and iron shovels.

The building program of the colonists postulates a technique of exact mensuration. The system used in the sixteenth century can be reconstructed in part from the documents bearing upon land-assignments in the cities. The *Pintura del Gobernador,* composed *ca.* 1566,[97] portrays a Spanish surveyor staking out a municipal lot with pegs and cords (Fig. 41). Within the enclosure, an Indian family is gathered around their dwelling, in protest against the expropriation. It is the process designated as "echar cordeles" or setting cords, as in the layout of new towns.

The minutes of the municipal council of Mexico City provide information about the units of measure employed. The earliest grants of city land involved square lots

95. *AC,* VI, 192–195.
96. *Epistolario,* VIII, 33.
97. M. Tellez Girón y Beaufort, duque de Osuña, *Pintura del gobernador, alcaldes, y regidores de México. Códice en geroglíficos mexicanas* (Madrid, 1878), fol. 469b.

seventy paces on a side; later, in 1537, this standard was reduced to square parcels, 150 feet on a side. The street widths were fixed at fourteen varas, and the garden lots at the edge of the city were assigned in parcels 40 x 100 *pasos,* or paces, in size.[98]

It appears that these units of measure referred to standard measures of length in the custody of the municipal council. At the time of the foundation of Puebla (1531), the Audiencia ordered that such standards be prepared and presented to the new city. They were probably made of cord and leather. All municipal grants were to be measured with these standards and no others.[99]

In 1537, furthermore, the metropolitan standards of measure were enforced for all New Spain. Viceroy Mendoza ordered that all municipal land grants be fixed at 96 x 192 *varas* (yards) of the standard of Mexico. This standard was established as containing three *varas de medir menos una ochava,* and the grantors in provincial cities were requested to come to the capital to take possession of suitable measures prepared from the standard. Similar standards for the measurement of building stones were specified and prepared. In 1537, four separate sets of these were in existence. One was kept in the municipal council, and another in Tlatelolco, and all were sealed with the insignia of the capital.[100]

These early land measures, however, either wore out or proved inadequate, for in 1543, the cabildo ordered the manufacture of a new standard. It was to be a staff of ten pasos, "de a doce puntos escasos" (twelve-unit paces), marked with the city seal, and specified for land grants. This measure was apparently meant for actual use, since another one was prepared for deposit with the municipal council.[101] Finally, in 1556, the cabildo secured an appropriation to send to Spain for copies of the standard weights and measures used on the Peninsula, including measuring staffs (*varas de medir*) made of copper or iron.[102]

In theory then, all grants of land were subject to measurement from uniform government standards. It is not unlikely that similarly uniform standards of measurement were used in construction, although we have no texts describing their character.[103]

The introduction of wheeled vehicles and beasts of burden did not immediately improve Mexican methods of transportation. The carts and wagons (Fig. 42) could

98. *AC,* I, 4; IV, 71. Vetancurt, *Chrónica, Tratado,* p. 1.

99. *AC,* IV, 69, ". . . paresce que la abdiencia real de esta nueba españa les dio la dicha medida quando se fundo e poblo la dicha cibdad e mandaron al mayordomo que envie a la dicha cibdad de los angeles por la dicha medida, para queste cabildo la tenga."

100. *AC,* IV, 72, 76.

101. *AC,* IV, 329 (Feb. 20, 1543).

102. *AC,* IV, 253.

103. That the Indians utilized methods of measurement is self-evident. Mendieta, in telling of the ingenuity of the Indians of Huaquechula when copying a Spanish loom, describes the way in which the Indians surreptitiously transferred the measurements of the machine to sticks of appropriate lengths, from which they were able to build it (Mendieta, *Historia eclesiástica indiana,* p. 255). León y Gama, furthermore, al-

not be used except in the capital until suitable roads had been built. The draft animals were few in number, and it was years before the Indians acquired the special skills necessary in the handling of horses, asses, and mules. In the rebuilding of Tenochtitlan, the Indians of Texcoco carried the materials in hods (*huacatl*); Ixtlilxochitl's own hod was made of tiger-skin, and he carried stone. The others were made of hides or wood, and were loaded with lime or sand.[104] Transportation continued long in the colonial era to depend upon human legs and backs. As late as 1555, Viceroy Mendoza held that the suppression of the Indian bearers (*tamemes*) would be highly prejudicial to the economy of New Spain, and he urged his successor to refrain from excessive legislation in these matters.[105] The viceregal government under Mendoza, did, however, restrict the exploitation of Indian bearers. Tamemes were not to be used in the tierra caliente; and in the mining areas of the north, their loads were limited to two *arrobas,* not to be carried more than five or six leagues daily. In architectural undertakings, we have the case of the materials for Cortés' palace in Mexico City. In 1533, some stones for this building were brought from the vicinity of Oaxtepec, and it is recorded that crews of one hundred men were engaged in the hauling of a single block over the mountains.[106]

In general, however, the transportation of building materials to and within Mexico City was greatly aided by the lake and canals. A main canal entered the city from the west, flowed from San Francisco past the main plaza (Figs. 62–65), and eastward into the lake. It also served as the central sewer and flood-drain, so indispensable that it was not paved over until 1753 and then only in part.[107] In the sixteenth century, other canals were built for specific purposes. The *Pintura del Gobernador* records the construction of an acequia from Ixtapalapa (Fig. 43), for the express purpose of conveying building materials for the fabric of the metropolitan cathedral.[108] In addition, lake-borne traffic was heavy at all times. In 1587 the stone and sand for the building of the Dominican convento were brought in canoes from Tlahuac by a crew of Indian boatmen expressly assigned for the purpose. It is interesting that recent droughts had made the acequias unnavigable, with the result that this particular undertaking lasted six months longer than planned.[109]

ludes to the fact that in Indian manuscripts, certain lines refer to standard measures, of which one was the *tlaquetzilantli,* equal to two-and-a-half Castilian varas. In Tlatelolco, a standard of measure was the distance from foot to hand, called *tlacaxilantli,* about one yard. (Cited by Boban, *Documents,* I, 399.) In the Nahuatl vocabulary by Alonso de Molina, we find a long list of measurements of length with Indian names. These are probably pre-Conquest lengths (Molina, *Vocabulario,* p. 83). The generic name for measures of length was *tlayeyecoloni* or *tlaoctaca anoni;* for measures of weight, *tlatamachiualoni.* A yardstick or its approximate length was *octacatl.* The act of measurement was designated by the operative *tamachiua.* An ell was designated as *ceninolicpitl;* and the Spanish *braço* as *cenciyacatl* or *cemacolli.*

104. Ixtlilxochitl, *Obras históricas,* I, 435.

105. Pérez Bustamante, . . . *Don Antonio de Mendoza,* pp. 129, 134.

106. *Epistolario,* III, 2, 121; Cuevas, *Documentos inéditos,* p. 45.

107. Marroqui, *La Ciudad de México,* I, 180.

108. *Códice Osuña,* folios 469, 501.

109. Zavala, *Fuentes,* III, 45.

Hence Mexico City, served by a network of waterborne traffic, was unique in New Spain. All other areas depended upon human transportation, or upon the gradual opening up of new roads. Until these road-systems had been established, the towns and buildings tended to the closest possible proximity to sand-pits, quarries, and lumber resources.

The earliest of the great Mexican wagon roads was built in 1530–31. It connected the capital with Veracruz, via Otumba and Tepeapulco.[110] A Franciscan friar, Sebastián de Aparicio (1502–1600) is intimately connected with the building of the first Mexican roads. He arrived in New Spain in 1531, and at first built wagons in the newly founded city of Puebla. He was the first European to yoke bullocks to a wheeled vehicle, thereby astonishing the Indians, who never before had seen such a combination. After a long period in which Sebastián supervised the wagon traffic to and from Veracruz, he opened the new wagon road to the province of Zacatecas in 1542. Without this road, the mining enterprises in the north would not have been possible. The frontier towns, such as Queretaro, Celaya, San Felipe, and San Pedro Toliman were all dependent upon the road for supplies and contact with the capital. Fray Sebastián took the habit of a lay Franciscan brother in 1574, after having gained a great reputation in New Spain as a trainer of draft animals.[111]

Without roads, many newly founded communities could not have survived. At Tiripitio, in 1537, the Augustinians were forced to build roads in order to convert the Indians in the tierra caliente to the south of them.[112] Naturally, in certain mountainous regions, the building of wagon roads was long delayed. Thus, the one from Mexico to Toluca was not undertaken until 1564, because of the rugged mountains to be crossed. By 1585, however, two great highways connected Veracruz with the metropolis.[113] Six other highways gave access to the capital from different directions. One led in from Amecameca and others from Tochimilco, Texcoco, and Tlalmanalco.[114]

As the roads were developed and extended, many of the communities served by them changed character. For example, the town of Cuitzeo, where salt for the Tarasca peoples had long been produced, became less important when the new roads made it possible in the sixteenth century to bring salt from Colima to Michoacan more cheaply than to produce it at Lake Cuitzeo.[115] Instances can be multiplied: the introduction of

110. *AC*, II (1889), 66, 67, 114.

111. Vetancurt, *Chrónica, Menologio*, p. 17; *Relación . . . Ponce*, I, 535–536.

112. Basalenque, *Historia . . . Michoacán*, pp. 19–20. "Hizieronse assimismo unas calçadas anchas, y buenas, para que de las Visitas, que caen del Pueblo hazia el Sur, viniessen."

113. López de Velasco, *Geografía*, pp. 192–193. One of them followed the course of the present auto highway: Mexico—Chalco—Texmelucan—Huejotzingo—Puebla—Venta del Pinar—Caceres. The other road followed a more northerly course: Mexico—Guadalupe—Santa Clara—San Cristobal—Tequesistlan—Tepetlaoztoc—Calpulalpan—Tecoac—Caceres. The northerly route was more level, and therefore better suited for wagon traffic. Both roads joined midway to Veracruz at the village of Caceres.

114. *Relación . . . Ponce*, I, 158–159.

115. Escobar, *Americana thebaida*, p. 662.

the new systems of communications made western Mexico accessible to the peoples of the east in a way which had never been possible before the Conquest.

An ambitious and abundant program of building; a backward and overburdened system of transportation; and the unskilled labor in Mexico are the factors that may be brought to account for the excessive scarcity and cost of building materials in the sixteenth century. Specially expensive were columns of stone. For the cutting, transportation, and setting of a stone column, the price in 1531 was ten pesos. The same sum of money, incidentally, would build a wall fifteen yards long by two yards high.[116] In Mexico City, where building activity was most intense, the shortage of building materials was so great in 1528 that the stone used for retaining walls at the edges of the island was being stolen. Heavy fines were imposed to discourage the abuse.[117] In 1532, even the paving stones in the streets were misappropriated; the offenders were both Indians and Spaniards, and the abuse continued in the 1540's.[118]

Hence the colonists made a diligent effort to conserve and use again the materials of older constructions. The primitive Cathedral of Mexico was built in part of blocks cut from the paving (Fig. 44) of the pre-Conquest temple precinct.[119] Innumerable cases of an economical re-use of archaeological materials are still to be seen. At San Esteban Tizatlan, the adobe bricks resemble those of the revetment of the pre-Conquest pyramidal structures. Toussaint reports that the chapel itself (Figs. 257, 258) was a fragment of the pre-Conquest palace of Xicotencatl.[120] At San Francisco Tlaxcala, to mention but one more case, the facing stones appear to come from pre-Conquest structures.[121] Not only were pre-Conquest materials used over, but when a colonial edifice became obsolete, its materials were carefully conserved for new construction, as with the slaughterhouse in the capital, whose materials were to be saved in 1537 for the construction of the new shops on the same site.[122]

Such practices were powerfully reinforced by ceremonial considerations. To the colonists, a special virtue resided in the use of heathen materials for the construction of Christian churches: symbolically, it signified that the Church stood in triumph upon the ruins of paganism. Thus the Franciscan church of Tlatelolco stands upon the platform of the great temple described by Bernal Díaz; recent excavations have re-

116. *CDIAI*, XII (1869), 524.

117. *AC*, I, 161. Offenders were fined one hundred pesos gold and were given one hundred lashes.

118. *AC*, II, 188; IV, 249.

119. A. García Cubas, "Las Estaciones en el valle de México," *México pintoresco* (Mexico, 1905), p. 27. A. A. Esteva, comp. The excavations revealed foundation blocks of an "artificial stone," in "una capa, del grueso de un decímetro, de una mezcla de cal, arena y pequeños guijarros, cubierta aquella con otra de pura cal, muy delgada, bruñida . . ." The individual blocks measured 40 x 35 x 10 cm.

120. M. Toussaint, "Un Templo cristiano sobre el palacio de Xicotencatl," *Revista mexicana de estudios históricos*, I (1927), 173–180.

121. *Ibid.*, p. 173.

122. *AC*, IV, 82. Cf. "Relación de fray Miguel Navarro," *NCDHM*, IV (1892), 120, on the rebuilding of S. Francisco in 1569 or thereabouts.

vealed its stairways.[123] In 1538, Viceroy Mendoza declared in a letter to Zumárraga and others that the stone from the destruction of Indian temples should be applied to the construction of churches or monasteries. Motolinia also reports the fact in 1540: not only building stones, but also the Indian idols were taken from Indian temples and put into the walls of churches, as we can see in many places.[124] The column bases in the primitive cathedral of Mexico were fashioned from the beautiful serpents of the pre-Conquest *coatepantli,* or serpent wall.[125] The vault over the altar of the primitive Franciscan church, completed *ca.* 1525, was built of stones taken from the stairs of the *templo mayor.*[126] In Culhuacan a stone figure of Atepanecatl was made into four columns for the altars of San Juan Evangelista before 1543.[127] And in Oaxtepec, a figure of Ometochtli was sent after 1534 from Tepoztlan, by fray Domingo da la Anunciación, to be built into the foundations of the church.[128] Finally, throughout the area of colonization, one sees pre-Conquest stone decorations worked into the walls of the churches (Fig. 180), standing in mute testimony to the presence of older civilizations.[129]

The production of architecture in the sixteenth century was further limited by the availability of local materials. In areas where good supplies of building stone were not available, there were no pre-Conquest monuments to be exploited, and the backward transportation system made it impossible to bring in the necessary materials. Even with great local populations, a deficiency of materials made building operations difficult. Such was probably the case in southwestern Mexico, in the region of Guerrero and western Oaxaca, as well as in southern Michoacan.

The Valley of Mexico was well supplied with quarries (Fig. 45). Each of the colonial organizations developed its own supply. The municipal council secured its paving stones from a quarry near Tenayuca, whence deliveries began in 1547. The citizens were required to pave their streets with these *tenayucas,* or flat stones, and the cabildo had the monopoly upon their quarrying.[130] Other stones for the public works sponsored by the cabildo came from the quarries at Sinbuque, some eight leagues distant, which were worked by the Indians of Ixtapalapa.[131] The Augustinians procured their

123. See P. Martínez del Rio, "Resumen de los trabajos arqueológicos," *Tlatelolco a través de los tiempos* (Mexico, 1944–45), IV, 16–19. The second episcopal palace also stood on a pre-Conquest platform. Cervantes de Salazar, *México en 1554,* p. 117, and *Crónica de Nueva España,* p. 318.

124. F. A. de Icaza, comp., "Miscelanea histórica," *Revista mexicana de estudios históricos,* II (1928), Apendice, 50; Motolinia, "Historia de los indios de la Nueva España," *CDHM,* I, 27.

125. Durán, *Historia de las Indias,* II, 83; García Cubas, *op. cit.,* pp. 13–41.

126. Vetancurt, *Chrónica, Teatro,* Pt. IV, p. 32; Zorita, "Historia de la Nueva España," *Colección de libros y documentos referentes á la historia de América,* IX (1909), 296. Murillo, *Iglesias de México,* II, by Toussaint, 22.

127. Zorita, "Breve y sumaria relación," *NCDHM,* III, 266, 287–288. The statue was originally composed of five great pieces.

128. Dávila Padilla, *Historia . . . Santiago de México,* p. 617; cf. Motolinia, "Historia de los indios de la Nueva España," *CDHM,* I, 27.

129. e.g., Tlalmanalco, Huejotzingo, Acolman, Xochimilco.

130. *AC,* III (1533), 10; V, 183, 201; VIII, 186.

131. *AC,* III (1533), 66.

materials from a quarry near Tacuba, operated by fray Agustín de la Coruña;[132] and the Franciscans were dependent upon supplies from a quarry near Los Remedios.[133] Other metropolitan quarries were situated at Santa Marta and Chiluca.[134]

The Mezquital district of Hidalgo provided the Augustinians and Franciscans not only with dense populations, but with the best building stone in Mexico.[135] Hueypoxtla, for instance, was the source of a rose-colored stone of great durability, favored for columns, bases, and other trim. Tlamaco possessed limestone and other quarries. In short, only such abundance of materials made possible the construction of the great establishments at Ixmiquilpan, Tula, and Actopan.

Puebla was likewise admirably situated for building materials. Lime, clay, and stone were immediately available in large quantities within the city limits. As the foundations for the buildings were dug, these very excavations provided the necessary materials, mainly a soft white stone which hardened immediately upon exposure, as well as a harder stone suitable for columns, doorways, windows, and moldings.[136] Nearby at Cholula was a good quarry of darker stone, within the town, and a fine black stone came from Calpan.[137]

But it is to be noted that where good supplies of material were found without large surrounding populations, these resources were useless. Such was the case at Zinapecuaro, where fine deposits of a smooth-grained black stone could not be worked for lack of skilled Indian labor.[138]

Two very striking kinds of building stone distinguished sixteenth-century Mexican architecture as much as they do the architecture of today. *Tezontle* (a porous igneous rock) and *tecali* ("Mexican onyx") have always been noted by observant travelers in Mexico; copious texts describe their use in the early days of the colony. The *casas viejas* were almost entirely built of tezontle; nearly seventy thousand square yards of wall are mentioned in the appraisal of 1531.[139] To the men of the period it seemed that tezontle was a gift of Providence to the ambitious builders of Mexico City. Clavigero provides a curious text pertaining to the Indians' own discovery of the stone. A great quarry was first opened near Tenochtitlan in 1499 or thereabouts under Ahuitzol; at first the stone was used for building temples, and many individuals followed suit. Ultimately, Ahuitzol ordered that all ruinous buildings in the capital be

132. Grijalva, *Crónica de la orden de N. P. S. Augustín*, p. 266.

133. Vetancurt, *Chrónica, Menologio*, pp. 11–12.

134. The Chiluca stone is famous for use as trim. Vetancurt characterizes it as "dura para vasas [bases], la blanda para cornijas, y capiteles. . . ." Vetancurt, *Chrónica, Tratado*, p. 2. Cf. J. B. Trend, *Mexico* (Cambridge [Eng.], 1940), pp. 26–27.

135. Hueypoxtla: *PNE*, VI, 30. ". . . Piedras que tiran a color rrosado de que se hazen colunas y vasas y portadas; es piedra rrezia, no se come jamás de salitre ni de otra cosa que las puede dañar." Tlamaco: *PNE*, I, 224.

136. Vetancurt, *Chrónica, Tratado*, p. 46; *Epistolario*, IV, 138; Motolinia, "Historia de los indios de la Nueva España," *CDHM*, I, 231–235.

137. *Diccionario universal de historia y de geografía* (Mexico, 1853–55), II, 714. *PNE*, V, 104. The writer has not noticed this material in actual use.

138. *Relación . . . Ponce*, I, 528.

139. *CDIAI*, XII, 520 f.

torn down and rebuilt in the lighter material.[140] Contemporaries claimed to have seen the stone float in water.[141]

On the other hand, the coarse grain and extreme brittleness of the stone made it unsuitable for fine carving or for bridging wide spans or for use at corners exposed to wear and erosion, even if its beautiful dark-red to light-brown color made it highly suitable for contrasting decoration or for wall-surfacing. Thus at Santo Domingo in Mexico City, the wall-facings were of tezontle on the exterior, and of white cut-stone on the interior.[142] A black tezontle was used at Tecamachalco. Large quantities of the material were assembled in the 1570's for the rebuilding of the metropolitan cathedral, but in 1572, the supplies were diverted for the building of the essential Santa-Fe–Chapultepec aqueduct.[143] The most abundant quarry of the *piedra liviana,* as it was sometimes called, was situated at Santa Marta, on the shore of the salt lake three leagues from the capital, where it was worked by one hundred fifty tributaries.[144]

The other important and specifically Mexican building stone was tecali, a metamorphic rock sometimes called Mexican onyx, of which deposits are widely distributed throughout the mountainous areas in Puebla, Oaxaca, and Lower California.[145] The most accessible quarry was situated at Tecali, in the present state of Puebla. Large quantities were used in the sixteenth century for altar-tables, and above all, for window-glazing. The striking transparency of the stone, when cut in thin slabs, made it a rich and sumptuous material serving many of the purposes of window-glass. Few of these windows survive; some seventeenth-century examples may be seen in the Academia de las Bellas Artes stairwell in Puebla, in the *parroquia* of Tecali, and other isolated examples in Oaxaca.[146] Another large quarry is still worked at Huitzo, near Etla in Oaxaca. The Dominican convento reputedly was built entirely of a coarse, opaque tecali before 1581. It is an ample establishment, with fourteen cells, and was

140. F. S. Clavigero, *The History of Mexico* (Philadelphia, 1817), I, 273–274. I. Sariñana y Cuenca, *Noticia breve de la solemne, deseada, ultima dedicación del templo metropolitano de México* (Mexico, 1668), p. 22a. The porous, light stone "arguye claramente la singular providẽcia, con q̃ la crío Dios en las cercanias de Mexico, proporcionãdola á su terruño, y previniẽdola à la constancia de sus edificios." J. McAndrew has remarked in correspondence upon Spanish use of light materials, as in the tufa webs of León Cathedral.

141. A. Vázquez de Espinosa, "Compendium . . . of the West Indies," *Smithsonian Miscellaneous Collections,* CII (1942), 156; Ojea, . . . *Historia religiosa,* p. 2: "piedra pomez, colorada y esponjada, y por esto tan liuiana que nada sobre el agua, á la qual llaman los indios *tezontl,* que es la comun de los edificios nueuos, y muy propria para edificar en tan mal sitio."

142. *Ibid.,* p. 10; Franco, . . . *Historia . . . Santiago de México,* p. 537.

143. *AC,* VIII, 120.

144. *PNE,* III, 26. Vetancurt, *Chrónica, Tratado,* p. 2; *Teatro,* Pt. IV, p. 88. Other quarries: Coatepec Chalco, *PNE,* VI, 59; Huexotla, Zavala, *Fuentes,* V, 180. See also E. Guillemin Tarayre, "Rapport sur l'exploration minéralogique des régions mexicaines," *Archives de la commission scientifique du Mexique* (Paris, 1867), III, 312; who calls tezontle a *basalte bulbeux.*

145. *Ibid.,* p. 311.

146. J. A. Villaseñor y Sánchez, *Theatro americano, descripción general de los reynos, y provincias de la Nueva-España, y sus jurisdicciones* (Mexico, 1746–48), I, 322–323. The stone from Tecali was used for "clarabollas de Iglesias para resguardo del ayre, tan luminosos, que dan la mesma claridad, que si fueran vidrieras. . . ."

once capable of housing twelve friars.[147] More commonly, however, the material was used for decorative structures and accessories, as in the great fountain in the cloister courtyard of San Francisco in Mexico City, described by Vetancurt.[148]

It should be noted that in sixteenth-century usage, the term *marmol* or *marmolejo,* does not always refer to the metamorphic stones, such as tecali, but to the column as an architectural element as well. Thus Molina lists *columna* and marmol as synonymous.[149]

The lime needed for the manufacture of mortar was an expensive item in the economy of sixteenth-century building operations. Contemporary accounts usually distinguished between *cal y canto* and *cantería.* The former referred to masonry construction of rubble and mortar; the latter term designated the fine cut stone of doorways, window-frames, and other trim.[150] Lime itself was a commodity in great demand, at least in the capital. In 1531 a *tapia* of rubble wall, two yards wide and one yard high, took one hod of lime, valued at a peso. But the cost of the labor and the stone together was but one peso, so that the lime itself was the most costly component.[151] In 1552, a shortage of lime was impeding the progress of works in the capital. The supply was controlled by those who received it in tribute, or who manufactured it on their encomiendas. The main operators were the encomenderos of Atlanpa, Hueypoxtla, Zumpango, Ajacuba, Tlapanaloya, Jilotzingo, and the corregidores of Tetepango and Citlaltepec. These men, frustrated by the low prices decreed for lime in the capital, created an illegal market where the material could be sold at prices of their own choosing. Thus, although the lime was customarily to be sold in the *plaza menor* in front of the bullpens, customers could obtain none at the regular posts.[152] The demand was enormous. Between 1555 and 1565, Indians brought 2,015 *cargas* or loads of lime to Mexico City at the order of the Viceroy. Of this amount, 1,615 cargas were used merely upon the repairs to the casa real, or viceregal palace, then situated, as we may presume, in the casas nuevas, recently sold by Martín Cortés (see p. 193).

Not only could builders get little lime, but the Indians themselves were unreliable in its use. Unless they were carefully watched, the Indian workmen would substitute ashes for lime in the mixing of mortar. The abuse was so common that in 1538 the municipal council felt the need of a foreman specially designated to supervise the mixing of mortar. The Indians' purpose is not clear, but it is readily seen that their action had serious consequences. Not only did buildings thus erected collapse in con-

147. *PNE,* IV (1905), 202.

148. Vetancurt, *Chrónica, Teatro,* Pt. IV, p. 33. Surviving examples of other ornamental work in tecali will be studied by Elizabeth Wilder in her forthcoming book on sixteenth-century sculpture.

149. Molina, *Vocabulario,* p. 82. See *PNE,* IV, 151.

150. See *PNE,* V, 104, with respect to the Franciscan establishment at Jalapa in Veracruz (1580). The walls themselves were of cal y canto, and the crestings (*cumbres*) and doorways were of cantería.

151. "Tasacion y autos de las casas que tenia el Marqués de Valle Méjico (1531)," *CDIAI,* XII (1869), 523.

152. *AC,* VI, 72–73.

struction, but the total expenditure of labor was increased by the necessity of beginning defective construction anew. Hence the use of lime was avoided, by recourse to other methods. A striking instance of the survival of pre-Conquest technique appears at Huejotzingo, where the nave walls are built of rammed earth and adobe bricks, cased between retaining walls of cut stone. The hearting of the wall, therefore, contains no mortar. A similar technique may be seen at the former site of Tehuacan (Fig. 46).

Lime was of course indispensable in the great projects of the period.[153] In the building of Santo Domingo in Mexico City, for example, the lime came directly to the site from the kilns in Zumpango. Otherwise, Mexico City drew most of its supply from the kilns of Calpulalpan, especially in the latter part of the century. The very fine lime for surface plastering was manufactured at Cuzcatlan in southern Puebla. This material was specially prized for outdoor floorings, as at San Gabriel in Cholula, where the entire atrio was paved with burnished red plaster (Fig. 196), as in pre-Conquest practice. Outside Mexico City, many settlements developed their own supplies of lime. In Puebla, about 1544, the lime quarries and kilns were located within a stone's throw from the city limits. The town of Cuitzeo was situated directly over a supply of limestone. And at Patzcuaro Cathedral, the masons used an adhesive substance extracted from clay, which commanded the admiration of European builders for its hardness and brilliance. On the whole, however, the high cost of lime had appreciable effects upon the style of building at the mid-century. In Chapter VII (specially pp. 347–349), we shall show how rubble masonry gave way to cut-stone techniques using less mortar.

At the end of the century, the price of lime seems to have dropped. A cartload was worth thirty pesos in 1598, at Izhuatepec, but the masons were paid fifteen pesos for raising two varas of wall. The contrast with prices in 1531 is striking.[154]

It is astonishing to note how slowly the fictile industries made their way into Mexican architecture.[155] Bricks and tiles are regarded in European building as indispensa-

153. Zumpango: A. M. Carreño, *Fr. Domingo de Betanzos* (Mexico, 1924), p. 254. Calpulalpan: *Relación . . . Ponce,* I, 72. Cuzcatlan: Motolinia, "Historia de los indios de la Nueva España," *CDHM,* I, 194. Cholula: Vetancurt, *Chrónica, Teatro,* Pt. IV, p. 55. Puebla: *Epistolario,* IV, 138. Cholula was supplied from here (*Diccionario,* III, 714). Cuitzeo: "Papeles de Nueva España," Vol. VIII, MS copy by F. del Paso y Troncoso, Library of Museo Nacional, Mexico City. Patzcuaro: Beaumont, *Crónica de Michoacán,* II, 389, writes of the mortar that it was "de singular consistencia, pues parece obra maqueada, y es que se valdrían los tarascos de alguna tierra argilosa que suele abundar en la sierra, y mezclada con arena y cal, forma un betún muy liso y transparente como el barniz . . . algunas de estas tierras argilosas . . . se endurecen sumamente con el tiempo. . . ."

154. The church at Izhuatepec was begun in 1598 and finished in 1616, costing 347 pesos. For lime, the value of 201 pesos was donated; the unmarried men of the community gave the white cut stone for the façade. See A. Peñafiel, ed., "Manuscrito americano no. 4 . . . de Berlin," *Colección de documentos para la historia mexicana* (1897), pp. 11–15, 59–63, titles of S. Isabel Tola, and E. Boban, *Documents,* II, 199, 265, 406.

155. Motolinia, *Memoriales,* pp. 201–202; *idem,* "Historia de los indios de la Nueva España," *CDHM,* I, 273.

ble elements of the architectural repertory. Where the material is abundant, the style of architecture conforms to the needs of brick construction. In Mexico, the clays for making brick and tile were abundant, but it was not until about 1580 that their use became common, perhaps because adobe was cheaper, and traditionally Indian. At the middle of the century, if we may believe Cervantes de Salazar, it was felt in Mexico City that fictile materials were "vile," and that the proper material, specially for doorways, was cut stone, although the roof-drains might fittingly be of wood or clay.[156] And in 1579, Diego Valadés commented upon the *paenuriam imbricum ac tegularum* in Mexico City. At Cholula, in 1581, there was not one tile on any house, although a few had been manufactured in Puebla as early as 1540.

The reasons for the late use of fictile materials in abundance are difficult to establish. Where there was any scarcity of water, the manufacture of bricks and mortar was, of course, impeded, as in certain sites of southern Mexico.[157] It is also to be remembered that the Indian ceramists were not accustomed to the manufacture of fictile elements in large quantities, and that their training to mass-production took time. At all times on the plateau, the Indian technique of roofing a building with a flat, thick layer of earth has proved perfectly adequate. Throughout the colonial epoch, such dirt roofs were customary even in the capital. One of the earliest exceptions to the rule was the roofing of the sacristy at Santo Domingo in Mexico City, which was covered with a double layer of tiles set in bitumen.[158] By 1581, however, the more elaborate metropolitan buildings were being roofed with tiles.[159]

In floors and doorways bricks were widely used after the mid-century. The Franciscan establishment at Huejotzingo probably had a brick floor in the sixteenth century;[160] and in 1585 at Cholula (cf. Fig. 22) the doorways were usually of brick, set into adobe walls. The sidewalks were also of bricks.[161]

Occasionally the bearing parts of a church would be built of bricks. A peripheral example was the church of San Salvador at Autlan in Jalisco *ca.* 1545. The walls between arches were built of adobe, but the roof was surfaced with bricks.[162] And at Santa

156. Cervantes de Salazar, *México en 1554*, p. 90: "Aedium antepagmenta non ex lateribus aut vili alia materia, sed ex magnis saxis artificiose positis constructa sunt . . . Culmina item plana sunt, prominentibus in viam ex subgrundiis canalibus ligneis et fictilibus, pluviam veluti evomentibus." Cf. Valadés, *Rhetorica christiana*, pp. 167–168. Note, however, that several arcades in the casas viejas of Mexico City were made of bricks in 1531. *CDIAI*, XII, 526, etc. Cholula: *Diccionario*, III, 714. Motolinia, "Historia de los indios de la Nueva España," *CDHM*, I, 235.

157. e.g., Zimatlan del Valle. Cf. Burgoa, *Geográfica descripción*, II, 29 f.

158. Ojea, . . . *Historia religiosa*, p. 12.

159. Murillo, *Iglesias de México*, II, by Toussaint, 13. Also Spain. Ministerio de fomento, *Cartas de Indias* (1877), p. 341. ". . . Como todos los ediffiçios de aqui son de terrados en lo alto y no está ladrillado el de la iglesia, como aora se haze en los buenos ediffiçios, sino solo tierra pisada sobre el maderamiento." On brick ribs in vaulted churches, see p. 184.

160. Vetancurt, *Chrónica, Teatro*, Pt. IV, p. 58.

161. *Relación . . . Ponce*, I, 162. *Diccionario*, III, 714. ". . . todas las aceras que miran a las calles están labradas de ladrillos."

162. Mendoza, *Fragmentos*, p. 65. Beaumont, *Crónica de Michoacán*, III, 62. *Relación . . . Ponce*, II, 91.

Maria Churubusco, near the capital, the Franciscans built a small church and convento of bricks, probably before 1530.[163] The famous *Rollo* of Tepeaca, built in 1559, was entirely of brick, upon an octagonal plan. The town of Tepeaca, furthermore, was supplied with water brought from sources six leagues distant, through clay pipes.[164] Such fictile products were naturally made at the site rather than imported. In Guadalajara, for example, the Franciscans built brick-ovens directly at the site of their intended construction.[165]

Once the techniques of brick and tile making had been diffused among the Indian populations, great savings could be effected. An interesting case in point may be inferred from the career of fray Juan de Alameda, the Franciscan builder. He is commonly assigned the construction of the establishments at Huejotzingo and at Huaquechula (Figs. *144*, 197). The latter undertaking was completed not long before his death in 1560. At Huaquechula, fictile elements play a much greater part than at Huejotzingo, where the dense and intricate ornaments (Fig. 385), worked in stone, must have consumed vast quantities of labor. At Huaquechula, such effects are secured with clay decorations in the atrio chapels (Fig. 389). This process is perhaps to be observed in Mendicant building generally: as the century drew near its end, the friars used fictile products more and more generously. The Franciscan establishments at Acatzingo, Totimehuacan, Tepeyango, or Atlihuetzia, to mention a few, are illustrations (Figs. 47, 48), as well as the brick architecture of the Dominicans in Chiapas (see pp. 281–282).

If plain fired bricks were slow to be introduced, polychrome tiles of Islamic origin were even more reticently used. The layman usually identifies Mexican architecture with a lavish use of glazed and colored bricks: actually these did not appear in great numbers until the seventeenth century, with the development of Talavera wares in Puebla. The sixteenth-century specimens of polychrome pottery or brick are extremely rare. One example among several is a baptismal font of glazed pottery, dated 1599, which stands in the church at Teppepan, near Xochimilco. It is festooned with garlands, Eros children, and angels, all bracketed by the Franciscan cord.[166] It may be compared to the green glazed clay fonts, in the popular art of the sixteenth century in Toledo and Seville.[167] Another instance in Mexico is recorded at the most sumptu-

163. *Ibid.*, II, 225–226. "Fué aquella casa de las primeras que se hicieron para frailes en la Nueva España y al principio fué visita de nuestros frailes observantes." Compare the small, late conventual cloister at Hueyotlipan in the State of Tlaxcala, also of bricks.

164. Archivo General de la Nación, *Ramo Padrones*, MS "Relación de Tepeaca," Vol. XXXVIII, fol. vi vo. The main doorway of the Franciscan church is also of brick, *PNE*, V, 18.

165. Simpson, "Studies," *Iberoamericana*, XIII, 82–83 n.

166. Dr. Atl (G. Murillo) characterizes the Puebla polychrome style of decoration as an economic expedient to satisfy an enormous architectural demand. Murillo, *Iglesias de México*, IV, 9. R. García Granados, *Xochimilco* (Mexico, 1934), p. 57 (Monografías mexicanas de arte, V). Another such font is at Zinacantepec.

167. J. Contreras y López de Ayala, marqués de Lozoya, *Historia del arte hispánico* (Mexico, 1931–), III (1940), 416, fig. 421. Such a *pila* also stood in the chapel of the Casa de la Contratación in Seville in 1536. P. Torres Lanzas, "La Casa de la contratación,"

ous of metropolitan churches, Santo Domingo, where the walls of certain lateral chapels were sheathed with polychrome tiles after 1560 and before 1607.[168]

Securely dated specimens of sixteenth-century adobe construction are not known to the writer.[169] It is safe, however, to assume that then as now, adobe and *tierra pisada,* or stamped earth, were the most common and the most fugitive of Mexican building materials. The manufacture of adobe bricks was known in pre-Conquest technology, and it continued throughout the colonial era. The texts note merely the prevalence of adobe construction at the periphery of New Spain. Burgoa states that in New Spain generally, the adobe bricks were very large, and that the clay was mixed with straw, as in European practice.[170] There is no evidence that the admixture of straw rather than grass was common in antiquity, for straw is derived from European cereals and postulates a stock-breeding economy, which was not practiced before the sixteenth century. Mexican fibres, such as cactus, have not so far been identified.

Not only in the metropolitan area, but in the high mountains, such as the Villa Alta district of southern Mexico, adobe construction was normal, and square bricks were made.[171] In the tierra caliente of western Mexico, adobe construction was everywhere practiced, in the absence of abundant labor and stone.[172] Along the Gulf Coast as well, local conditions demanded adobe construction, as the expense of stone was too great. At Veracruz, the early city was built of adobe, and it was repeatedly destroyed by floods.[173] All through Jalisco, moreover, adobe was the standard material. Clay deposits for the manufacture of fired bricks were abundant, but the manufacture of fired bricks was rarely possible in Jalisco, as at Zacoalco, *ca.* 1550, when an artisan brought for the purpose from Zapotlan, taught the Indians the craft.[174]

One of the glories of the Valley of Mexico early in the sixteenth century was its immense stands of timber. Many Valley communities derived income from the sale of timber: Ojea reports that there were large stands not only of cedar, but also of pine, holm oak, and *ayacahuitl.*[175] These were rapidly exhausted by the colonists, and many of the ravages of deforestation were experienced long before 1600. Girava speaks of great *cedros* which were once available, so large that timbers twelve feet square and 120 feet long could be taken from them. Such a timber was fashioned into an immense cross in the courtyard of San José in Mexico City at Christmas, 1527. The Indians

Boletin del centro de estudios americanistas de Sevilla, III, no. 8 (1915), 10.

168. Ojea, . . . *Historia religiosa,* p. 10.

169. J. McAndrew informs me that the upper parts of Etzatlan in Jalisco may be of the sixteenth century. Adobe walls are mentioned in the southern portions of the casas viejas in the capital in 1531. *CDIAI,* XII, 520 f. In 1540, it was specified that an inn at Perote should be built of adobes upon thick stone foundations; the walls themselves to be two-and-a-half bricks thick. *AC,* IV, 196, 197.

170. Burgoa, *Geográfica descripción,* II, 169.

171. Dávila Padilla, *Historia . . . Santiago de México,* II, 549. No lime whatever was available in the Villa Alta district.

172. Basalenque, *Historia . . . Michoacán,* p. 16b; Escobar, *Americana thebaida,* p. 128.

173. *Epistolario,* III, 39–41.

174. Ornelas, *Crónica . . . Xalisco,* p. 34.

175. Ojea, *op. cit.,* p. 2. "*ayaquahuitl,* ques madera excelente y mui semejante al cedro o cipres." G. Girava, *Dos libros de cosmographia* (Milan, 1556), p. 199.

took it from a cypress at Chapultepec, which yielded an upright member two hundred feet high.[176]

The quantities of timber needed for the rebuilding of Tenochtitlan may be estimated from the report that Cortés used 6,906 cedar beams merely in the building of his own houses.[177] By 1625, Thomas Gage, the English Dominican, saw the cedar forests "much decayed by the Spaniards, who have wasted and spoiled them in their too too sumptuous buildings."[178]

The immediate consequence of deforestation was the silting of the lake. The run-off from the mountain slopes was increased; the processes of atmospheric erosion were hastened, and great floods arose to endanger the island city.[179] As early as 1533, the municipal authorities displayed great alarm, and a commission was appointed to set aside restricted areas where no further lumber might be cut. It was noted that the districts of Cuajimalpa and Tepeaquilla, near the city, had been specially maltreated, and that an agent of Cortés, Juan Cano, had been one of the worst offenders. In 1538 the cabildo also prohibited the cutting of any trees within the city, and in 1539, a license had to be secured to cut any wood, as with the request of Cristobal de Oñate for four hundred timbers to build his house.

In the meanwhile, however, the radius of exploitation expanded beyond the control of the municipality. A special danger to the forest reserves was offered by the charcoal industry. The European population, needing heat in the chill highland atmosphere, demanded great quantities of this fuel. The cabildo could only register the danger. In the exploitation of lumber, the Indians were very wasteful. Not only did they cut green trees, but when cutting for boards, they adzed the trunk, with tools

176. "Carta de Fr. Pedro de Gante al rey," *NCDHM,* II, 224, 232. The tree had long been venerated by the Indians for its height. About 1590 it was taken down, and a smaller cross, made of the transverse arm, was erected in its place in the courtyard of San José de los Naturales. This smaller cross, finally, was blown down in 1671. See Vetancurt, *Chrónica, Teatro,* Pt. IV, p. 41.

177. Valued at 1,716 pesos, used in the casas viejas alone. *CDIAI,* XII, 520 ff.

178. Gage, *The English-American,* p. 58.

179. On sixteenth-century floods, see Marroqui, *La Ciudad de México,* I, 112 ff. In an analysis of extraordinary perspicacity, the Dutch geographer-engineer Henrico Martínez (*Reportorio de los tiempos y historia natural desta Nueva España* [Mexico, 1606], pp. 185–186) assigned the floods to complementary causes: "Bien sabido es de todos, que antes que los Españoles viniessen a esta tierra, los naturales della no tenian cauallos ni ganado, tampoco se araua la tierra, y las cuestas y laderas eran poco cultivadas; per que los Indios, segun dizen, labrauan sus sementeras y milpas en tierra lana y junto à sus casas, con lo qual el agua que llovia y las vertientes de las sierras, como estaua la tierra dura y apretada, descendía menos turbias q̄ agora en estos tiempos. Mas despues que este Reyno está poblado de Christianos, como la tierra se ara por muchas partes, y la huella continuo el ganado y los cauallos, es causa de estar mouida, y de que los aguaceros que vienē aparar à los llanos vengan embueltos con mucha lama y tierra, la qual se assienta en las partes mas baxas, las quales con esto van creciendo y subiendo poco à poco hasta que vienen à emparejar con las demas tierras circumstantes . . . la laguna . . . no mengua, pues siempre entran en ella las aguas que solian entrar, sino que el suelo y la tierra ala redonda della crece, haziendo que se estreche y leuante el vaso della. . . ." If the Valley of Mexico is today a dust-bowl, the phenomenon is not new. Cf. Ricketson on the formation of *bajos* in the Peten district of Guatemala, citing Cook. O. G. Ricketson, Jr., *Uaxactun, Guatemala. Group E (1926–31). Part I: The Excavations* (Washington, 1937) (Carnegie Institution of Washington, Publication no. 477).

that allowed them to secure no more than one or two boards per tree. The cabildo then ordered that the Indians use saws, which they themselves were to provide, in order that the number of boards secured from a single tree might be increased. At the same time, the council decreed that no tree might be cut within five leagues of the city without license; that the lighting of fires in forest areas was to be forbidden, and that forest guards were to be appointed.[180]

The early abundance of forest reserves probably favored the tendency to build three-aisled churches during the first campaign of evangelization (see pp. 299–300). With easily available timbers, a capacious three-aisled church could be built quickly. The columns of San José de los Naturales were wooden, and it is recorded that other multiple-aisled churches of the earliest period (Fig. *214*) had wooden columns.[181] With vaulted construction large amounts of lumber still were needed for centerings and stagings. Thus, when the Dominicans in Oaxaca finally occupied their new convento in the seventeenth century, the vaulted service rooms still had all the centerings in place, a condition perhaps made necessary by the long drying or seasoning period of the mortar. Other reports as well, from Mexico City and from the Indian towns, give us an indication of the great quantities of lumber used in this way.[182] In addition, many sixteenth-century churches were built with wooden ceilings. Such are the *iglesias de tijera,* with their wooden trusses, or the roof of San Agustín in Mexico, before 1585 (the second church on the site), which was made in large part "de madera mozayca dorada y de azul añigal,"[183] probably not unlike the present ceiling (Fig. 49) of San Francisco in Tlaxcala. Throughout the western and southern provinces, far less pretentious wooden roofs were the rule. At Etzatlan in Jalisco, for example, the Franciscan church was beamed, as Tello says, "con can y sobre can," signifying a system of doubled corbels upon which the beams rested.[184]

Today, specimens of sixteenth-century woodwork may be seen in the cloisters at Huexotla, Tlaxcala, and perhaps Calpulalpan. Carved doors survive at Tlalnepantla, Huejotzingo, and Culhuacan; stair trim at Yuriria and Zinacantepec; wooden moldings at Huejotzingo and wooden ceilings at Epazoyucan and Erongaricuaro. This listing is random and fragmentary; many other specimens may easily be identified. In

180. Cano; *AC,* III, 56–57, 58, 59: Oñate; *AC,* IV, 115, 161: Cabildo; *AC,* VI (1554), 141–142: saws; *AC,* VII (February, 1570), 470: guards; *AC,* VII, 470. Cf. J. Soustelle, *Mexique, terre indienne,* 1936, for a report upon the modern Indian habit of setting fire to a live tree trunk for warmth or for catching animals.

181. Cervantes de Salazar, *México en 1554,* pp. 131, 133; see p. 293.

182. On Oaxaca, see Burgoa, *Palestra historial,* p. 440. Cf. *AC,* VIII, 121; Sariñana, *Noticia breve,* p. 12; Torquemada, . . . *Monarchia indiana,* III, 212.

183. Burgoa, *Geográfica descripción,* I, 415–417; Zorita, "Historia de la Nueva España," *Colección de libros y documentos referentes á la historia de América,* IX, 184.

184. Mendoza, *Fragmentos,* p. 32. Tello wrote *ca.* 1652, so that this is probably not the roof built in 1538. J. Stevens, *A New Spanish and English Dictionary* (London, 1706), translates "can" as follows, "In architecture, the end of Timber or Stone jutting out of a Wall, on which in old Buildings the Beams us'd to rest, call'd Cantilevers."

general, however, surviving examples represent but a minute fraction of the sixteenth-century work. For the destruction of so much, we may blame the many rebuildings, in more permanent materials, that were common during the period. Of course, the rebuildings were often made necessary by the simple processes of decay.

Often the wood could not be properly seasoned, with the great hurry to complete a serviceable building. This is still the condition in Mexico today: it is nearly impossible to find properly seasoned woods for building or cabinet making. At Cuitzeo late in the sixteenth century (*ca.* 1590), it was found that the wooden roofs of the convento had to be replaced every twenty years. The period is strikingly short for timbers of *cedro y guayameles,* as they are described by Escobar.[185] Occasionally we find the authorities legislating a due seasoning period for commercial woods. In 1537, for instance, the municipal council of Mexico City ordered that the wood for wagons must be seasoned at least eight months after cutting.[186] But there is no record that such prescriptions ever were drawn for building woods.

In the choice of lumber, moreover, the European builders were often confused by the unfamiliar Mexican species. Near Etla in Oaxaca, for example, a local variety of mountain pine, called *pino de la sierra* proved to be too soft to endure, although it became evident that the boards cut from *pino blanco* were virtually indestructible.[187]

In addition to all their other troubles, the Mexican builders encountered new and formidable insect enemies of wooden construction. At Nejapa, in Oaxaca, the beams of the roof of the Dominican establishment had been attacked by wood-boring insects, with the result that the beams were hollow, housing colonies of bats, "con indecible indecencia." Father Burgoa, as prior, was obliged to vault the entire edifice, and to replace all wooden objects such as altars and statues with new ones made of cedar.[188]

There is little real evidence that the Spaniards were especially familiar with shingles or shakes before their arrival in New Spain.[189] The Indians nevertheless used large quantities of fir and pine shakes in their own domestic architecture during the sixteenth century. Called *tejamaniles,* the shakes were produced in large quantities in the forested regions of western Mexico, especially in Michoacan. Although the Europeans preferred their traditional beams and boards to the light Indian shakes, the tejamaniles rapidly found use as roofing material. Before 1531, tejamaniles were used in the roofing of the town house of Diego de Ordaz in Mexico City.[190] By 1584, they were being exported from Michoacan to other areas of Mexico, notably to Jalisco and

185. Basalenque, *Historia . . . Michoacán,* pp. 64a, b; 121b; Escobar, *Americana thebaida,* pp. 671–672. Note, on the other hand, that Burgoa praises the careful seasoning given the timbers used in the construction of the convento at Tlaxiaco (*Geográfica descripción,* I, 309–310). Possibly the event was so rare that it deserved special notice.

186. *AC,* IV, 106.

187. Burgoa, *op. cit.,* II, 5.

188. *Ibid.,* II, 234.

189. Contrast P. Carrasco, in *Houses and House Use of the Sierra Tarascans* (Smithsonian Institution, 1945), p. 34.

190. *CDIAI,* XII, 530.

Durango.[191] A text of 1584 gives us an accurate description of their use: "They roof many houses with little boards the size of tiles or a little longer, and about that width, flat and as thick as a finger. These they nail upon the timbers of the house at an angle sufficient to shed water. In Mexican they are called *taxamaniles.* They last ten or twelve years, made of a certain kind of pine in Michoacan, a pine which splits readily and very straight. . . ."[192] Shakes are also illustrated in the *Códice florentino,* illustrated for Sahagún *ca.* 1575 (Fig. 51).

The visitor to Mexico is impressed today by the Indians' skilful use of the organ cactus for architectural purposes. Fences, corrals, and even houses are frequently built of the straight, thick, and tall trunks of this plant, set vertically in the ground, and evoking log construction. We have few sixteenth-century texts for the architectural use of cactus. In the region about Izucar, where wood was so scarce that it had to be brought from the slopes of Popocatepetl, the houses at Tepeoxuma and Tlatequetlan were built of cactus in 1554. And Cervantes de Salazar reported that the concave leaves of maguey plants were used as roof-tiles, as they still very commonly are.[193]

In the sixteenth century the house with a thatched roof (Fig. 52) bore the generic name of *jacal.*[194] In moist areas, such thatched roofs were indispensable, for the flat roofs of the arid highland were ineffective, and the paucity of labor and materials made framed or vaulted roofs impractical. In humid climates, moreover, the thatched roof provides necessary ventilation, and the material is so inexpensive that it may easily be replaced when infested or decadent. Thus, in Jalapa de Veracruz in 1580, the walls of the casas de comunidad were built of rubble masonry, but roofed with thatch (*paja*).[195] Burgoa tells us that in the Villa Alta region of Oaxaca, the climate and the lack of skilled labor made it impossible to build anything but jacales. An effort to waterproof flat roofs with resin did not endure over two years, and the Dominican builders therefore reverted in their church construction to extremely steep thatched roofs.[196]

A striking aspect of sixteenth century Mexican technology is the abundant use of metal in architectural undertakings. We are told that the Augustinian church in Mexico City was roofed with sheets of lead; the same was true of the Dominican

191. Paso y Troncoso, comp., "Papeles de Nueva España," MS, VIII.

192. *Ibid.*: "munchas [sic] casas cubren conciertas tablillas del tamaño de las tejas un poco mas largas y casi del propio anchor, enpero son llanos e gruesas de un dedo, las quales clavan sobre el maderamiento de la casa, y danle suficiente corriente para que no rrebaren ellas el agua; llamanse en lengua mexicana Taxamaniles y dura su cubertura diez y doze años, y hazense de un cierto jénero de pino que ay en la provincia de Mechuacan que hiende muy façil y derecho. . . ."

193. Izúcar: *PNE,* I, 211, 213. "unos arboles que tienen de espinos en sus cerros se provechan . . . para hazer sus casas." Cervantes de Salazar, *México en 1554,* p. 146.

194. Dávila Padilla, *Historia . . . Santiago de México,* p. 549.

195. *PNE,* V, 104. The meaning of the term "jacal" varied geographically. In the Spanish southwest, particularly in Texas, the term was applied to palisaded construction.

196. Burgoa, *Geográfica descripción,* II, 169. Cf. Bevan, *The Chinantec,* 1938, pp. 53–64.

church, and later on in the century, of the Franciscan church.[197] In the sixteenth century as today, the supplies of lead were probably the by-product of the silver-smelting operations, and the great bulk of it came from the mines in the region of Zimapan, in the Mezquital district.

At Xochimilco, according to Vetancurt, the roof of the great church, with its enormous span, was braced not only by wooden trusses, but also by "tirantes de cadenas de fierro con gruessos eslabones."[198] In 1554, San Agustín in Mexico City had a fence of stone posts and lions supporting an iron chain; throughout the city, moreover, the houses of the rich had iron door-pull rings.[199] Iron was also used in quantities in public works of various kinds. An interesting case is that of the water-gauges used to control the issue of water to the householders. The city granted water in quantities measured by the diameter of the stream; this was governed by perforations in an iron plate at the point where the main conduit was tapped. Some iron came from Europe. Vetancurt tells of a great iron screen, or *reja,* fifteen by eight yards, for the ornament of the Franciscan church in the capital. It came from Cantabria, probably in the seventeenth century, and cost ten thousand pesos.[200]

The great Mexican centers of metal-smithing were Xochimilco and Atzcapotzalco. At Atzcapotzalco, many bronze objects, such as church bells, nails, and door-hinges were made. Xochimilco was famous for iron-smithing, producing grills and balconies. Still another center for iron-smithing was at Huamantla, in Tlaxcala province, where the Indians manufactured metal horse gear, such as stirrups, bits, and so on, in great quantities.[201]

Elsewhere, the friars were specially zealous in the confiscation of pre-Conquest metal objects. These were used for casting church bells. The bells cast from Indian metals at Tiripitio survived in the eighteenth century; in Michoacan, fray Francisco Lorenzo melted down enough idols in the tierra caliente to cast sixteen bells for the churches he built. In Jalisco as well, copious supplies of pre-Conquest metal were collected for the manufacture of church bells.[202]

The use of glass in windows appears to be a seventeenth-century development in Mexican building. It may be noted that glass was also uncommon in Spanish domestic

197. Zorita, "Historia de la Nueva España," *Colección de libros y documentos referentes á la historia de América,* IX, 184. San Augustín: "en lugar de tejas tiene planchas de plomo, por manera que todo lo alto donde avia de estar tejado, está emplomado, y de la misma manera esta lo alto de la yglesia de Sancto Domingo, y tienen ambas una misma traça." Cf. Franco, *Historia . . . Santiago de México,* pp. 538–539, for the second church of the Dominicans, and Vetancurt, *Chrónica, Teatro,* Pt. IV, p. 34, for the Franciscan church built by Francisco de Gamboa between 1590 and 1602. On sources of lead, see Guillemin Tarayre, "Rapport," *Archives de la commission scientifique du Mexique,* III, 308.

198. Vetancurt, *op. cit.,* pp. 56–57.

199. Cervantes de Salazar, *México en 1554,* pp. 131, 157, 159.

200. Vetancurt, *op. cit.,* p. 34.

201. Villaseñor, *Theatro americano,* pp. 77, 165, 309.

202. Escobar, *Americana thebaida,* p. 155; Rea, *Crónica de la orden de N. serafico P. S. Francisco,* p. 56; Mendieta, *Historia eclesiástica indiana,* p. 755.

architecture; Jacob Sobieski, the Polish traveler, noted in 1611 at Logroño in Old Castile, that cloth was used in the windows, "para evitar los calores del sol é impedir su invasion en el interior de las casas. . . ."[203] In Mexico, windows were glazed with wax paper or painted cloth, if not with the translucent, alabastrine tecali. The primitive Cathedral of Mexico (Figs. *211–213*) had painted and waxed cloth windows in 1585, and in 1574 the large window in the council chamber of the ayuntamiento was covered with a "marco con un lienzo encerado."[204] Cervantes de Salazar makes no mention of glass in his description of the plate-traceries in the windows of S. Agustín in Mexico City, nor is glass mentioned by Burgoa in the bar-traceries of the nave (Fig. 381) of Yanhuitlan.[205] In 1697, however, Vetancurt could speak of a Mexican glass industry whose products, in his opinion, rivalled those of Venice. It was originally situated in Cholula, and later transferred to Puebla.[206] Such seventeenth-century glass was used, not only for windows, but also for the protection of the holy objects in the churches.

Contemporary reports upon the procedures actually used in Mexican construction are extremely rare. The methods of preparing foundations, or building vaults, are never recorded in great detail, and even casual allusions to procedure are far from common. Numerous Spanish texts of the sixteenth and seventeenth centuries, however, permit us to document the usual field observations upon the methods employed, at least in their general outline (see also pp. 179, 181).

Very ambitious leveling and filling operations sometimes prepared the site of a permanent edifice. At Yanhuitlan, for instance, about 1570, the Dominicans directed the construction of a great terreplein, to serve as a pedestal for the church (Fig. 161). The sloping ground necessitated such a platform, and it covered an area five hundred yards square. The terreplein supported the atrio (see p. 316), and it was approached by flights of stairs on three sides.[207] The analogy between this procedure and the pre-Conquest habit of building great pyramidal platforms is obvious. The form of labor was one to which the Indians were fully accustomed. Usually, however, a pre-Conquest

203. K. Liske, ed., *Viajes de extranjeros por España y Portugal en los siglos XV, XVI y XVII. Colección de J. Liske (Año de 1878)* (Madrid, 1879), pp. 241–242. Cf. J. W. Thompson and E. N. Johnson, *An Introduction to Medieval Europe* (New York, 1937), p. 312, and C. Borromeo, *Instructions on ecclesiastical building* (London, 1857), p. 20, G. J. Wrigley, tr. The late colonial parroquía at Tecali has thin-plate onyx windows that admit a pleasing, diffused light, and may have been brought over from the nearby three-aisled church at the time of its dismantling in the nineteenth century.

204. Toussaint, *Paseos coloniales*, p. 16; *AC*, VIII, 135.

205. S. Agustín, Mexico: "quam gratus ex earum fenestris prospectus! Quam longae lataeque viae lapideis reticulis, per quae lux transmittitur, illustratae!" Cervantes de Salazar, *México en 1554*, p. 154. Yanhuitlan: "cada ventana tiene cuatro varas de luz, que entra per celogías de lata labradas, con cincel y variedad de taladros." Burgoa, *Geográfica descripción*, I, 292–293. Cf. B. Cobo, "Dos cartas," *Revista histórica*, III (1928), 34–35.

206. Vetancurt, *Chrónica, Teatro*, Pt. IV, p. 55.

207. Burgoa, *op. cit.*, I, 292. J. McAndrew has suggested that the friars merely adapted a pre-Conquest platform (correspondence, 1946).

platform was already available for the church; such was the case at Molango in Hidalgo. But at Tlalmanalco, the problem of the sloping ground-level was solved in the sixteenth century by excavating a level site from the hillside, for church and convento.[208]

On the platform, the next step was to open suitably deep foundations for the building. Occasionally the haste of builders to advance with wall-building led to expensive consequences. At Patzcuaro, for instance, the cathedral was given such shallow foundations in 1550, that the walls soon opened and cracked. In addition the site itself was poorly chosen, being inadequately drained. The ultimate failure of the entire cathedral project at Patzcuaro may in part be assigned to these initial errors.[209]

In the capital, conditions were far more demanding of the colonists' ingenuity than elsewhere in New Spain. The marshy subsoil of the island platform constantly moved, with the result that buildings sank, squirmed, and slid about on their foundations. Several important edifices were completely lost in the sixteenth century. The great monastic churches, for example, settled so deeply into their swampy foundations that the buildings became virtually submarine.

An interesting document of the 1560's shows the operations used in establishing a firm platform (Fig. 53) for the fabric of the new metropolitan cathedral. A water-pump constantly drains the excavation; into it, cross-timbers have been laid. Over these a platform of masonry is being built. Indians bring up stone in wheelbarrows; others mix the cement at the edges of the excavation. The preparation of these foundations lasted many years; ultimately a subterranean platform of great mass and depth was completed, upon which the cathedral has stood, without notable deformation, ever since.[210] We also have a contemporary description of this operation, from Alonzo de Zorita. According to him, the first foundations that were opened had to be abandoned, because of the great cost and because of the constant flooding to which they were subjected. Then the effort was made again, by a new method of driving stakes

208. Vetancurt, *Chrónica, Teatro,* Pt. IV, pp. 62–63. Cf. Chap. VII, p. 316.

209. Beaumont, *Crónica de Michoacán,* II, 388.

210. *Codice Osuña,* p. 300. The Aztec inscription reads, in my translation: "Here is displayed the work at the place where the iglesia mayor shall arise. The majordomo, Juan de Cuenca, neither assigned the labor, nor was it paid for." Zorita, "Historia de la Nueva España," *Colección de libros y documentos referentes á la historia de América,* IX, 176. "El cimiento que primero se avia abierto para ello costó ochenta mill pesos y se dexo por no se poder proseguir por aquella orden, a causa del agua, que no se podia agotar avnque a la contina andavan trabajando en ello con sus bombas, y se mudó a otra parte y se haze de estacada el cimiento, por vna orden sutil y de buen ingenio con que se hincan las estacas y todas quedan parejas a rrayz del agua, y de alli adelante sobre la haz de la tierra se a de hazer vn plantapie de argamasa que tome todo el edificio de la yglesia, porque con el peso se sumen los edificios de la laguna y quede que se poder sumir, y tambien porque no lleguen los cuerpos de los difuntos en las sepolturas al agua." Cf. L. G. Ansorena, "La catedral de México," *Anales de la asociación de ingenieros y arquitectos de México,* XX (1913), 68–69; Murillo, *Iglesias de México,* II, by Toussaint, 19. Vetancurt, *Chrónica, Tratado,* p. 1, specifies that the stakes were of cedar; five to six varas in length, and that upon them "hicieron una cepa entera sobrandole quatro varas de cimiento por cada lado."

into the building site in very great numbers. This was a pre-Conquest custom in Tenochtitlan, and it worked as well in the sixteenth century as it had for the Aztecs. Over the platform created by these close-set stakes, another platform of clay was built, upon which the entire edifice rested. It is not clear whether the illustration in the *Pintura del Gobernador* refers to the first or the second of these campaigns; the date, however, suggests that the first, or unsuccessful campaign is shown. We know from the minutes of the municipal council that the change of technique probably occurred early in 1563;[211] and the *Pintura del Gobernador* refers to unpaid work performed by various Indians in the decade prior to 1566. Ultimately, the mat of stakes was used for many important metropolitan buildings. The more modest edifices, of course, were not given deep foundations.[212]

The methods of building wall may be reconstructed both from monuments and from the texts. The computation of the thickness of the bearing walls was, of course, made with respect to the span of volume, height of wall, and nature of material. In this connection a sixteenth-century Spanish text is available, by the architect Rodrigo Gil de Hontañon.[213] As it was not published until 1868, the treatise was probably not available to builders in Mexico, yet it incorporates a body of highly traditional knowledge about computation, of a character surely known to the more experienced friars and civilians. Since the Mexican vaults, and the ones built by Hontañon belong to the same family, we cannot go far wrong in citing his computational methods as being fairly representative of those used in Mexico. Other writers of later periods also record such traditional knowledge, and in their work, a sharp division is always apparent between the artificial Vitruvian lore and the living heritage of late medieval practice. This is strikingly the case with the writing of fray Lorenzo de San Nicolás,[214] whose empirical recommendations have a conciseness and authority lacking in the dilute chapters derived from Vitruvian scholarship.

According to Hontañon, several methods were available for calculating the necessary thickness of the bearing walls. The most elaborate methods concerned the walls

211. *AC*, VII (Feb. 19, 1563), 105: "los cimientos que se abren para la obra de la yglesia desta cibdad se abren diferentamente de como esta trazado y señalado. . . ." Cf. pp. 111, 118, 121. The cabildo was perennially concerned over these foundations: in 1570 its members again voiced fears that they might be inadequate. They also questioned the choice of site. *AC*, VII, 487–488.

212. *Relación . . . Ponce*, I, 177: "hacen unas estacas de maderos muy juntos y hincados, y en medio dellos fundan el cimiento."

213. See J. Agapito y Revilla, "Un laborioso arquitecto castellano . . .," *Arquitectura* (March, 1923), pp. 57–63. Simón García, "Compendio de arquitectura," *Arte en España*, VII (1868). See also J. Camón, "La intervención de Rodrigo Gil de Hontañon en el manuscrito de Simón García," *Archivo español de arte*, no. 45 (1941), 300–305. Hontañon's share in the text includes chapters i through vi. Camón observes that a new edition of the manuscript is currently in preparation in Spain, from the manuscript in the Biblioteca Nacional in Madrid. Simón García compiled the treatise between 1681 and 1685.

214. Lorenzo de San Nicolás, *Arte y uso de arquitectura* (Madrid, 1796), II, chap. xxviii, 78, reveals his long acquaintance with, and dependence upon the highly original *Medidas del romano*, by Diego de Sagredo (1526).

intended to support stone vaults. In one, the radius of an arch or barrel vault was taken as the side of a square at the impost level (Fig. 54). The normal to the diagonal of the square at its intersection with the semicircle of the arch profile was then constructed. A line through the other diagonal, from the impost to the keystone, was also constructed. The normals and the line then intersected. The distance from the impost to this intersection was used as a radius with the center on the impost, to strike off, on the impost line, the necessary thickness of bearing wall or buttress.[215] Another rule, with an even higher safety factor, suggests taking the thickness of the bearing wall as one quarter of the desired diameter of the vault.[216] Neither of these rules, however, takes the height of the bearing walls into account, but Hontañon advances several others, of which the most interesting recommends the following. The thickness of the desired buttress is computed by taking the square root of the sum of the height of the bearing wall (to impost level) and the radius of the vault. It is to be noted that these rules all pertain to the thickness of the bearing wall or buttress at impost level; at ground level, according to Hontañon, increments must be made to provide the "taluses y demás adornos."

In practice, the Mexican builders sometimes far improved these cautious recommendations. At Cuitzeo, for example, the walls were originally built thick enough so that, although the original roofing for the convento was of wood, it was possible later on (*ca.* 1590), to impose stone vaults without changing the walls.[217] Elsewhere, for military reasons, as at Yuriria, or for protection against earthquakes, the bearing walls were made extraordinarily massive. At Yuriria, for instance, and at Santo Domingo in Oaxaca, the walls in construction were so thick that carts could be driven, as upon a road, over them.[218] Thus great wall thickness in Mexico is not necessarily a sign of amateur design or even of preparation for damage by earthquakes; it may also relate to anticipated changes of structure, as at Tiripitio (see p. 265).

In any case, several techniques unknown in Spain were devised in Mexico, in contact with pre-Conquest Indian practice. At Huejotzingo and old Tehuacan (Fig. 46), for example, the bearing walls of the church consist of rammed earth and adobe brick between massive facings of cut stone. This is an old Indian technique in the building of pyramidal platforms. The bonding of the corners of certain churches,

215. García, "Compendio de arquitectura," *Arte en España,* VII, 175–179. The normal is constructed to AC at D. The normal to BE is constructed at E. Their intersection at K is taken as radius from E to strike F.

216. Lorenzo de San Nicolás, *op. cit.,* I, 46, offers other rules of thumb. He distinguishes among stone vaults; domical vaults of brick (*rosca de ladrillo*), and an unclear type designated as a vault *rubricada de ladrillo.* In the first instance, unbuttressed walls must total one-third the inner span of the vault; in the second they must total one-seventh, and in the third, one-eighth. The wall thickness may be substantially reduced by the addition of buttresses.

217. Basalenque, *Historia . . . Michoacán,* pp. 64a,b.

218. Yuriria: González de la Puente, ". . . Choronica augustiniana," *Colección de documentos F. Plancarte y Navarrete.* Oaxaca: Gage, *The English-American,* p. 121. See also Burgoa, *Geográfica descripción,* II, 41.

moreover, evokes ancient Indian practices. An example is seen at Atotonilco de Tula (Fig. 457), where the corners are bonded by vertical and horizontal stretchers and headers, in a manner recalling Yucatan, Tula, or Tenayuca (Fig. 35). In the colonial epoch such bonding was often executed in materials different from those of the wall mass. At Atotonilco de Tula, for example, the corners of a wall of *tepetate* were reinforced with blocks of *cantera colorada.*[219]

Ribbed vaults were not generally built in Mexico until after 1540. Before this date, Motolinia records only the sanctuary of S. Francisco in Mexico City, and two small chapels in Tlaxcala[220] (Figs. 254, 256).

Before approaching the problem of construction, we shall need to examine the nomenclature of the various types of vaults and their members. In sixteenth- and seventeenth-century Spanish, the terms used to designate the various kinds of vault vary from author to author. Basalenque, for example, distinguished rib vaulting from other forms by the term *clavería,* and he speaks of it, out of his own experience as a builder, as the most elaborate, expensive, and time-consuming form of covering.[221] Father Burgoa, on the other hand, speaks of rib vaults as *bóvedas de arista,* or *bóvedas de lacería,* or more reconditely, as *artesonería de lazos* or *cantería.* In all authors, the term *bóveda de cañón* alludes to barrel-vaulting. The term *artesonado* does not specify the type of structure other than by geometrical form: it signifies a coved or concave ceiling, regardless of material or technique.[222] *Tijera* always signifies a wooden roof composed of joined timbers in an openwork and concave form (Fig. 49); special forms are the *techo de ochavados* or *de una tercia de hueco.* A full discussion of these wooden roofs pertains to the treatment of seventeenth-century architecture. In the sixteenth century, the ceilings usually were simple trabeated constructions (Fig. 400) rather than the elaborate geometric carpentry (Fig. 49) of Moorish antecedents.[223]

An exact terminology for the parts of the rib vault is also provided by Rodrigo Gil de Hontañon. The fundamental members of the rib vault are, of course, the ogives (or cross ribs) intersecting diagonally across the bay; the wall ribs adjoining the bearing walls, and the transverse ribs, spanning the bay. Hontañon analyzes the behavior of these various ribs, designating the transverse ribs as *arcos pripiaños,* exercising the greatest thrust. The ogives (*arcos cruceros*) and the wall ribs (*arcos de forma*) thrust obliquely and, therefore, according to Hontañon, may be of thin, light construction.

219. See *Catálogo . . . Hidalgo,* I, 159 ff.

220. Motolinia, *Memoriales,* p. 184. "No creo hay otras en esta tierra."

221. Basalenque, *op. cit.,* pp. 56a, b. Burgoa, *op. cit.,* I, 292, 403–404. Dávila Padilla, *Historia . . . Santiago de México,* p. 571, also speaks of rib vaults as *bóvedas de arista,* as distinguished from *bóvedas de cañon.*

222. Stevens, *A New Spanish and English Dictionary.* A good classification of Spanish ceilings is found in Bevan, *Spanish Architecture,* p. 116.

223. For a full discussion, see D. López de Arenas, *Carpinteria de lo blanco y tratado de alarifes* (3d ed. Madrid, 1867), E. de Mariátegui, ed. (*Biblioteca de el arte en España,* IV); see also J. F. Ráfols, *Techumbres y artesonados españoles* (2d ed. Barcelona, 1930) (Colección Labor. Sección IV: Artes plásticas, no. 86).

Finally, the intermediate or tierceron ribs from impost to keystone (*arcos terceletes*) exercise the same order of thrust as the ogives. Therefore, he compares the bundle of ribs to the human hand (Fig. 55): the various ribs must be scaled proportionally to the thrust they exercise. The ratio of the transverse ribs is to the ogives and tiercerons as the thumb is to the middle finger and index or ring finger; the wall rib, finally, is scaled as the little finger. In arithmetical measures, the relative sectional dimensions of the various ribs are determined from the overall width or side of the bay as a whole. For example, the sectional height of the transverse rib is one-twentieth the width of the bay, where the width is equal to the height of the bearing walls. The cross ribs or ogives are one-twenty-fourth the width; the tiercerons are one-twenty-eighth; and the wall ribs one-thirtieth. In the case of rectangular bays, the designer must take one-half the sum of the two dimensions as the base from which to compute the sectional heights of the various ribs. Given the dimensions of the bay and the number of ribs he intends to use, the designer may then compute the thickness of wall-buttressing necessary to absorb the thrusts of the rib-clusters. The sum of the linear lengths of the ribs, from impost to keystones, is taken, including cross, wall, transverse and tierceron ribs. Their sum is reduced by its third; the intended height of the buttress is added to the remainder, and the root of the result divided by three. The quotient yields the width of the buttress; and two-thirds of the quotient gives the depth of the buttress, including the buttress itself, the wall thickness, and the pilaster on the interior. Any talus or glacis (setback molding) is to be added to these basic measurements. Thus the overall dimensions of the bay control the size of the ribs, and through them, the dimensions of the buttressing.

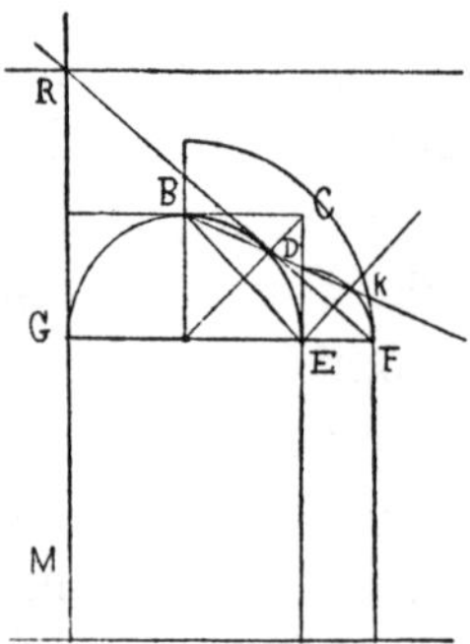

54. Diagram for computation of barrel-vault thrusts

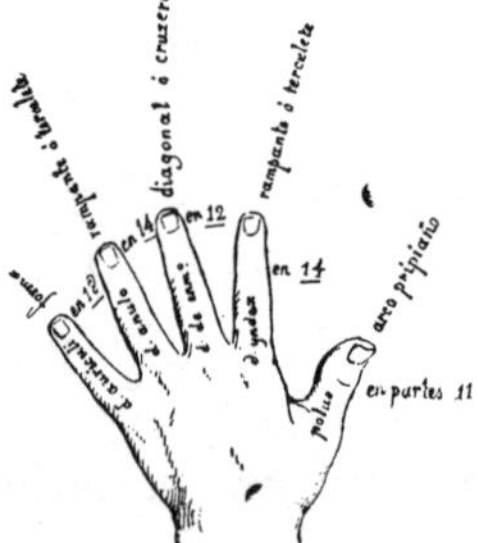

55. Diagram showing relative rib thrusts

A glance at the plates will immediately reveal the complexity of the ribbed decoration of the Mexican vaults (Figs. 60, 276). Tiercerons and liernes complicate the fundamental structural pattern of six ribs in almost all examples. This is also true for the Spanish examples of rib vaulting in the sixteenth century, and Rodrigo Gil de Hontañon describes the way in which these complex patterns were constructed. Fig. *56*, from his treatise, shows a simultaneous plan and section of such a vault, with one ogive, the impost, the keystone, and pendant secondary keystones. In the haunches

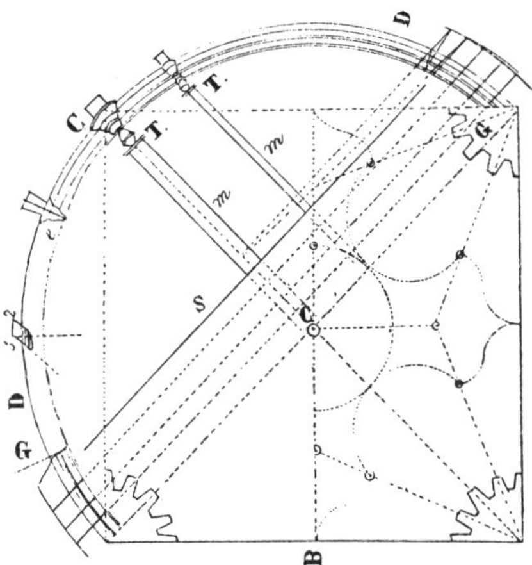

56. Scaffolding used in rib construction

of the vault, a little above impost level, a platform scaffold was built, and on it, the entire vault design of ribs and keystones was laid out in line drawing. Wooden centerings were then constructed to locate the various keystones and pendants in their designated places. The stones were supported in position by wooden columns of correct lengths. The ribs were then built, and finally the masonry web spanning the spaces between the ribs. Hontañon also indicates that the keystones and pendants were drilled longitudinally, and that, as in Europe generally, the perforations were useful for cleaning the intrados of the vault; for hanging lamps; and for taking down the scaffolds after completion. He also provides a method of computing the optimum weight of the keystone from the dimensions of the bay, and the weight per foot of the diagonal rib or *crucero*.[224]

In Mexican practice, however, it is a fact of considerable importance that the ribbed vaults were often not borne upon stone or brick at all, and that the ribs were

224. García, "Compendio de arquitectura," *Arte en España*, VII, 173–184. On the value of Hontañon's computations in medieval archeology, see G. Kubler, "A Late Medieval Computation of Rib Vault Thrusts," *Gazette des beaux-arts*, ser. 6, Vol. XXVI (1947), p. 135. The rule for keystones involves taking the square root of the difference between the lengths of the two diagonal ribs and the length of one ogive from impost to key. This root, expressed in *quintales*, or 100-pound units (one quintal = weight per foot of the normal ogive), equals the optimal weight of the keystone, at which the key will function properly in resisting the upward thrust of the stones in the arch of the rib.

sometimes constructed of plaster, serving as purely ornamental additions to the vault soffit. This was the case at Huejotzingo (Fig. 57), and at S. Francisco in Puebla.[225] Such shortcuts were surely intended to conserve labor and reduce the number of complicated operations described by Hontañon in the construction of true bearing ribs. In the Cathedral of Mexico, nevertheless, the manufacture of plaster ribs, before 1627 in the chapel of S. Isidro Labrador, was meant to reduce the weight of the building upon its uncertain foundations.[226]

Elsewhere, as at Tecamachalco (Fig. 58) or Acatzingo, the ribs were built of thin, fine bricks. That these served a bearing function, and were built more or less according to the precepts of the time, is probable, although it has not been possible to conduct any thorough examination of the properties of these ribs *in situ*. It may be noted that the webs of Tecamachalco are also of brick.

The construction of barrel and groin vaults and domical vaults of all kinds is described in detail in various seventeenth-century treatises. With the exception of the barrel vault (cf. pp. 262–263), such forms were not commonly built in the sixteenth century, so that we may dispense with any detailed discussion of the otherwise important treatise by Torija.[227]

A recurrent problem in the study of sixteenth-century building operations is the extremely slow rate of construction. The Franciscans, for example, began the building of San Andrés in Cholula as early as 1557, but the vault of the sanctuary was completed only with the aid of donations in 1670. At Charo, in Michoacan, the Augustinians began work about 1550, but they did not finish the establishment until the middle of the seventeenth century. At Jacona, fray Sebastian de Trasierra began an ambitious edifice which was not roofed until 1626. Here the reason given is the diminution of the Indian populations. When beginning work in a populous area, the friars laid plans, in other words, for a suitably large church. During construction, serious losses of population not only retarded the rate of construction, but entailed changes of design. Such was the case also at Poncitlan in 1586; although the sanctuary was finished and the walls were built to a high level, Ponce thought the building would never be finished because of the paucity of inhabitants and their lack of devotion. At the other extreme, however, we find the remarkable cases of rapid construction, as at Epazoyucan (Fig. 167) or Ucareo. Both were Augustinian foundations: Epazoyucan was built *ca.* 1541 in seven months and some days, including both convento and church; Ucareo was built in one year by fray Juan de Utrera. These instances

225. Vetancurt, *Chrónica, Teatro,* Pt. IV, p. 58: S. Miguel Huejotzingo, the church was roofed with "bobedas con lazeria de yezo muy hermosa." *Ibid.,* p. 48: at S. Francisco, Puebla, *ca.* 1567–70, in the church, "las bobedas se registrá de hiezo labradas molduras. . . ."

226. Sariñana, *Noticia breve,* fol. 7 vo. ". . . se varió la obra, disponiendo . . . se hiziesse mas ligera . . . respecto de la inconstancia del suelo . . . todo su convexo se hermoseó con lazos, tarjas, y figuras de medio relieve en yezo, con perfiles dorados."

227. Juan de Torija, *Breve tratado de todo genero de bobedas* (Madrid, 1661). See, however, p. 181.

49. Tlaxcala, S. Francisco, gilded cedar ceiling towards choir

50. Angahua (Michoacan), ceiling in parish church

51. House with shakes on roof

52. Indian thatched huts (*jacales*). A. Hipped roof B. Peaked roof

57. Huejotzingo, detail of rib cluster, north nave wall

53. Mexico City, laying of the Cathedral foundations

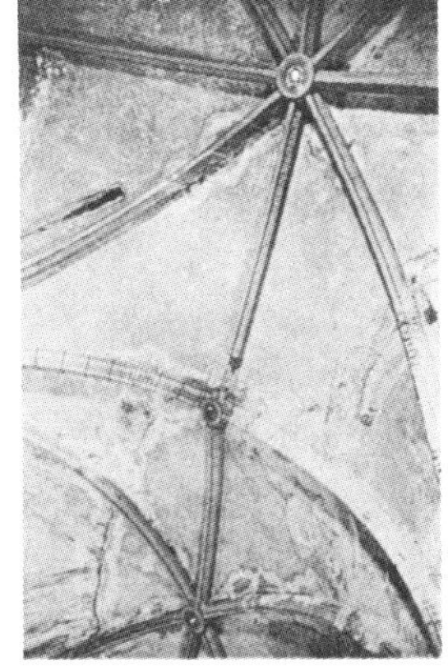

58. Tecamachalco, nave vaults

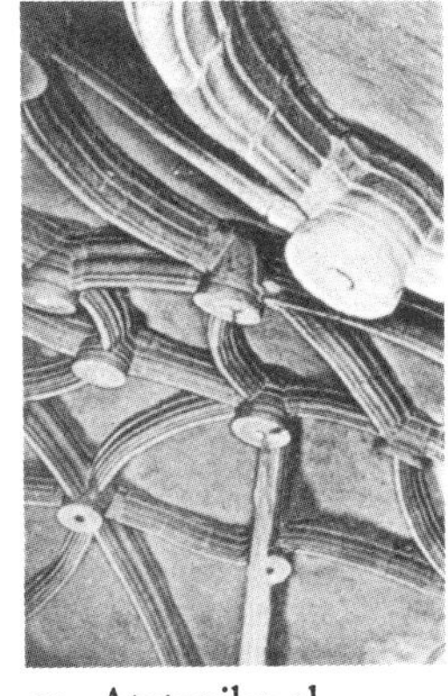

59. Atotonilco el Grande, sanctuary vault

60. Yuriria, sanctuary vault

61. Uruapan, Hospital, view of chapel and court from northeast

are, of course, exceptional,[228] but they do confirm the otherwise perhaps too general declaration by Mendieta that the Indians worked rapidly to build for the friars. According to him, villagers would often complete the monastic buildings in their settlement according to plan in less than half a year. Mendieta perhaps exaggerated, but it is in all likelihood true that the Indians worked more zealously for the friars in rural environments than for civilians in the urban centers.[229] In the former case, they stood to benefit from the spiritual comfort, temporal protection, and technological instruction afforded by the missionaries.

In the missions, nevertheless, the triennial changes of guardian or prior often interrupted the work of building. An exceptionally detailed example is found at Zacoalco in western Mexico. In 1585, the buildings were to be built anew; the foundations were laid by one guardian, and before he could bring the walls to any height, another guardian took over, finishing the walls and building the façade. The vaulting went on under still another supervisor, when the whole edifice collapsed because of the poor quality of adobe construction. Four more guardians saw to the rebuilding of the walls and roofs. Thus no one man was in office long enough to complete his designs, and his work was subject to revision by his successors.[230]

Still another factor of delay is perhaps to be found in the presence of a subsidy. If the subsidy were granted annually until completion of the edifice, an incentive was given to delay or postpone the date of completion. Thus the Augustinians accepted in 1544 a royal grant of three thousand pesos annually for the rebuilding of the church and convento in the capital. This work was not completed until 1587. Although many other factors of delay may be invoked, the wish of the Augustinians to continue to benefit from the subsidy should not be overlooked.[231]

In all matters pertaining to Indian participation in building operations, it is interesting to revert to the invaluable *Códice del Tecpan de Tlatelolco*.[232] There we see that when the Indians were working for themselves, they labored swiftly and

228. Cholula; Vetancurt, *Chrónica, Teatro*, Pt. IV, p. 90; Charo; Basalenque, *Historia . . . Michoacán*, pp. 67–69: Jacona; *ibid.*, p. 79b: Poncitlan; *Relación . . . Ponce*, II, 23–24: Epazoyucan; *PNE*, III, 86; Basalenque, *op. cit.*, p. 22a; Grijalva, *Crónica de la orden de N. P. S. Augustín*, pp. 157–158; *Catálogo . . . Hidalgo*, I, 248: Ucareo; Basalenque, *op. cit.*, pp. 22a, 69b; Ricard, *La "Conquête spirituelle" du Mexique*, pp. 205–206. Remesal gives, as an average building period for substantial edifices of permanent character and comparable to Spanish buildings, a term of seven or eight years. He speaks of course, for the Dominicans. Remesal, *Historia . . . Indias*, II, 247. F. Ximénez, *Historia de la provincia de San Vincente de Chiapa y Guatemala de la orden de predicadores* (Guatemala, 1929–31) (Biblioteca "Goathemala" de la sociedad de geografía e historia), I, 482.

229. Mendieta, *Historia eclesiástica indiana*, pp. 408, 427, 527.

230. Mendoza, *Fragmentos*, pp. 99–107 (written by Tello, 1652).

231. Grijalva, *Crónica de la orden de N. P. S. Augustín*, pp. 211–212. Viceroy Mendoza awarded a subsidy of two hundred pesos towards the Franciscan foundation at Chietla in 1550. See "Mandamientos del virrey D. Antonio de Mendoza," *Boletín del archivo general de la nación*, X (1939), 269.

232. "Códice . . . Tlaltelolco," *Investigaciones históricas*, I, no. 3 (1939). The construction schedule proceeded as follows: viceregal quarters by Aug. 11, 1576; travelers' quarters by Nov. 20; Audiencia wing by Feb. 14, 1577; inner partitions by July 3; upper floors by Jan. 4, 1578; gardens by June 3; and the entire edifice completed and ready for the archepiscopal con-

efficiently, through the worst plague in the history of Mexico, and during the greatest single depletion the Indian race experienced, to produce the buildings which were to prevent their humiliation by the Spaniards. Between 1576 and 1581, the Indians built a relatively magnificent public building (Figs. *90–92*), of which the remains survive today.

The striking complaint by Viceroy Mendoza to his successor in 1550[233] alludes without question to the shocking number of technical failures that had occurred in Mexican building. Long after Mendoza, however, the disasters, collapses, and cave-ins continued.[234] The second church of San Francisco in Mexico City lasted less than two generations, and collapsed in 1590. At Tehuacan, the vaults of the church collapsed and were replaced with wooden roofs after 1568. In Xochimilco (Fig. 180), the upper part of the doorway and main façade collapsed, and had to be rebuilt shortly before 1585. And the great Capilla Real in Cholula (Fig. *264*), one of the most imposing edifices of its day, caved in about 1581.

Some failures were of course due to causes other than the incompetence of builders. At Xiutepec in Morelos, the newly completed convento was damaged by an earthquake shortly before 1585, and at Chilapa, in 1537, a quake completely leveled the new work. Naturally, the colonists were unaccustomed to seismic destruction; and it is not until well after the mid-century that we encounter devices of construction meant to withstand tremors.

Sheer incompetence must be assigned a large part in accounting for numerous mistakes. A notorious case in 1572 was that of the aqueduct designed to bring water from Santa Fe and Cuajimalpa to Chapultepec. Miguel Martínez, the municipal alarife, was in charge of the work, until it was noticed that he had built some fifty-one arches seriously out of line. One of these was a whole foot out of the vertical, and the footings for the arches were generally insufficient.[235]

On the whole, it is remarkable that so much sixteenth-century building has withstood destruction and collapse. As we have seen, amateurs and handymen were the designers and engineers. The work was accomplished by a manual labor not entirely in sympathy with the campaign of construction, and the buildings have suffered long neglect or abuse. But it is probably true that amateur design, if inelegant and clumsy, tends towards a massive and stable architecture which, if it stands at all, has great longevity.

secration by June 24, 1581. The edifice was declared to have cost 33,600 pesos, of which 5,600 pesos were contributed by wealthy Indians. The remainder of the valuation accounts for the labor and the materials donated by the Indian workmen from the various wards or districts.

233. See Chap. III, n. 27.

234. Mexico; *Annales de . . . Chimalpahin*, p. 311: Tehuacan; Vetancurt, *Chrónica, Teatro,* Pt. IV, pp. 29–30; *Relación . . . Ponce,* I, 262: Xochimilco; *ibid.*, I, 171–172: Capilla Real, Cholula; *ibid.*, I, 162–163: Xiutepec; *ibid.*, p. 189: Chilapa; Grijalva, *op. cit.*, pp. 86–88.

235. *AC*, VIII, 72.

V

CIVIL ARCHITECTURE

Casas . . . las ay muchas y mui buenas y mui grandes y fuertes y de mui buenos edificios y aposentos altos y bajos, y con buenos patios, y algunas o las mas tienen agua de pie y huertas, y no ay tejados sino açoteas.

Zorita, *Historia de la Nueva España,* I, 200.

SIXTEENTH-CENTURY Mexican society called for fewer civil buildings than churches. The functions that would today take a score of specialized structures were satisfied by the church and its dependencies. The few thousand white colonists, moreover, could be housed with little effort, but each Indian community needed a church as the center of its communal life. Hence we shall find many fewer civil buildings in sixteenth-century New Spain than our own needs would suggest; religious architecture was the dominant mode, and secular buildings rarely assumed durable and monumental forms.

In sixteenth-century Europe, on the contrary, the need for churches had long since been satisfied by many generations of medieval builders, and the century was one of great secular undertakings in palaces and municipal edifices. It is likely that the reduced volume of religious architecture in Renaissance Europe was a consequence of too many medieval churches, as much as of reduced piety. In America, an initial need for religious edifices demanded satisfaction, with the result that sixteenth-century building in America bears many sociological resemblances to the pattern of activity in northern Europe in the eleventh and twelfth centuries. And yet, the secular component is much like that of sixteenth-century Spain; the main differences are of volume and intensity, for the building of churches absorbed energies that otherwise would have been dedicated to civil edifices. Away from the metropolis, Mexico had very few imposing civil buildings. In the capital itself, physical and economic conditions have brought about the disappearance of virtually the entire sixteenth-century city. We are therefore confined to reconstructing the meager pattern of civil architecture from a few texts and ruins. But even were the texts and sources more abundant, the volume of civil architecture would still be insignificant.

We lack a definitive study of Spanish domestic architecture, perhaps mainly for the reason that highly distinct or conventional types are difficult to identify. The plan and structure of the Spanish rural house are closely determined by available materials. The outlines of a diversity of types appear chiefly in the contrast between north and south: the occasional solid block dwelling of stone or wood in the north, and the dominant courtyard dwelling of the south, with its Moorish and Roman antecedents.[1] In Mexico, in spite of the paucity of surviving examples of rural architecture of any importance, the texts suggest that the southern "Andalusian" courtyard type was dominant in the sixteenth century, with occasional exceptions such as the courtless Palace of Cortés in Cuernavaca (Fig. 79). Nowhere do we find traces of the Catalan courtyard with its exposed staircase (example: Torre Pallaresa, Barcelona), the Catalan *masía,* the Basque *celta,* or the Valencian *barraca.* In the lake towns of Michoacan, however, a rustic house-type (to which churches often approach: cf. Fig. 61) with hipped roofs, wooden balconies, and projecting eaves strongly recalls the sixteenth-century Asturian houses (example: Las Rozas) of northern Spain. The houses in Michoacan cannot be dated exactly, but it is not unlikely that some of them survive from the seventeenth century, especially in Patzcuaro, Uruapan, or the smaller towns such as Erongaricuaro and Tzintzuntzan.[2]

The foregoing distinction between block houses and courtyard houses pertains, of course, to detached rural and village dwellings. In the cities, on the other hand, we are poorly informed about types and variants. Probably, as in Spain, the solid block house was characteristic of the accommodations of the lowest income groups (Fig. 84); the texts, however, tell us of such great courtyard houses as the casas nuevas (Figs. 71, 72) and viejas (Figs. 66, 67) in Mexico City. In Mexico, as in Spain, the urban courtyard or patio plan was associated with the privileges of wealth.[3] This courtyard plan was generically designated as the "patio castellano," fundamentally distinct from the plan of the Moorish house. It is such a "Castilian" patio to which Cervantes de Salazar alluded in 1554 when describing the sumptuous house of Dr. López in Mexico City (see p. 194).

In sixteenth-century building, it is always difficult to draw firm distinctions between religious and civil architecture, or between domestic and institutional edifices.

1. See V. Lampérez y Romea, *Arquitectura civil española de los siglos I al XVIII* (Madrid, 1922), I, 66–67. The northern type occurs from the Bay of Biscay and the Pyrenees to the Ebro and Duero rivers; the southern group is found south of the rivers, including southern Catalonia, Lower Aragon, the Castiles, Valencia, Murcia, Extremadura, and Andalusia. Cf. R. Lino, *L'Evolution de l'architecture domestique au Portugal* (Lisbon, 1937), p. 1.

2. See Mendieta y Núñez, ed., *Los Tarascos* (Mexico, 1940). P. Carrasco has suggested a derivation of the Tarascan *tejamanil,* or roof of shakes, from Basque sources. R. L. Beals, P. Carrasco, and T. McCorkle, *Houses and House Use of the Sierra Tarascans* (Washington, 1944) (Smithsonian Institution. Institute of Social Anthropology, I), p. 34. Cf. our p. 174.

3. Lampérez, *Arquitectura civil española,* I, 118–120, bases the distinction upon the *Ordenanzas de Sevilla,* compiled in 1527. The "casa con patio central" belonged to the wealthy bourgeois or lesser nobility. Lampérez (*ibid.*) also points out that the Castilian type has direct ingress from the street through the house to the patio; the Moorish patio, on the other hand, is isolated from the street view by tortuous passages. The Castilian patio has colonnades on three or four sides; the Moorish patio has colonnades only on the two facing walls. According to Lampérez, "las diferencias son esenciales, constitutivas."

As we shall see, it was the rule that dwellings could be converted to institutional purposes, as with the houses built in the capital by Fernando Cortés. And the edifices destined specifically for institutional purposes were often used for residential needs, for instance, the Ayuntamiento (Fig. 89) in Mexico City, which housed the *corregidor* and his family. The modern divorce of residential and institutional or commercial architecture is a recent phenomenon; in the sixteenth century, stores were places of residence; workshops were also the homes of the artisans, and it is rarely possible clearly to distinguish between domestic and industrial architecture. Virtually all urban functions fitted into the basic dwelling type, consisting of simple buildings in one or two stories, disposed around a colonnaded or arcaded courtyard.

The same difficulties are present in the treatment of certain aspects of religious architecture. For the purposes of this discussion, we shall regard as religious edifices only those buildings dedicated to the cult itself and to the personal accommodation of its ministers in their ritual capacities. Monastic churches and conventual buildings; parish churches and rectories; cathedrals, chapels, oratories and all their immediate cult-dependencies will be treated as religious architecture in the following chapters. But here the discussion concerns not only the clear instances of civil architecture, but also the conventual schools, hospitals, prelates' dwellings, and public utilities, such as water-conduits, reservoirs, communal housing, etc., built under religious auspices. In short, ecclesiastical building not directly connected with the cult and its ministers is a part of the civil architecture of the sixteenth century. The distinction will often seem artificial, as with the archepiscopal palace, or the Colegio de Santa Cruz in Tlatelolco, or with the conventual hospitals. In the latter, the care of the sick was so closely allied to the cult that it would seem as reasonable to treat this service under the heading of religious building. Yet the morphology of the hospitals, however incompletely it may be reconstructed, strongly suggests the forms of civil rather than religious architecture.

The rarity of intact survivals among civil monuments enforces a tedious and discursive form of treatment, by textual analysis and reconstruction from fragments. In this section it will therefore not be possible, as in the chapters on religious architecture, to relegate such passages to an appendix; for knowledge of the buildings depends more upon the devices of textual reconstruction than upon physical evidence. Under such circumstances, it is also difficult, even impossible, to trace convincing connections with contemporary Spanish civil architecture. On the other hand, it will be possible, in the final chapter on ornament, to analyze numerous physical remains of sixteenth-century civil architecture, not otherwise amenable to architectural discussion.

The most sumptuous private dwellings in New Spain were, of course, built by

Fernando Cortés. He appropriated two sites at the main plaza of Tenochtitlan (Figs. 17, 62–65). One upon the site of the present Monte de Piedad buildings, in the northwest corner of the plaza, comprised some twenty-five solares, more or less. The other, upon the site of the present Palacio Nacional, included another twenty-four solares.[4] The Monte de Piedad site was designated as the casas viejas, and Cortés built a dwelling there for immediate occupancy when Tenochtitlan was reoccupied. The Palacio Nacional site was called the casas nuevas; the names refer to the pre-Conquest palaces. The Monte de Piedad site stands upon the palace of Axayacatl, where the Spaniards were originally given hospitality, and where Motecuzoma was kidnapped; and the casas nuevas were the dwelling-area of Motecuzoma himself.

The history of both buildings is of some interest, for it reveals the way in which Cortés housed the colonial government on his own properties. Both buildings were originally planned on an immense scale, comparable to that of the pre-Conquest buildings on those sites, not merely for residence, but also as commercial and governmental buildings. Cortés himself lived in the casas viejas, apparently through 1529. But when it became necessary in 1530 to provide the Audiencia with official quarters, the Oidores moved into the casas viejas. Cortés himself moved to the casas nuevas about 1531; these in turn were also to become government buildings.

In 1531, the casas viejas contained a rich variety of accommodations. The plan was an immense rectangle (Fig. 65), bounded by the Empedradillo, the Calle Tacuba, the Calle San Francisco, and the Calle de S. José el Real. Within the rectangle stood other buildings, separated by courtyards. An appraisal of 1531 mentions audience chambers, an arsenal, apartments for the members of the Audiencia, many shops and workshops, and two different kitchens. Later on, after 1535, the Viceroy also occupied suitable apartments. Parts of the edifice rose two stories (Figs. 66–67), of which the upper story served as a *piano nobile* for audience chambers and official apartments. The courtyards within were surrounded by covered walks, supported upon colonnades and arcades of brick, wood, or stone, depending upon the importance of the courtyard. On three sides of the main rectangle, the shops had egress to the street.

The eastern façade, overlooking the plaza just west of the Cathedral, contained no shops, and was more handsomely built than the other façades. At each corner stood a tower; the north tower contained the municipal clock; and between them was the main portal or *zaguan,* which gave access to the inner courts. Across the upper part of the central façade an imposing arcade of stone window frames lightened the mass, as in the contemporary urban palaces of Spain (cf. Palacio Monterrey, Salamanca,

4. *Archivo mexicano. Documentos,* I, 111, 187, 225. The texts are unclear; in one place the sites are described as having but sixteen solares, and in another twenty-four solares are given. In any case, the two lots comprised some fifty solares. The grant was astronomical in comparison to the grants made to other colonists, who were assigned one or two solares at a time. On the size of the individual solar, see p. 160.

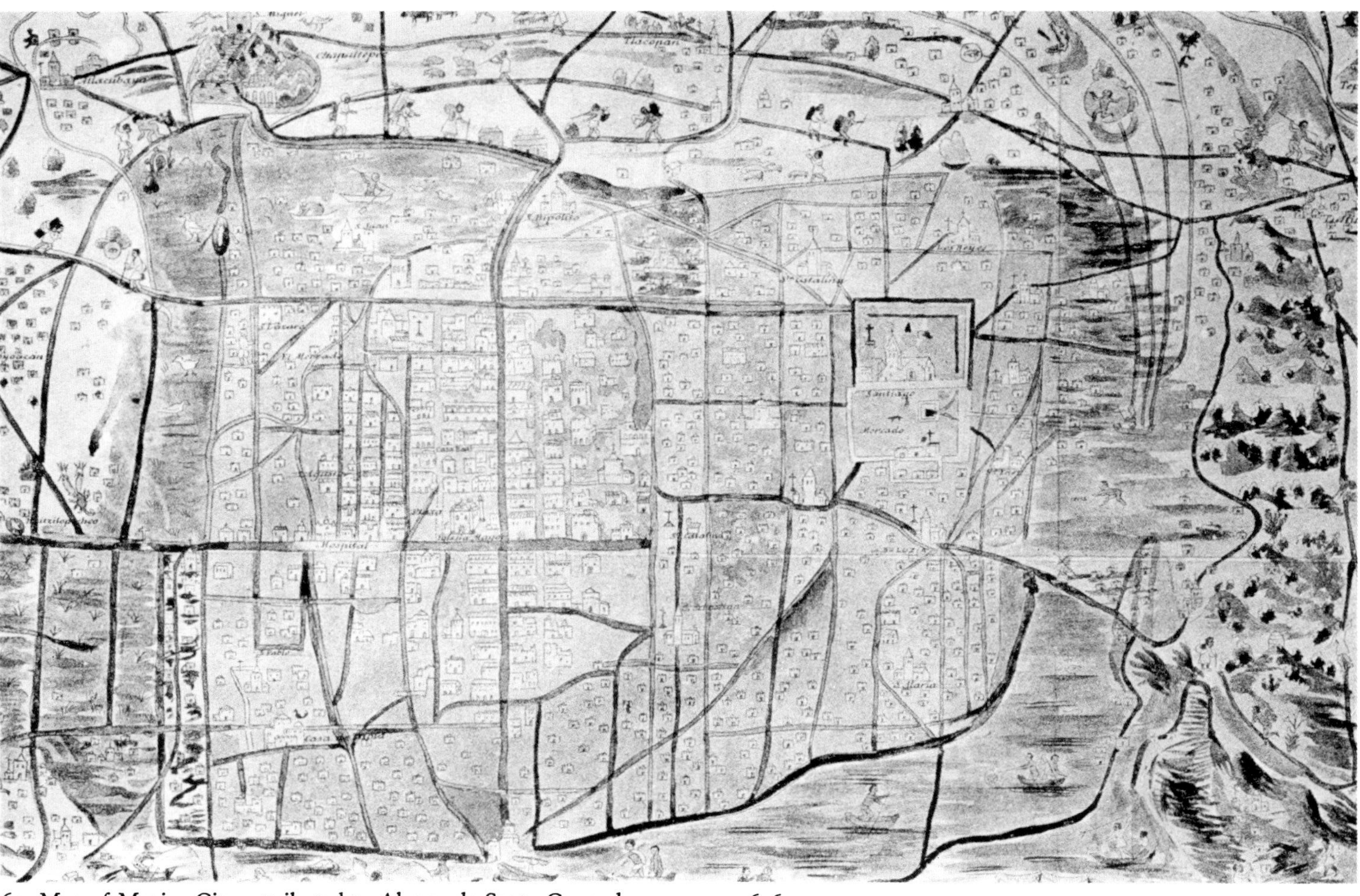

62. Map of Mexico City, attributed to Alonso de Santa Cruz, drawn *ca.* 1556–62

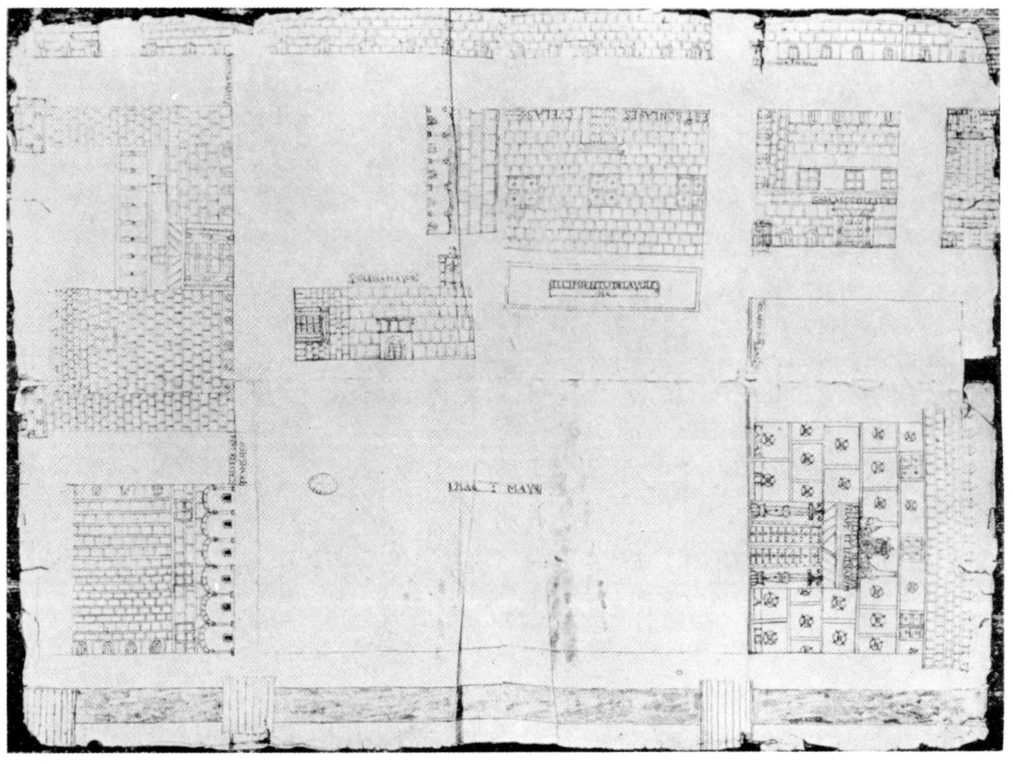

63. Mexico City, the main plaza in 1563

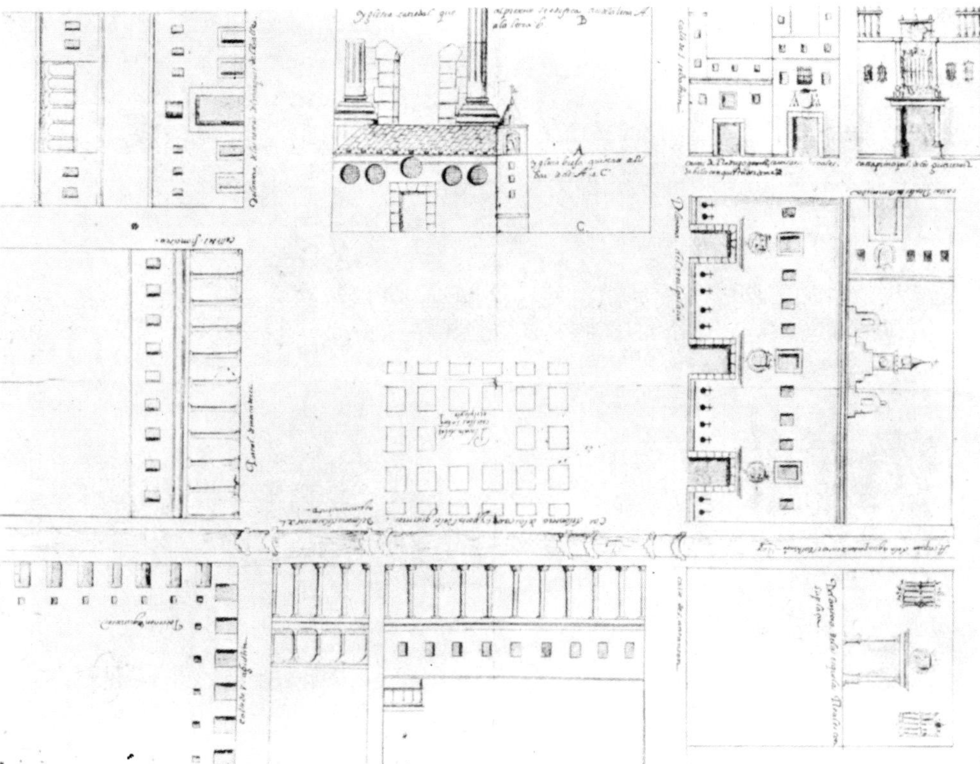

after 1539). The north façade on Calle Tacuba was less imposing, with shops in the ground floor. But in the upper story a range of large, square windows dignified its appearance. The southern and western façades were probably of more common construction, and less coherently designed.[5]

The approximate appearance of the casas viejas shows in the two famous drawings of the plaza mayor. In 1563 the façade displayed turrets, crenelations, and suggestions of plateresque detail in balustrade and doorway (Fig. 66). A few square, mullioned windows perforated the blank and forbidding masonry. In 1596, the height of the façade is shown as much greater; a loggia or *adarve* is indicated across the top, and the number of windows had been increased (Fig. 67), bringing the building into the fashion of the Renaissance palaces of the mid-century in Spain proper, as for instance, in Ayerbe.[6]

About 1531 the Audiencia was ready to purchase the casas viejas, or that part of the complex occupied by them, for nine thousand pesos.[7] Ultimately, the Crown purchased instead the casas nuevas for this purpose. But the incident is of interest, in that it demonstrates Cortés' far-sighted policy of speculative building. The only suitable edifices for governmental occupancy were his own dwellings, and the Crown depended upon his properties for proper housing of the colonial government. Therefore, official and domestic architecture may be identified in the early years of the colony.

The building history of the casas nuevas (Figs. *68, 69, 70,* 71, 72) reveals the same general pattern. Cortés intended to erect private accommodations of great magnificence which should ultimately be suitable for governmental purposes. The original layout upon the site of the Palacio Nacional was made in 1523.[8] In 1531, construction

5. This description is contained in two separate accounts: the appraisal of 1531 (*CDIAI*, XII, 520 f.) and the colloquy of 1554 (Cervantes de Salazar, *México en 1554*, pp. 92–96). The tourists in the colloquy, *Mexicus interior,* first behold the building when standing northwest of it, presumably in the Calle Tacuba, and describe it as "altior et munitior caeteris, tot infernae tabernas habens . . . Regiae membrum est, et ejus alterum est hoc quod respicit in alteram hanc viam: utrumque, quae est in latere copulat turris. . . ." In the upper part was "superiora hujus membri, tam magnis fenestris decorata . . . Regi consiliarii; et membrum aliud interius, quod magnificentius est, Prorex." At the northeast corner was the clock-tower "In editaque hac turri quae etiam utrumque aedium latus communit, eo est collocatum, ut com sonuerit, undequaque ab incolis audiatur." The east façade, "superiora illa deambulacra, tam multis et magnis columnis speciosa. . . . Teretes sunt columnae, nam quadrangulas, et in his striatas et medianas, non perinde commendat Vitruvius."

6. R. del Arco, *Provincia de Huesca* (Madrid, 1942) (Catálogo monumental de España), I, 114; II, fig. 224.

7. F. Cortés, *Cartas y otros documentos de Hernán Cortés* (Seville, 1915), pp. 87–89, M. Cuevas, ed. In 1531, the value of the casas viejas was officially assessed at 48,449 pesos; the parts occupied by the Audiencia were worth 20,417 pesos. *CDIAI*, XII, 522; Ternaux-Compans, *Voyages*, II, v, 145 (1531). The later history of the Monte de Piedad site is intricate and obscure. The Cortés family long retained ownership. The original eastern façade, as described by Cervantes de Salazar, was probably destroyed in the fire of 1636. The groundplan of the buildings, which recalls the layout of certain great Spanish hospitals, was established *ca.* 1611 by Andrés de Concha, and approved by the Cortés estate. After the fire of 1692, the viceregal government returned to the site of the casas viejas, when their quarters in the casas nuevas became uninhabitable. See Alamán, *Disertaciones*, II, 222–226; González Obregón, *Mexico viejo*, p. 321.

8. Cortés himself, Luis de la Torre, and Juan Rodríguez participated in the making of the plan. The use of *cordeles* is mentioned. "Documentos . . . Cortés," *Publ. AGN*, XXVII, 321, 335. That this most interesting document, which presents the complaint

had advanced sufficiently for Cortés to occupy the buildings, while the Audiencia resided in the casas viejas. Abundant details are recorded. The work was done by the Indians of Coyoacan. In the 1530's they provided the materials and labor, and built a water-wheel in the garden. Seven hundred cedar beams are mentioned, as well as 15,200 boards, and sixty window shutters. Five carpenters worked constantly in the manufacture of door and window frames. It appears that the original plan comprised two wings at right angles; one facing the present plaza, and other facing north, and running east, on land which is now roughly at the center of the Palacio Nacional. The east-west wing overlooked a garden on the north, and defined a courtyard to the south.

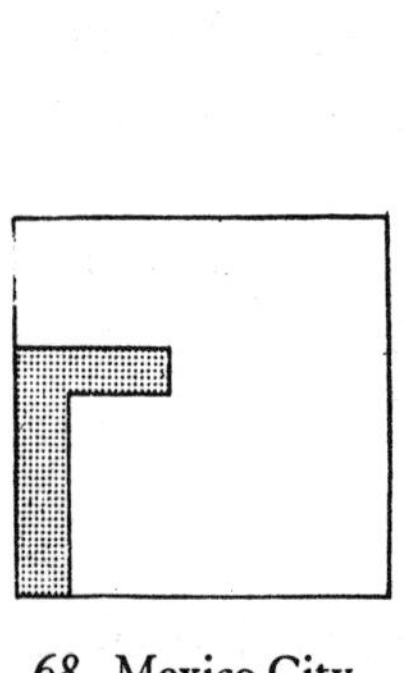

68. Mexico City, diagram of wings of *casas nuevas* in the 1530's

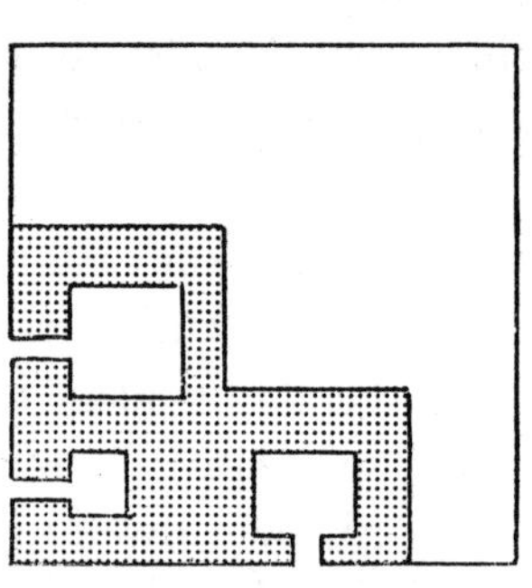

69. Mexico City, reconstruction of *casas nuevas* as of *ca.* 1550, following Sariñana

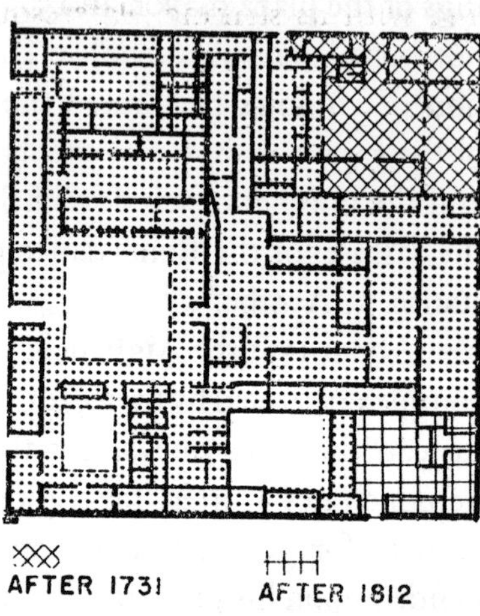

70. Mexico City, plan of the Palacio Nacional (formerly *casas nuevas*)

of the Indian laborers of Coyoacan, pertains to the casas nuevas is proved by internal evidence. On progress in 1531, see Ternaux-Compans, *op. cit.*, II, v, 156–157. Cervantes de Salazar (*México en 1554*, p. 112) speaks of *atria tria*, but only of one *antepagmentum et vestibulum*. The drawing in Seville has been discussed by Toussaint (Murillo, *Iglesias de México*, VI, by Toussaint). The doorway inscriptions are quoted by González Obregón, *México viejo*, p. 313. See I. Sarinaña y Cuenca, *Llanto del occidente* (Mexico, 1666), and J. M. de San Vicente, *Exacta descripción de la magnifica corte mexicana* (Cadiz, 1768). See also Zorita, *Historia de la Nueva España*, pp. 176–178. ". . . se a labrado en su circuito la carcel de Corte, y casa de fundicion y casa de moneda, y casa de armas; tiene tres puertas a la plaça principal; por la primera se sirve el Visorrey y Avdiencia; por la segunda la carçel, y por la tercera los oficiales de la rreal hazienda; tiene otra puerta por donde se sirve la casa de la moneda; tiene quatro patios grandes: en el primero, que es del Avdiencia rreal, ay tres salas grandes. . . . En el segundo patio bibe el Visorrey. . . . El tercero y mayor patio es donde biben los oficiales de la rreal hazienda. . . . El otro patio es el de la casa de la moneda. . . . La traça desta casa es quadrada . . . hazia la casa de la moneda, ay otros solares, donde se an de hazer otras casas para rrenta." The viceregal palace retained the plan with three courts until the nineteenth century. J. de Cassini reported in 1778 that "The Viceroy's palace is in a spacious and pretty regular square with a fountain in the middle. . . . The only merit of this palace is, that it is built very solid. . . . Within its circumference are three handsome court-yards, with each a fountain in the middle." J. Chappe d'Auteroche, *A Voyage to California* (London, 1778), p. 41 (the voyage took place in 1768).

The approximate relationship of these wings is indicated in Fig. *68*. Martin Cortés later declared that these apartments (*delantero* and *de la huerta*) were ready for occupancy as early as 1524, but that the corridors, roofs, doors, and windows of the second floor remained to be finished. The roofing began in 1531. On the plaza façade, however, the completion of a great entrance-way was delayed until after 1551. Hence the façade shown upon the drawing of 1563 (Fig. 71) is posterior to 1551, and records an extremely stenographic notation of the appearance of the building at that time. In reality, however, the casas nuevas grew very considerably by 1550. Three great courtyards (Fig. *69*) were entered through one portal on the plaza. This portal was finally completed in 1563, as we know from the inscription recorded by Sariñana in 1666. It read "Philippus Rex Hispaniarum, et Indiarum 1563," much as in the drawing, incorrectly ascribed to 1562. On the basis of Sariñana's text, however, we must reassign the drawing at least to 1563. According to Sariñana, again, the other great doorway bore the inscription "Philippus Hispaniarum et Indiarum Rex, Anno 1564." This suggests that our drawing was executed exactly in 1563, and that the façade was substantially altered towards greater symmetry in the following year. The approximate date of the final façade in the drawing of 1596 is suggested by Zorita. He specifies that the façade had three doorways (Fig. 72) and four courtyards, whence we infer that the whole complex was thoroughly rebuilt after the drawing of 1563, but before his writing, *ca.* 1585.

In 1562, Martín Cortés, the son and heir of the first Marqués del Valle, sold the entire edifice to the Crown for a government palace, for thirty-four thousand castellanos. Its later history does not pertain to this volume, for the buildings we have discussed perished in the great fire of 1692.[9] At the beginning the casas nuevas, intended for a private dwelling, were designed for rapid conversion. The completion of the buildings followed with great magnificence, which equipped the edifices once and for all for government use. Fernando Cortés did not live to see both his houses occupied by the government, but we can hardly doubt that this was his intention from the beginning. The enterprise was audacious. A remote precedent is afforded by the great *cortijos* of southern Spain (see p. 202); a closer precedent may be seen in the royal buildings of the Reconquest monarchy in Spain, designed to house not only the person of the ruler, but his court and government as well. The casas nuevas and viejas are the correct measure of the grandiose scope of Cortés' political thought.

The houses built by the other colonists were far less splendid. If the appraisal of the casas viejas in 1531 was nearly fifty thousand pesos, the assessed value of the fine house built by a civilian, Diego de Ordaz, was not over five thousand pesos. It is true,

9. A. Valle-Arizpe, *El Palacio nacional de México*, pp. 399–424. On the value of the *castellano*, see *Diccionario*, V, 911. On the fire of 1692, see Alamán, *Disertaciones*, II, 207.

of course, that in the market, the Ordaz house brought only nine hundred fifty pesos, or one-fifth its assessed value, but the proportion remains significant: Cortés' dwellings were each worth at least ten times the price of any other colonists' houses.[10]

Between the palaces built for Cortés, and such houses as were built for Diego de Ordaz, there seem to have been few intermediate kinds. Examples are the episcopal palace (Figs. 74, 75), and the fine Guerrero dwelling, with its striking plateresque façade, figured upon the drawing of 1596 (Fig. 73). The close affinities between this façade and that of the University (Fig. 96) suggests that it, like the University, was built in the decade of the 1590's. Striking is the contrast between the plateresque refinement of the Guerrero building, and the bare simplicity of the much older house (Fig. 75) belonging to Guerrero's father-in-law, Rodrigo Gómez.

Cervantes de Salazar, finally, gives us one more glimpse into the palatial houses of mid-sixteenth-century Mexico City. Referring to the palace of Dr. López, in the street leading north from the plaza towards Santo Domingo, he speaks of the view through the portal into the garden of the house. The lofty stone façade and the stone colonnades of the garden court are also mentioned.[11]

The primitive episcopal dwellings were located in the street which led from the plaza mayor towards the atarazanas (Fig. 17); it is now Calle Guatemala. The houses in question were some distance from the entrance to the plaza. This we know from two sources. In 1530–31, Zumárraga paid 1,280 pesos for certain houses for the Church and for his own residence. Payment was made to Hernán Medel, Manuel Flores, and Diego de Soria.[12] Nothing is known of their appearance, but Zumárraga spent some money upon their decoration and furnishing. A staircase was installed, as well as new floors and doors, an altarpiece, and a confessional, amounting to one hundred pesos.[13]

Writers have always assumed that the Medel houses stood on the site of the archepiscopal palace, described by Cervantes de Salazar in 1554 and 1560, and which endured throughout the colonial era, near the plaza mayor, across the present Calle de la Moneda (Figs. 74, 75) from the north façade of the Palacio Nacional.[14] This is in

10. *CDIAI,* XII, 531.

11. Cervantes de Salazar, *México en 1554,* p. 120. "Quem habent dominum aedes istae quarum facies tanta majestate, quod in aliis non animadverti, ex secto marmore et ad perpendiculum continuato surgit? Amplissimum est atrium, et multis etiam ex lapide, quae ad latera porticus faciunt, columnis ornatum. Hortus, ut apparet, satis amoenus, hinc perspicuus fit, januis, ut nunc, apertis." López was probably a friend whom Cervantes wished to compliment.

12. F. Ocaranza, *Capítulos de la historia franciscana* (Mexico, 1933–34), I, 356–357. Alamán, *Disertaciones,* II, 249. *AC,* I, 9, 11–12, 62. Marroqui, *La Ciudad de México,* I, 468. Medel's neighbor was Francisco de Orduña, and the houses faced on the Calle de los Bergantines.

13. Ocaranza, *op. cit.,* I, 356–357. Payment was made by Cristóbal de Valderrama, majordomo of the Cathedral, on April 10, 1530. Since the sale was dated Feb. 12, 1530, the work of remodelling must have progressed rapidly, and have been rather modest, given the small cost of the work.

14. e.g., Alamán, *Disertaciones,* II, 250. Marroqui, *La Ciudad de México,* I, 468. The error may be traced to C. de Sigüenza y Góngora, *Piedad heroica de D. Fernando Cortés* (Mexico, 1898), fol. 66. J. García

65. Mexico City, plan in 1628, after Vingboons

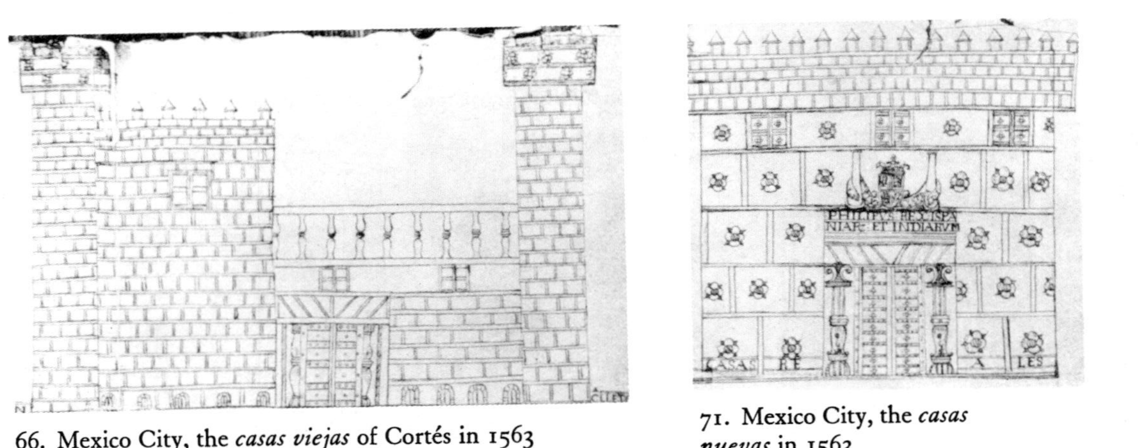

66. Mexico City, the *casas viejas* of Cortés in 1563

71. Mexico City, the *casas nuevas* in 1563

74. Mexico City, the arch-episcopal palace in 1563

67. Mexico, the *casas viejas* of Cortés in 1596

72. Mexico City, the *casas nuevas* in 1596

73. Mexico City, the Guerrero house in 1596

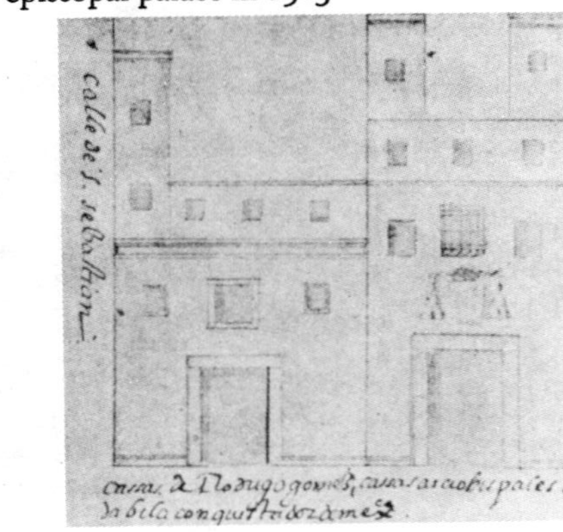

75. Mexico City, the arch-episcopal palace in 1596

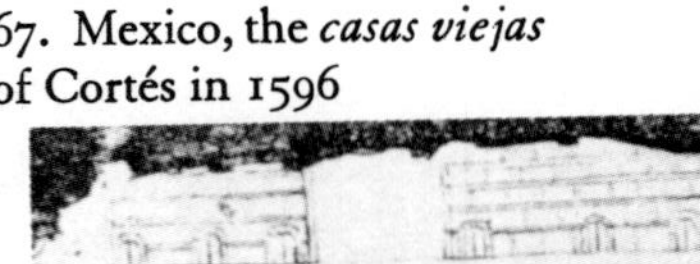

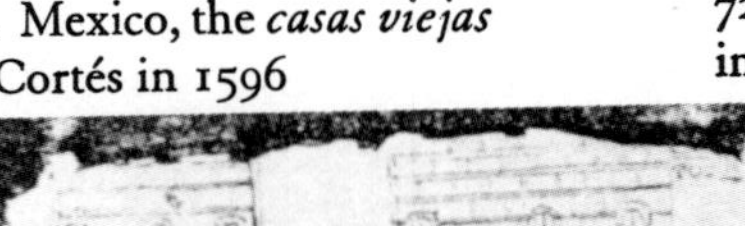

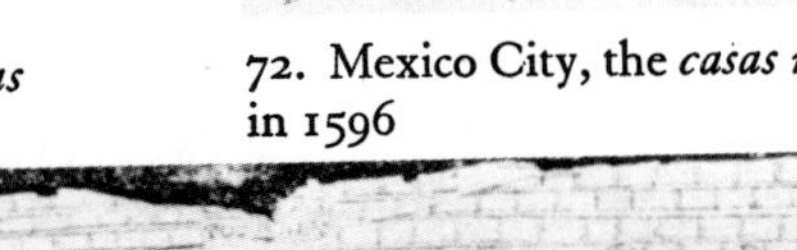

76. Mexico City, town houses north of the Cathedral, in 1563

error, for the great episcopal palace described by Cervantes and figured upon the drawing of 1563 has no connection with Zumárraga's original dwelling, but stands much farther west, upon land acquired by the bishop at another time altogether. In 1534, the Crown awarded Zumárraga an important source of income: one fourth the episcopal tithes "para que con parecer del Presidente de la Real Audiencia la gaste en casa para la dignidad obispal."[15] The implication is obvious that the bishop was not adequately housed according to his dignity; that the houses purchased from Medel and refurnished for one hundred fifty pesos were insufficient. It is apparent, furthermore, that the construction of suitable quarters had not progressed by 1537, for on December 20 of that year, Zumárraga requested the permission of the Crown to bequeath the Medel property to a school for Indians, which he had founded next door to the Hospital del Amor de Dios. The school, it will be noted, was housed next door to the Hospital; and it occupied the Medel purchase. But the Hospital has always been east of the site occupied by the second episcopal palace. Therefore no doubt persists that the property was distinct from the final episcopal dwelling. That no such final dwelling was built until late, is shown by the wording of the petition of 1537; Zumárraga requested permission to bequeath the Medel property, "pues con la iglesia mayor juntamente se han de edificar las casas obispales con todos sus complimientos contiguos á ella."[16] In 1541, Zumárraga formally bequeathed the houses bought from Hernán Medel and the other men to the Hospital del Amor de Dios. The donation (recorded in 1545) was approved by the Emperor in 1546, and there is no valid record that the property did not pass into the possession of the Hospital.[17] The transfer was acknowledged, furthermore, by Lorenzana, writing before 1769 (Zumárraga "dexó sus Casas Arzobispales para fundar el Hospital Real de el Amor de Dios").

By 1546 a new episcopal palace was in being, probably upon the Moneda site. This we know from the fact that the Crown alluded in 1546, on November 8, to "unas casas en que al presente morais," which were distinct from the earlier donation of the Medel-Flores-Soria property.[18] Thus the primitive episcopal palace was near the site of the Hospital del Amor de Dios, later the Academia de Bellas Artes. The inference is that Zumárraga acquired the new site in or before 1541, whereupon he deeded the old buildings to the Hospital. Since a document of 1550 speaks of the building in the Calle de la Moneda,[19] we may assume that it was then already occupied,

Icazbalceta followed Sigüenza in his biography of Zumárraga, *Don fray Juan de Zumárraga.*

15. García Icazbalceta, *op. cit.*, Appendix, p. 49.

16. *Ibid.*, Appendix, p. 109.

17. Marroqui, *La Ciudad de Mexico*, I, 316–317. A later seventeenth-century interpretation reported by Sigüenza y Góngora, *Piedad heroica*, f. 66, asserts that the bequest was annulled, but the pertinent documents have never come to light. See n. 23, and A. Lorenzana y Butrón, cardinal, *Concilios provinciáles, primero y segunda, celebrados en la ciudad de México* (Mexico, 1769), p. 214.

18. García Icazbalceta, *op. cit.*, Appendix, p. 168.

19. "Documentos . . . Cortés," *Publ. AGN*, XXVII, 302 ff. From this investigation of 1550, the following points emerge: (*a*) the property neighboring that of Martin López in the present Calle de la Moneda belonged to the Archbishop in 1550. (*b*) The gate to

and that it is substantially the building (Fig. 74) described by Cervantes in 1554, and figured upon the drawing of 1563.[20]

It is apparent, therefore, that Zumárraga occupied two palaces: the confusion may arise from the fact that the earlier, inadequate dwelling retained the title of episcopal palace, even after being deeded to the Hospital del Amor de Dios, and after the construction of the new edifice in Calle de la Moneda. The new edifice may have been in existence as early as 1546; it is certain that the episcopal palace with which we are concerned, the palace figured on the drawing of 1563, was built before 1554, when Cervantes de Salazar described it.[21] Cervantes described it again in 1560, and his remarks do not betray that the building had undergone any important changes. Its main distinction was an emplacement upon the pyramidal platform of a pre-Conquest temple. Zumárraga dwelt upon the elevated ground floor behind a façade which Cervantes approved as "elegant"; therefore, in classicizing taste, and symmetrical, with towers "muy altas" relative to the modest size of the building.[22]

The curious fact is that the drawing of 1563 corresponds less closely to Cervantes de Salazar's description than the drawing of 1596 (Fig. 75). Perhaps the 1563 drawing is systematically conventional, showing essential relationships in an extremely abbreviated and abstract notation. In any case, the harmonic towered façade mentioned by Cervantes and shown in 1596 conveys an admirable idea of the incipient symmetry and regularity of design in urban domestic building after 1550, without the entire sacrifice of the turreted and military aspect of an earlier architecture. The interior disposition of the building is totally unknown; it may be that Zumárraga's account books, which were available to Sigüenza, will, if discovered, yield more information

Cortés' stables faced the episcopal palace (p. 308). An extremely small interval separated the palace from the stables, across an ill-defined street whose existence was in question (p. 413). (*c*) From Guerrero's house east to the Hospital was a wide street, but there was none in the block between Guerrero's house and the plaza mayor (p. 326). (*d*) In 1550, however, there was a "Calle del Obispo" (p. 336). It presumably ran north and south between the present Escalerillas and Moneda. This street, together with the Calle del Hospital, had long been in existence (p. 341).

20. Alamán, *Disertaciones,* II, 254, strongly suggests that the deed of 1545 pertained to the Calle de la Moneda site; Marroqui, *La Ciudad de México,* I, 320, on the other hand, cites the actual deed, in which the houses in question are mentioned as neighboring the property of Francisco de Orduña. Since the Medel house flanked Orduña's, it was the Medel house which was transferred in 1545, and not the Martin López property, as suggested by Alamán.

21. A reasonable *terminus ante* may be 1548, for Cervantes specified that the dwelling of his day (1560) was built by Zumárraga (*obit* 1548). See Cervantes de Salazar, *Crónica de la Nueva España,* p. 318.

22. Cervantes de Salazar, *México en 1554,* p. 116, "Cujus est tam edita illa domus quae est ad sinistram, antepagmento eleganti, et cujus suprema solaria, multo editiores media, turres amplectuntur? Archiepiscopi habitatio est, in qua, quod mirabere, prima illa contignatio seu compages ferreis clathris variata, et a solo procul distans, firmo fixoque usque ad ipsas fenestras innititur fundamento."

Idem, Crónica de la Nueva España, pp. 317–318, "aunque no son muy grandes, son muy fuertes, con dos torres de cal y canto muy altas; edificada toda la casa sobre un terrapleno, que antiguamente era cu, tan levantado de la calle que hasta el primer suelo, donde el Arzobispo tiene su aposento, hay una pica en alto . . . las . . . hizo Don fray Juan de Zumárraga." In 1550, a witness declared that he had seen many old buildings on the site at the time the traza was prepared. "Documentos . . . Cortés," *Publ. AGN,* XXVII, 336.

upon this extremely important monument of the semi-official architecture of the capital at the mid-century.[23] The controversy continued unabated through the eighteenth century, with the voices insisting upon two sites refusing to be quelled. All the documents, excepting the proof of annulment of Zumárraga's bequest, were reviewed again in 1778 by Mariano Fernández de Echeverría y Veytia.[24]

In 1554, the main streets were lined with low houses of durable construction, carefully obeying the rectilinear streets (Fig. 76). Cervantes de Salazar specifies that the houses, excepting the occasional towered buildings, were of uniform height, in order that they might not overshadow one another. Only Cortés' casas viejas rose above the level rooflines of the town houses. The finest buildings, belonging to the great encomenderos, flanked the present Calle Argentina, and Calle de San Francisco (now Avenida Madero).

As we have already seen, the city imposed fairly strict regulations upon the residential use of municipal land. The city wished to stimulate rapid construction of durable buildings. The recipient of any grant was obliged to reside in the city or lose his title. He was forbidden to sell or convey his property to the clergy or any ecclesiastical institution or establishment. He must build surrounding walls within six months, and as owner reside upon the property within a year from the date of the grant. Finally, he was forbidden to use the lot as a source of building materials for construction upon another site, although he was not prevented from doing so for construction upon the spot.[25] The houses on such grants were designated as *pares de casas* (pairs of houses); the term probably refers to the separation of masters' and servants' quarters. The main house faced the street, with a stone façade, and the servants' building hugged the rear property line. Between them was an open courtyard. That they were regarded as ostentatious forms of dwellings is shown by Zumárraga's complaint to the Crown in 1529 that the members of the First Audiencia were building great palaces "de muchos quartos y trasquartos para vivienda."[26] When eight grooms in Cortés' service built such pares de casas for their own use on the Calle San Francisco (the principal thoroughfare: now Avenida Francisco Madero), others felt that these citizens had exceeded their rank.[27] Such houses were built for their owners by

23. Sigüenza y Góngora, *Piedad heroica*, p. 30. See Alamán, *Disertaciones*, p. 248. Sigüenza's pamphlet was reprinted in 1898 by "La Semana Católica." Sigüenza's purpose in denying the fact that the episcopal palace occupied two distinct sites is connected with a seventeenth-century controversy over the exact site of the meeting between Juan Diego and Zumárraga, in the matter of the miraculous apparition at Tepevaca.

24. *Baluartes de México*, MS transcript made in 1801 with notes by Francisco Sedano, New York Public Library, Manuscript Division. See especially fols. 42–57. Echeverría y Veytia reports upon the many different sites assigned to the first episcopal palace.

25. *AC*, IV, 44 ff. (1536), 126 (1538), 345 (1543).

26. "Cartas de Fr. Juan de Zumárraga," eighteenth-century MS transcript, New York Public Library, Rich Collection 40, fol. 904.

27. *Archivo mexicano. Documentos*, I, 158. The grooms were "mosos de espuelas."

encomienda Indians. An unusually full record (Fig. 77) of services is preserved in the *Códice Kingsborough,* written by or for the Indians of Tepetlaoztoc, about 1553.[28] The Indians built a city dwelling for Gonzalo de Salazar about 1526, providing all the materials and artisans without pay. In 1530 they were obliged to build another house for their encomendero's foreman, Luis Baca, and in 1534, still another foreman ordered a turreted house. Then they built a country house near the capital for Salazar, as well as a residence upon the encomienda, at Tepetlaoztoc, in 1547–48. Similar demands upon the respective Indians probably came from many other encomenderos living in Mexico City.

At first these houses presented a formidable military appearance. In 1529, most of the conquistadores' dwellings were turreted, with artillery embrasures, arches, and crenelations. Facing the Cortés palace (casas nuevas), which was itself a fortified enclosure, Pedro de Alvarado built an even larger fortress, with towers and embrasures whose fire covered the Cortés palace. Although Crown officials attempted to arrest the work, it went forward, and in 1529, two towers had been completed, facing the casas nuevas.[29] Other persons also built urban fortresses: in his own defense, Cortés explained that he had permitted them for the protection of the colonists against hostile Indians. The forbidding appearance of these street façades may be estimated from the drawing of 1563, showing the buildings around the main plaza (Fig. 76). Masonry façades appear with extreme economy of detail; at regular intervals, arched doorways give access to the interiors. The appearance of the streets was probably not unlike that seen today along the south wall of the Franciscan conventual buildings in Morelia (Fig. 78). The owners indulged in an ostentatious display of ironwork window grills (Fig. 73). These were so low, and they projected so far into the narrow streets, that traffic was impeded. The municipal council then decreed that the grills be removed or raised to a suitable level.[30] Iron door-rings further distinguished the houses of the rich; one encomendero, Alonso de Villaseca, had gilded ones.

28. *Códice Kingsborough,* fols. 221, 229, 230, 234, 239. Tepetlaoztoc was held in encomienda by Cortés in 1521–24; then by Diego de Ocampo (1525), Miguel Díaz (1526), and the notorious Gonzalo de Salazar (*ca.* 1526–53). The codex is a complaint of excessive duties, addressed to the Audiencia.

29. *Archivo mexicano. Documentos,* I, 18, 47, 90, 120, 148, 192, 332, 354, 379, 410; II, 33. The meaning of the controversy over these fortified houses is clear: Cortés was accused of encouraging feudatory tendencies among the colonists. It is interesting to recall that Indian society, according to Tezozomoc, was regulated by sumptuary laws in the building of houses, not unlike the attitude to which the Cortés investigation alludes. Tezozomoc reports that ostentation and distinction in the dwellings of the Indian nobles in the time of Motecuzoma the Elder were strictly regulated, ". . . otro ninguno de el rey, para abajo podia tener en su casa, como si digésemos un hidalgo almenas, ó torre dorada en su casa, sin gran merecimiento de su persona y valentia . . . tener sus casas con sobrados altos, y en los patios de sus casas tener un buhiyo como sombrero, con un remate en la punta del xacal puntiagudo, y pasado el xacal ó buhiyo con flechas grandes largas como decir casa de chichimecas, y tener un mirador muy alto . . . so graves penas, que era apedreado y muerto el que se atrevia á hacerlo en su casa." F. Alvarado Tezozomoc, *Crónica mexicana* (1598) (Mexico, 1878) (Biblioteca mexicana), pp. 352–353. M. Orozco y Berra, ed.

30. *AC,* IV, 77 (April, 1537). The effect of the grilled street windows may be estimated today in the older quarters of Monterrey, where the window grills

77. Town and country houses built by the Indians of Tepetlaoztoc for their encomendero and his foremen

78. Morelia, street façade of the Franciscan foundation

79. Cuernavaca, palace of Cortés, view from south

80. Hacienda de Baños (Hidalgo), loggia

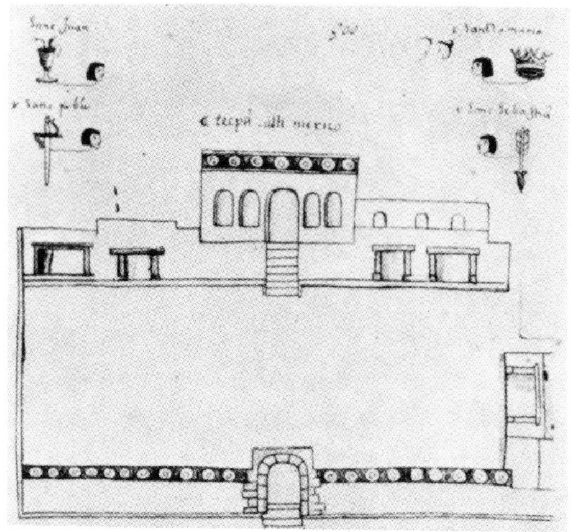

81. The *tecpan* of Mexico

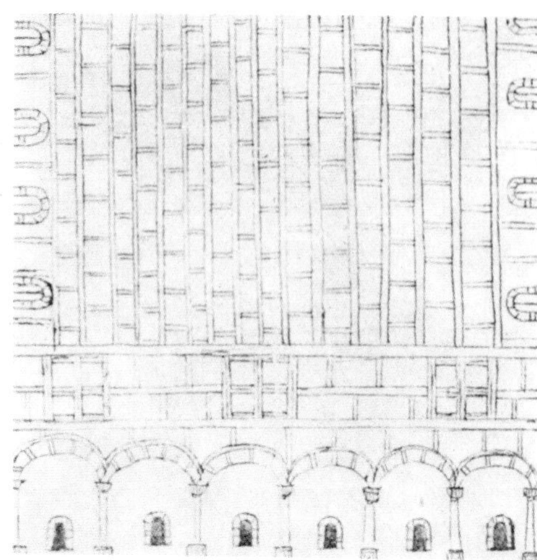

82. Mexico City, merchants' *portales* in 1563

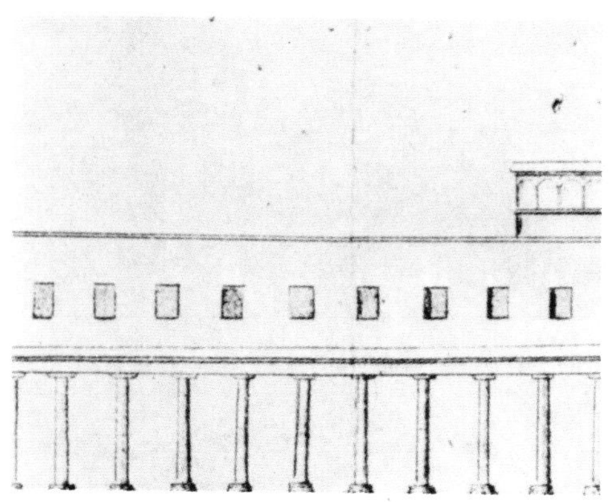

83. Mexico City, merchants' *portales* in 1596

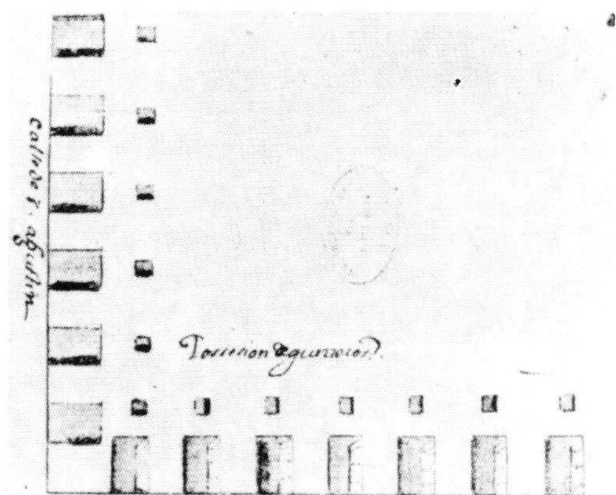

85. Mexico City, shops in the southwest corner of the main plaza in 1596

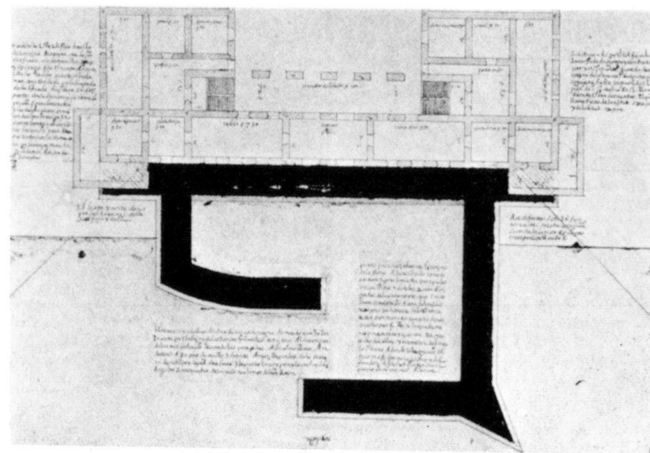

87. Plan of the *atarazanas* projected for Veracruz *ca.* 1586 (Detail)

88. Tepeaca, the *rollo*

Another levity graced the hardness of the early houses. Rosettes are painted upon the façade of the palacio real in the plan of 1563 (Fig. 71); of great size relative to the single stones, and probably executed in red or brown paint. The speakers in the colloquy by Cervantes de Salazar mention such decorations when admiring certain buildings in the vicinity of the Monasterio de la Concepción. The allusion is to painted cornices.[31] Throughout New Spain, these wall decorations were common (see pp. 362–363); their traces may still be seen on the façades of many monastic buildings and churches, such as Atlixco and Tepeaca. Sometimes the paint imitated the coursing of masonry (Yautepec); sometimes edifying inscriptions were painted in red and black Gothic letters (Tepeaca cloister), and frequently simple rosettes were used. The painting of masonry or stucco exterior walls is, of course, a commonplace in Mediterranean countries, but it was also an Indian habit before the Conquest.

Sixteenth-century dwellings in provincial cities are rare. Puebla preserves the fragments (Fig. 428) of a few, but nowhere can an intact sixteenth-century town house be identified. Only the doorways of the houses in Puebla have survived; one is situated in the Hotel d'Italia; a Purist façade was built by Dr. Tomás de la Plaza in 1580 (Fig. 445); and still another sixteenth-century doorway may be seen at No. 505, Calle del 16 de Septiembre.[32] Strict Herreran forms prevail at No. 125, Poniente 5. Here, the doorway shows signs of having been recut. The basic forms are Manueline, in the attenuation of the countersunk colonnettes, but the framework has been reset to conform to a stricter classicizing canon of composition. At the Hotel d'Italia, however, the doorway jambs are carved with hunting scenes. It is one of the rare specimens of secular sculpture in the period, perhaps derived from European tapestries.[33] In Cholula, an isolated fragment survives in the so-called "eagle-knight" consoles of what was perhaps an Indian household doorway.[34]

Of the great country houses built by the early colonists, few remain, and the most notable is the palace built by Cortés for his own use in Cuernavaca (Fig. 79). Heavily rebuilt and frequently restored, few parts of the original campaign of construction survive, although the fundamental plan of wings embracing and enclosing a colon-

are unusually prominent and numerous, although most of them date from the nineteenth century.

31. Cervantes de Salazar, *México en 1554*, pp. 126, 213. García Icazbalceta interpreted the mention of *depictae summitates*, after much hesitation, to mean painted or tiled roofs. Actually, there can be little doubt that the phrase alludes to painted cornices, in the absence of gabled roofs.

32. E. A. Cervantes, *Puebla de los Angeles en el año de mil novecientos treinta y tres* (Mexico, 1935), p. vi. Opposite San Agustín in Puebla is a doorway of sixteenth-century style, brought to my attention by J. McAndrew. On this and the Alhóndiga doorway, see M. Toussaint, "Joyas de arte renacentista en Puebla," *Anales del instituto de investigaciones estéticas*, no. 8, II (1942), 75–76.

33. At the periphery of New Spain, sixteenth-century urban dwellings are to be found in Yucatan and Chiapas. See I. Rubio Mañe, *La Casa de Montejo en Mérida de Yucatan* (Mexico, 1941), and S. Toscano, "Chiapas: su arte y su historia coloniales," *Anales del instituto de investigaciones estéticas*, no. 8, II (1942), 27–43.

34. See p. 203.

nade in two stories is probably of our period. The date of construction is nowhere given explicitly. The palace was not built before 1529, for in that year, an enumeration of Cortés' houses makes no mention of a residence in Cuernavaca.[35] A *terminus ante quem* is given by an inventory of Cortés' belongings; in 1549 his widow, the Marquesa Juana de Zuñiga, lived at Cuernavaca in a house with many servants, gardens, and stables, probably the house we are discussing.[36] Another text suggests that Martín Cortés, rather than his father, built substantial portions of the palace as it stood in 1589. In his testament, bequeathing the property to his son Fernando, Don Martín specified that these were the houses he had built.[37] Hence Lucas Alamán's suggestion, which has found wide currency, that Cortés' palace was built before 1531[38] can be only partly true, since substantial portions were erected by Martín Cortés, after 1547 and before 1589.

Late in 1532 and in the first weeks of 1533, on the other hand, Cortés had about one hundred Indians bringing stone and lumber from the mountains "para una labor y edificio de casa . . . en la dicha villa," as well as many others working on the fabric.[39] It seems reasonable to identify this undertaking with the beginnings of the palace under discussion. A further suggestion concerning the date of the extant portions of the sixteenth-century edifice may come from the remarkable colonnade overlooking the Valley of Cuernavaca. Such porticoes framed by parallel wings derive from classical Roman villas, and had no currency in European architecture before the fifteenth century. Early examples are the Villa Belvedere, built for Pope Innocent VIII, and many others.[40] The type was not imitated in Spain until the decade 1520–30, when such a villa (Palacio Saldañuela) rose at Sarracin in Burgos province.[41] In America,

35. S. Baxter, *Spanish Colonial Architecture in Mexico* (Boston, 1901), p. 203, reports that "an inscription on one of the walls records that the palace was finished in the year 1531," without describing or transcribing the statement. It is possible that the inscription in question was prepared at the time the house was converted into a state palace, in 1872.

36. "Documentos . . . Cortés," *Publ. AGN*, XXVII, 225 ff. In the house were 21 tapestries, 8 doorhangings, 14 rugs, 15 gilt leather hangings. In the house and its dependencies lived 27 Negro and Indian slaves, including a miller, a tailor, a cook, a butcher, and their various families. In the stables were kept 52 swine and 24 horses and mules. There was also a sizable arsenal. Cf. pp. 229–249.

37. *Ibid.*, p. 402. ". . . las casas principales que yo tengo en la mi villa de Cuernavaca, que son mías propias e labradas a mi costa."

38. Alamán, *Disertaciones*, II, 35; cf. V. Riva Palacio, ed., *México a través de los siglos* (Barcelona, 1888–89), II, 146.

39. F. Gómez de Orozco, "Monografia del convento e iglesia franciscanos de Cuernavaca" (Congresso terciario franciscano, El Santo Evangelio, Mexico). *Conferencias literarias* (Mexico, 1943), p. 346.

40. See H. Willich, *Die Baukunst der Renaissance in Italien bis zum Tode Michelangelos* (Berlin, 1914–29), I, 107.

41. Lampérez, *Arquitectura civil española*, I, 56–59. Lampérez describes the Saldañuela palace as "una joyita algo exótica e inadaptada al lugar y al clima." The type remained uncommon in Spain; another rare example is the Casa de los Fonseca (La Salina) in Salamanca (J. Camón Aznar, *La Arquitectura plateresca* [Madrid, 1945], I, 253, says it was not begun until 1538). Lampérez, in *Los Palacios españoles de los siglos XV y XVI* (Madrid, 1913), p. 14, says the Saldañuela palace was begun *ca.* 1530, and postulates an older period for the construction of the tower. A. Byne and M. Stapley, on the other hand, prefer a date for the palace façade "well in the latter half of the century," because of its *estilo desornamentado* and the "fact that the corner consoles in the ball-room windows have portraits said to be of Philip II and the intriguing Princess Eboli." *Spanish Architecture of*

the palace of Diego Columbus in Santo Domingo, and the ruined Palacio del Engombe (built 1553) in the same city, are further adaptations of this type originally defined in Roman villas, revived in the Villa Belvedere, and imitated in Spain. It is most unlikely that the relevant colonnades in Santo Domingo were designed or built much before the Saldañuela palace at Sarracin; the colonnade at Cuernavaca, accordingly, may have been built in the decade of the 1550's, a date suggested by the Palacio Engombe in Santo Domingo,[42] which in turn is probably coeval with the colonnade of the palace of Diego Columbus. Until excavations and archive studies of the Cortés palace are available, no final decision can be reached. It is regrettable that no systematic study ever has been made of this most remarkable building (see p. 188).

On Indian lands the white colonists often built country houses which prefigure the great haciendas of the nineteenth century. Such country houses lacked permanence and luxury, but they were built in fairly large numbers. Cortés, the greatest encomendero of them all, built many: one was begun shortly after 1521 in Tepeapulco, but the Audiencia put a stop to the work because, as they declared, it was being done without royal license.[43] Another great encomendero was Alonso de Avalos, in New Galicia. He built a casa fuerte, a fortified dwelling near Amacueca, and lived there many years, fearing an Indian revolt. He had few white neighbors, and his residence was probably the only center of civilian authority within a great radius.[44]

Another revealing case is that of the widow of Pedro Ruiz de Haro, Leonor Arías. She inherited property near Compostela in New Galicia, and when the mines of Espiritu Santo were discovered *ca.* 1543, she was enabled to marry her three daughters to the most eligible gentlemen in western Mexico. Each of the husbands then built fine houses near their mother-in-law's rancho. One of these, like the casas nuevas in the capital, was reputed to have had a patio large enough for bullfights.[45] The story calls to mind the plan of the hacienda houses of the great latifundias of the nineteenth century in Mexico. The example in New Galicia perhaps imitated the Andalusian cortijos of the sixteenth and seventeenth centuries, near Seville and Cordova, with their high peripheral walls, immense courtyards, pretentious gateways, and innumerable de-

the Sixteenth Century (New York, 1917) (Publications of the Hispanic Society of America, CIX), p. 407.

42. See M. J. Buschiazzo, *La Arquitectura colonial en Hispano America* (Buenos Aires, 1940), p. 16, and T. T. Waterman, "The Gothic Architecture of Santo Domingo," *Pan-American Union Bulletin*, LXXVII (1943), 312–325; E. W. Palm, "Engombe," *Arquitectura* [Mexico City], no. 20 (1946). Cf. Robert Smith, "The First History of Latin American Art," *The Americas*, II (1946), 363.

43. *Catálogo . . . Hidalgo*, II, 235.

44. Beaumont, *Crónica de Michoacán*, III, 183, ". . . fabricó una casa fuerte, en un cerro, que está junto a Chichiquila, como media legua, poco más, retirado de Amacueca, en la que vivió mucho tiempo, por el recelo que tenía de alguna invasión de los indios, a causa de no estar la tierra poblada de españoles."

45. *Ibid.*, III, 68 ff. The sons-in-law were Manuel Fernández de Hijar, Alvaro de Tovar, and Alvaro de Bracamonte. The hacienda with the great patio was called the "milpas de Miravalles." The mines, however, from which the family derived income, ceased to yield after 1562. Beaumont does not record whether any remains of these houses were visible in his day. Henry Hawks wrote, in 1572, that the miners were "princes in keeping of their houses, and bountifull in all manner of things." Hakluyt, *Voyages*, III, 554.

pendencies (example: the fifteenth century cortijo "La Reina," Cordova).[46] Such latifundarian establishments surely also spread out over the Valley of Mexico, in Morelos, and in Hidalgo, where, for example, the Hacienda de Baños unquestionably incorporates fragments (Fig. 80) of late sixteenth-century construction.[47] In any case, the great haciendas of the nineteenth century have a long history in Mexico, and it is not unlikely that a continuous tradition from the *al-muniat* of the Saracens in southern Spain, to the cortijos of Andalusia, and through the colonial haciendas, to the nineteenth-century latifundias can be demonstrated.

The physical remains of early colonial Indian housing are difficult to identify. Their form probably persists in such towns as Mixquic and Milpa Alta. The dwellings of only the Indian nobles and officials approximated European types. In 1554, the Indian governor of Tlatelolco lived in handsome houses fronting upon the main plaza.[48] The Indian governor of Coyoacan in 1560 enjoyed the services of ten bricklayers and ten masons, for the building and maintenance of his house, which when built was to face upon the main plaza and market.[49] In Texcoco, the Indian nobles preserved their traditional symbols of prestige. No Indian who pretended to social distinction in 1582 could afford not to live upon a terreplein (cf. Fig. 81). Small his house might be, if only enthroned upon an earthen platform.[50]

In the capital, Indian houses were arranged without order (Fig. 17), forming a shabby slum around the Spanish traza.[51] Most huts were built of adobes (Fig. 52) and fenced about by wattles. Canals and irrigation ditches meandered irregularly through the settlement.[52] Certain sections, nevertheless, presented a pleasing appearance. Henry Hawks, who spent many years in Mexico City, wrote in 1572 that the Indians were using small windows (a European trait), stone walls, and elaborate and intricate arrangements of many small rooms. One room was reserved for the entertainment of guests, with floormats, chairs, and holy images, but the family ate and slept upon the

46. Lampérez, *Arquitectura civil española,* I, 96–97.

47. A serviceable history of Mexican domestic architecture in the sixteenth century cannot be written until the haciendas of the nineteenth century have been analyzed in exhaustive detail.

48. Cervantes de Salazar, *México en 1554,* p. 150: "E regione eorumdem gubernatoris quem ipsi *cacique* vocant, permagnifice erectae sunt aedes, quibus adhaeret carcer, in quem, cum peccant, detruduntur indi."

49. F. Fernández del Castillo, *Apuntes para la historia de San Angel* (Mexico, 1913), p. 26.

50. Pomar, "Relación de Tezcoco," *NCDHM,* III, p. 69. ". . . lo tienen por punto y blasón . . . el preciarse de proceder de casa conocida con terrapleno."

51. Cervantes de Salazar, *op. cit.,* p. 136. Just west of San Francisco, at the edge of the traza: "Hinc redduntur apertae indorum aediculae, quas quia humiles sunt et humi serpunt, intra nostratia aedificia obequitantes, conspicere non potuimus." Alfaro adds, "Sine ordine," to which Zuazo replies, "Ita semper tulit ipsorum consuetudo."

52. D. de Cisneros, *Sitio, naturales y propiedades de la ciudad de Mexico* (Mexico, 1618), p. 110. "En los arrabales de esta Ciudad ay infinitos Barrios y calles de Indios, que viuen en su antigua forma sin auer dexado la criança y usso de sus antiguos, y passados en Casas de adobes con sus azequias, y cercadas de cañas."

ground. Hawks estimates between forty-five and forty-six thousand Indian households in the capital in 1572.[53]

Away from the capital, the Indians sometimes approximated the European type of dwelling. In Cholula, for example, the doorways were carefully fashioned of masonry or brick (Fig. 22); the corners were bonded with stone, and the rooms were separated by function. On the walls hung mats and paintings. Rojas specifies that it was the best Indian housing in New Spain.[54]

Both in the capital and in the larger Indian cities, then, the better native housing tended to conform to European models. Striking is the use of windows and specialized rooms. The texts just cited suggest the rapidity with which the Indians assimilated the use of European furniture, such as chairs and religious images. The same process is documented for certain missionary towns; at Tiripitio, the Augustinians made a determined effort to amplify and diversify the living quarters of the Indians in the new town. The dwellings remained low, one-story huts, but they were augmented with a living room (*sala*), a kitchen, and an oratory, all separated from one another.[55]

At the periphery and in the inaccessible regions, however, few changes took place. In the Llerena-Sombrerete region of Durango, for instance, about 1585, the houses were built of rammed earth on platforms. Only three walls were built: one side of the dwelling was open to the outdoors. The roof was intricately built. A layer of earth covered the rafters. Over the earthen layer, small columns of adobe brick supported another roof of rafters, crossboards, and shakes. The purpose of such elaborate roofs is unclear, but it does not seem that they were of European origin.[56]

53. Hakluyt, *Voyages,* III, 549. "The building of the Indians is somewhat beautifull outwardly, and within full of small chambers, with very small windowes, which is not so comly as the building of the Spaniards." Hawks, of course, knew the city after its plateresque transformation from a grim military citadel of private fortresses. He continues (p. 557) with a remarkably detailed ethnological description of Indian housing. "The wals of the houses of the Indians, are but plaine, but the stones are layd so close, that you shall not well perceiue the ioynts betweene one stone and another, they are so finely cut: and by the meanes that the stones are so workmanly done, and finely ioyned together, there is some beautie in their wals. They are marueilous small and light, as Pumie stones. They make their doores very little, so that there can go in but one man at a time. Their windowes, and roomes within their houses are small, and one roome they haue reserved for their friends, when they come to talke one with another, and that is alwayes faire matted, and kept marueilous cleane, and hanged full of images, and their chaires standing there to sit in. They eate their meate upon the ground, and sleepe on the ground vpon a mat, without any bed, both the gentlemen, and other."

54. G. de Rojas, 1581, in *Diccionario,* II, 714. "Las casas están edificadas y se labran al modo que labran los españoles, de piedra tosca, ladrillo y adobe, cubiertas de azoteas, encaladas, las portadas son todas o de piedra parda y negra labrada de sillería ó de ladrillo que aquí se hace. . . . Las esquinas de las calles son todas de la dicha piedra labrada, tienen las salas y aposentos (que son mas pequeños que los que labren españoles) bien adornados por de dentro, lucidos con cal y con una tierra amarilla lustrosa, y con historias pintadas ó colgados y esterados con petates muy pintados, y no hay casa donde no haya un altar con muchas imágenes de santos . . . en general es la mejor casería de indios que hay en toda la Nueva España."

55. Basalenque, *Historia . . . Michoacán,* pp. 19–20; Escobar, *Americana thebaida,* p. 144. See also Beals, Carrasco, McCorkle, *Houses and House Use of the Sierra Tarascans.*

56. Paso y Troncoso, comp., "Papeles de Nueva España," MS, VIII, 151: ". . . hazen las dichas casas

In New Galicia, at the turn of the seventeenth century, Bishop Mota classified the Indian dwellings in three categories:[57] the very poor lived in thatched huts; the more prosperous Indians in clay-daubed, palisaded houses, and the wealthiest occupied adobe houses with timbered roofs. In every yard draft animals were stabled. Even in the best houses, the rooms were small; their number rarely exceeded four to six. Such economic stratification probably reflects acculturation.

Even the greatest town houses of early Mexico accommodated commercial facilities, such as stores and shops, on the ground-floor level. In the casas viejas (Fig. 66), fifty-two such shops on three sides of the building yielded a substantial income to the Cortés family all through the sixteenth century.[58] Few were the buildings that did not contain shops: the archepiscopal palace (Fig. 74), the Guerrero palace (Fig. 73), and perhaps a few others, including the casas nuevas (Fig. 72). In the drawing of 1563 (Fig. 63), shops line the various streets on both sides, indicated by small, arched doorways at regular intervals. Such is still the custom in Mexican cities as in most Latin and Mediterranean countries; places of trade and small factories of all kinds occupy the ground floor of important buildings.

Around the plaza, colonnaded porticoes advanced beyond the façades; within these colonnades, called portales, were more shops. Over the shops dwelt the storekeepers and artisans (Figs. 82, 83). The earliest portales on record are those for which a municipal permit was issued on April 15, 1524. Each householder was allowed to take a width of twenty-one feet into the plaza for his section of the colonnade; the householder was responsible for maintenance, cleanliness, and amenity of the covered thoroughfares about the plaza. Later on, the Audiencia decreed that these portales belonged, not to the householders, but to the city. But the houseowners continued the custom of collecting rent from the small tradesmen who set up their wares in the portales. Hence individuals and organizations eagerly sought the privilege of building portales at their own expense. In 1539–40 the Augustinians built a series which, however, protruded into the street at the corners, so that the council ordered their removal. In 1549 again, the Auditor Tejada was allowed to build portales fifteen feet wide at the market place. It is to be emphasized that the portales fronted upon rows of shops extending deep into the buildings behind the portales. These shops were provided

de obra de tres tapias en alto, y el simiento; y lo cubren de bígas e tablas, y encima hechan una torta de tierra, y despues hazen unos pilares de adobes y echan unas tigeras y ençima unas latas que se asierran de las mismas vigas, de tres e quatro dedos en quadra, las quales se ponen clauadas, y sobre estas se cubre de tajamanil, ques unas tablas de pino muy delgadas . . . de Mechoacan." The tapia was a measure of area, two varas wide and one vara high. (*CDIAI,* XII [1531], p. 523.)

57. Escobar, *Descripción geográfica,* pp. 33–34. The three types were "fabricadas de paja a manera de tugurios; . . . de palizada y embarradas de barro; . . . de adobe cubiertas de vigas."

58. "Documentos . . . Cortés," *Publ. AGN,* XXVII, 13, 16, 22, 347; *CDIAI,* XII, 520 ff.

with living quarters, so that we are dealing with a special form of domestic architecture, restricted to urban environments, and combining the dwelling with a place of business.[59]

Thus the shop, or *tienda,* often comprised three principal elements: the portal, the shop proper within the building, and the *trastienda,* or living quarters, which might be behind or above the shop. Many such tiendas surrounded the main plaza; a whole block of them in the northwestern corner of the plaza (Fig. 63) faced the casas viejas. In 1579, another new block of twenty-nine appeared at this desirable spot in the plaza menor.[60]

Towards the western edge of town were the so-called "tiendas de Tejada," one of the most highly specialized buildings in the city. It was triangular in plan; two sides were lined with portales, and the third faced upon a navigable moat or canal. Each shop was a complete dwelling with entry-way (zaguan), courtyard, stable, kitchen, dining room, and bedrooms on the upper floor. One whole side of the building opened out upon the great Indian market of San Juan; the second floor of the façade was perforated by large windows.[61]

Elsewhere, free-standing, self-contained shop buildings were not uncommon. A drawing in the *Codex Aubin* (Fig. *84*) shows the groundplan of a commercial build-

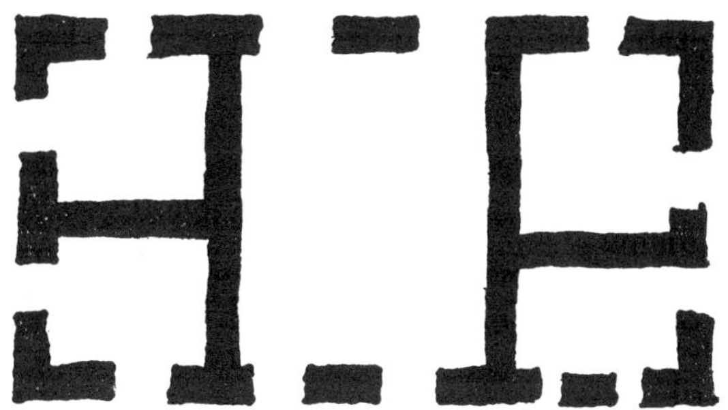

84. Mexico City, plan of a shop building

ing put up in 1573. It contained five rooms on the ground floor, and thirteen doorways or windows. No clue is given to the disposition of the rooms in any upper story; the absence of stairs suggests a one-story edifice.[62]

Although it is the only building of its class of which we possess such a detailed

59. *AC,* I, 8 (1524); V, 16 (Nov. 5, 1543). Such tradesmen were the tailors, shoemakers, scribes, barbers, sword-makers, and vendors of all kinds. *AC,* V, 26, 67; *AC,* IV, 193 (1540); V, 265 (1549).

60. *AC,* II, 128, 130, 144, 146. They belonged to the city, but their income was enjoyed by one Francisco de Baena in 1531. *AC,* X, 81.

61. Cervantes de Salazar, *México en 1554,* p. 138.

62. *Codex Aubin,* fol. 114. The Aztec text reads: "ynyc mopeualtia motlallana dienta Sant ypolito tianguizcoca [how the foundations of the shop at the marketplace of S. Hipolito were begun]."

record, many of its kind were built in or near the marketplaces of the sixteenth-century city. The main metropolitan marketplace was the Parián (Fig. 64) in the plaza mayor: the gridiron layout of its buildings was first established in 1533, but all was destroyed in a fire in 1658.[63] Another great marketplace took the name of an Indian chief, Juan Velázquez by baptism. The market was outside the traza, upon the site of the later Convento de S. Isabel, bounded on the east by the Hospital de Terceros, and on the west by the later Alameda.[64] Another famous marketplace in Tlatelolco, described briefly by Cervantes de Salazar, is best known in its pre-Conquest form from the narrative of Bernal Díaz del Castillo.[65]

Thus commercial functions were accommodated within the domestic envelope, and only the finest houses, such as the archepiscopal palace, lacked shops in the ground floor. The combination of the impregnable townhouse with the craftsmen's quarters (Fig. 76) expressed the ambiguous and semi-military character of urban life in the early metropolis.

By 1579, however, many of these grim street façades had given way to more civilized dwellings. Diego Valadés emphasized the fact that the town houses were no longer fortified in his time, and that they were exceptionally handsome buildings.[66] The change of appearance is also recorded in the view of the main plaza prepared about 1596, in which elaborate and delicate plateresque façades replace the dour walls of the primitive capital (Fig. 64).

But even after this change of style, which probably occurred about 1560–70, the capital retained one of its most distinguishing pre-Conquest features, a feature that not only excited comment from many European visitors, because it distinguished Mexico City from many contemporary European cities, but today still lends to the city an unusual and exotic silhouette, like that of Andalusian and North African cities. That feature was the flat roof. In 1554, Cervantes de Salazar felt that the roofs of Mexico (Fig. 85) were different from those of the mother country, for his eye was accustomed to the gabled houses of Castile, with their overlapping semi-cylindrical tiles. He explained the flat roofs of Mexico by the fear of earthquakes, by the insecurity of the foundations, and by the wish to promote salubrious currents of air.[67] Twenty-

63. González Obregón, *México viejo,* pp. 394 ff. *AC,* III, 61–62.

64. González Obregón, *op. cit.,* p. 370. Marroqui, *La Ciudad de México,* I, 25, cites Gómara, *Historia de las conquistas de Hernando Cortés,* II, cap. 51, in asserting that the market was named for Juan Velazquez Tlacotzin Cihuacoatl, to whom, as we know, Cortés entrusted the resettlement and rebuilding of the island city. H. Berlin has discovered the plan of this market, signed by Cristóbal Carballo in 1588.

65. Cervantes de Salazar, *op. cit.,* p. 150. Díaz del Castillo, *True History,* pp. 176–177.

66. Valadés, *Rhetorica christiana,* pp. 167–168. "Domus Hispanorum sunt in praesentia sumptuosissimae & splendidissimae, nec munitae atque commode, admodum architectonice & ad perpendiculum confectae."

67. Cervantes de Salazar, *op. cit.,* p. 90: "Culmina item plana sunt, prominentibus in viam ex subgrundiis canalibus ligneis et fictilibus, pluviam veluti evomentibus." "Decuit etiam . . . domos . . . non multum surgere; salubrior ut esset civitas, non impedientibus editissimis aedificiis flantibus et reflantibus ventis, qui

five years later, Valadés praised the low, level silhouettes of the capital, which he regarded as a source of great beauty.[68] The flat roofs also served an important function, in that they served as living space, where flowers and vegetables might be raised,[69] as in pre-Conquest Tenochtitlan.

In the sixteenth-century world, Mexico was unique by virtue of the pacific appearance of its cities. No fortifications encircled the towns, and the only military feature of the inland settlements was the massive church, suitable for defense, but dedicated primarily to the Christian cult. The exceptions were the maritime cities, such as Veracruz or Acapulco, where great fortifications arose to repel attack from the sea. In Europe, the century was marked by unparalleled activity in the arts of war, but in America, the Spanish colonies developed pacifically excepting at their sea-girt periphery.[70]

These maritime fortifications are essentially defensive, intended to offer protection against piracy. The French and English attacks availed only against unfortified cities; they began about 1570 and culminated in 1586 with the sack of Santo Domingo and Cartagena. Somewhat belatedly, the Crown undertook in the 1580's to establish a coherent plan for the military defense of the Caribbean ports. Italian military engineers were called to the task. Most notable among these was the Antonelli family, originally from the vicinity of Rome. Bautista Antonelli, who died in 1616, established the master plan. He entered the service of Philip II about 1570, and spent many years after 1586 in the Caribbean. The first great project in his campaign was the rebuilding of the fort called El Morro at San Juan on Porto Rico. Fortification also began in 1589 at Santo Domingo and Havana. Antonelli then visited the island of San Juan de Ulua, where he amplified the earlier sea-wall fortifications (which had been begun after 1552) in 1590. One consequence of these operations at the island was the removal of Veracruz from its earlier position to a plain facing the island, in which Veracruz stands today.[71]

In Mexico, Cortés built one substantial military edifice in 1523, to house the fleet of brigantines used in the siege of Tenochtitlan. It was the only monumental and

una cum sole, pestiferos quos palus, quae in proximo est, vapores emittit, discutiunt longeque arcent."

68. Valadés, *Rhetorica christiana,* pp. 167–168. "Suntque tectae delapidatis vel stratis propter imbricum ac tegularum paenuriam ea aequalitate, ut per tecta sine ulla impedimento ex aedibus ad finem plateae ingredi liceat, quae res tant ornamentum & amplitudinem civitati Mexicanae cōciliat."

69. P. Murillo Velarde, *Geographia historica,* Libro IX (Madrid, 1752), p. 74. Called *azoteas,* the flat roofs were used "como de jardines para el desahogo, y diversion, con otras comodidades."

70. *Relación . . . Ponce,* I, 189–190. *Epistolario,* VI, 180 ff. In Europe, after Madrid became a great city under Philip II, the absence of peripheral fortifications excited comment, as from the Polish traveler Jacob Sobieski in 1611. See Liske, ed., *Viajes . . . colección de J. Liske,* p. 263.

71. Angulo Iñíguez, *Bautista Antonelli.* Antonelli later went overland to the Bay of Fonseca, and planned the fortification of the Isthmus of Panama.

permanent military structure ever to be brought to completion in the sixteenth-century capital. Cortés describes it in a letter relating the events of 1523–24. "After the capture of this city, I took steps to establish a fort in the water where the brigantines might be kept safely, and from where I might control the whole city should there be an occasion for it, and the exit and entrance remained in my hands. It was constructed in such wise that, although I have seen some forts and arsenals, I have seen none that equals it, and many others affirm the same as myself; and it has been built in this wise: on the side towards the lake, it has two very strong towers, provided with loop-holes: one tower projects with loop-holes whose fire covers the entryway, and the other tower is likewise armed in the same way; these two towers are joined by a building in the form of three naves, where brigantines are kept, and which have doors towards the

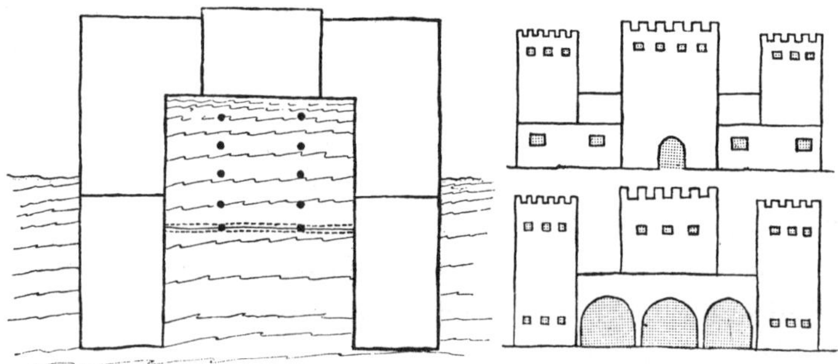

86. Mexico City, reconstruction of the docks

water for going in and out; and all this building is provided also with loop-holes, and on the end towards the city there is another large tower, with many rooms above and below for offensive and defensive operations."[72] From this description it is clear that Cortés wished to establish a fortified bridgehead upon the island, at which he might have a point of ingress or egress, as desired. The building is figured in an extremely abstract notation in the plan attributed to Alonso de Santa Cruz (Fig. 62); as well as in the *Códice en Cruz.*[73] Cortés' remarks suggest the approximate plan (Fig. *86*).

72. F. Cortés, *Cartas y relaciones de Hernán Cortés al emperador Carlos V* (Paris, 1866), P. de Gayangos y Arce, ed., pp. 309–310: "Puse luego por obra, cómo esta ciudad se ganó, de hacer en ella una fuerza en el agua, á una parte desta ciudad en que pudiese tener los bergantines seguros, y desde ella ofender á toda la ciudad, si en algo se pudiese, y estuviese en mi mano la salida y entrada cada vez que yo quisiese, y hízose. Está hecha tal, que aunque yo he visto algunas casas de atarazanas y fuerzas, no la he visto que la iguale; y muchos que han visto mas, afirman lo que yo; y la manera que tiene esta casa, es que á la parte de la laguna tiene dos torres muy fuertes con sus troneras en las partes necesarias; y la una destas torres sale fuera del lienzo hácia la una parte con troneras, que barre todo el un lienzo, y la otra á la otra parte de la misma manera; y desde estas dos torres va un cuerpo de casa de tres naves, donde están los bergantines, y tienen la puerta para salir y entrar entre estas dos torres hácia el agua; y todo este cuerpo tiene asimismo sus troneras, y al cabo deste dicho cuerpo, hácia la ciudad, está otra muy gran torre, y de muchos aposentos bajos y altos, con sus defensas y ofensas para la ciudad."

73. C. E. Dibble, ed., *Códice en cruz* (Mexico, 1942), p. 120.

The building also served as an arsenal and as a prison for special political offenders. An effort was made to locate it upon another, more suitable site in 1531, but the project was abandoned and the original buildings survived into the seventeenth century. By 1567, the fabric was badly decayed, and the settlers regarded it as useless. The building continued to molder, but still stood when Thomas Gage visited the city in 1625.[74]

Elsewhere in Mexico, the only edifice comparable to the atarazanas was never executed, but its plan is preserved in the Archives of the Indies in Seville. Designed about 1586, it was intended as a dock and warehouse (*casa de descarga y contratación fortificada*), to serve the ships arriving at the mainland opposite San Juan de Ulua. The plan (Fig. 87) indicates a two-storied edifice, with a heavily-built breakwater offering shelter from northerly winds. Behind it, and attached to it, were two buildings containing vaulted storage rooms, and enclosing a central court for the loading and unloading of carts or wagons. At the corners of the edifice towers, presumably for defensive fire, stood against attack from land or sea.[75]

In Spanish medieval architecture, such fortified docks were far from uncommon. The defense of the coasts and rivers of the Peninsula necessitated their building, as at Seville, where the atarazanas protected the fleet from north winds between 1248 and 1252. Fragments of the edifice still survive, showing five docks of an original total of sixteen at right angles to the flow of the Guadalquivir River. The docks were vaulted upon columns of brick. Similar thirteenth-century docks were an important part of the military architecture of Barcelona, ample enough to contain thirty vessels, and surrounded by moats and walls. Other atarazanas are recorded in the northwest, at Santander and Urdiales. From these medieval naval yards, fortified and equipped for the storage of a fleet, Cortés undoubtedly derived the idea of the atarazanas of Tenochtitlan. The dock and warehouse at Veracruz also stem from the same tradition.[76]

One of the most astonishing monuments of mudéjar art in Mexico is the famous rollo of Tepeaca (Fig. 88). An inscription still visible in the eighteenth century recorded that the work was begun in 1559.[77] Built of brick, upon a pedestal of seven

74. Marroqui, *La Ciudad de México*, I, 476–477. On the proposal to rebuild in 1537, see Ternaux-Compans, *Voyages*, II, v, 234. Francisco Gómez Triguillos to His Majesty, March 15, 1567: ". . . está una casa en esta cibdad que se dicen las atarazanas que ellas no hacen servicio . . . porque ellas se están cadal día cayendo: están todas apentaladas por de dentro . . . ni hay necesidad de ellas aunque fuera casa fuerte porque esta cibdad es tan fuerte que cada casa es fuerte. . . ." *Epistolario*, X, 192. Gage, *The English-American*, p. 81. He describes ". . . fair docks covered over with arches."

75. See Angulo Iñíguez, *Planos de monumentos arquitectónicos*, I, pl. 2, and his *Bautista Antonelli*, p. 40.

76. On the Spanish atarazanas, see Lampérez, *Arquitectura civil española*, II, 227, 228.

77. *Ramo Padrones*, MS, XXXVIII, fol. vi vo, 1791. The inscription was located near the doorway to the rollo, ". . . en donde aun que con dificultad se persive que es obra que mandó hazer el señor Franco Berdugo el año de 1559 siendo su Justicia mayor. . . ."

steps, the tower displayed an octagonal plan. At the center of the structure a winding stone staircase gave access to the upper parts. Eight twinned windows of Moorish style (*ajimeces*) pierced the walls. The edifice was vaulted.[78] Toussaint records and affirms a local tradition to the effect that the Rollo was connected with the Franciscan convento some hundreds of yards distant, by a subterranean passage.[79] Another local tradition assigns the construction of the Rollo to fray Sebastián de Trasierra, the builder of roads and wagons, at the time he was working on the road from Tepeaca to Tecali.[80]

In Spain, the closest analogue to the Tepeaca Rollo is the tower in Seville, the Torre del Oro on the banks of the Guadalquivir. From its embankment, many vessels set sail for Mexico, and there can be no doubt that the builder of the octagonal structure in Tepeaca had the Sevillan tower or one of its counterparts in mind. It was a Moorish construction, originally forming part of the fortifications of the Alcazar of Seville, and built *ca.* 1120 by the Cid Abu-el-Ola. The twelve-sided tower gained its name from the brilliant sheathing of glazed tiles in the second story. The building was restored in the fourteenth century, and again in 1760, when the large windows were opened in the twelve-sided walls.[81]

Although the Rollo of Tepeaca is derived from the Moorish towers of Seville, it remains unclear how the building gained its name. In Spain, the term rollo signifies a boundary marker, which indicates either a territorial or a jurisdictional limit. In its Spanish form, the rollo is a simple columnar monument, consisting of pedestal, shaft, and an armorial headpiece. The Spanish rollos, which were specifically Castilian, enclosed no spaces. The oldest example is the one originally in Villalón, but now located in the Instituto de Vitoria, and bearing the date 1434. In the Renaissance, the rollo in Spain usually consisted of a classicizing column. From the Spanish boundary-marker, therefore, to the Moorish tower in Tepeaca, is an unexplained gap. And yet the term rollo was applied to the Mexican building in the sixteenth century, as we know from the account by Cerón Carbajal.[82]

It would seem reasonable to suppose that the Mexican form, like its Moorish ancestor, was intended to serve a defensive function, supplementing the fortress-like

78. Thus Jorge Cerón Carbajal in 1580: ". . . subese a el por una escalera de caracol con ocho bentanas grandes con sus pilares, çerrado lo alto de boveda y con sus escalones a la rredonda y pie de todo el, quen efeto puede serbir de morada: es todo labrado de cal y canto. . . ." *PNE,* V, 23.

79. Toussaint, *Paseos coloniales,* p. 128.

80. P. Vera y Zuría, abp., *Cartas a mis seminaristas en la primera visita pastoral de la arquidiócesis* (2d ed. Barcelona, 1929), p. 534.

81. *Enciclopedia universal ilustrada* (Espasa-Calpe, Barcelona), LV, s.v. Sevilla, p. 851.

82. See *PNE,* V, 23. Lampérez, *Arquitectura civil española,* II, 369–373, provides a discussion and bibliography for the Peninsular rollo. Another Spanish example of Moorish construction is the octagonal tower at Badajoz. Built of brick, it originally pertained, like the Torre del Oro, to the castle defenses. See J. R. Mélida y Alinari, *Provincia de Badajoz* (1907–10) (Madrid, 1925–26) (Catálogo monumental de España), III, pl. CLVII, no. 2204.

church. Dominating the plaza, and bristling with crenelations, the tower in Tepeaca is an unique survival of a class of monuments which may have been more widespread in sixteenth-century Mexico.

As early as 1527, the cabildo of Mexico City discussed the construction of a rollo. A traza or plan was prepared, and the edifice was to be built by Rodrigo de Pontesillas. Nothing came of the project, although discussion continued during the 1530's. Sometime before 1551, the foundations for a rollo were actually dug in the plaza mayor; the edifice was to follow a suitably prepared plan, on a site chosen by Viceroy Velasco in front of the cabildo. Intended for "autos publicas asy de justicia como de almonedas publicas," as in Valladolid and other Spanish cities,[83] a building rather than a simple column or *picota* was probably planned.

The buildings specifically designed for public use were few in number. Their form rarely departed in any significant way from the patterns of domestic architecture. The fundamental disposition remained the same: a colonnaded courtyard surrounded by buildings one room deep; flat roofs; simple and symmetrical street façade. The great difference was the size of the rooms. A town-hall, for instance, required large chambers, of an amplitude not customary in residential building.

The town hall or Ayuntamiento (Fig. 89) in the capital is fairly well documented. The building has always adorned the south side of the plaza mayor (Fig. 64). It is perhaps the most venerable site of municipal government in America: the present edifice is of recent construction, but it occupies the soil and continues the tradition of the primitive buildings. According to the residencia of 1529, the original cabildo was begun about 1527 by Cortés upon land recently expropriated by the Crown from Alonso de Estrada.[84] The program included accommodations for the council, for a town jail, and for the municipal meat market. Reliable witnesses inform us that the buildings were near completion in 1529. During the rest of the century the edifice was constantly improved.[85] Plans for a thorough rebuilding were under discussion in 1530, and in 1531, a daily crew of sixty Indians was assigned to the work. The design prepared, it seems, by maestre Martín, was executed by Juan Entrambasaguas. The main ornament, a fine doorway of cut stone, came from materials originally quarried for a fountain in the plaza. The renovated edifice was ready for use by May, 1532. When the portales were added is not clear, but the jail was given a new doorway by Entrambasaguas in 1537. Later on, a granary arose in 1567–80, upon designs by Miguel Martínez, and in 1574, a design for still another rebuilding of the Ayuntamiento was submitted by Claudio de Arciniega.

83. *AC*, I (April 12, 1527), *et seq.*, VI, 30–32: cf. Alamán, *Disertaciones*, II, 295–296.

84. González Obregón, *México viejo*, p. 394.

85. *Archivo mexicano. Documentos*, I, 62, 91. *AC*, II, 44, 142, 148, 178; IV, 66; VII, 365, 367; VIII, 136.

About 1585, the complex included many separate functions. Colonnades overlooked the plaza. In the ground floor were the assembly rooms for the corregidor and the alcaldes, as well as the jail and a number of shops, from which the city derived income. The mint also once occupied part of the town hall; it was moved to the casas nuevas in 1567 (Fig. 72), and its place was taken by the meat market and the assay offices (*platería*). In the upper floor was the handsome council room of the cabildo. Above the granary the apartments of the corregidor overlooked the plaza. The exact arrangement of these rooms and halls cannot be reconstructed from the texts.[86] The essential disposition, however, was of large rooms in a building one room deep, with colonnades overlooking both the plaza and the inner court. The important social use of the upper-story colonnades is given by a description of the great city festival of San Hipólito, in 1595. All the officials of the city were assigned seats in these colonnades, from which to view the ceremonies and processions. Some twenty-one such posts are enumerated, and the plan of the plaza mayor in 1596 gives the appearance of the colonnades at this moment (Fig. 89).

The case of the Mint differs in no essential particulars, but it has the interest of revealing the gradual specialization of official architecture. The need for such buildings existed from the first years of the colony; originally the Mint was housed just west of the town hall, and acquired new buildings in 1528. The *Casa de Moneda,* formally established by Viceroy Mendoza in 1535, then moved to new quarters in the Ayuntamiento buildings. By 1567, the Mint had outgrown its quarters, and in 1569, it was transferred to a handsome new building (Fig. 72) in the northeast corner of the giant rectangle occupied by the Palacio Nacional.[87] This is the building figured on the plan of 1596, and it is the fourth courtyard mentioned by Zorita in his description of the layout of the viceregal palace (Figs. *69, 70*). Thus the special functions of colonial government tended gradually to be housed in separate and properly designed structures. The Mint is one of the earliest instances; other specialized buildings came into being in the seventeenth century. On the whole, however, government was accommodated in the sixteenth century within structures planned to serve the needs of domestic residence.

86. Zorita, *Historia de la Nueva España,* p. 179 (written before 1585): ". . . tiene vnos corredores sobre la plaza principal y en lo alto mui buena sala del Ayuntamiento, y en lo bajo haze audiencia el corregidor y alcaldes ordinarios, y está alli la carcel publica, y tiendas, de que tiene mui buena rrenta la cibdad, y la carniceria y la plateria está en vna casa donde solia estar primero la fundicion, y tambien es rrenta de la cibdad." In 1623, A. de Villalobos gives further details (A. de Villalobos, "México en 1623," *Documentos inéditos ó muy raros para la historia de Mexico,* X [Mexico, 1907], p. 162). "El corredor que hace entrada á la sala del Ayuntamiento" had "pilares y roscas de arcos." Within was the "sala de los asientos de Justicia y Regimento . . . de aqui se salía á un grande y espacioso balcón que vuela sobre la Plaza y Audiencia Ordinaria, por centanas rasgadas de la misma sala, con cobertizo muy curioso, de mazonería, y barandas de reja . . . al salir de la sala y corredores de Cabildo, se entra en las casas y balcones del Corregidor, que esta sobre la Alhóndiga. . . ." *AC,* XII, 193, 303.

87. See A. M. Carreño, "Las primeras Fundiciones

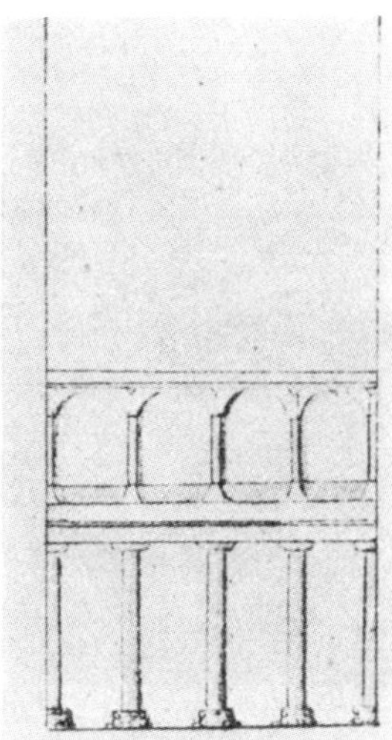

89. Mexico City, detail of the town hall in 1596

91. Indian drawings of the *tecpan* at Tlatelolco

92. Fragment of the colonnade facing on the court of the *tecpan*

94. Mexico City, the university in 1563

96. Mexico City, the university in 1596

98. Mexico City, view of east range and the corner window of the Hospital de Jesús

99. Santa Fe (Valley of Mexico) *ca.* 1555–62

100. Zempoala, the aqueduct from the southwest

101. Tepeapulco, the fountain

102. Tecali, cistern from the northeast

103. Tochimilco, fountain

105. Waterwheel

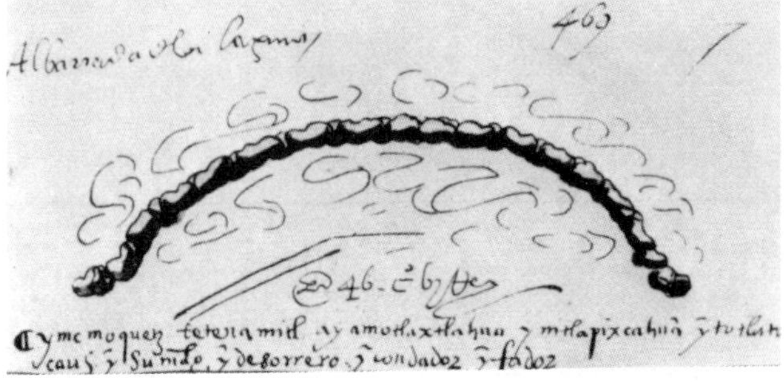

106. Mexico City, the dike

The same considerations hold for the town halls in the Indian communities. Fortunately, fragments of one or two of the tecpan buildings still survive, and texts permit some discussion of the general form. The general situation of the municipal buildings was described by Diego Valadés in a lapidary passage about 1579, "In frontispiciis templum forumque versus erant porticus tam supra, quam infra. In superioribus & excelsis habebatur senatus & cōsilium & ius reddebatur. In inferioribus & humilioribus existunt multae habitationes & carceres; nam fiunt eiusmodi aedificia in opidis excalce & immensis saxis fabricata eadem forma cum structuris Hispanicis."[88] The most ambitious and the most interesting of the Indian municipal buildings was the famous Tecpan of Tlatelolco. It was entirely an Indian enterprise, built to maintain the dignity of Indian town government. The program (Figs. *90, 91*) included facilities for entertaining the Viceroy and other distinguished visitors, in an apartment of nineteen rooms, with colonnades and gardens. The large rooms faced south on a

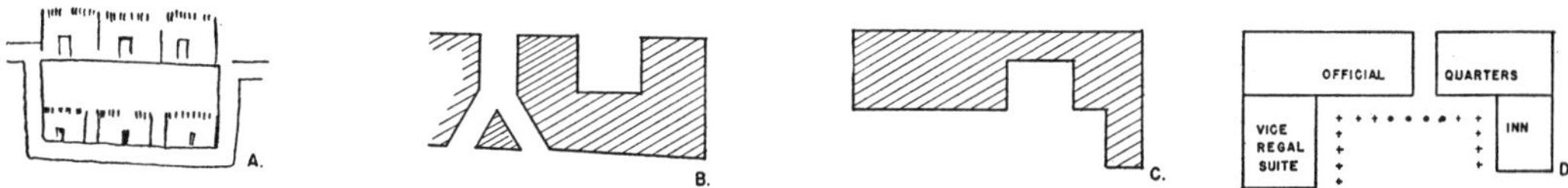

90. Tlatelolco, plans and sketches of the *tecpan* from various sources. A. *ca.* 1555–62, according to the map attributed to Alonso de Santa Cruz B. In 1628, according to Vingboons C. In 1793, according to the map by García Conde D. Author's reconstruction, based on the *Códice del Tecpan*

plan about 170 feet long. The cost of these apartments was four thousand pesos. Another suite was set aside for lesser travelers, containing a community room and twelve chambers, with provision for public scribes. This unit, and the reception rooms, defined the wings of a courtyard, and ran east and west. Between them was the main body of the building, over six hundred feet long, and intended to house the courts, the Audiencia, and the jail (*telpiloyan*) on two floors. A latrine building stood on the grounds, as well as a bath-house, and conduits for providing drinking water. The construction lasted from 1576 to 1581: a small fragment (Fig. 92) of the main building still survives.[89]

Of some significance is the cost of the enterprise. The total expense was 33,600 pesos, of which 5,600 pesos were donated in cash by wealthy Indians, and the remainder was contributed in labor and materials by the community at large. When it

y amonedaciones en México," *Investigaciones históricas,* I, no. 1 (1938–39), 70.

88. Valadés, *Rhetorica christiana,* pp. 109–110. Valadés probably had in mind the situation in Mexico City, and was describing the plaza mayor, but the passage is of interest in that it describes Spanish intentions for generalized urban situations.

89. J. Fernández, ed., "Códice del tecpan de Santiago Tlaltelolco (1576–81)," *Investigaciones históricas,* I, no. 3 (1939), 243–264. Does the "tecpancalli Mexico" (our Fig. *84*) represent an earlier version of the building, or is it another metropolitan tecpan altogether?

is recalled that the most sumptuous building in Mexico City, the casas nuevas belonging to Cortés, was sold to the Crown in 1562 for thirty-four thousand castellanos, it will be seen how lavish and luxurious was the Indian undertaking. It is not impossible, of course, that the Indian accounts were inflated to bring the expense to a figure so significantly near to the famous sale price of the casas nuevas. But there can be no doubt that the Tecpan of Tlatelolco was the most sumptuous Indian communal building in New Spain.[90]

Elsewhere, the tecpan was often a building of durable structure and lavish form.[91] Thus at Yanhuitlan in the Mixteca Alta, the Indians built durable edifices during the third quarter of the century, at about the same time the church was in construction. The tecpan was of masonry, with an entrance court ample enough for bullfighting. Within were two smaller, cloister-like courtyards with stone arcades. Some of the chambers were vaulted, and had fireplaces.

In Tepeaca, the Indians built a Casa Real after 1543. The conditions at Tepeaca were unusual: it was an Indian community, but some sixty Europeans resided in the town. The town hall was on the west side of the plaza, solid and massive, two stories high, with many rooms, including a dwelling for the municipal justice; a prison and an inn. It seems, however, that these buildings were reserved for the use of whites, for in the rear court, a single-story building housed the meetings of the Indian officers of the community. The walls of the Casa Real subsisted until 1791, when murals displaying scenes of the Conquest were still visible.

A situation similar to that of Tepeaca is reported for several other communities. In Jalapa (Veracruz), two houses of rubble construction, and roofed with thatch, served as the municipal building, and housed the court of justice. In Tepeapulco, two well-built houses were available for the corregidores, and served as municipal buildings. At Tlaxcala, the casas reales, facing on the plaza, were under construction in 1539. Only at Metztitlan have fragments of such buildings been studied. A small,

90. The *Códice del Tecpan* gives the following table of costs (*Investigaciones históricas*, I, no. 3 [1939], 243–264).

Viceregal quarters	$ 4000
Travelers' quarters	4001
Audiencia building	4200½
Inner partitions	4800
Upper floors	2800
Gardens	400
Miscellaneous	10000
	$30201½

Miguel García donated 4000 pesos in cash, and Juan Mihuatototl gave 1600. About 3398 pesos are unaccounted for in the table above; it may be that these were spent for furniture, wall-painting, and decoration.

91. B. Cobo visited Yanhuitlan in 1638; his account was reprinted in 1928. See C. A. Romero, "Dos Cartas inéditas del P. Bernabé Cobo," Instituto histórico del Perú, Lima, *Revista histórica*, VIII (1928), 26–50. See also *Códice de Yanhuitlan*, p. 49. Fragments may survive in the present school.

Tepeaca: *PNE*, V, 23; Archivo general de la Nación, *Ramo Padrones*, MS Vol. XXXVIII, vi vo. Murals also adorned the walls of the Indian tecpan in Quecholac. See F. A. Lorenzana y Butrón, cardinal. *Concilios provinciales, primero y segundo, celebrados en la . . . ciudad de México* (Mexico, 1769), p. 15. Jalapa: *PNE*, V, 104. Tepeapulco: *PNE*, VI, 303 (1581). Tlaxcala: Motolinia, "Historia de los indios de la Nueva España," *CDHM*, I, 87; Metztitlan: *Catálogo . . . Hidalgo*, I, 463–464.

vaulted, two-room structure (Fig. *93*), with a loggia and fine details was built during the 1540's. Local tradition identifies it as a counting-house or treasury, perhaps part of the tecpan, in which tribute and tithes were received.

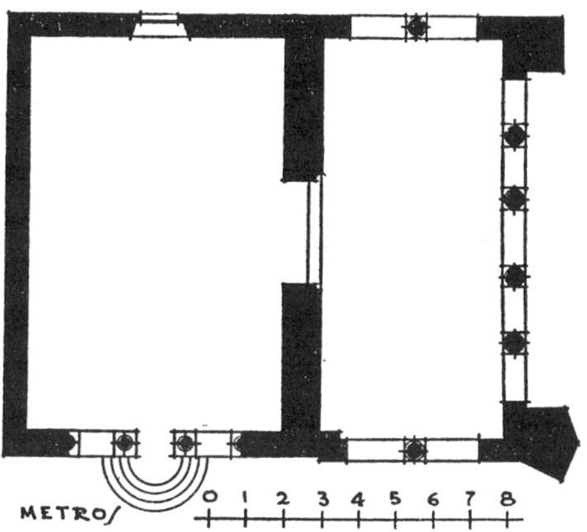

93. Metztitlan, plan and elevation of the *Tercena*

The establishment of casual inns for European travelers in the Indian towns was a common sixteenth-century practice, designed to safeguard racial segregation. Travelers were forbidden to lodge with Indians in towns with inns by a royal cédula of 1563, and the statute passed into the Recopilación. The remains of such inns are not securely identified, although one façade near Actopan has been published as a sixteenth-century mesón.[92]

Along the highways of New Spain, taverns were built for the accommodation of European or creole travelers. A fairly detailed history of one of the *ventas* may be reconstructed from the minutes of the municipal council of the capital. In 1537, the maestro mayor of the city, then Juan Entrambasaguas, was relieved of all other duties while laying out the plan for the venta at Perote, near Orizaba. The labor was donated by the Indians of Jalacingo, and the building was completed in 1538. The operation of the inn was a municipal monopoly, which the city let out to the highest bidder. This first edifice burned in 1540 and was abandoned, whereupon it was decided to renew the undertaking upon another site. Ultimately, after 1543, a masonry building arose. Other inns of this class appeared as early as 1529 at Texcoco, Calpulalpan, and other towns. Gage, visiting Mexico in 1625, describes his comfortable visit in one of these hostelries. There is no indication that their plan or structure departed significantly from the usual pattern of the modest provincial dwelling.[93]

92. E. O'Gorman, *Reflexiones sobre la distribución urbana colonial de la ciudad de México* (Mexico, 1938), pp. 21–22. See Mexico. Secretaría de educación pública, *Tres siglos de arquitectura colonial,* p. 19. Cf. L. de Palacio Magarola, *Mesones y ventas de la Nueva España* (Mexico, 1944), pp. 12–18.

93. *AC,* II, 14; IV, 99, 101, 135, 141–142, 196–197; V, 6. Gage, *The English-American,* p. 43.

The position of the theater in colonial society is difficult to classify by modern standards. In spite of the importance of theatrical performances, no highly specialized theater buildings such as we know in Europe after Palladio were built in sixteenth-century America. Yet the theater fulfilled a social function, and like the school and the hospital, it was accommodated within the forms either of religious or of domestic building.

As González Obregón has pointed out in a valuable essay, dramatic performances were an important part of early colonial life; formal representations of secular character were produced as early as 1588, and we know of at least two edifices which served as theaters. A third theater-building in Puebla is traditionally and wrongly assigned to the sixteenth century. But no part of this highly specialized building of octagonal form, with fully developed stage, orchestra pit, and peripheral boxes, is of sixteenth-century design.[94]

In Spain proper, the only housing given the theater until long after the sixteenth century was in the courtyards or patios of edifices originally dedicated to other purposes. According to Lampérez, the theater of the Golden Age played in the *corral;* the specialized form of the Renaissance Italian theater did not appear in Spain until the beginning of the eighteenth century.[95]

Nothing, unfortunately, is known of the plan and exact appearance of the theater (*casa de las comedias*), which existed in Mexico City in the house of Francisco de León. It was located in the Calle de Jesús, across the street from the Augustinian convento, and it would appear that many plays were presented.[96]

Another metropolitan theater was more intimately associated with religious life; it was located in the courtyard of the Hospital Real de los Indios, the establishment founded by Pedro de Gante. It was called the *Coliseo,* or *corral de comedias,* founded during the reign of Viceroy Montesclaros (1595–1603) to raise income for Indian welfare. Consisting of tiers of wooden benches, with some form of cover for spectators and actors, the institution flourished all during the colonial era, in spite of a fire in 1722, which destroyed most of the hospital buildings. The theater itself was rebuilt in 1725.[97]

Thanks to Cervantes de Salazar, we have a better knowledge of the primitive buildings of the University than of the permanent edifice built for it after 1589. It is

94. Gonzálex Obregón, *México viejo,* pp. 333–341. Cf. Ricard, *La "Conquête spirituelle" du Mexique,* II, chap. v, for a masterly study of the Indian performances of religious plays under the supervision of the clergy. According to E. Gómez Haro, *Historia del teatro principal de Puebla* (Puebla, 1902), pp. 15 f., the Coliseo was begun *ca.* 1742, and modelled upon the Teatro Principal in Mexico City.

95. Lampérez, *Arquitectura civil española,* II, 341–343, 353–357: ". . . corral: es decir, el patio de una casa, con sus característicos dos pisos de galerías circundantes sobre columnas, y las gradas debajo."

96. González Obregón, *Epoca colonial,* pp. 335 ff.

97. *Ibid.,* pp. 81, 339; Vetancurt, *Chrónica, Tratado,* pp. 3, 44; Vázquez de Espinosa, "Compendium . . . of the West Indies," *Smithsonian Miscellaneous Collections,* CII, 161–162; *PNE,* III, 25 (1571).

only recently that the location of these primitive buildings has been ascertained.[98] Not until the discovery of the plan of 1563, showing the buildings in the plaza (Fig. 63), did it appear that the University, like the Cathedral, stood in the plaza itself. Icazbalceta, because of a faulty reading of Cervantes, supposed that the original University buildings were on the western edge of the plaza, next to the episcopal palace. But the drawing of 1563 makes the situation clear, and Cervantes de Salazar's dialogues account for many details of the appearance of the buildings.

Awarded to the newly founded University by Viceroy Velasco in 1553, the buildings were residential quarters, hastily adapted for the purpose of housing students

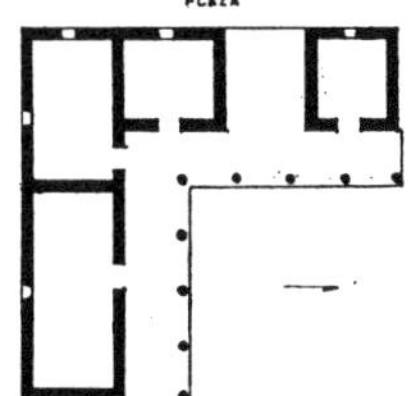

95. Mexico City, plan of the university *ca.* 1554, reconstructed according to description by Cervantes de Salazar

and classes. In 1554, the appearance of the University was probably substantially the same as that recorded in 1563 (Fig. 94). The north façade overlooked the continuation of the Calle de Tacuba; the south façade commanded the plaza itself.[99] It was a two-storied building, with large windows on both floors. A narrow portal, presumably in the north façade, gave access to the courtyard, with its wide colonnades on both floors. The courtyard, however, was incomplete in 1554, for Cervantes describes it as having land enough for the construction of another wing to the east which should complete the square of the courtyard (Fig. 95). Classrooms occupied both floors;

98. Mexico (City), Universidad nacional. Instituto de investigaciones estéticas, *La primera Universidad de América* (Mexico, 1940). Icazbalceta was misled by the fact that the buildings were near the corner of the Calle del Arzobispado and the Calle del Seminario. He thought the buildings must, therefore, be on the edge of the plaza, instead of in it, as given by Cervantes de Salazar, *México en 1554*, pp. 8–9. Vetancurt, moreover, leaves no doubt: the buildings, which formerly belonged to Doña Catalina de Montejo, were "cercanas al Palacio Real, con su plazuela." Vetancurt, *Chrónica, Tratado*, p. 32.

99. Cervantes de Salazar, *op. cit.*, p. 20: ". . . quae sit haec domus quae altero membro, tot ac tantis supra subterque factis fenestris, forum, et facie publicam viam respicit. . . ." Cervantes de Salazar was professor of rhetoric in the newly founded University, and he describes it with enthusiasm and authority, p. 22: "Atrium, pro frequentia et discentium numero, satis capax, et loci nimium a sinistro hoc latere, quartum ut membrum, dextro non inferius, erigi possit." See also p. 12.

grammar was taught on the ground floor, and upstairs were halls for sacred theology, civil and canon laws, dialectic, etc. No library is mentioned; the students utilized the various conventual libraries. This was not to be the permanent home of higher studies. The opening of the foundations of the Cathedral made it necessary for the University to move from place to place until new buildings were available for it in 1589. In 1561, its quarters were established in an unidentified building belonging to the Hospital de Jesús. Thus the primitive buildings were occupied but eight years. The significant fact is that private residential quarters satisfied the needs of professors and students; the genuine flexibility of the residential plan of contemporary Spanish domestic building accommodated many functions.

In 1584, the Audiencia granted the University part of the site of the Volador marketplace (Fig. 64), just south of the Palacio Nacional. The land was purchased from the Cortés estate, and construction began under the direction of Melchor de Avila. Progress was hindered by legal obstacles until 1589; at that time, the buildings housing the University collapsed, and the studies were moved to the one-story building then in construction on the new site.[100] By 1596 the handsome building shown in the drawing (Fig. 96) was in existence, with the plateresque details of the façade. Little is known about the interior disposition: a chapel was provided, of which the decoration attracted much comment. The furnishings were not completed until the seventeenth century.[101] One valuable indication of the drawing of 1596 pertains to the history of Mexican ornament. From the dates just given, it is apparent that the façade shown on the drawing was built between 1589 and 1596. The execution cannot have been completed much before 1596. This dating yields an accurate indication of the metropolitan style of the decade of the 1590's, with its severe, symmetrical forms, which recall a simplified plateresque style more old-fashioned than the massive Herreran doorways then esteemed in Spain.

In Patzcuaro, at the Real Colegio de San Nicolás Obispo, the educational institution also occupied domestic quarters. Bishop Quiroga founded the school *ca.* 1540, and he bequeathed his dwelling to it in 1565. This dwelling was provisional, but it incorporated a chapel and a room suitable for a library.[102]

100. Alamán, *Disertaciones*, II, 216–222.

101. See *La primera Universidad de América* for the reprint of the history of the University, written in 1668 by M. de Solís y Haro. García Icazbalceta, in the addendum to his edition of *México en 1554*, cites a manuscript by Carrillo y Pérez, which appears to contain many details concerning the later history of the buildings (p. 13, n.).

102. Cuevas, *Historia de la iglesia en México*, I, 398–399. "Se le queda . . . todo el aposento nuestro, que está junto al Colegio, que hicimos de prestado, hasta que se hagan los aposentos, que han de ir encorporados en nuestra Iglesia Catedral, conforme a la traza de ella, que ha de ser el Episcopio e aposento para Nos e nuestros sucesores y el aposento para los prebendados de la dicha santa Iglesia Catedral, a la otra parte. Y déjoselo todo al colegio así como va y está edificado y cercada . . . con el edificio de la capilla de San Ambrosio y de la sala grande en que está la dicha capilla que podrá servir de libería en el dicho colegio hasta que otra mejor se haga, aderezándose como convenga para ello"

Of the other metropolitan schools, little is known. By 1537 Zumárraga had evidently founded a school for the instruction of Indian children, and it was his wish to endow the school by the gift of the houses he had bought for his own residence in 1530.[103] Such a school actually functioned for several years; in 1549 the Crown alluded to the fact that Zumárraga had founded and built a school for girls in houses adjacent to the Hospital del Amor de Dios. In 1549, however, the buildings were vacant, and the school no longer functioned.[104] It is another instance of the conversion of domestic accommodations to institutional purposes.

Still another school at the western edge of the traza was founded under the patronage of the cabildo in 1529 for the instruction of mestizo children. Under the advocacy of San Juan de Letrán, the school came under royal patronage in 1548. In the nineteenth century, monolithic columns of sixteenth-century manufacture were discovered and identified as belonging to the fabric of this early school,[105] which did not acquire its own building until well after 1552.

The founders of the Colegio de Santa Cruz at Tlatelolco, at the time of its inception in 1533, intended to provide a school of higher studies for Indians, where they might learn "gramática romanzada en lengua mexicana." On January 6, 1536, the institution formally received Indian pupils, under the direction of the Franciscan friars of Tlatelolco. The pupils dwelt at first in some adobe buildings, which, however, threatened ruin the following year. A new edifice was needed, and the sponsors proposed that it should be built of stone with two stories, to house a library, dormitory, workshops, and classrooms. In 1538, steps were taken to advance such a building. We know nothing about its appearance, and in the 1560's, the edifice was in great disrepair. For various reasons, the establishment had decayed, and it was not until the last quarter of the century that its fabric was built up again. Fray Bernardino de Sahagún and fray Juan de Torquemada were instrumental in seeing to the repairs. In the late sixteenth century, the buildings housed between two and three hundred Indian pupils. A refectory was maintained for them, as well as a dormitory, presum-

103. García Icazbalceta, *Don fray Juan de Zumárraga,* Appendix, p. 109. Dec. 20, 1537. There is no reason to identify this undertaking with the coeval church school of the Franciscans, Santa Cruz de Tlatelolco.

104. *Ibid.,* Appendix, p. 208 (Aug. 21, 1549). Zumárraga ". . . me ha hecho relacion que junto al Hospital Real de las bubas que él hizo é fundó . . . está una casa donde se solian dotrinar las niñas hijas de caciques y principales, en la cual dizque al presente no mora nadie, é que él á su costa edificó lo mejor della. . . ." By this decree, the Crown awarded the buildings in question to the Hospital. Perhaps this building is the one indicated upon the plan of 1563 as "la maese escuela." The location is correct, but we have no other text referring to the continued operation of a school in this region of the city.

105. See García Icazbalceta, *Obras,* II, 421–425; F. Osores y Sotomayor, *Historia le todos los colegios de la ciudad de México desde la conquista hasta 1780* (Mexico, 1929 (Nuevos documentos inéditos ó muy raros para la historia de México [II]. C. E. Castañeda, ed.), p. 9, n. 11. *Diccionario,* II, 369–370. Mexico, *Gaçeta de Mexico* (September 1737). In 1578 the colegio instructed some seventy or eighty youths. *Epistolario,* XII, 51. Cf. *AC,* V, 180, 182, 222, 242, and F. V. Scholes, "Documents," *The Americas,* II (1945), 99–106.

ably on the second floor, where the students slept upon low wooden platforms (*tarimas*). It is interesting to find the Arabic term used in this connection; the sleeping platform was common in Spain, but it is not recorded as an Indian custom, and at Tlatelolco probably constituted a step in the Hispanicization of the Indians. Each pupil, furthermore, had his own chest for his belongings, with its lock and key. In 1728, the school still existed, but very little survived of the sixteenth-century buildings. A wall, presumably the entrance of the older buildings, still displayed the arms of Charles V. The precinct flanked the south side of the church, bordering the atrio, and measured 103 by 114 yards, with all buildings showing signs of great antiquity, in spite of the fact that many rooms had been recently rebuilt. In short, the Colegio de Santa Cruz was the greatest Indian school of its day, and gave an example for the more modest monastic schools in the Indian towns away from the capital.[106]

Of these many monastic schools, little or nothing remains. But each establishment had an annex built by the Indians, and destined for the instruction of the children, with a classroom, dormitory, refectory, and oratory. Torquemada informs us that these buildings usually formed part of the atrio precinct. The Augustinians had similar schools. Grijalva describes them, and explains more fully the way in which secular and religious education were constantly intermingled. Between the school and the catechetical activities in the atrio there was little real difference, for the educational activities of the missionaries were not restricted to particular times and places. The whole community was a school, and the education to Christian life was constantly in progress.[107]

In addition to these modest monastic schools without particular architectural pretensions, a few urban schools were built in the Spanish towns. We have already spoken of San Nicolás in Patzcuaro (later resettled in Morelia); there is also the school for girls in Puebla, endowed by a private citizen, Luis de León Romano, with ten thousand pesos about 1570. The buildings went up about 1571 and were very solid.[108]

106. F. B. Steck, *El primer Colegio de América, Santa Cruz de Tlaltelolco* (Mexico, 1944), 5, 31–32. F. Ocaranza, *El imperial Colegio de indios de la Santa Cruz de Santiago Tlaltelolco* (Mexico, 1934), p. 23, attributes the earliest buildings to fray Arnoldo de Basaccio. See also Mendieta, *Historia eclesiástica indiana*, p. 415; Torquemada, . . . *Monarchia indiana*, III, 113–114, and Ocaranza, *op. cit.*, pp. 16–17. The most valuable study of the Colegio is the scrupulous investigation by Ricard, *La "Conquête spirituelle" du Mexique*, pp. 262–276. The study by Ocaranza presents many new documents, and photographs of the fragments of the old buildings.

107. Torquemada, *op. cit.*, III, 28. See the letter by Zumárraga, written in 1532 to the Franciscan chapter in Toulouse: "una quaeque Domus fratrum Francisci habet aliam domum sibi conjuntaem pro pueris docendis ab artificibus indorum constructam cum lectorario, Dormitorio, Refectorio, et devoto Sacello." Reproduced in Beaumont, *Crónica de Michoacán*, II, 148.

Grijalva, *Crónica de la orden de N. P. S. Augustín*, p. 226. "En todos ellos [los conventos] ay escuelas, que caen al patio dela Yglesia; donde se enseñan los niños, à ayudar à Missa, à leer y escriuir, à cantar, y à tañer instrumentos musicos. La Doctrina Cristiana se enseña siempre en los patios de la Yglesia; por que como à de ser tan general para todos, es bien, que el lugar sea publico. Alli se diuiden por los angulos, à vna parte los varones, y à otro las hembras, y vnos Indios viejos, que les enseñan segun la necessidad."

108. López de Velasco, *Geografía*, p. 209; L. García Pimentel, ed., *Relación de los obispados de Tlax-*

Fernando Cortés founded a great hospital in Mexico City in 1524 or earlier, a hospital which even within his lifetime was to become a vast establishment comparable to the great hospitals of Spain and Italy. Its full name became the Hospital de la Purísima Concepción y Jesús Nazareno, commonly known as the Hospital de Jesús. It has been the subject of several detailed studies, and this treatment can add nothing new to the history of the building excepting to emphasize the architectural form and antecedents.[109] The plan of the hospital (Fig. 97) resembled that of the casas viejas,

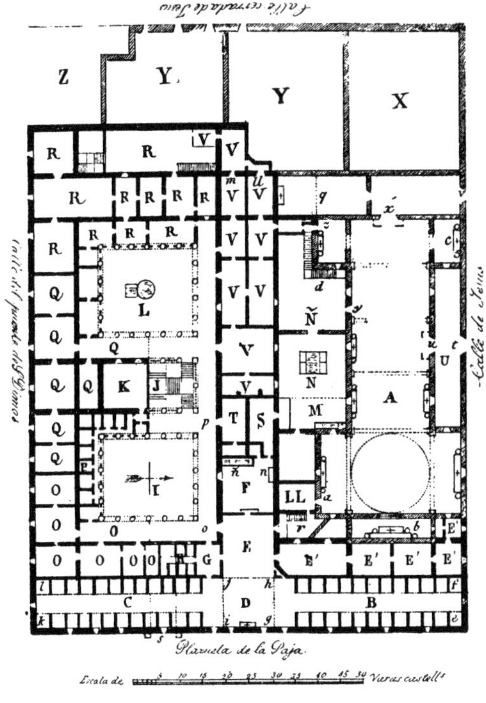

97. Mexico City, plan of the Hospital de Jesús

covering a large tract (93 by 128 varas) in the southeastern quarter of the traza. The final form was to consist of a church and four great ranges of buildings, defining two large courts. How much of this formed the original plan by Pedro Vázquez, who is mentioned as its author in Cortés' testament, is unclear, but we do know that the east range, running north and south (Fig. 98), was built, at least in part, by 1535, because of a famous inscription still in place in 1833. The edifice was incomplete at Cortés' death; his testament provided that the work was to be completed according

cala, Michoacán, Oaxaca y otros lugares en el siglo XVI (Mexico, 1904) (Documentos históricos de Méjico, II), p. 2.

109. Sigüenza y Góngora, *Piedad heroica;* Alamán, *Disertaciones,* II, 83–109; Zavala, *Fuentes,* III, 7–8; J. Enciso, "Los Frescos cortesianos del Hospital de Jesús," *El Hijo pródigo,* I (1943), 344–345.

to a wooden model prepared by Pedro Vázquez. Building progressed slowly during the century, and in 1578, ten Indian carpenters and twelve masons were regularly assigned to the work. A provisional church served the religious needs of the residents, until 1601, when the construction of a permanent building was confided to Alonso Pérez de Castañeda. In the hospital proper, the colonnaded walks in one court undeniably contain work of the sixteenth century, for frescoes in the style of the period still adorn the walls. The great multiple-court plan inevitably evokes such Spanish exemplars as the Hospital Real at Santiago, designed by Enrique Egas and built between 1501–11, which in turn depends upon the plan by Filarete for the Ospedale maggiore in Milan (*ca.* 1457). But the closest Spanish parallel for the Mexican hospital founded by Cortés is the Hospital de la Sangre in Seville, begun in 1546 on plans by Martín Gainza, and finished in 1591.[110] It is not impossible that the plan mentioned in Cortés' testament directly followed this model.

Many other hospitals were founded in the capital, but none of them showed the highly specialized form of the Hospital de Jesús. The asylum for venereal sufferers, known as the Hospital del Amor de Dios (or H. de las Bubas), was founded *ca.* 1534 by Zumárraga, and as we have seen, it was originally housed in nondescript buildings which had previously served other purposes.[111]

The general hospital for Indians was endowed in 1553, with substantial royal gifts; construction remained incomplete in 1556.[112] Like the Hospital de Jesús, it was later sustained in part by revenue from theatrical performances, held in the courtyard of the hospital (see p. 216). In 1583, it was regarded as the best hospital building in the capital, although it lacked a church.

All told, the hospitals were about twelve in number; little information has been preserved about their sixteenth-century housing, but a useful description of the institutions, as they functioned about 1612, was written by Antonio Vázquez de Espinosa.[113]

Far more numerous and far less pretentious monastic hospitals served the Indian

110. Camón Aznar, *Arquitectura plateresca,* I, 167–168.

111. See García Icazbalceta, *Don fray Juan de Zumárraga,* p. 144. Zumárraga purchased a house from Manuel Flores on July 8, 1530, to be used as an ecclesiastical prison. Icazbalceta thought this was situated in the Calle S. Teresa la Antigua; the text, however, suggests that it was the site of the present Academy of San Carlos, where the Hospital del Amor de Dios was once located. On April 17, 1540, Zumárraga informed the Crown that this prison building had been converted to use as a hospital ("primero era carcel la que es agora hospital"), Appendix, p. 137. See also Cuevas, *Documentos inéditos,* pp. 107, 325; Tomson, *An Englishman and the Mexican Inquisition,* pp. 81, 112; Ocaranza, *Capitulos de la historia franciscana,* II, 120–127.

112. Puga, *Cedulario,* II, 220–221, 282–283; J. Fernández, "El Hospital real de los indios de la ciudad de México," *Anales del instituto de investigaciones estéticas,* I, no. 3 (1939), 25–47. See Cuevas, *op. cit.,* p. 325.

113. Vázquez de Espinosa, "Compendium . . . of the West Indies," *Smithsonian Miscellaneous Collections,* CII (1942), 161–163. See also a list of metropolitan hospitals in Cuevas, *op. cit.,* pp. 325 f., compiled in 1583.

towns, hospitals founded by the Mendicants and by the secular clergy. Of these the most famous, in the Dominican establishment at Oaxtepec, was founded by Bernardino Alvárez about 1573. It depended upon alms gathered by the Hermanos de San Hipólito. The buildings housed various convalescents and venereal sufferers, chiefly Europeans. The construction of elaborate buildings was under way in 1580; by 1585, Father Ponce reported that the buildings were finished.[114] The hospital at Oaxtepec, however, was but one unit in an extensive system operated by the brothers of San Hipólito. Their primary purpose seems to have been the care of disabled travelers; the brown-garbed brothers maintained other roadside hospitals at points along the difficult journey from Veracruz to the capital; one at Perote, and another in Mexico City called the Hospital de Convalecientes and founded *ca.* 1563.[115]

Among the Franciscans, part of the conventual buildings served as an infirmary.[116] At Cuernavaca, for instance, the Indians received medical care in buildings on the north side of the convento; and similar infirmaries adjoined the conventos in Mexico City and in Puebla. At Tlaxcala, a hospital accommodating 140 patients was built in 1537; and Motolinia tells us that it was dedicated to the Incarnation, and built "al modo de los buenos de España." Another important Franciscan hospital, founded *ca.* 1566 by fray Juan de Mansilla in Jalapa, served white and Indian travelers. The hospital in Tepeapulco was also very likely a hospital for travelers, founded by fray Andrés de Olmos about 1528–29; and at Acambaro, a Franciscan hospital appeared presumably *ca.* 1532. The Augustinians also maintained infirmaries; their chroniclers, however, are not so explicit as the Franciscan historians. At Cuitzeo, for instance, Francisco de Villafuerte established the hospital in an adobe building about 1550.[117] In the village of Angahua, a small sixteenth-century hospital chapel still stands, founded in 1570 by a canon of the cathedral chapter of Michoacan:[118] thus the secular clergy also took part in the creation of asylums for the sick.

In the Indian towns, and particularly at the hands of the secular clergy, the concept of the hospital acquired connotations with which we are not familiar in the

114. *Relación . . . Ponce,* I, 187, 202; Cuevas, *op. cit.,* pp. 327–328; Zavala, *Fuentes,* II, 245.

115. The Hospital de Convalecientes was under construction in 1581, and was halted at that time for lack of wood and woodcutters, *ibid.,* II, 402, 408–409. By 1612, Vázquez de Espinosa, *op. cit.,* p. 162, called it "one of the finest and wealthiest in the Indies." At that time the brothers of San Hipolito were more generally known as the Brethren of Oaxtepec. Cf. A. Ortega, "Fray Juan de Paredes y la fundación de los hospitales de San Juan de Ulua-Veracruz," *Archivo ibero-americano,* XXXIV (1931), pp. 266–277.

116. Cuernavaca: Vetancurt, *Chrónica, Teatro,* Pt. IV, p. 59. Mexico: *Relación . . . Ponce,* I, 180. Puebla: (founded about 1551), R. Ricard, "Une Lettre de Fr. Juan de Gaona à Charles-Quint," *Revue d'histoire franciscaine,* III (1926), 120. The hospital in Tlaxcala was formally established in 1546 (Motolinia, "Historia de los indios de la Nueva España," *CDHM,* I, 151; Vetancurt, *Chrónica, Teatro,* Pt. IV, p. 54), and its advocacy changed to the Annunciation. Jalapa: *PNE,* V, 104; Torquemada, . . . *Monarchia indiana,* III, 330; cf. Cuevas, *Documentos inéditos,* p. 412. Tepeapulco: *PNE,* VI, 302–303. Acambaro: Beaumont, *Crónica de Michoacán,* II, 298–306.

117. Escobar, *Americana thebaida,* p. 672: the two-storied masonry hospital at Tiripitio is described on pp. 158 ff.

118. See Toussaint, "Angahua," *Journal of the Society of Architectural Historians,* V (1945–46), 24–26.

twentieth century. There can be little doubt that the fundamental notion of the hospital as a center of religious life stems from Bishop Quiroga, but the Mendicants also claimed credit for the idea, and realized it in many monastic foundations.[119] In any case, the nature of the Mexican community hospital is best defined by the documents pertaining to the two original hospitals of Santa Fe, founded by Bishop Quiroga, and established both in the Valley of Mexico (Fig. 99) and in Michoacan. Quiroga manifestly intended the hospital to serve as a center for the propagation of the Catholic faith. It was created for the indoctrination of both kinds of Indians: the unbaptized tribes who were to be brought to Christian polity; and baptized Indians, in whom the doctrine was to be implanted. Among the latter, the teaching of Christian doctrine would advance, not only by instruction, but by the performance of charitable works, such as the reception of travelers and the curing of the sick.[120] Another important activity of the Quirogan Hospital was the *hospital de cuna,* where foundlings were reared. The association school cared for their later education.[121] In practical terms, therefore, Quiroga's hospitals differed little from the missionary foundations by the Mendicants.

Before Quiroga, the Mendicants held the initiative in the creation of such centers of colonial indoctrination. Their mission had especially equipped them for such activity. But the secular clergy lacked the tradition and the training with which to undertake genuine colonization. It is not unlikely that Quiroga attempted to remedy the shortcomings of the secular clergy as active missionaries by the creation of the instrument of the hospital, which provided the parish priest with an institutional framework roughly analogous to the one used with such skill by the Mendicants. The Quirogan Hospital may, therefore, be equated with the monastic Mendicant foundation, as a center of urbanizing activity within the concepts of Christian polity. Hence the claim by the Mendicants that the Hospital credited to Quiroga was in reality their creation, has some justification.

Quiroga, nevertheless, gave the fundamental concepts of missionary activity a fresh interpretation and equipment which entitle his hospitals to be considered as a category distinct from the Mendicant foundations. For example, the Quirogan hospital was coterminous with the community. To participate in the hospital meant to participate in the life of a community. The property was communally held; the assignment of labor was carefully regulated with respect to the division between work in the fields and work in the town. The relations between laborers and chiefs were care-

119. Grijalva, *Crónica de la orden de N. P. S. Augustín,* p. 216; Rea, *Crónica de la orden de N. serafico P. S. Francisco,* p. 45b, assigns the "invention" to fray Juan de San Miguel.

120. In Quiroga's concept, the performance of Christian works was designated as a process of civilizing the Indian through "la moral exterior." See Aguayo Spencer, ed., *Don Vasco de Quiroga,* p. 30.

121. Grijalva, *op. cit.,* pp. 54–55.

fully prescribed; the practice of individual trades was supervised by the authorities of the hospital in relation to a far-sighted program of communal thrift. The members of the community were dedicated to the achievement of Christian perfection; the Indian settlers were in effect induced to behave as members of a religious retreat. The leisure of the settlers passed in prayer and doctrinal exercises; in the singing of hymns in the streets, and in the service of the sick. Thus Quiroga extended the concept of monastic dedication beyond the clergy to the entire community. To dwell in a hospital was for the Indian tantamount to entering a religious community not unlike the Mendicant Orders. The Indians' sense of monastic dedication was encouraged and enhanced by their exemption in 1547 from all forms of personal service, and from the payment of tribute. If the Church in America ever achieved a program for the full incorporation of the Indian to Christian life, it was in the Hospitals established by Bishop Quiroga.

The first foundation at Santa Fe, near Mexico City, occurred in 1531 or 1532. Then an Auditor, Quiroga purchased the necessary lands from his own funds. The sixteenth-century population of the settlement was estimated at some twelve thousand persons, housed in substantial buildings, which lasted well into the seventeenth century. Indian laborers, under the aegis of their *tlatoani,* provided the materials and labor at a very low rate of pay. An interesting view of the establishment is preserved in the map attributed to Alonso de Santa Cruz, as of about 1555, showing the Indians gathered in the atrio of the church (or Hospital) for instruction (Fig. 99). An open chapel is shown, and it is not easy to differentiate the appearance of the buildings from that of the usual Mendicant foundation. In effect, Grijalva tells us that the conventual buildings of Santa Fe were actually Augustinian buildings, serving a foundation established by fray Alonso de Borja, about 1534.[122]

Quiroga's settlement in the Valley of Mexico, however, rapidly encountered vigorous opposition. The encomenderos felt that its existence jeopardized the capital, by offering the Indians a more attractive environment than that of the crowded reservoir of low-paid labor huddled at the fringe of the metropolitan traza.[123] The colonists wished to augment the population of the capital, and thus to fortify it against possible Indian rebellions. But this purpose was defeated by the presence of large Indian centers of population in the immediate vicinity of the capital. The colonists therefore maintained a policy of preventing the growth of large Indian settlements in the Valley of Mexico other than the metropolitan one itself. Opposed to the colonists, and allied with Quiroga, however, was the Audiencia, which favored Quiroga's purpose

122. *Ibid.*, pp. 54–55, 56, 58. Beaumont, *op. cit.*, II, 161; Aguayo Spencer, *op. cit.*, p. 26. Gómez de Orozco, "Monasterios," *Revista mexicana de estudios históricos*, I, 46.

123. Beaumont, *op. cit.*, II, 162, 259. See p. 74.

by further grants of land to the new Indian community in the Hospital.[124] Although Grijalva indicates that the enterprise was abandoned by Quiroga about 1536 because the community had already fulfilled its original purpose of converting and instructing the Indians, there can be no question that civilian opposition led to its decay. The site of Santa Fe was highly strategic, situated at the source of a supply of water most important to the well-being of the capital, and the colonists were vitally interested in preventing the growth of a large Indian city in the vicinity of this essential strategic point.[125]

Quiroga, nevertheless, did not abandon the effort to institute the principle of the hospital as a mode of Christian community life. In Michoacan, where Quiroga became the first bishop, the community of Santa Fe was founded anew, as a center for the conversion and indoctrination of the western Indians. On the north shore of Lake Patzcuaro, it flourished greatly, and served as an example for the foundation of other, modified hospitals throughout the bishopric. Moreno records that in the eighteenth century the Indians of the region of Patzcuaro still preserved "sus distribuciones, sus asambleas y lo demas que se acostumbraba. . . ."[126] The population of the Michoacan settlement is not known with certainty; according to its apologists, Grijalva, Moreno, and Beaumont, Santa Fe contained some thirty thousand persons, but the rector of the community reported only five hundred in 1570.[127]

A constant preoccupation of the colonists is found in their concern for water. In Mexico City, they were perennially concerned with its excess and with its defect: potable water had to be brought from the mainland by aqueducts, but surface water had to be pumped away from the island. Wherever colonial activity was undertaken, such hydraulic questions absorbed much of the energy of the settlers and natives. Aqueducts and public fountains often assumed monumental forms of great beauty (Figs. 100, 101, 103). The storage of water made it necessary to devise tanks and cisterns, upon whose construction much knowledge and labor were expended.[128]

The building of suitable aqueducts for the supply of the capital lasted through the sixteenth century. In its final form, the system comprised three main *caños de agua:* one coming from Atzcapotzalco, another from Santa Fe, and a main aqueduct from Chapultepec, the traditional pre-Conquest source of water for the capital. The most ambitious aqueduct entered from Santa Fe; in the seventeenth century it comprised nine hundred arches rising five yards above ground level, and it fed into the city along the north side of the present Alameda (Fig. 65). The minutes of the mu-

124. Aguayo Spencer, *op. cit.*, p. 30.

125. Grijalva, *op. cit.*, p. 56.

126. Zavala, *La "Utopia" de Tomás Moro en la Nueva España*, p. 15, n. 70.

127. Aguayo Spencer, *op. cit.*, p. 36.

128. F. Gómez Pérez, "Mexican Irrigation in the Sixteenth Century," *Civil Engineering*, XII, no. 1 (1942), 24–27.

nicipal council swelled with discussions of this enterprise.[129] It was extremely slow in building: we have already examined the problem of the Indian community founded by Vasco de Quiroga at the source of the water (see p. 85). The Chapultepec aqueduct was also carried upon arches, originally built about 1543. Their bad condition in 1591 made rebuilding imperative. The project was awarded in competitive bidding to Diego de Aguilera, who offered to rebuild at a cost of thirty thousand pesos in four years. He planned to use the labor of three hundred Indians, in building stone foundations one and one-half yards deep, with arches and columns of tezontle. The work actually began in 1592, when the city purchased materials from the Jesuits for the aqueduct. Thomas Gage, who saw it in 1625, describes two conduits, built in order that one might be cleaned while water flowed in the other. These conduits were carried upon arches of brick and stone.[130]

The water flowed in many public fountains. In 1560, according to Cervantes de Salazar, nearly every street corner had its *arca de piedra,* and ducts led into many institutions and private houses. A central water-distribution station, designed and built by Claudio de Arciniega in 1560, has disappeared;[131] a stenographic record of its rough form survives in the *Codex Aubin* (Fig. 32). The Indian draughtsman, in making the entry for the year 1560, recorded a simple pumphouse or fountain edifice. The accompanying Aztec words have never been translated satisfactorily. The edifice is designated as a great antheap (*ve tziccatl*); and the term *quiyauac* is ambiguous, signifying either a position near a door or gate, or an allusion to water falling from above. A plausible translation would be, "October 8 [1560]: the new antheap [*caja de agua*] at the door of the tecpan [alternate: the house of rain]."[132] At intervals elsewhere, various stations allowed the Indians to approach the aqueduct in their canoes or punts; in 1554, they had the custom of filling the canoes with potable water from an overhead tap at the aqueduct.[133]

In the missionary towns, very elaborate systems supplied the establishments with water for domestic and industrial purposes. The *locus classicus* among Mexican hy-

129. Cf. specially *AC,* VII, VIII (1564–71).

130. *AC,* X (1896), 54, 118, 174. Gage, *The English-American,* p. 70.

131. Cervantes de Salazar, *Crónica de la Nueva España,* pp. 320–321. "Y porque las insignes ciudades para el proveimiento de los vecinos han de tener agua de pie y esta ciudad la tenía por algunas calles della, al presente se trae por todas, y en cada esquina se hace un arca de piedra, donde los vecinos pueden tomar agua, sin la que entrará en muchas casas. El edificio donde se rescibe para hacer el repartimiento della es muy hermoso y de gran artificio. Hácele Claudio de Arceniega, maestro mayor de las obras de México." An eighteenth century painted screen in Spain shows such an edifice, perhaps analogous to the design by Arciniega (E. Marco Dorta, "Un Biombo mějicano," *Archivo español de arte,* no. 62 [1944], 70–76).

132. *Codex Aubin,* p. 101, "viii Octubre in yancuicā ve tziccatl tecpan quiyauac."

133. Cervantes de Salazar, *México en 1554,* p. 126: "Verum, quid sibi vult illud ut supra aquam aqua etiam imbutae indicae cymbae natent? . . . quae fert trabes aqua, non est potui, quae autem fertur, ex fonte per ligneam, sicuti continuo inspicies, magnam canalem in subjectas cymbulas, ex alto, magno strepitu cadit." It is possible that this is the "high place" seen by Robert Tomson in 1556, "where come every morning at the break of the day twentie or thirtie canoes." (Hakluyt, *Voyages,* III, 539; Tomson, *An Englishman and the Mexican Inquisition,* p. 20.)

draulic works of this class was the great aqueduct of Zempoala (Fig. 100), built by fray Francisco de Tembleque between *ca.* 1541 and 1557 (see p. 117).

The Franciscans built another ambitious aqueduct in this period to supply Tepeaca. The water came nearly twenty miles from the Sierra de Tlaxcala near Acatzingo, where mountain springs were tapped about 1543. Before that time, the community took water from local wells. But the new supply came in clay conduits, with pressure held by the introduction of cisterns at intervals along the lengthy passage.[134]

At Epazoyucan the Augustinians brought water in 1567 from a point nearly eight miles distant. The conduits led to two outlets; one in the churchyard, and another in the cloister court, where the water ran in elaborate fountains.[135] An intricate system served the Augustinians at Tiripitio in Michoacan. After 1537, the friars brought water in an *acequia,* or open ditch, from a point some six miles distant. Part of the distance they bridged by a raised aqueduct. At the entrance to the town, subterranean conduits took the water at a level low enough to feed many points of emission. Four branches led from the plaza to the various public fountains and taps; other streams were fed to the fulling mill owned by the encomendero. The pressure sufficed to drive the hammers of this mill, and it is interesting to note that its ruins survived until the eighteenth century. Still other streams were fed to the encomendero's house, to the convento and the hospital.[136]

Similar arrangements provided the Dominicans at Cuilapan: the water, brought from a nearby mountain, served both the convent and a flour-mill.[137] At Tepeapulco, the handsome caja de agua (Fig. 101), built after 1541, is fed by springs some sixteen miles distant.[138] The form of this caja de agua evokes none of the fountains or cisterns usually built for communal use in contemporary Spain.[139]

At the terminal points of such aqueducts, facilities for storage were needed. The pre-Conquest Indians had developed tanks called *xaveyes.*[140] The Spaniards improved them further, lining the tanks with stone, and multiplying their number. It was usual for a conventual establishment to maintain two tanks, one for drinking-water, and the other for breeding and raising fish, as at Cuautinchan, Yanhuitlan, or Tecali (Fig. 102). At Cuitzeo and Ucareo, the *algibes* were beneath the cloister, with access

134. *PNE,* I, 207; V, 18.

135. See J. M. Romero, "Memoria sobre el distrito de Pachuca," in R. Almaraz, ed., *Memorias de los trabajos executados por la comisión científica de Pachuca en el año de 1864* (Mexico, 1865), p. 160. The springs were situated south of the settlement. The same source contains an interesting view of the aqueduct of Zempoala (opp. p. 168).

136. Basalenque, *Historia . . . Michoacán,* pp. 19–20; Escobar, *Americana thebaida,* p. 144.

137. Burgoa, *Geográfica descripción,* I, 403–405. Burgoa also notes an *arquería* supplying the convento at Etla. *Ibid.,* II, 7.

138. *PNE,* VI, 294. Gómez Pérez, *op. cit.,* p. 26, says the Tepeapulco conduits were finished in the eighteenth century.

139. Lampérez, *Arquitectura civil española,* II, 520–530.

140. *Relación . . . Ponce,* I, 140; Vetancurt, *Chrónica, Teatro,* Pt. IV, pp. 69–70.

by a stairway at Ucareo. Occasionally, earthquakes displaced the watertable and emptied the tanks, as at Zapotitlan in Jalisco during the 1580's.[141]

At Tepeaca, Tecali, or Ucareo, the form of these conventual cisterns may be studied in detail. Another ruined specimen is behind the church at Totolapan in Morelos, stone-lined, immediately adjacent to the church, and fed by the runoff from the church and conventual roofs. Hence a functional dependence between the flat-roof systems and the cisterns can be proposed.

Urban fountains of some ornateness still stand in Chiapa de Corzo (finished before 1562), in Texcoco, Tochimilco (Fig. 103), Tepeapulco (Fig. 101), Ocuituco, etc., and a record of the elaborate municipal fountain built in Patzcuaro has been published.[142]

104. Mexico City, waterlift

The water in the settlements was often harnessed for industrial purposes. In Mexico City in particular, the marshy subsoil necessitated the use of waterpumps in preparing the foundations for buildings. A pump is shown in connection with the laying of the foundations for the Cathedral (Fig. 53), and constant pumping was necessary in the excavation for the foundations of San Agustín before 1554.[143] A fairly detailed drawing of a water-lift appears in the *Codex Aubin* (Fig. *104*), as of the year 1562. A belt, with pots attached to it at intervals, traveled over a wheel, raising water from one level to a higher one.[144] Since the text pertains to repairs to the church, involving the preparation of mortar, this lift may have been devised to raise water for the preparation of mortar on the scaffolds.

141. Basalenque, *op. cit.*, p. 70a; Cuautinchan, *Relación . . . Ponce*, I, 139; Cuernavaca, Vetancurt, *op. cit.*, p. 59; Tecali, *ibid.*, pp. 69–70, *Relación . . . Ponce*, I, 140; Teotihuacan, *ibid.*, I, 214; Zapotitlan, *ibid.*, II, 99; Yanhuitlan, C. A. Romero, "Dos Cartas inéditas del P. Bernabé Cobo," *Revista histórica* [Lima], VIII (1928), 35.

142. *Relación . . . Ponce*, I, 532–533.

143. *Pintura del gobernador, alcaldes y regidores de México* (Madrid, 1878), p. 30; Cervantes de Salazar, *México en 1554*, p. 155.

144. *Codex Aubin*, fol. 103. The text reads, "Viernes a 7 dias del mes de agusto amotenextin yn [iglesia] caltepotzco yn oncan amatlacatl ollo [On Aug. 7, lime was placed behind the church where it joins (?)]."

Water-power also drove sawmills and crushing mills at the silver mines. Numerous waterwheels of this type figure in the *Códice Kingsborough* (Fig. 105), where they appear as Indian constructions, built for the benefit of their encomenderos and their foremen.[145] Finally, the great hydraulic project of the sixteenth century was the construction of the *albarradón,* or dike, separating the waters of the eastern and western halves of the lake in the Valley of Mexico (Fig. 106).[146]

145. Romero, *op. cit.,* pp. 29–37, mentions water-powered sawmills in Guatemala and at Rio Frio near Mexico City. B. Dorantes de Carranza, *Sumaria relación de las cosas de la Nueva España* (Mexico, 1902), p. 298, specifies that Juan Baeza de Herrera "hizo la invencion de los ingenios de agua para la molienda de los metales de la plata." These technological devices are common property in the Renaissance. See W. B. Parsons, *Engineers and Engineering in the Renaissance* (Baltimore, 1939), pp. 138, 139, 207.

146. Clavigero, *History of Mexico,* I, 240. *Annales de . . . Chimalpahin,* p. 251. *Pintura del gobernador, alcades, y regidores de México,* p. 469.